The teaching of basic sciences

New trends
in integrated science
teaching

Volume VI

1990

Unesco

Published in 1990 by the United Nations Educational,
Scientific and Cultural Organization
7 place de Fontenoy, 75700 Paris
Typeset by Unesco
Printed by Imprimerie Bietlot - Fleurus

ISBN 92-3-102665-8

Preface

This publication is the sixth on the subject of integrated science teaching in the Unesco series 'The teaching of basic sciences'. The first two (New Trends in Integrated Science Teaching, Volumes I and II) attempted to analyse world-wide trends in a rapidly-evolving field. The third and fourth addressed themselves to two crucial problems, namely the education of teachers (Volume III) and the evaluation of integrated science education (Volume IV). Volume V was based on the proceedings of a conference organised in April 1978 at the University of Nijmegen (Netherlands) by the International Council of Associations for Science Education (ICASE) and the Netherlands Association for Science Education (NVON) with the support from Unesco and other bodies. Its main aims were to take stock of the developments in integrated science education over the previous ten years and to provide an opportunity to look forward to new trends in science education in the 1980s and beyond.

The present volume is based on the proceedings of a Unesco consultation, held in conjunction with a worldwide conference in Canberra in 1988 on Science Education and the Quality of Life, organised by ICASE and the Australian Science Teachers Association (ASTA). The consultation came 10 years after the conference held in Nijmegen and was designed to look at developments in integrated science teaching over the interim period, to take stock of trends in the teaching of integrated science, and to discuss key issues and problems. The proceedings of the consultation, produced for Unesco by ICASE, included region and country reports to indicate how far integrated science teaching had spread around the world. These form a substantial base for section 2 in this volume.

The readership for which this publication is intended is a wide one, including practising teachers and teachers in training, as well as teacher educators, curriculum developers and research workers, and officials of Ministries of Education. It is hoped that it will provide the opportunity for many of the key people working in integrated science teaching to know about what each other is doing and to establish bonds that will be strong enough to continue in the future. It is also hoped to reflect the 'flavour' of integrated science teaching from different parts of the world. Just as we have English with an Oxford accent or a Caribbean accent, so we have many 'flavours' of integrated science teaching.

Much has happened in the science teaching world in the decade of the 80s. Many initiatives have been taken to emphasise the importance of primary science education, even pre-primary education. Major integrating themes such as 'energy' and environment have received much prominence. Technology is coming to occupy a more important place in the curriculum, links with school and industry are stronger. All these and indeed many other developments enrich the flavour of this publication.

We have deliberately, in the past not, tried to 'define' integrated science teaching in order to not 'confine' it. But at the same time we need to distil out of this diversity, the unity of purpose and of conviction that has led many countries along the integrated science teaching path. I suspect that we shall find that many of the key issues and problems are much the same as they were ten years ago. But maybe we shall also find that some new solutions have evolved.

Contents

Foreword

This book is an outcome of a consultation meeting held on the theme 'Recent Developments in Integrated Science Teaching Worldwide' from 8 to 10th July, 1988 in Canberra, Australia. The meeting was organised by the Australian National Commission for Unesco, in co-operation with the International Council of Associations Science Education (ICASE) and with the Australian Science Teachers' Association.

In preparation for the meeting, ICASE had undertaken a review of integrated science courses worldwide: data were collected from about 40 countries describing some 128 courses, about half of which were new courses or major revisions of the courses analysed at the last major Unesco international meeting on integrated science held in Nijmegen, Netherlands in 1978.

The chapters in the first part of this book, some of which have been specially commissioned, describe key issues in integrated science and broad trends in the approaches to integrated science teaching worldwide. They include the conclusions of five working groups set up during the Canberra meeting to discuss the key issues in the following areas: content (developments in science and technology and their implications for science education); curriculum and resource materials; teaching, learning and assessment; equipment and science teaching facilities; and teacher education.

The second part of the book describes national and regional developments in the teaching of integrated science and is based largely on the reports and discussions at the Canberra meeting. The third part contains some examples of topics and modules of integrated science courses taken from recent courses.

The annotated bibliography on integrated science teaching is supplementary to the bibliography in *New Trends in Integrated Science* Vol. V and attempts to sample the literature relevant to integrated science in the last ten years.

I would wish to thank the authors of the principal papers and express my gratitude to all those participants at the meeting in Canberra whose contributions have been reflected in this volume. The views expressed in this publication are those of the editor or the individual authors and not necessarily those of Unesco.

Dennis G. Chisman, Editor, ICASE

Part 1

A general review
of trends in
integrated science teaching

Chapter 1

What is integrated science teaching: its beginnings and its place today

Dennis G. Chisman

Introduction - 20 years retrospect

The first major international conference on integrated science education, sponsored in part by Unesco, was held in 1968 in Droujba, Bulgaria in co-operation with the International Council of Scientific Unions (ICSU) Committee on the Teaching of Science (CTS). This was preceded, in 1967, by a symposium in Lausanne, Switzerland on the co-ordination of the teaching of mathematics and physics.

The Droujba Conference produced 15 conclusions and recommendations in the form of ideas and guidelines reflecting international opinion at that time of science educators. These ideas and guidelines have, over the period of 20 years, stood the test of time and they still provide useful guidance for those involved in developing courses in integrated science education.

The five main conclusions of the Droujba Conference were:

The teaching of integrated science contributes towards general education, emphasizes the fundamental unity of science and leads towards an understanding of the place of science in contemporary society. It avoids unnecessary repetitions and permits the introduction of intermediate disciplines.

A course of integrated science should emphasize the importance of observation for increased understanding of the environment; it should introduce pupils to logical thinking and scientific method.

As it may be necessary in an integrated course to omit some details, it is essential that the content of a course be judiciously chosen. It must be carefully compiled by collaboration between the different teachers and other specialists.

The extent of integration and the balance between integration and co-ordination will depend on the age of the pupils, the type of educational institution and local conditions. At the earlier stages of secondary education, a totally integrated course in experimental science appears generally desirable. At the higher stages of secondary education such a course may also be desirable, especially for those students who have decided not to specialize in science.

Science is an important part of primary education, particularly in arousing scientific curiosity and in developing scientific attitudes and skills.

Other ideas and guidelines referred to the need for further experimentation with integrated science courses, for wide dissemination of the results of such experiments and projects, and for special attention being given to the training of teachers for integrated science.

There were also some suggestions about the need for correlation and co-ordination of physics and mathematics courses at school level.

In 1973, the problems of education and training of teachers for integrated science were addressed at a major international conference in Maryland, USA. This was sponsored by the ICSU CTS in collaboration with Unesco and the University of Maryland. The various approaches to evaluation and assessment of integrated science education were considered at a smaller international symposium held in Oxford, England in 1975.

The development of integrated science education worldwide was the subject of another major international conference — held in Nijmegen, Netherlands, in 1978 — organised by the International Council of Associations for Science Education (ICASE), in collaboration with Unesco.

The proceedings of each of these major events — in 1973, 1975 and 1978 — were published in the series of Unesco New Trends in Integrated Science Teaching (Volumes III, IV and V respectively).

Interdisciplinary science

The notion of integration can be applied at the highest levels of scientific research, where interdisciplinary science implies work which originates from the joint and continuously integrated efforts of two or more specialists or teams of specialists having different disciplinary backgrounds and training. The results resemble a chemical compound, where the individual constituents or elements can no longer be recognised or physically separated. It differs from multidisciplinary science where collaboration, often in parallel, leads to a physical mixture; here the ingredients can be seen and disengaged. The properties of a compound transcend those of its elemental parts, whereas those of a mixture never do.

The Journal *Interdisciplinary Science Reviews* contains in the Editorial of Volume 1 No. 1 the following reference to interdisciplinary science:

Increasing orientation towards interdisciplinary topics within the scientific community requires an understanding by specialists in one field of the needs, problems and terminology of another field. There is significant difference between information and understanding and, for the future of science, the latter is as important as the former. Understanding is achieved through collating critical reviews of contributions from a variety of fields. These will enable the scientist to use information retrieval systems, specialist reviews and research papers in the most rational manner.

But how is this novel interdisciplinary compound to be synthesized? How can the representatives of different disciplines be inspired to a joint creative effort? Or is it better perhaps to give individuals a chance to master a second discipline? Two outstanding historical examples come to mind: The Honourable Robert Boyle (1627-1691) and Alexander von Humboldt (1769-1859) certainly achieved excellence in more than a single field of science, and modern scientists may well be able to learn from their experience.

In more recent times, Interdisciplinary Research found its most widespread use in Operations Research, or Operational Research as it is called in the United Kingdom where it was originated by A P Rowe in 1937. He and his distinguished scientific colleagues started by teaching the intricacies of radar and such was their success that by 1945 operational research activities had become a truly interdisciplinary effort of scientists and industrialists. It is defined as the application of scientific method to the management of organised systems in which human behaviour plays in important part.

Systems Engineering, using a similar interdisciplinary approach tends to concentrate on technological innovation with less emphasis on the human factor. Systems Analysis, which again includes humanity in all its aspects, differs today but little from Operations Research as both fields developed and matured through their outstanding achievements in industrial, military and space activities. The essence common to all is Interdisciplinary thinking and a fusion of effort.

This understanding of integration can be enlarged to embrace many more scientific and human activities in many fields including education.

Although the basic recommendations about integrated science, adopted at the Droujba Conference in 1968, describe in broad terms what integrated science is, educators in recent years have tried deliberately not to define integrated science too precisely in order not to confine it. But, at the same time it is necessary to distil out of the diversity of approaches to integrated science the unity of purpose and of conviction that has led many countries along the path of integration of science. Now, twenty or more years later, many of the problems and issues are much the same as they were when integration of science at school level was just beginning; nevertheless, some new approaches and novel solutions to problems are emerging.

Even the word 'integration' is under scrutiny. In some countries the notion of 'integration' has other—more political—connotations. In many others, the approach to integration of science is reflected in other titles, such as 'general science' (a resurrection of a term used widely in the 1930s in some countries), 'balanced science', 'environmental science' 'science and society', 'basic science' and so on.

The place of integrated science teaching today

The continuing interest and debate on integrated science teaching is a reflection of the present state of flux in science education. Perhaps the very word 'integration' is evocative itself, and sufficiently magnetic or arresting enough to continue to attract attention. For some, integrated science provides a means of studying old but unresolved problems and issues in science education. For others, integrated science is a convenient platform for drawing attention to some research findings relating to learning and teaching of science. For yet others, integrated science is a timely device for gaining some say in the fate or destiny of science education in a field that has traditionally been firmly held by scientists of the established subject- orientated disciplines.

Among the trends and forces influencing integrated science today are the following:

(a) persistent attempts to introduce science into the primary school curriculum;
(b) the widespread acceptance that integration of science at lower secondary level should be part and parcel of general education;
(c) increasing attention being given to the training of teachers for integrated science;
(d) the inclusion of social issues, especially environmental issues, in secondary school science curriculum as a deliberate attempt to relate science teaching to social concerns;
(e) the need to arouse scientific curiosity in students in schools and to develop a positive attitude towards science;
(f) recognition of the existence of children's science before the students are exposed to science in schools. The ideas and concepts held by children — gained from a variety of external sources, including parents, the media, etc — are firmly held and cannot be so easily changed or diverted into traditional subject disciplines.

Modern approaches to integrated science, therefore, have to take into account the trends and forces outlined above. Curriculum models for integrated science at primary and secondary level should, according to Fensham (1983), cover five broad areas of concern:

• concerns for the factual and theoretical knowledge of science
• concerns for the process of scientific investigation and reasoning
• concerns for practical (laboratory) investigation in science
• concerns for attitudes towards science and attitudes associated with science
• concerns for the relation of science to society.

Issues in integrated science teaching

What are the main issues in integrated science education today?

In addition to the familiar problems that beset many systems i.e. overburdened teachers, lack of status of teachers, lack of adequate training of teachers, the following issues are among the most important:

The apparent dichotomy between the wish to provide scientific literacy for all, and the need to prepare future scientists and technologists. Whether one should teach science — or about science — and at what level, and to what extent, are demanding questions for those involved in designing integrated science courses. There are conceptual mismatches between the teaching of science and about science. In some cases the science is complex (e.g. AIDS), whereas, in others the economic and social issues are complex when the science is less so (e.g. acid rain).

The need to orient the content towards future trends in science and technology, including those trends that have an international dimension (e.g. population, energy, environmental), as well as those that affect individuals within specific societies. Thus different content topics will need to reflect different types of scientific and technological processes.

A recognition of the disintegrative nature of content-based testing in integrated science courses. Even though the course is designed as an integrated science course, the testing — often only for recall — leads to superficial learning of individual topics. Assessment should encompass all the objectives of integrated science courses at levels other than straight recall, and should embrace both formative and summative evaluation.

The limitations of the teacher training systems worldwide in preparing teachers adequately to teach integrated science, at primary and secondary level. This, coupled in some countries, with the problems of recruitment, motivation and resources, is the single most serious problem facing science education in general and integrated science teaching in particular. The solution is not easy or obvious, but massive programmes of in-service teacher education on the content and techniques of integrated science teaching coupled with professional support and incentives for teachers (resource centres, networking of science teachers' associations etc) is an essential prerequisite.

The genuine fear of many teachers of the challenges of change in science and technology and a lack of motivation to tackle integrated science, especially by those (the majority) who feel more comfortable with the single-subject discipline of their own initial training. One solution here is to encourage colleagues in other disciplines, such as language teachers, to introduce aspects of science in their own teaching.

These issues affect all countries in varying degrees according to local circumstances. The problems involved can be alleviated to some extent by a sharing of concerns worldwide through international agencies, Governmental and non-Governmental, through exchange of curricula and testing procedures, through harnessing resources for science and technology teaching from local communities (i.e. self-help basis) and generally by providing maximum support for the teachers involved.

Specific recommendations for action might include:

Establishing show-case schools in particular regions where exemplary practice of integrated science teaching can be seen.

Encouraging teachers to take a hard look at integrated science programmes in a specific country, with the help of international experts and local teachers who develop such programmes.

Developing hands-on experience of integrated science teaching rather than allowing teachers just to read about it.

Assisting teachers to understand the rationale of integrated science teaching in the 1990s by studying the interrelationships depicted in topics such as:

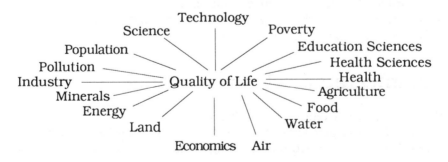

Debating with teachers the parameters of integrated science teaching i.e. what does integration encompass? Does it cover - technology? - economics? - social concerns? - ethical factors?

Encouraging the need to consider science in the community rather than in isolation in the laboratory or the classroom?

Ensuring that higher educational levels (Universities, Polytechnics etc) should show that at these levels there is genuine regard for integrated science at the secondary school level and that developments in integrated science are fully recognised.

Developing links and communication among teachers through science teachers' associations.

Discouraging the tendency of some teachers to look at integration as a little bit of biology, a little bit of chemistry, a little bit of physics. This is a rather narrow definition and is best avoided. Maybe it is now time to drop the word 'integrated' from junior secondary or secondary science courses. Is integrated science the same as combined science? Are primary science courses the same as integrated science? It would appear that relying on a name is unlikely to lead to the philosophy of teaching one would wish to advocate. There is a need to go beyond the name. Now is the time to give more attention to this area.

Encouraging students to acquire the appropriate technology of a country through a Technology Process Model geared to needs/problems, research design, student knowledge, skills and attitudes by reference to

  (a) Functional efficiency,

  (b) Economic aspects,

  (c) Artistic aspects,

  (d) Social aspects,

  (e) Political aspects.

Developing in the population a public understanding of science/technology.

Chapter 2

Review of integrated science education worldwide

Introduction

This review is based on replies to questionnaires issued to member associations of ICASE and on replies from other organisations and individuals. It also draws on the global survey of Unesco (1986): *The Place of Science and Technology in School Curricula.* There were 90 replies from 34 countries. Altogether, 128 courses were identified for review. This compares favourably with 130 courses analysed in a similar review in 1978. About half of the courses reviewed were new courses or revisions of courses since 1978.

The review aims to provide an overall view of the state of integrated science education today and to identify trends worldwide in the development of teaching of integrated science.

The analysis of the raw material and the presentation in this review follow the pattern adopted for the Nijmegen Conference 1978 which is reported in Chapter 5 of Unesco's New Trends in Integrated Science Vol.V. For purposes of definition use has again been made of the matrix proposed by Abraham Blum (1973) as a criterion for including or excluding particular courses. Blum's matrix has two axes: *scope* and *intensity*. The scope of a course is the range of disciplines, scientific or social, which it includes, while the intensity measures the extent to which the subjects have been blended together to give a deliberate synthesis of the material.

This review then, contains essentially those courses which have a substantial amount of both 'scope' and 'intensity' of integration. Thus, only those courses are included with two or more scientific disciplines and where a substantial amount of interweaving has taken place.

The definition of course or curriculum in this review has also followed the practice in the Nijmegen review. The main criteria are:
(a) evidence of publication or intention to publish and
(b) trials of material before publication.

Thus an individual school devising its own curriculum with no thought of wider use would be excluded on criterion (a), whilst a textbook written and published as a commercial venture with no development or implementation programme to support it would be excluded by criterion (b).

The areas or aspects of courses for which replies were called for include the following:
- date of inception,
- grades for which course is intended,
- ability range i.e. all students or selected groups,
- expected teaching time,
- language of course,
- country of origin of course,
- initiating authority,
- organisation of course,

- flexibility of course,
- scope of integration (as defined above),
- extent of integration (as defined for intensity above),
- printed material available,
- audio-visual, including computer software, available.

Age range

The age range has been used as a rough measure of the educational level since in many countries the assigned age range may bear no resemblance to the actual age of members of a particular class or educational group. There may well be the case where a project for a particular age range is used in a different context.

The age ranges considered were:

Primary. This covers the ages 5-11 years or grades K-7 years. Although most courses at this age range can be considered as integrated, there are some nature study courses which do not cover the physical science areas and are not counted as integrated e.g. *Living Science.*

Lower or junior secondary. Covering ages 12-15 years, grades 7-9. This is the age range with the greatest representation. In the UK, courses for this range have been boosted by the policy document *Science 5 -16* and the move to balanced science for all.

Senior secondary. Again the ages must be regarded as approximate but covering 15-17 years or grades 10-12. As might be expected, there is some specialisation at this stage and the number of integrated courses decrease.

Teacher education. Materials for integrated science remain scarce at this level.

University level. Except for some materials produced for general students in North America, materials for this level are thin on the ground, possibly because specialisation is regarded as usual and integrated materials are not always regarded as academically respectable.

Analysis by age range

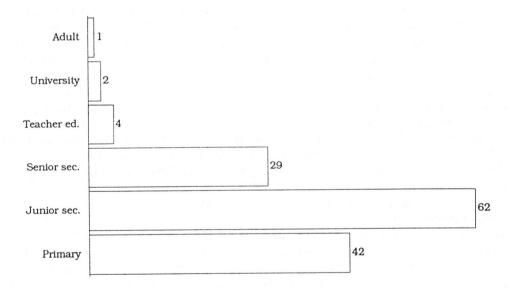

Total of 140 indicates that some projects fall in two different age ranges. e.g. *Science 5 -13.*

Ability

Nearly all the courses claimed to be for all abilities or average ability. Many courses made the claim that they were suitable for 'mixed ability', perhaps a reflection that streaming still exists in many schools. However, there was a great difference between the intellectual demands made by the different courses. In the UK, many courses are designed for low ability or non-examination classes. Examples of this approach are: *LAMP Project and Heinemann Core Science.*

The three ability levels identified and the percentage of courses relating to them are:

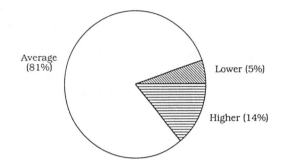

Average.	81 per cent
Lower	5 per cent
Higher	14 per cent

The allocation to ability groups was a little arbitrary; unless otherwise stated, the course was taken to be for average ability.

Country

As in the 1978 survey, it was not felt helpful to analyse the geographical distribution of courses. Some areas such as Eastern Europe and South America were underrepresented. From the Unesco survey of countries, there were indications of integrated science courses for China, Bulgaria and Romania. It would be interesting to compare a 'western' course with an 'eastern' one. Unlike many developing countries where the courses have had a considerable 'western' input, the 'eastern' courses will probably have developed entirely in isolation. An assessment of courses region by region is given in the next chapter.

Language

A large majority of the courses were in English, perhaps reflecting the language of the questionnaire. No attempt was made to pursue this dimension further.

Origin of the Course

To give a straightforward comparison, the same four measures of originality were taken. There was a marked tendency to overrate the degree of originality and some circumspection is required when interpreting the results. It was often difficult to classify courses from the amount of information given.

(a) Adapted from elsewhere, with few modifications.
(b) Adapted from elsewhere with major changes.
(c) Mostly original material.
(d) Original.

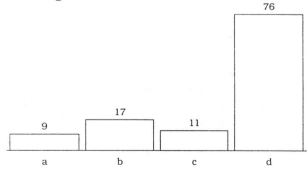

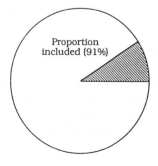

Initiating Authority

This dimension shows how the curriculum arose and the agency or organisation that gave rise to it. In many cases it is not possible to distinguish one single agent of change; a number of different bodies may be involved in the innovation.

School level. In practice it is very difficult for a school to make an individual integrated science curriculum. What is more likely is the adaptation of one or more courses to provide a coherent course for a particular school. In practice, there does seem to be an increasing direction as to which course to adopt within the schools of a local education authority. The only example in the UK of the initiative of one school remains the *Wreake Valley project.*

Middle administrative level. At this level it is perfectly feasible to devise a curriculum for a local education authority working through a group of schools or a Teacher's Centre. Recent examples in the UK of projects at this level include: *Suffolk Co-ordinated Science* and the ILEA *Modular Secondary Science Resources.*

National level. This is much more likely to be the level for developing countries where there may well be a shortage of teachers able to act as curriculum initiators. For large countries, e.g. Nigeria, the development may take place at federal or state level. No attempt has been made to distinguish between country or state.

Teacher's Association. Science teachers' associations may encourage or participate in curriculum development, through the involvement of some of their more active teachers. In the UK the ASE was responsible for producing *Science in Society* and *Science in a Social Context* courses. In Nigeria, the Science Teacher's Association (STAN) was the initiator of the Nigerian Integrated Science Project (see Chapter 9).

Universities. Universities have played an important role in curriculum development, either through their Science or Education Departments of Faculties.

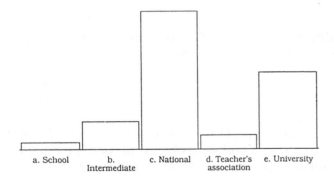

a. School   b. Intermediate   c. National   d. Teacher's association   e. University

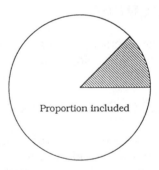

Proportion included

Organisation of the course

The following approaches were identified in the 1978 report:
• Concept,
• Topic,
• Process,
• Environment.
These approaches continue to reflect the main characteristics of new courses, but without seeing the original materials it is not always easy to decide how the course is organised. Some examples are given in the section on specific regions and countries. There seems to be a trend towards more courses based on the process approach and for more to be orientated towards the environment. This latter reflects the growing concern with science and society issues. Part III gives one approach to the inclusion of various factors in the development of one course.

Flexibility

The degree of flexibility allowed to the teacher varies widely with each course. A course for which there were: texts, workbooks, teacher's guides and curricular guides will be more prescriptive than one for which a general philosophy exists. Most teachers, given a wealth of written materials, would follow the course, but even with such a structure it is not possible to say exactly what will be taught.

An attempt is made to classify courses as:

Prescriptive. A course with a complete set of written materials and where all elements are compulsory must be regarded as prescriptive. An example of such a course is *Gambia Grades 1-6 Science.*

Series of units with different paths. Here greater flexibility has been introduced and there is some choice for the teachers as seen in *Primary Science for Botswana* (see Chapters 9 and 14).

A modular course. The use of modules has been seen in a number of recent UK courses. These modules are either used at different levels of ability or to satisfy different examination boards and allow candidates to gain either a single or double award. *Nuffield Science 13-16* in the UK is an example.

A resource bank. Here the teacher is presented with a bank of materials from which to make his or her choice. Often some guidance is given. Examples in the UK include *Warwick Process Science* and the *Modular Secondary Science Resources* (MSSR) of the Inner London Education Authority.

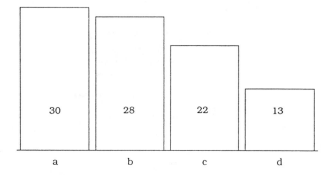

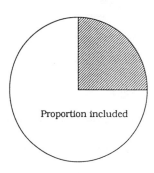

Proportion included

Scope of integration

To be included in the survey, a curriculum must contain at least two sciences. Greater *scope* is given by increasing the number of components in the course. The materials were analysed for scope as follows:

Two science disciplines. Common examples of these are Physical Science courses, but as has been pointed out, there must also be a degree of integration.

Three science disciplines. These courses present the largest number of courses at senior secondary level, but the degree of integration is often low.

Two or more sciences plus non-science areas. With increasing emphasis on the social relevance of science and a move away from specialisation, it has become popular to include social and environmental issues in a course. Many examples exist such as the Pakistan Grades 9-10 course and the integrated science course from the Philippines.

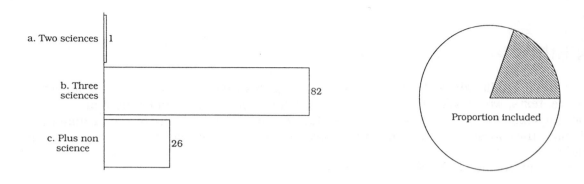

Intensity of integration

There is a tendency to exaggerate the intensity of the integration but without examining the materials in some detail, it is not possible to categorise the courses precisely. This explains why the 'not known' sector is quite large. Three types of courses are identified.

Co-ordinated. In this case it is possible to distinguish separate sections of chemistry, biology and physics. An example is Nuffield Co-ordinated Science.

Combined. Although the separate sciences are the starting point, the course is so designed that the three sciences are blended together.

Amalgamated. Here the ideas associated with the separate sciences are used as required to give a unified whole, or a high degree of integration.

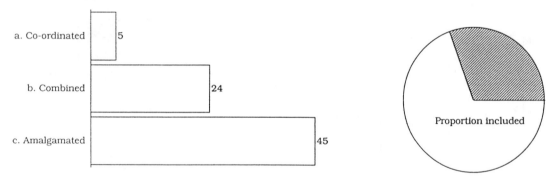

Printed and other materials

Most courses provide some written material, if only to give the aims of the course and a sense of direction. Written materials included:
• Textbooks,
• Workbooks/worksheets,
• Teacher's guides,
• Curriculum guides,
• Unit or topic tests.

Audiovisual material is also an important part of many courses. These include:
• Slides,
• Audio tapes,
• TV or radio programmes,
• Video tapes,
• Films,
• Games or simulations,
• Computer software.

Increasingly, computer software is now part of the course, but with notable exceptions. This use is mainly in developed countries. There might well be a problem with maintenance of hardware in many developing countries. In some countries apparatus kits are also available to teachers as part of the course (eg. the ZIMSCI Kits in Zimbabwe for junior secondary schools).

Practical work

All the courses claimed practical work took place, but the amount of practical work varied from less than 25 per cent of the time to more than 75 per cent.

It has not been possible to study in detail the provision of apparatus for practical work or where this work actually takes place. It is also not possible from the information at present available to determine whether the practical work is demonstration experiments by the teacher or actual practical work by students working alone or in groups.

Chapter 3

Reflections on the development of integrated science teaching

Reflections on the development of integrated science teaching projects for 4-16 year olds

Kerst Th. Boersma, Rob J. de Kievit, Paul M. Pilgrim,
National Institute for Curriculum Development, Netherlands

Introduction

This is a description of two projects sponsored by the National Institute for Curriculum Development in the Netherlands (SLO) as examples of creative curriculum development. The two projects are Natural Science at Primary Level and Integrated Science for 12-16 year olds.

In the first place, both projects have a strongly innovative character. Both projects are aimed at the development of a curriculum for integrated science, a subject which is new or at least almost new in the Netherlands. Innovative development work also implies that solutions must be found for subject didactics, as well as curriculum related issues not clearly defined at the outset of the project. This in itself demands strong creative ability on the part of the developers.

Secondly, both project groups decided upon a completely different development strategy. As a result of this, i.e. because of the fact that the curriculum products were developed at different levels and due to the fact that subject integration creates new problems, a situation emerged in which the chosen development strategy could not be followed without certain problems arising. This also inspired a certain degree of creativeness, although in the first instance this was not appreciated as such by the developers themselves. It was not until afterwards, when the development strategy had to be defined and executed, that the problems which had emerged were appreciated as creative moments, at least as far as satisfactory solutions could be found to those problems.

Thirdly, an account on the successes and failures of a curriculum development project which, in many ways, has pursued a creative course, may well succeed in stimulating the creativeness of others. Creativeness cannot be compelled, although it is possible to create certain conditions which could spark off creativeness. A reflection of the successes and failures of both projects could be one of those conditions.

Merely on account of the fact that both projects have been directed towards the development of Integrated Science, can both projects be considered as being distinctly innovative.

But subject integration is not the only innovative characteristic. The innovative characteristics of Natural Science at Primary Level and Integrated Science for 12-16 year olds were not established independently of the developments abroad or in the Netherlands. Both project groups were strongly influenced in their definitions by views on innovation as they are and were already defined in other countries. The projects themselves are described in para. 2 below. The innovative characteristics of both projects are described in para. 3 below; and the development and implementation strategies of both projects are compared in paras. 4 and 5. Some of the problems which were encountered will also be pointed out.

Projects of a strongly innovative character run the risk of producing educational programmes that may become very difficult for the majority of teachers to relate to. It is therefore significant that consideration is given to the way in which both project groups approached the problems relating the implementation of the educational programmes they developed.

The projects at work

The project Natural Science at Primary Level

The project 'Natural Science at Primary Level', designated by the SLO as the 'NOB-project' started in 1978. The central focus of the development strategy was that teachers and curriculum developers contribute equally to a joint curriculum development process. This opinion of the project group was well-matched with the spirit of the 1970s. The 1970s were the years of discussions on open and traditional education and curriculum development based on practical situations. The NOB-project followed this general trend and opted for a practice-oriented point of departure: the development of a school's curriculum starts with the teacher in the classroom.

The first round of the development activities (1978-1984) was set up in six schools, situated all over the country. Each school formed a development group which consisted of teachers and co-workers from the NOB-project and the local regional schools advisory service. If possible also a school biologist and a teacher trainer were involved. The school work can be characterised as 'Incentive Action': teachers developed their own curricula on a small scale while developers observed and analyzed. This title emphasized that the final proposal for a curriculum should grow from a variety of small concrete activities in the classroom, chosen by the teacher himself or herself. The result of this development work was the so-called 'School Description of Natural Science', published in 1986.

After 1984, the information obtained from the six school descriptions was supplemented by the project group with information concerning subject content from national and international projects.
This resulted in three experimental publications:
A broad outline of Natural Science education, providing a programme of study for 4-12 year olds.
A sourcebook of National Science, which includes a plan of lessons as an elaboration of the programme of study.
Lessons in Natural Science, which includes 32 examples of learning activities.

The set-up of these publications was also influenced by a change in views within the project group. It had become clear that teachers need more guidance in the form of concrete lesson material than originally was intended.

During a second round lasting two years (1986-1988) the ideas in these publications were subjected to a practical assessment in 25 pilot schools. Conferences and local training workshops were organized in order to prepare teachers for the implementation of the described lessons.

In the meantime, the SLO was requested to draw up a statement for attainment targets for all subject areas in primary education. Co-workers of the NOB-project undertook that task for Natural Science. Of course, they made use of the experience acquired during the project. In the process of the development of this statement several groups and individuals were consulted. The result may be regarded as a rather widely accepted set of attainment targets for Natural Science, which has had its impact on the further adjustment of the programme of study.

The project Integrated Science for 12-16 year olds

The project Integrated Science for 12-16 year olds was initiated by SLO in August 1983. The body which applied for the initiation of the project was the Dutch National Association for Science Education, NVON. The request of the NVON was a result of the ICASE/Unesco conference on Integrated Science Education, which was held in Nijmegen, the Netherlands, in 1978.

In the project Integrated Science for 12-16 year olds, an attempt has been made to overcome two obstacles in current science education at junior secondary level.

The first one is that pupils must learn all kinds of scientific concepts without being able to relate such concepts to daily life situations. Topics like 'the insulative and protective characteristics of clothing' or 'electrical appliances in the home' receive hardly any attention at all in lessons.

A second obstacle in current science education, is the lack of coherency between the various individual science subjects, physics, chemistry and biology.

Key concepts, such as energy, molecules and substances, apply to each of the individual subjects in their own specific way and are treated at different stages in the learning process. Systematic discipline separation by pupils is the result of this. To pupils, the molecules discussed in physics are different from the molecules discussed in chemistry classes. If the biology teacher speaks of nutrients, these substances are different from the 'chemical substances' discussed by the chemistry teacher.

An important objective of the project was to design a programme which appeals to pupils and from which they can profit at a later age. The principal objective is that pupils should be able to use their scientific knowledge and skills in daily life situations. One therefore speaks of 'context-orientated education', whereby integrated science is considered as an integral school subject containing contributions from the subjects biology, chemistry, physics, physical geography and agricultural technology.

The big problem at the beginning of the project was that there was no exemplary teaching material available, nor was there a basic structure available for a programme of study. The project group attached great value to the development of teaching material in collaboration with pilot schools. What teaching material was the question that was posed, and if a certain amount of teaching material had been developed, how then would it be possible to conceive a programme of study on the basis of such material?

Looking back, one can distinguish three stages in the project work. The first phase ran from August 1983 until the Spring of 1985. It was decided to opt for a simultaneous development of exemplary teaching material for the first two years of the project and a first draft of a programme of study. The project worked together with ten pilot schools, situated all over the country.

The development of the exemplary teaching material was intended as a further examination of a number of characteristics of the type of integrated science education the project group had in mind. The most important characteristics were:
• the curriculum must be context-orientated and integrated;
• the curriculum should motivate pupils;
• the teaching material must be appropriate to all pupils.

At the beginning of 1985, the first version of the programme of study was ready.This first programme of study contained a further elaboration of points of departure for an integrated science curriculum and a catalogue of objectives. There was no relationship with the material that had already been developed. The proposal had been specifically based on desirability and hardly at all on attainability. The function of the document was to correlate the many different views with regard to the content of an integrated science curriculum.

The second phase was begun in 1985 when the Dutch Ministry of Education requested the SLO to draw up the contents of a science curriculum for a new type of school: Advanced Primary Education for 12-16 year olds. The result of this work was the provision of a detailed description of a science curriculum in the form of minimum requirements. This provided the project group with an excellent aid for the development of a programme of study and a first draft proposal was subsequently drawn up. From that moment onwards, the project group also based the development of the exemplary teaching material on this proposal.

The third phase ran from August 1986 until completion of the project in August 1988. During this particular phase, two pilot schools joined the project as new participants. The project group wanted to verify whether the teaching materials, as they had been developed during participation of the first series of schools, could also be applied in other schools.

A total of 7 teaching units were compiled. All the topics had been chosen from the everyday world of the pupil: My Clothes, Pets, Your Home, Soil, Milk, Maize and Weather Report. Each topic follows the pattern: orientation, core part, optional parts. They have been tested once, some even twice.

As a result of the project work a number of studies have been conducted in which the opinions on and experience with specific subjects in the project have been described e.g. studies on environmental education and fieldwork.

Based on the experiences with the schools, a second draft programme of study was drawn up (June 1987) for the first three years of secondary education. This draft programme of study was based on the description of contents as mentioned in the second phase.

The programme of study is arranged according to context areas; four subjects contribute to integrated science: biology, physics, chemistry and physical geography (see Table 1).

Context area	Topics	Subjects	School year
1.	Plants and animals	B	1
2.	Health	B-Ph.-Ch.	1
3.	Shelter	B-Ph.-Ch.-G	1
4.	Energy	Ph.-Ch.	1
5.	Machines	Ph.	2
6.	Food	B-Ch.	2
7.	Communication	Ph.-B	2
8.	Materials	Ph.-Ch.	2
9.	Sexuality	B 2	
10.	Transport	Ph.-G	2
11.	Environment	B-Ph.-Ch.-G	2

Table 1. The context areas of the proposed programme of study

The final curriculum proposals were completed in 1990. These proposals lay specific emphasis on attainability by teachers and pupils, based on the comments received from the participating schools.

Characteristics of innovation

Natural science at primary level and integrated science teaching for 12-16 year olds

The characteristics of innovation in the project 'Natural Science at Primary Level' ('NOB project'), were strongly influenced by developments outside the Netherlands. The most important decisions had in fact been made prior to the establishment of the SLO and were greatly influenced by British projects such as the Nuffield Junior Science (1967) and Science 5-13 (1967-1970). With this, the NOB project had joined the first wave of innovative projects to emerge in the USA and Great Britain during the 1960s. Many of these projects share common characteristics of innovation, such as:
• Science should be investigative → learning by discovery;
• Children should choose what they want to investigate;
• Science should be more than nature study;
• Child-centred emphasis;
• Piagetian ideas prominent.

29

The above criteria can indeed be distinguished in the NOB project. Moreover, the NOB project group has always endeavoured to adhere to and uphold these principles. However, developments in the Netherlands, and especially abroad, have not stopped at 'Learning by Discovery'. Partly due to the long course of development of the NOB project, a certain discrepancy has occurred between the principles chosen and the principles which are considered as desirable. An example of this is the emphasis which is now laid on development of concepts and the lack of emphasis on the development of scientific skills. Another example of this is the emphasis now laid on the functionality of knowledge in context-related fields relevant to the pupils themselves. The NOB project group has not chosen to follow this principle. Additional complications stemmed from the project group's decision to retain, as long as possible, the principle that 'Children should choose what they want to investigate' which in fact meant that the project group did not wish to prescribe or dictate the content of lessons. The choice of relevant knowledge within specific context areas would signify the desertion of this basic philosophy.

The project for Integrated Science for 12-16 year olds has, to a further extent than the project Natural Science at Primary Level, inclined towards more recent philosophies of innovation. Integrated Science for 12-16 year olds focuses on context orientated science education that views subject integration as a means rather than as an objective in itself. In a way, this approach to context orientation follows international developments, whereby social relevance is advocated. (Ref. NSTA, 1985; Pennick & Jager, 1986).

However, the concepts 'context-orientated' and 'socially-relevant' are by no means identical. The development of context orientated science and mathematical education can be seen as an important Dutch contribution to international education developments. Therefore. the project has, to a large extent, followed the trail of innovations that have taken place in Dutch physics education. An example of this is the project Curriculum Development for Physics Education (PLON). (Kortland 1987; Lijnse & Hooymayers).

In deciding to focus on subject integration, the project group for Integrated Science for 12-16 year olds has been strongly inspired by the Australian Science Education Project (ASEP), initiated in 1970. ASEP developed material designed to help students (Cohen & Fraser; 1987):
Acquire skills and concepts that will encourage them to try to interpret their physical and biological environment.
Initiate and pursue their own inquiries while retaining a balance between their needs and obligations as individuals and as members of a group.
Adapt to change.
Ask about the consequences of scientific concepts.
Develop creativeness.

Certainly in the initial stages of the project, following the ASEP, the philosophy has been to develop a series of more or less independent series of lessons taking specific account of the Piagetian theory of Cognitive Development. At a later stage, stronger emphasis was placed on the wider structure of the programme as a result of the increasing interest with regard to concept development in the Netherlands.

The following will now be discussed in more depth:
• subject integration,
• context and environment,
• equal opportunities and intercultural education,
• field of interest and for knowledge of students.

Subject Integration

The similarities and differences that exist between both projects in relation to subject integration become visible when we take a look at integration at the level of the programme of study and integration at the level of the teaching material. The project group NOB has decided in favour of a so-called 'phenomenological approach': objects and phenomena as perceived by students are taken as the starting point of science education. Science lessons would then be principally directed towards objects and phenomena. When we look at the strongly inductive development strategy which was followed (see below), this meant that the structure chosen at the level of the Programme of Study was also based on the structure and arrangement of objects and phenomena. Since the sciences are, to a significant extent, directed towards certain types of objects and phenomena, the situation occurs in which only a limited part of the lessons can be integrated. The project group has therefore developed an integrated programme of study whereby the individual subjects are not integrated.

The project group for Integrated Science based its approach on the fact that subject integration can be the result of the elaboration of certain pre-selected topics. In particular, the project group has attempted to select lesson content which might be expected to be functional to the pupils in their own daily environment. On the other hand, the project group also based its approach on the view that it would be meaningless to offer subject matter which can only be significant in a limited number of situations. In other words, therefore, great importance was attached to the possibility of making flexible use of the teaching material.

Consequently, this meant that both the course of reasoning relating to the personal environment of pupils (context areas) and subject matter were used as a basis for compiling the programme of study. The above approach resulted in the fact that the programme of study, as a whole, became clearly integrated, but that the series of lessons which had been distinguished within the programme of study contained only 40 per cent of the subject matter ascribed to other subjects. The different directions chosen by the two project groups clearly demonstrate that the nature of subject integration is to a large extent a reflection of didactical views.

It may be suggested that, in view of cognitive development, it is essential that the programme of study at the lower levels should incline towards a phenomenological approach, whereas at higher levels, the material could be further integrated within context fields relevant to the pupils. As such, it can be concluded that it would be desirable to interrelate the nature of subject integration with the level of cognitive development of pupils.

Context and environment

The content of the programme of study for Natural Science at Primary Level focuses on the pupil's immediate environment (i.e the school environment). This is where children encounter and are confronted with objects and phenomena in their daily surroundings. The project group has always emphasized the importance of fieldwork. Contexts in the sense of everyday life situations relevant to the children were never used by the project group for Natural Science at Primary Level.

For the project group for Integrated Science on the other hand, context areas have always formed the basis for the significance of science education to pupils. The selection of relevant context areas, therefore, has been one of the project group's major problems. The project group recognized that, in order to be able successfully to introduce scientific concepts, it would be sufficient to present these concepts within contexts which could be understood by and which would be familiar to the pupils. Yet on the other hand, teaching material was not merely selected on the basis of relevance within selected context areas. It was essential that a balance be achieved between contexts and concepts in such a way that, on the one hand, concepts could be related to contexts and, on the other hand, that specific attention could be paid to ensuring that students would also be able to apply the knowledge they acquire outside the learning context (Boersma & De Kievit, 1987). Apart from the emphasis the project group laid on contexts, it also appreciated the significance of fieldwork on the basis of similar arguments as brought forward by the project group for Natural Science at Primary Level.

The question then arises to what extent the views of both project groups actually differ in relation to environment and contexts and whether the age difference of the pupils has perhaps been an important contributory factor towards the choices which were made. Context-orientated education takes place in a school environment too. The question arises whether context-bound education in itself offers sufficient guarantees for applying that which has been learned within the scope of contexts in everyday life. This is where fieldwork can make an important contribution. If fieldwork is not considered only in strictly biological sense, it can contribute to learning within the contexts of everyday life. It would then be logical to focus initially on objects and phenomena spontaneously arising from within these context fields.

31

It goes without saying that attention should first be paid to the orientation on the objects and phenomena which are apparent and of relevance. As far as this is concerned, we may conclude that the project group for Natural Science at Primary Level has drawn insufficient content from context areas. On the other hand, it can also be concluded that, at the other end of the learning process, the project group for Integrated Science for 12-16 year olds has paid insufficient attention to the application of knowledge in the everyday life of the pupils, for example, by developing homework assignments.

Equal opportunities and intercultural education

Both project groups addressed the issue of intercultural education only incidentally. The question therefore remains to what extent the developed curriculum proposals published will require adaptation from an intercultural point of view.

The situation with regard to equal opportunities between boys and girls is quite different. In the Netherlands, as well as abroad, it has been frequently observed that the way in which boys and girls develop in our society apparently seems to lead to discrepancies in study performance at secondary school, in particular with regard to Physics. It can be expected that the differences in interests and performance stem from or are strengthened by the primary school period. Meanwhile, an initial investigation into this situation has been conducted among grade 8 pupils. This survey has in fact confirmed the outcome of the British Assessment of Performance Unit (APU) survey, which concluded that the differences in performance between girls and boys at this level are only nominal and that differences of any consequence are found primarily in technical and scientific subjects (Van den Akker et al., 1987). The project group for Natural Science at Primary Level has therefore initiated research aimed at uncovering the discrepancies in the behavioural pattern of boys and girls and at developing proposals for remedial didactics.

At the request of the project group for Integrated Science, a survey was also conducted into the field of interest and fore-knowledge of pupils with regard to 40 context descriptions compiled on the basis of a draft curriculum developed by the project group. The survey points out that the preferences of girls and boys do show characteristic differences and that these differences have been confirmed by other sources. For example, girls appear to have a greater interest in the functioning of the human body. Topics like health and healthcare, a balanced diet and the control of body weight are themes often mentioned by girls, but hardly ever by boys. It also appears that girls are more interested in carrying out experiments themselves.

In addition, it was found that 17 subjects gained more interest from girls, whereas only 7 were more popular with the boys. This perhaps indicates that girls will be more positively encouraged by education offered in the form of contexts (Deetman & Timmer, 1988).

As yet, we may conclude that, although information is available concerning the differences in interests and knowledge between girls and boys, it is not quite clear how curriculum publications should be adapted to meet these differences. It may be suggested that adaptation should be possible at primary level, this in view of the relatively small differences which occur at that level.

It remains to be seen whether didactic differentiation or adaptation would suffice. The argumentation here is based on the fact that sex-related differences in interests are undesirable and that it should be the task of science education to contribute to reducing these differences. If these views were to be accepted, this would also mean that another didactical view held by both project groups should be abandoned, namely that it is important to relate to the interests of the pupil.

Field of interest and foreknowledge of pupils

Both project groups have attempted to take serious account of the interests and foreknowledge of pupils. The crucial question is therefore, to what extent the interests and foreknowledge of specific groups of pupils can also be taken into account in curriculum publications. Can you base a curriculum on average interests and foreknowledge of pupils? Or is taking account of the interests and the foreknowledge of pupils only momentous?

As previously mentioned, the project group for Natural Science at primary level has always been in favour of an open curriculum in which space is created for the momentous interests of the pupils. This has been demonstrated in the various stages: introduction - discovery - assimilation - understanding.

The project group for Integrated Science 12-16 has taken the view that differentiation according to interests is of essential importance. This idea has been further developed by the inclusion of optional sections in the exemplary teaching material based on generally accepted or the known interests of pupils. Moreover, the project group has endeavoured to incorporate subjects of general interest in the core of the curriculum. The results of the research which was conducted with regard to the interests and foreknowledge of pupils (Deetman & Timmer, 1988), as was previously mentioned, could provide a source of reference for this.

In relation to foreknowledge, a totally different picture emerges. Neither of the projects have specifically focussed on momentous foreknowledge as was the case for example in the British project entitled 'Childrens' Learning in Science' (Driver, 1987). However, after having accepted the inevitability of formulating a curriculum, the project group for Natural Science at Primary Level had posed the question of how account can be taken of the phase of cognitive development on the basis of Piaget's Theory. On the one hand, the project group was confronted with developments such as the 'British Science 5-13', whereas on the other hand, it was gradually becoming a widely accepted view in international circles that the specific attitudes and ideas of pupils are of greater significance than the purely logical mathematical definitions of the Piagetian phases. Yet the question remains how specific conceptions of pupils can be dealt with when designing a programme of study. After making an inventory of the literature on the views and attitudes of pupils at primary school level, the project group reached no other conclusion than that it would perhaps be better not to introduce certain concepts (for example: energy and the molecule). In the development of the project Integrated Science for 12-16 year olds, no account was taken of available literature relating to alternative frameworks of pupils. However, an attempt was made to develop a series of concepts on the basis of required foreknowledge. It can be concluded that both project groups have approached the interests of pupils from different angles. The issue of how, if at all, account should be taken of the preconcepts of pupils in a programme of study, is a question which, as yet, has only been partially answered, even at international level.

Development: design and evaluation

Natural Science at Primary Level and Integrated Science for 12-16 year olds

A remarkable fact is that although both project groups have produced comparable curriculum products, they have in fact employed quite different development strategies in order to develop these products. Both projects have, at certain stages, carried out curriculum development in a 'school environment- orientated' manner. However, the ways in which these school environment-orientated strategies have been implemented are strikingly different. These differences in strategies have been determined by a number of factors.

The project group for Natural Science at Primary Level commenced in a period when the development of an open curriculum development was strongly propagated in response to the failure of research-development-diffusion strategies. On the one hand, it was the general view that curriculum development ought to be undertaken by the teachers themselves, but on the other hand, it was considered necessary to focus primarily on the current interests of pupils (see para. 3.5.). The initial group of developers of the Natural Science curriculum had certainly projected these views and ideas with great enthusiasm. The results of these views were the so-called 'incentive actions': teachers developed their own curricula on a small scale while developers observed and analyzed. An important factor here was the fact that, prior to the activities of the project group, no tradition had been established in Dutch schools in relation to science studies. Science education was a new concept and consequently had to be structured right from scratch.

The situation with regard to the Integrated Science project for 12-16 year olds was quite different. To begin with, most developers had gained their experience from large scale and rather successful innovation projects for chemistry and physics. In these projects, the development of good quality and highly innovative teaching material stood in high regard, especially for the subject physics, and they themselves developed the teaching material. Influenced by these successful projects, the ambitions of the majority of the developers was directed towards producing good quality teaching material. This ambition could only be partly met with, since it was determined by the SLO that no complete methods could be developed. The development of exemplary teaching material should be designed to support the empirical basis of curricula. Secondly, the participating schools were experimenting with self-developed science curricula, the innovative aspects of which were primarily found in subject integration and to a much lesser extent in various new subject content or didactical innovations (see para. 3.1.).

At the start of the project, the educational-political context for the development of integrated science education had been quite favourable. A major difference between science education at primary level and at secondary level, is the role of subject knowledge.

Subject knowledge at primary level is less relevant than it is at secondary level, and teachers at primary level are not usually subject experts — they teach everything. Although teachers at secondary level are not trained to teach integrated science, they are nearly always subject experts.

Inductive and deductive courses

Two stages are distinguished in the course of development of the project for Natural Science at Primary Level. In the first stage, incentive actions were carried out at six schools. These incentive actions resulted in the structure of a complete school curriculum for the development schools. On the basis of these school curricula, and based on information obtained from external sources. e.g. from the Education Department of the State of New York, a programme of study was produced. During the second stage of the project, new lessons were designed on the basis of this programme of study and after being re-included in the school curricula, will be incorporated in a final programme of study. The final programme of study will also contain the attainment targets that were established during the course of the development. The first stage can certainly be regarded as a strongly inductive method of work. Due to generalization, the experiences with the schools had to be included in the programme of study. The next course pursued was a deductive one — from a programme of study to lessons — and a partially inductive- deductive course — from lessons, attainment targets and a draft programme of study to a final programme of study. It was during the first inductive course in particular that serious problems occurred when the generalization of the school curricula failed to result in a structure for a programme of study.

Moreover, the assessment and incorporation of contributions by parties not directly involved with development proved to be a time consuming task.

During the course of development of the Integrated Science Project, as yet, three stages can be distinguished.

During the first stage, activities were focussed both on a programme of study as well as the development of teaching materials: the two were not interrelated. The first draft programme of study was drawn up on the basis of attainment targets which had been previously established (Boersma & de Kievit. 1987). School curricula were then developed based on the series of lessons and previously developed teaching material, after which a second draft of the programme of study was completed. During the second stage, the developers followed a deductive course.

It was during the third stage of the project that the attainment targets were actually developed for the second time, but now within a different educational-political framework, which is the reason why a final programme of study still has to be finalized. Lesson material based on that programme of study will not be developed by the SLO.

In view of the development strategies followed by the SLO with regard to both projects, it has been concluded that, for reasons of efficiency, it would be advisable to start with a draft programme of study and to base the development of teaching material on such a programme of study. One condition however, is that this draft programme of study will require thorough verification.

The role of the teacher

The role assigned to the teachers by the project group for Natural Science varied at each stage of development. During the first stage of development, when incentive actions took place, the teachers assumed the role of the developers of their own programme of study. The members of the project group made an attempt to limit their role to that of observer and evaluator. During the second stage, the project group designed lessons based on the draft programme of study whereby the role of the teachers was limited to the implementation of the written teaching material.

In the project for Integrated Science, carefully defined tasks were assigned to teachers and developers in the pilot schools. Although the teaching material was primarily designed by the developers, this was only done after close consultation with the teaching staff. Many of the ideas were also forwarded by the teachers.

The experiences of both project groups indicate that one should not always assume that teachers function successfully as developers, in particular when this is related to the development of teaching material which is also to be applied outside of their own schools. Various skills play an important role in the development of teaching material: practical teaching experience, writing skills, development experience and subject-related expertise. The available time is also an important contributory factor. Such skills are often only adequately at one's disposal if such a development team includes teachers and developers. It would be advisable therefore, to allocate various tasks within the development teams according to specific skills. In order to stimulate the personal involvement of teachers and to prevent the re-occurrence of some of the practical problems, in most cases it would seem wise only to confine the role of the teachers to the implementation of the developed teaching material. A different situation exists when curriculum products other than teaching materials are developed. Experiences both in the Netherlands and abroad, for example with ASEP, (Cohen & Fraser, 1987) indicate that discussions about attainment targets do not often provide the most suitable points of connection for teachers. Curriculum proposals should obviously be verified by teachers. but teachers usually demonstrate little enthusiasm towards this task.

Organization of the curriculum

With regard to the development of curricular products, it is the general view that developers possess a large amount of creativity and make implicit use of a variety of design principles. This also is also characteristic of the project group for Natural Science at Primary Level. This meant that, although the project group was in a position, on completion of the project, to indicate how the product was developed, this was not done on the basis of a pre-contemplated design strategy, derived or not derived from learning theories such as that of Ausubel (for ref. see Novak & Gowin, 1984; Boschhuizen, 1987).

This also means that the structure of education, in particular the sequential structure, took place during the course of the development of the project as a whole. On analysis, it appeared that the project group for Natural Science applied the following structure procedure:
a. the programme of study is described in principles, inspired by the Elementary Science Syllabus of the State of New York. whereby a distinction is made between knowledge, skills and attitudes each of them elaborated according to age periods of two years.
b. the programme of study is described in terms of the seven defined contexts.
c. within the various contexts, learning activities are arranged according to increasing complexity.
The project group for Integrated Science employed a distinctly different method in developing the first draft programme of study: at the start of activities, a design strategy was first devised and applied after minor adjustments had been made (Boersma & De Kievit, 1987). The design procedure comprised the following steps:
a. the selection of attainment targets based on a matrix consisting of social roles and a scale — from 'individual' to 'world orientation';
b. a selection of key concepts from pre-selected attainment targets;

c.   the construction of a conceptual network in such a way that if knowledge of one concept was essential to the understanding of another, connecting arrows were drawn between them. Clusters were distinguished in the conceptual network;

d.   a link between attainment targets and context areas;

e.   the inclusion of skills;

f.   the conversion into a proposed programme of study whereby choices were made for the amount of curriculum time to be allocated to each context area and a sequence was then established between the various context areas.

For the time being, it seems worthwhile to attempt to formulate design procedures based on learning theories such as that of Ausubel. If these learning theories contribute to creating an optimal learning process, it can then be expected that if use is made of the design principles derived from such theories, the sequences developed in this manner will indeed contribute to an optimal learning process.

Evaluation and Verification

The rule applies to all curriculum development projects that if insufficient attention is paid to formative evaluation, teaching material will be developed which insufficiently guarantees that the objectives aimed at will in actual fact be achieved. A similar rule applies to curricula and programmes of study. If these are inadequately verified, the project runs the risk that the proposals will be insufficiently implemented.

During the first years of the project for Natural Science at Primary Level, when incentive actions were developed, much emphasis was laid on formative evaluation. All lessons were recorded on video and discussed with the teachers. In the second round in the collaboration with the pilot schools, lessons were evaluated using evaluation forms. Due to lack of available time only a part of the lessons could be observed. Experience shows that these evaluation forms usually only produce comments of a general nature from teachers and that insufficient information is collected, in particular in relation to study results. Meanwhile, an evaluation project has been started by the University of Twente which is specifically aimed at visualizing study results.

Formative evaluation of the Integrated Science lessons was carried out by the CITO (National Institute for Educational Assessment). Both the pupils and the teachers were presented with questionnaires relating to the objectives of the lessons and the organization of the classroom. Lessons were only occasionally observed by members of the project group. Although formative evaluation carried out by people from external organizations can be of great value, in this event a number of problems occurred on account of dislocation and differences of opinion. The most significant problems which occurred included the following:

a.   CITO evaluators claimed that their evaluation data had been inadequately used for the adjustment of the material.

b.   Some project group members expressed the view that educational methods largely based on statistics had fallen short in producing relevant information.

c.   According to the CITO, the project group had failed to provide clear information at an early stage about the attainment targets which were to be evaluated.

d.   In many instances it had been unclear to project group members how evaluation data should be interpreted and how, on the basis of these data, decisions could be made for adjustment.

In consideration of formative evaluation, it can be concluded on the basis of the experiences of both project groups that in the process of developing innovative teaching material, it is essential for developers (or external researchers) to observe lessons, particularly with regard to the characteristics of innovation.

Both project groups have adequately addressed the issue of verification. In this respect, however, their experiences have been rather ambivalent. Experiences indicate that it is not sufficient to have draft programmes of study verified by teachers, since the terminology and formulations applied are often too abstract and teachers are not sufficiently motivated.

On the other hand, it would also be unwise if verification were to be carried out only by experts (training institutes, post-training institutes, developers, researchers etc.), as they often have difficulty in distinguishing desirability from attainability. Nor is it wise to bring teachers and experts together in verification meetings, since the chances are great that the teachers will be forced to succumb to the verbal dominance of the experts.

Curriculum development and implementation

Natural science at primary level and integrated science for 12-16 year olds

The time when it was assumed that curriculum products could first be developed and that dissemination could then take place is long gone.

During the last two years in particular, the SLO is explicit in its attempts to take account of the possibilities of actually implementing the products on completion of the project during the first stages in the preparation and the characterization of the products to be developed. The following strategic choices have been made in support of this policy:

a. 40 per cent of the SLO budget is allocated to projects initiated in response to applications from the field. Another 40 per cent is committed to applications from the government and guarantee compliance with government policies.
b. Market research and research into the demand for projects is carried out to an increasing extent prior to the initiation of a project.
c. During the implementation of projects, a network of experts and teachers is set up who can play a supportive role during implementation.
d. Increasing emphasis is placed on a public relations policy which is specifically defined for each individual project.
e. Explicit features of curriculum products are continuously chosen in order to promote the capability of implementation.
f. Increasing efforts are made to reach agreements with educational publishers.
g. Particular emphasis is laid on the verification of curriculum proposals.

The curriculum for Science at Primary Level in particular, and to a lesser extent the curriculum for Integrated Science for 12-16 year olds, were developed at a time when these strategic choices were made to a much lesser extent than they are at present. However, this does not mean that both project groups have not made choices directed at implementation. On the contrary. A brief outline of the above designated strategic policies is:

a. The project for Integrated Science for 12-16 year olds was initiated in response to demand from the field; moreover, in 1983 the project also ran in correspondence with the proposed policy of the government.
b. The project group for Natural Science at Primary Level in particular, but also the project group for Integrated Science, have invested a great deal of time in setting up and maintaining a network. The work carried out by the project group for Natural Science at Primary Level resulted in the foundation of educational workshops.
c. The project group for Natural Science at Primary Level has spent little time and effort on public relations: the project group for Integrated Science frequently published its findings in professional journals. The educational publication entitled 'De Grabbelton' containing suggestions for teachers, formed an important medium for the distribution of those findings.
d. Research was conducted into the explicit features of teaching material for Natural Science at Primary Level (Van den Akker, 1988). Systematic attention has also been paid to the explicit features of the curriculum for Integrated Science.
e. Both project groups have attempted to establish an agreement with one or more educational publishing houses; at present, only the project group for Natural Science has achieved success. Since then, many of the ideas of the project group for Natural Science have been incorporated in concise form in recent teaching methods.

Despite the above, it must be observed that the implementation of both projects will not occur without a struggle. Based on the estimations made in relation to the possibilities for the implementation of both projects, the following general provisional conclusions may be drawn.

In the first place, the dilemma occurs in development projects directed towards a considerable degree of innovation that, on the one hand, innovation must be given sufficient opportunity to crystallize; this requires time and a certain degree of isolation. However, on the other hand, for successful implementation, it is necessary to involve those who play a role in the later implementation of the project as early as possible. Although working in isolation for a prolonged period of time is, to a certain extent necessary, it may be unwise.

Secondly, a development project can only contribute to innovation sufficiently if, on the one hand, it corresponds with the government policy that is to be implemented (and preferably if it is also supported by sufficient pressure from society, e.g. the movement of environmental education) and if, on the other hand, it is adequately linked with the requirements indicated by teaching staff. Implementation will be successful only when there are sufficient top-down and bottom-up processes to support it. As far as this is concerned, the project group for Integrated Science started its work under favourable conditions; however, government policy in relation to subject integration has changed somewhat since 1986.

Teaching material and preparation of implementation

Successful implementation nearly always requires the availability of high quality, practicable teaching material. In this respect, the role of the SLO in the development of teaching material is restrained by government policy. In order to avoid competition with commercial educational publishers and to ensure that the SLO does not give the impression that it prescribes state pedagogics, it has been determined that the SLO shall only develop exemplary teaching material. Successful implementation therefore, largely depends on whether educational publishers make use of the material developed by the SLO in the development of complete methods.

A consequence of this is, on the one hand, that the group at which the material is aimed quite often consists primarily of educational publishing houses and not teachers, and on the other hand, that it must be made clear why the exemplary teaching material looks the way it does.

Both project groups have applied considerable efforts to the development of exemplary teaching material, the project group for Natural Science particularly during the second stage of development. The purpose was twofold; to invite comments from others on the proposals, but also to consider whether it should prepare and organize the process of implementation itself. This was preceded by research work (Van den Akker, 1988) which was aimed at investigating how the teaching material should look in order to stimulate implementation. Procedural directives for the benefit of teachers also seems to be of essential importance.

The role of teaching material in the project for Integrated Science was quite different. In response to requirements from practice, the teaching material was aimed primarily at being applied in the pilot schools.

As such, the material was not effective enough in its function as exemplary material for educational publishers, in particular because the series of lessons contained insufficient information with regard to the specific questions and problems which had to be answered and solved. The project group for Integrated Science has attempted to develop practicable teaching material for mixed ability classes. The teaching material is largely self-guiding.

Degree of innovation and school practice

There is often a remarkable relationship between curriculum development and school practice since curriculum development is directed towards a practical school situation which does not yet exist or is only present to a limited extent. Consequently, a number of problems may arise.

The objective of curriculum development therefore. is to contribute to the quality of education, in particular to the quality (nature and efficiency) of what pupils learn. In consideration of this, curriculum development should be primarily directed towards optimizing the effects of learning. However, there are a number of reasons that make it impossible to do this directly.

In the Netherlands. the principal responsibility for the organization and provision of education, including the choice of subject matter, rests with the school and only in the last instance with the teachers themselves. The school and the teacher form the necessary link and it is they who decide whether or not methods of a higher quality will be used or whether relevant subject matter will be taught. Consequently, there is a certain degree of tension between the choices teachers make and the optimization of the learning process and, of course, the question is then in fact how innovative a curriculum should be, in particular when one speaks in terms of didactical innovation. Learning by discovery, the learning of research skills and fieldwork such as were initially emphasized by the project group for Natural Science at Primary Level are quite remote from the school practice in most primary schools.

It has become clear that the extensive innovative step which both project groups have attempted to make, has had an adverse effect on the possibilities of successful implementation. It is, therefore, recommended that projects which are directed to a large extent towards innovation are not only aimed at the development of ideal situations in education. In addition, specific attention shall have to be paid to the further realization of the intermediate stages which can lead to these ideal situations.

Conclusion

There are no illusions that natural science for primary level education, as described, will be implemented in the Dutch educational system on a large scale, only as a result of the activities of a curriculum development project. Specifically defined and approved teaching materials constitute only one of the essential factors for such a large scale implementation. Even when this is realized, there will still remain much work to be done by others following the initiatives of the NOB, in particular as far as materials for use by pupils is concerned.

In addition, the implementation of a natural science curriculum in primary schools requires the following:

active school management and support, stimulated by way of special attention provided by the government;

specific and continuous post-training/guidance by school advisory services, school biologists and training institutes;

the stimulation of mutual collaboration and team development, possibly with the aid of a specialist-colleague as a pioneer;

a selective use of external sources (people and means).

Integrated Science for 12-16 year olds has not yet been generally implemented in junior secondary education. In fact, the use of the experimental teaching materials is limited only to a small group of pilot schools.

There are several reasons for its limited introduction. As far as policy is concerned, the situation with regard to junior secondary education has been unclear, for some years. During the second half of the 1970s, there was talk of introducing a different structure of education for pupils between 12 and 16, but so far, no political decision has been taken. The government proposals with regard to the restructuring of school subjects have varied greatly during the past years. At first, there was question of introducing a new structure of education in the way of learning fields (like integrated science), but the latest government proposals (1988) tend to be directed more towards a structure in the way of two science subjects: physics and chemistry together, and biology.

Teacher qualifications also form an important obstacle. At present, there is no adequate agreement on the qualifications of teachers of integrated science. Hardly any provisions have been made for post-training schemes either.

Although the project group has produced a proposed programme of study as well as exemplary teaching material, no close relationship exists between the two. No teaching materials have been compiled on the basis of the proposed programme of study, which means that there is an important instrument missing which could help teachers cross the threshold.

It is well known that the development of educational programmes is a matter of perseverance. However there are a number of tendencies indicating a change in the climate of integrated science education in the Netherlands:

At a large conference on integrated science education held in 1988, 93 per cent of the participating teachers appeared to be in favour of introducing an integrated science curriculum in schools. The previously mentioned obstacles prevented about half of these teachers from actually beginning such a programme of study.

Just recently, a forum for integrated science education has been set up, in which the NVON teachers' association and a number of institutions and training colleges collaborate.

In 1989 an association has been established whose primary objective is to develop teaching material for integrated science.

On request of the teacher's association NVON the SLO will do further curriculum development for Integrated Science for 12-16 year olds in the 1990s.

The declaration of policy of the new government (October 1989) proposes a greater coherence between subjects in basic education; schools will be given the opportunity to introduce integrated subjects.

In order to stimulate a context-orientated curriculum for integrated science, it is recommended that a distinction be made between short and long-term objectives. A context-orientated integrated science curriculum, therefore, would be a long-term objective. In the short term, one could pursue a more efficient adjustment between the individual subjects and a more contextual approach to these subjects. This would result in an important contribution being made to the general improvement of science education in schools.

The projects Natural Science at Primary Level and Integrated Science for 12-16 year olds are of major significance to the development of science education in the Netherlands. Neither of the projects has provided conclusive answers. However, a lot can be learned from both projects: positive things to derive from, as well as mistakes which must be avoided. The successes and failures of the projects for integrated science are certainly not only of significance to science education. Hopefully, they will also provide a source of inspiration for other developers.

References

AKKER, J.J.H. van den (1988), *Ontwerp en implementatie van natuur-onderwijs*. Swets & Zeitlinger, Amsterdam/Lisse.

AKKER, J.J.H. van den, L.W.F. BONEKAMP, P. KEUSTEN & A.C.M. NIES (1987), *Volgscholen in beeld. Verslag van een beginsituatie-onderzoek bij de volgscholen van het NOB-project.* Faculteit Toegepaste Onderwijskunde. Universiteit Twente, Enschede.

BOERSMA. K.Th. (1986), The innovation of junior secondary science education in the Netherlands. In: E.O.I. Jozefzoon (ed.) *Co-ordinating Curriculum Policy and Practice.* SLO, Enschede. 81-120.

BOERSMA, K.Th. & R.J. DE KIEVIT (1987), Development of a syllabus and programme of an integrated STS-curriculum for lower secondary education. In: K. Riquarts (ed.) *Science and Technology Education and the Quality of Life.* Vol. 2., 571-582.

BOSCHHUIZEN, R. (1987), *Van vakinhouden naar leerinhouden.* VU uitgeverij, Amsterdam.

COHEN, D. & B.J. FRASER (1987), *The Process of Curriculum Development and Evaluation. A retrospective account of the process of the Australian Science Education Project.* Curriculum Development Centre, Canberra/Australia.

DEETMAN, A.J. & J. TIMMER (1988), *Onderzoek voor het SLO-project Natuuronderwijs voor 12-16 jarigen,* SCO. Amsterdam.

DRIVER, R. (1987), Changing conceptions. Paper: International Seminar Adolescent Development and School Science, Kings College/Londen.

KORTLAND, K. (1987), Curriculum emphases in the PLON physics curriculum. In: I. LOWE (ed.). *Teaching the Interactions of Science. Technology and Society.* Longman, Cheshire/Melbourne. 231-240.

LIJNSE. P.L. & H.P. Hooymayers (1988), Past and present issues in Dutch secondary physics. *Education* 23 (3), 173-179.

NOVAK. J.D. & D.B. GOWIN (1984), *Learning How to Learn.* Cambridge University Press, New York.

PENICK, J.E. & R.E. YAGER (1986), Science Education: New Concerns Issues. *Science Education* 70 (4), 427-431.

PLOWDEN, J.P. (1976), *Children and their Primary Schools.* A report of the Central Advisory Council for Education. Vol. I: *Report.* Her Majesty's Stationary Office, London.

National Science Teachers Association (NSTA) (1985), *NSTA Handbook 1985-86* Washington D.C.

State Education Department (z.j.), *Elementary Science Syllabus + Supplement, Level 1.* Albany, New York.

Reflections of a science teacher

J.N. Mattoo, India

When, almost a decade back, a seemingly concerned voice suggested that we have gone too far into compartmentalisation of what was plain science, it stirred our conscious and gave thought to modifying our own doing. Whether this was right or wrong is a separate question altogether.

To my mind what emerges naturally through evolutionary thought, is almost always, an effective, necessary and successful answer to either an existing problem or, more interestingly, to one that is likely to occur in future.

If integrated science teaching' does not evolve on its own then surely it will disappear after some time. Enquiries, personal experience and extensive interviews have indicated a rather bleak picture in this direction.

It is the rare, few science teachers, who display sensitiveness to a problem and effect a possible solution. Most others follow a dictat almost mechanically. Whether science is presented through an integrated teaching procedure', or in a compartmentalized structure, has very little relevance for the classroom teacher, who has to wrestle with an unmanageable pupil-teachers ratio of mixed ability students, some simply first generation learners.

Philosophically, we can still impress on teachers that students need interrelated experiences, which make learning effective and meaningful. Even research has established, (which it need not, as it is a self-assertive opinion and outcome) that through interrelated study patterns, student's insight, understanding and motivation multiply, resulting in positive attitudes and enhanced performance levels. But this is true in general and not specific for science education alone.

Integrated science teaching has developed most successfully at the primary or the upper primary levels, even without expert advice, as the teachers have the freedom to amble back and forth to the advantage of students. The teacher has less pressure and time constraints imposed by heavy syllabuses and the demand of a desirable performance in an external examination.

But it is time that we faced up to unpleasant facts which are different from those expected.

At the primary stage, environmental studies is surely an effective and successful means to foster a foundation for integrated science teaching (IST). To my mind the only professional satisfaction of IST can be had at the primary stage, as here the real intention of integrating various hitherto compartmentalized disciplines could exist, although it is usually not dealt with. Integrated pattern is something which occurs or can be suggested naturally at this stage.

At the upper primary stage we find teachers using division into existing disciplines, because of the '*existing practices and general inclinations*'.

Even if an orthodox integrated science teaching programme attempt was made, it would become a casualty — because of a lack of adequate in-service training. Many Bachelors of Science teachers, catering to the upper primary students, have studied a combination of subjects, where at least one of the main areas of integrated science was missing. And there are instances where students have had two teachers teaching a combination of science subjects, thus defeating the possible outcome of a single teacher schedule, which could, to some extent, promote an 'integrated system'. This is perhaps, not so difficult a problem, as the content and courses at the upper primary stage are not too advanced and do not involve much derivations or numericals.

At the secondary level, the compartmentalization emerges despite pedagogically feasible plans like integrated science teaching.

The only national apex educational body in India (the National Council of Educational

Research and Training, directly under the Ministry of Education, as an autonomous body) has faithfully tried to carry out plans to guide teachers and science educators towards an integrated science teaching methodology.

In this connection workshops and seminars have been held; curriculum, syllabus and text-books have been written and a guidelines for 'Science Education in the First Ten Years' have been published.

There are some voluntary agencies committed to bringing science to the villages where IST' has been attempted.

It is sad that a representative cross-section of the intellengentsia, i.e. experts, teacher educators and even sensitive parents have expressed disenchantment with the expected outcomes of the steps taken to improve science education. Almost all agree that even the minimum possible has not been achieved.

After introducing integrated science teaching, the teachers, for convenience, fall back into the existing compartmentalized pattern and teach a chapter as a unit by itself, thus making additional bifurcations.

There is another dichotomy also. Perhaps we are in danger of churning out science slogans so fast that they are not fully noticed. That is how approaches to school science education, acceptable in the fifties, have been found wanting in the sixties and the science processes of the sixties found irrational in the seventies.

There has been a vacillation in school science policies. Recommendations to counteract this include action plans and decisions each closely succeeding the other. In some countries under the simple 'human failing' of 'keeping up with the Jones', educational planners have simply created local adaptations of overseas curricular projects in integrated science teaching'. It was only after some time that extensive evaluation of the adapted integrated science programmes were found 'inappropriate', both in content and general aims and goals.. There was thus a massive waste in manpower, materials and resources just to ape an idea. Above all, the deviation in teaching directions by the teaching force now needed another massive effort to retrain them to the desirable goals.

The above could be a most revealing and shocking experience to some, such as those who are only aware of the cosmetic compilations giving rosy pictures. Let us think of India: on the one hand we have 'the third largest scientific manpower in the world...', but on the other, the grassroot conditions are bad and they nurture dissatisfaction, disenchantment and utter failure in achievement that is 'even less than adequate' as far as the goals of science education are concerned. Thus 'quantitatively' we may have 'numbers' to 'advertise', but qualitatively, it is a hollow frame.

Again, on the one hand, we proclaim that India is the largest working democracy in the world, yet we wish our citizenry to be equipped with 'scientific literacy' which includes traits like being honest, truthful, co-operative, etc. Has the 'democratic spirit' proliferated in spite of its absence? Then where is the need?

With regard to an integration of science teaching it is interesting to note how Thailand has created a different pattern of integration which can be seen from the following sets:

Life experiences: social studies, science, health education;

*Basic skills:*mathematics and Thai language;

Work education: agriculture, carpentry, needle work, home economics;

Character education: civics, physical education; moral education;

Special experiences: foreign languages.

With the publication of a number of authoritative documents e.g. Challenge of Education; Science Education for the First Ten Years of Schooling; Guidelines for Upper Primary and Secondary stage; Syllabi for the Upper Primary and Secondary Stage; National Curriculum for Primary and Secondary Education: a Framework; National Policy on Education etc. a number of issues and problems have come to focus, along with the goals set before science education in general.

Almost all our science teachers have come from 'examination oriented studies' and they pass on the same techniques to the next generation to achieve an identical goal, e.g. to prepare students for an external examination, rather than for life:

a.   There are of course a number of concerns and beliefs in the teaching of science. There is a belief that young students, being immature, cannot think like a scientist.
b.   We do not know what level of scientific literacy is required to become a worthy citizen of a democracy.
c.   We do not know what is the best way to integrate science.
d.   Against the desirable, experience-centred science education, resource restraints and an apathy for change result in school teachers continuing a textbook-centred approach. They crush the IST concept, by titling a particular chapter of an IST text book as physics/chemistry/biology etc.
e.   Doubts about teaching and science education have been expressed such as:
     We do not know what and how much to teach at what level and why;
     There is not an adequately defined and delineated field of scientific competency and literacy projected as an expected outcome of general science teaching;
     There is not much light given as to what depth concepts should be treated at different levels;
     Much needs to be done to compile a science curriculum for the low and high ability students;
     With teaching as a last resort of employment, teacher competencies have a low profile, giving rise to a rather mechanical, routine and dull classroom atmosphere than one desired under ideal conditions.
     There are theoretical and ideological clashes of priorities between the plans for economic development and educational development;
     There are allegations that science education policies swing from one idea to another, result in half-hearted ambiguous decisions leading only to faulty or wrong outcomes.

The state of science education in India can well be grasped from the Government's own confession, that, 'in spite of the efforts made by various governmental and non-governmental agencies, in the area of science education, the impact of all this has been less than adequate. The scientific temper has remained a far cry'.

Let us analyse a simple criterion for science curriculum,, e.g. 'the science curriculum must be need-based and relevant to life'. It would be difficult to certify what is need-based and how much it is related to life. Causes, championed without strong indications of felt need, have to meet failure or remain satisfied in a lackadaisical existence. Such incongruities later emerge in some other formats, e.g. whereas the Pakistan Planning Commission projected a 'need' for having a big scientific manpower resource, thousands of them remained under-utilized for want of jobs.

Equally, with about 3 per cent enjoying the hereditary prerogative of education, what is the validity of 'our plans for implementations and conclusions'.

It is time that we try on ourselves as science educators some of the avowed outcomes of science education (e.g. to develop scientific attitudes) to appreciate scientific truths and instil a regard for accuracy.

What I wish to achieve is to muster the moral strength to convey through this rather crudely put approach that:

We need to request teachers to come out with the 'truth of the IST status' in their respective countries.

There is a natural tendency to extrapolate a small achievement at an individual level to a whole group which gives birth to misleading data.

We need to take a hard-core decision to stop any more 'science slogans' which, presented in high academic garb, wipes out old slogans as it makes room for itself.

Individuals and institutions soon pick those who can project themselves as conversant with 'most modern ...' or 'working in the frontiers of ...' or having the 'state of art...'

It is not always necessary to have progress per se, year after year. Discovery of a 'failure' may be more meaningful in helping stall expenses false or incorrect reports.

An evaluation team to investigate, in depth, the successes and failures of the 'IST process' would be better than maintaining a schedule of conferences and publishing reports.

If after a decade's action plan, including various serious steps taken towards the success of a project, result in dissatisfaction and disenchantment, to the extent that an evaluation was found unnecessary, then it poses itself as a moral question of deep significance.

Chapter 4

Science, technology, society: trends in the integration of science education

Science, technology, society: a major trend in science education

Robert E. Yager, University of Iowa

Rustum Roy, Director of the Science/Technology/Society (STS) Program at Penn State University, has proclaimed that STS is a megatrend in science education today (Roy, 1983, 1985a, 1985b). Such designation suggests that the STS descriptor captures much more than new materials for teachers to use in their day-to-day teaching. It emphasizes goals more concerned with science that meet the personal needs of students, assist in developing graduates prepared to deal with current societal issues, and produce students with awareness of current careers and occupations associated with science and technology. It suggests instructional strategies that make the teacher a facilitator and model of learning. Assessment focuses on indicators for all goals. STS is one reform effort which transcends a single discipline. It certainly affects science, mathematics, social studies, and technology as facets of the typical school curriculum.

The National Science Teachers Association has proclaimed STS as the focus for school science:

The goal of science education during the 1980s and 90s is to develop scientifically literate individuals who understand how science, technology, and society influence one another and who are able to use this knowledge in their everyday decision-making. The scientifically literate person has a substantial knowledge base of facts, concepts, conceptual networks, and process skills which enable the individual to continue to learn and think logically. This individual both appreciates the value of science and technology in society and understands their limitations (NSTA, 1982).

The NSTA has published two yearbooks which consider STS parameters for exemplary science instruction; it has conducted two searches for exemplary STS programmes nationally; and its teacher education affiliate has produced two monographs dealing with issues to prepare science teachers for STS instruction.

STS is also central to reform efforts in social studies education. One of the major task forces of the National Council for the Social Studies is on STS. The National Social Science Association devoted its 1987 meeting to STS issues. The Social Science Consortium has produced a definitive rationale and framework for STS education. STS is becoming a central theme in the social studies, emphasizing the centrality of science and tech nology to current culture.

STS is a major force in bringing traditional disciplines together, and, as such, can be directly related to trends in developing integrated science courses. STS means a relevant curriculum where students focus upon locally relevant issues, problem resolution, and community action. STS requires students to seek knowledge for use, i.e., use in decision making, problem resolution, problem identification, formation of possible explanations, the identification of suitable tests of the validity of personal explanations.

In 1988 the National Science Teacher Association decided it was important to define STS broadly as a means of defining current reform efforts as the U.S. public clamours for such reforms. The Special Task Force established for this purpose defines STS in the following manner:

STS is the term applied to the latest effort to provide a real-world context for the study of science and for the pursuit of science itself. It is a term that elevates science education rhetoric to a position beyond curriculum and the ensuing debate about scope and sequence of basic concepts and process skills. STS includes the whole spectrum of critical incidents in the education process, including goals, curriculum, instructional strategies, evaluation, and teacher preparation/performance. One can not 'do' STS by adding certain topics and lessons to the curriculum, course outline, or textbook. Students must be involved with goal setting, with planning procedures, with locating information, and with evaluating them all. Basic to STS efforts is the production of an informed citizenry capable of making crucial decisions about current problems and taking personal actions as a result of these decisions. STS means focusing upon current issues and attempts at their resolution as the best way of preparing people for current and future citizenship roles. This means identifying local, regional, national, and international problems with students, planning for individual and group activities which address them, and moving to actions designed to resolve the issues investigated. Students are involved in the total process; they are not recipients of whatever a pre-determined curriculum or the teacher dictates. There are no concepts and/or processes unique to STS; instead STS provides a setting and a reason for considering basic science and technology concepts and processes. It means determining ways that these basic ideas and skills can be seen as useful. STS means focusing on realworld problems instead of starting with concepts and processes which teachers and curriculum developers argue in terms of future usefulness to students (NSTA, in press).

The same Task Force offers a more specific listing of the qualities of a scientifically literate person. The development of such a person is a major goal of STS programs. The scientifically literate graduate is one who:

uses concepts of science and of technology and ethical values in solving everyday problems and making responsible everyday decisions in everyday life, including work and leisure;

engages in responsible personal and civic actions after weighing the possible consequences of alternative options;

defends decisions and actions using rational arguments based on evidence;

engages in science and technology for the excitement and the explanations they provide;

displays curiosity about and appreciation of the natural and human-made world;

applies scepticism, careful methods, logical reasoning, and creativity in investigating the observable universe;

values scientific research and technological problem-solving;

locates, collects, analyzes, and evaluates sources of scientific and technological information and uses these sources in solving problems, making decisions, and taking actions;

distinguishes between scientific/technological evidence and personal opinion and between reliable and unreliable information;

remains open to new evidence and the tentativeness of scientific/technological knowledge;

recognizes that science and technology are human endeavours;

weighs the benefits and burdens of scientific and technological development;

recognizes the strengths and limitations of science and technology for advancing human welfare;

analyzes interactions among science, technology, and society;

connects science and technology to other human endeavours, e.g., history, mathematics, the arts, and the humanities;

considers the political, economic, moral, and ethical aspects of science and technology as they relate to personal and global issues;

offers explanations of natural phenomena which may be tested for their validity (NSTA, in press).

To deserve designation as a megatrend STS — and integrated science courses reflecting STS — must offer specific differences from traditional science. Some of these major contrasts include:

Traditional (non-STS)	STS (integrated trend)
Survey of major concepts found in standard textbooks	Identification of problems with local interest/impact
Use of laboratories and activities suggested in textbooks and lab. manual	Use of local resources to locate information that can be used in problem solving
Passive involvement of students assimilating information provided by teacher and textbook	Active involvement of students in seeking information for use
Learning being contained in the classroom for a series of periods over the school year	Teaching going beyond a given series of class sessions, a given meeting room,
A focus on information is proclaimed important for students to master	A focus upon personal impact — often starting with student curiosity
A view that content is the information included and explained in textbooks and lectures	A view that content is not something that merely exists for student mastery simply because it is in print
Practice of basic process skills — but little attention to them in terms of evaluation	A de-emphasis on process skills- just because they represent glamourised skills of practising scientists
No attention to career awareness other than an occasional reference to a scientist and his/her discoveries	A focus on career awareness, especially careers that relate to science and technology and not merely to those related to scientific research and engineering
Students concentrate on problems provided by teacher and textbook	Students performing in citizenship roles as they attempt to resolve issues they have identified
Learning occurring only in the confines of the classroom	Study being visible throughout an institution and in a specific community
Science being a study of information where teachers determine the amount students acquire	Science being an experience students are encouraged to have
Learning focussing on current explanations	Learning with a focus on the future
'Learning' is principally for testing	Learning occurs because of activity
Retention is very short lived	Students who learn by experience retain it
Students see science processes as skills scientists possess	Students see science processes as skills they need and can use

• Students see processes as something to practice as a course requirement	• Students see processes as skills they need to refine and develop
• Teacher concerns for process are not understood by students, especially as they rarely affect course grades	• Students readily see the relationship of science processes to their own actions
• Students' interest declines at a particular grade level and across grade levels	• Student interest increases in specific courses and from grade to grade
• Coursework seems to decrease curiosity	• Students become more curious as they learn and do more
• Students see teacher as a purveyor of information	• Students see teacher as a resource and guide
• Students decline in their ability to question; the questions they ask are often ignored because they do not fit into the course outline	• Students ask more questions, such questions are used to develop STS activities and materials
• Students rarely ask unique questions	• Students frequently ask unique questions that excite their own interest
• Students are ineffective in identifying possible causes and effects in specific situations	• Students are skilful in suggesting possible causes and effects of certain observations and actions
• Students have few original ideas	• Students seem to effervesce with ideas
• Students see no value or use of their study to life	• Students can relate their study to their daily life
• Students see no value in their study for resolving current societal problems	• Students become involved in resolving societal issues

Specific assessment of results in classrooms produce major differences when STS is a focus. Some of these contrasts between STS efforts in the middle school contrasted with outcomes obtained in more traditional conceptually-organized courses suggest exciting differences. The differences emphasize the advantages and the power of STS.

Twelve teachers in Iowa (as a party of the Chautauqua Program which has operated statewide for seven years) were identified with special interest in contrasting an STS focus with the more traditional one in grades 6-8. All were interested in the extent to which concepts were mastered and the ability of students to use the. Some were especially interested in stimulating and measuring growth with respect to process skills; others were more interested in the development of creativity skills; others were concerned with student attitudes.

When teachers express interest in such areas and expect students to grow, exciting results emerge. We believe that teacher ownership and their expectation of student achievement are more important than an STS format and/or the exclusive focus on typical topics. Nonetheless, the Iowa Chautauqua programme permits the following observations that contrast STS and non-STS learnings. It is important, however, to emphasize the teacher belief that student growth in the particular domain was important and possible.

The contrasts include:

STS students achieve just as well as students enrolled in a more typical courses. In about 25 per cent of the classrooms students out perform non-STS students at the 0.05 level of confidence.

STS students outperform non-STS students in their mastery of process skills by two times (on all 13 of the S-APA processes).

Attitude is three times better for STS students than non-STS students.

Student creativity as observed in terms of quantity of questions generated, predictions of certain consequences, and ideas about possible causes for given phenomenon are increased by a factor of two in favour of STS students.

Student creativity in terms of quality/unique questions, prediction of consequences, and ideas about possible causes are six times greater for STS students than non-STS students.

The ability of students to utilize information and processes in new situations is three to four times greater for STS students than non-STS students.

Some have argued that STS efforts in integrated science in schools will fail because they do not affect standard test scores — or that the claimed advantages cannot be measured. The evaluation of Iowa students seems to refute these concerns. To date there have been no significant gains with respect to student acquisition of information. However, the improvement with respect to student attitude, the ability to use process skills, growth in terms of some features of creativity, and the ability to use information in new situations are impressive and positive advantages of STS instruction for even the most hardened skeptic. As more teachers are involved, as more time is spent in given courses and over grade levels, and as long-term studies give students the chance for even more impressive results arising from STS instruction, specific advantages for STS instruction are likely to be even more impressive. In fact, the assessment information may be as exciting for many as are the positive student, teacher, and parent testimonies which are first produced. Testimonies tend to wane; however, real evidence exists for all to see and to interpret.

References

National Science Teacher Association. (1982) *Science-Technology- Society: Science education for the 1980s.* Position Paper. Washington, DC: Author.

National Science Teachers Association. (in press). *The NSTA Position Statement on Science/ Technology/Society (STS).* Washington, DC: Author.

Roy, R. (1983, May 19). Math and science education: glue not included. *The Christian Science Monitor,* pp.36-37.

Roy, R (1985, Winter/Spring). Bright vision/impossible dream. *SSTS Reporter,* 1-2.

Roy, R. (1985). The science/technology/society connection. *Curriculum Review,* 24(3), 13-16.

Yager, R. E. (1989). STS results in significant gains. *Chautauqua Notes,* 4(7), 4.

The integration of science teaching through science-technology-society courses

John Holman, Watford Grammar School, UK

Why science-technology-society?

Science-technology-society (STS) is a relatively new field in secondary science education, yet in a short period of time this approach has had a significant influence on science curricula around the world.

The benefits of a science curriculum that emphasises social and technological aspects have been well documented. In volume V of 'New Trends in Integrated Science Teaching', John Lewis described the Science in Society Project, one of the earliest moves in this field. He pointed to the need to show students the relevance of science to their everyday lives, to show that scientific and technological activities can be both beneficial and detrimental to society and the environment and to understand the nature of decision-making within a scientific context (Lewis, 1979).

Since then, there have been many developments in the STS field. The SATIS projects from the Association for Science Education in the United Kingdom have developed a large number of STS units designed to link to the science curriculum (Hunt, 1988). These units show the manifestations of science and technology in fields as diverse as agriculture, food, industry, biotechnology and energy provision. Part 3 of this book gives examples of pages from SATIS units. Table 1 lists just 10 of the hundred units within the SATIS project.

Table 1. Titles of units in SATIS Book 4

Fluoridation of water supplies
DDT and malaria
Britain's energy sources
How would you survive? — an exercise in simple technology
The label at the back — look at clothing fibres
Blindness
Noise
Industrial Gases
Dam Problems
Glass

A particular feature of SATIS publications is that they are all interactive: they require students to play an active part in their learning through role-plays, simulations, discussion, data analysis, decision-making exercises and similar activities. Such active learning is successful in motivating pupils and in broadening the context of science, and it is an important feature of successful STS courses.

STS approaches such as those adopted by SATIS and similar projects have proved successful in a number of ways. They:
motivate pupils by engaging their interest;
help pupils develop relevant scientific knowledge and skills that will be useful in their future lives regardless of whether or not they become specialist scientists;
help pupils evaluate statements made in the media and elsewhere that claim to be scientific;
help pupils evaluate the benefits and drawbacks of scientific and technological activity to society and the environment.

How can STS bring about the integration of science teaching?

STS is concerned with the application and issues of science in society. Taking such applications and issues as starting points is an effective way to integrate a science course. This is in contrast to a conventional science course, which might start with a particular scientific fact or theory — such as the properties of acids, or the Laws of Motion. With STS, the starting point might be an issue, such as 'Do we need food additives?' or 'Can we build a dam without harming the environment?' From these starting points, relevant scientific facts and theories can be developed, as and when they are needed for an understanding of the issues concerned.

Such issues are by their nature interdisciplinary. The question of food additives certainly involves both chemistry and biology, and could also involve physics and some ethical issues as well. The impact of dams on the environment involves earth science and physics as well as biology.

Figure 1 illustrates the point in a more general way. 1A represents the areas of study involved in considering a particular scientific issue. 1B represents the science curriculum as traditionally conceived. 1C represents the situation that might arise when 1A and 1B are superimposed.

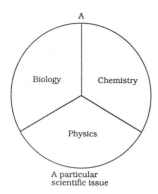

A particular
scientific issue

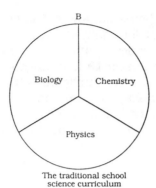

The traditional school
science curriculum

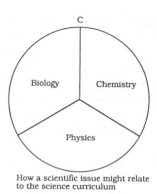

How a scientific issue might relate
to the science curriculum

As the figure illustrates, a particular scientific issue is unlikely to fall wholly within one of the traditional scientific disciplines. It is much more likely to overlap and span a number of disciplines — and indeed it may well spread outside the realm of 'science' altogether, so that teachers find themselves considering something of, say, the geographical, historical or ethical aspects of a particular issue.

The STS approach, beginning with scientific applications and developing the relevant scientific principles from them, thus serves to integrate, not only within the sciences, but within the curriculum as a whole. An issue-based science course can indeed become a way of covering large areas of the curriculum — though the constraints of the timetable or the particular teachers' inclinations or expertise may in fact make this impracticable.

Putting ideas into practice

In addition to the SATIS approach in the UK, the ideas of STS have been put into practice in many countries. Examples of these are contained in Section 2 and Section 3 of this book, and special reference is made to new projects in Botswana and the Philippines. The following section describes a further development in the UK.

The Salters science course from England

The Salters science course is under development at the University of York in the UK. It is a science course for 13 to 16 year olds which begins from science issues and applications in the ways that have been described. Table 2 gives the titles of foundation course units, for 13-14 year olds, together with the major science topic developed within the unit.

Each unit in the course develops a specific science topic, as shown in Table 2. Between them, the units provide a comprehensive and integrated science curriculum. Although each unit concentrates on a particular area of science, the units have been selected to give coverage of the major areas where science, technology and society interact, thus providing between them an integrated science curriculum. What is more, this curriculum also extends to a consideration of a number of social issues, such as noise pollution, traffic safety, alcohol abuse and heart disease, that are not covered in a traditional science course. The Salters Science course thus aims to teach pupils science that will be useful in their future lives, whether or not they choose to study science further.

A particular feature of Salters science is the variety of teaching and learning activities it includes, all designed to involve students actively in their own learning. Thus discussion exercises, problem-solving, data interpretation, decision-making and active reading exercises are all included, in addition to laboratory practical work. This range of learning activities reflects the wide range of skills and processes that are involved in learning about science in the real world.

Table 2 . Foundation units in the Salters Science course

Unit title	Major science topic
Babies	human reproduction
Being me	variation in people
Body care	maintaining good health
Child's play	energy and energy transfers
Drinks	particles and pure substances
Fire, Friend and foe	combustion
Full of Beans	seed germination
Food	food and tests for food
Green machine	photosynthesis
Metals	uses and reactivity of metals
Music and noise	ideas about sound
Neighbours	plant and animal habitats
On the rocks	introducing geology
Out of this world	astronomy and space travel
Painting and decorating	testing materials
Safe as houses	structures
Safe journey	ideas about speed
Seeing the light	uses and properties of light
Skin deep	skin function and hygiene
Switched on	electricity and simple circuits
Wear and tear	properties and structure of fabrics

There are further units, planned on a similar basis, for 14 to 16 year olds.

Integration of the sciences means a broadening and a bringing together. This is true of context and content: integrated science is broader than just physics, chemistry and biology — it needs to show the everyday context in which science operates, and it includes earth science, environmental science and other areas too. But the broadening applies to skills and processes as well: a truly integrated science course provides pupils with opportunities to develop a wide range of skills that will be useful in future life. To achieve such broadening of skills implies a broadening not just of contexts and content, but of the range of learning activities also.

An action plan for developing an STS-based integrated science curriculum

The experience of those who have been involved in developing STS-based integrated science curricula shows that certain key stages are involved. They can be summarized as follows:
1. Decide the curriculum framework. Who is the curriculum for? What does it aim to achieve? Who will teach it? What facilities are available?
2. Decide the starting-points for curriculum units. Will they be familiar and interesting to pupils? Will they enable pupils to learn knowledge and skills that will be of value in the future? Will they provide a context through which to develop important scientific principles?
3. Plan the curriculum units in outline. What topics will they include? What teaching and learning activities will be involved? What knowledge and understanding will be gained? What skills will be developed?
4. Review the coverage provided by the curriculum units. Do they make a coherent whole? Are there gaps or omissions? Will the planned curriculum match the aims identified in stage 1? Revise the outline curriculum units to take account of any problems identified.
5. Use the revised unit outlines to produce a working curriculum.
These stages are likely to be modified in practice and a good deal of overlap is likely to occur.

Effective curriculum development of this kind is unlikely to be achieved by curriculum planners working alone. A partnership is needed, and key members of this partnership are teachers and outside experts. Teachers are needed to make the decisions about what is within the capabilities of pupils, to develop learning activities, and ultimately to write the curriculum materials. Outside experts — industrialists, doctors, nutritionists, farmers, craftsmen — are needed to provide information and expertise about the ways that science is applied in the real world.

References

LEWIS, J.L. 1979, *Science in Society*. New trends in integrated science teaching, Volume V (Unesco).

HUNT, J.A. 1988, SATIS approaches to STS. *International Journal of Science Education*, Volume 10 ,No. 4.

NGANUNU, M. 1988, An attempt to write a science curriculum with social relevance for Botswana. Ibid.

TAN, M.C. 1988, Towards relevance in science education: Philippine context. Ibid

GOVERNMENT OF BOTSWANA. 1985, *Integrated Science Syllabus for junior secondary schools*.

Further information

SATIS. Information and publications are available from: Bookselling Department, Association for Science Education, College Lane, Hatfield, Herts, UK.

Salters projects. Information about Salters Science and other Salters curriculum projects can be obtained from: Science Education Group, Department of Chemistry, University of York, York, UK.

Science/technology/society interactions: teaching in the secondary school

E. Joseph Piel, State University of New York

Introduction

Among the various questions raised by recent reports of the 'State of Education' is the question of technological literacy and the related question of the value of teaching Science/Technology/Society (STS) interactions in science classrooms. Even the definition of 'technological literacy' is unclear in the minds of many. There is a tendency among some groups to equate it with computer literacy while others agree that computer literacy is a sub-set of technological literacy.

In their study of science teaching, the STS focus group of Project Synthesis agreed that among the areas of STS study were:

Energy
Population
Human engineering
Environmental quality
Utilization of natural resources
National defense and space
Sociology of science
Effects of technological development.

The last topic obviously includes anything a teacher would wish to include as long as it relates to the technology/society interface. This category was included because the dynamic nature of the STS area makes much curriculum obsolete as important technological developments occur in areas not originally included.

As we try to outline areas of study which are not presently being offered we are faced with the problem of acceptance by student, teacher, administrator, textbook publisher, and budget director.

The simplest problem to overcome is student acceptance. There seems to be no order of difficulty for overcoming the reluctance of the other groups since this varies from school system to school system. It is appropriate, therefore, to propose a set of desired student outcomes. These desired student outcomes may be described for each of the areas listed above with suggestions on how they might be accomplished. The first two will be described briefly, as examples of areas of concern.

Areas of concern

Energy

Desired student outcomes

Describe/demonstrate specific ways to decrease energy/waste.
Evaluate various tradeoffs associated with decisions involving energy conservation plans.
Apply rational processes of thought to a proposed solution to problems related to energy resources and their efficient use.
Describe and compare the relationship of energy consumption to quality of life, economics, and future development in developed and developing countries.
Describe the role of interest groups and the tradeoffs associated with the development of an energy plan.
Evaluate the short and long-range effects of proposed solutions to the energy problem.
Make realistic assessments of potential technical problems involved with various energy scenarios.

Suggested approach

Have students do a survey of energy use in the home and suggest ways in which it might be reduced.
Conduct a survey evaluating personal and family tradeoffs of energy saving decisions.
Have students examine various personal uses of energy intensive devices and propose less intensive ways to accomplish the same task. Various devices from electric toothbrushes to autos and bicycles should be compared for energy cost and benefits.
Through text material, periodicals, and media present STS relationships. Discuss these and have students graph energy use against GNP for various countries, as one example of a comparison. There are many others.
With guest lectures, films, and/or simulations present the views of conflicting groups on nuclear plants, oil versus coal powered plants, gasahol compared to gasoline and diesel fuel for cars, mass transit or personal autos for commuting, and so on. Have the students discuss the strength or weakness of the arguments based on their understanding of the technologies involved.
Make calculations of oil resources and use. Even if the top ten miles of the earth's crust was completely saturated with oil it can be shown that if oil use continues to increase, the world will run out of oil in approximately 200 years. Compare this with other suggested long-range energy sources.
Conduct studies of chemical situations involved in acid rain, biological effects of high and low level radiation, physics of mass of auto and energy use per mile. Discuss how these various science concepts are involved in decisions regarding the technology-society interaction.

These various desired student outcomes can be considered at different levels in the secondary schools. The level at which the student is expected to perform will depend on the maturity of the student, science background, and time spent. This will, of course, depend on whether the material is taught as part of a full course in STS or is infused into the existing science course. The other areas of concern are treated in a similar manner.

Population

Desired student outcomes

Discuss the implications of alternatives regarding population planning on a national scale.
Describe the impact that technological advance has had on the family unit.
Describe the impact that over-population and population distribution have on service elements of society (i.e. energy transportation, health care, supplies).
Describe how over-population will affect environmental quality.
Describe the long-range consequences that population control will have on other structures of society.

Suggested approach

Study the Rumanian situation in which a governmental decision to halt all abortions resulted in a doubling of the number of babies born from 1966 to 1967. Implications for various facets of the society including education, baby carriages, toys, and marriage patterns 18 to 22 years hence should be discussed. Contrast with the Chinese decision on the one-child-per-family programme and its consequences.
Through films and simulations show how improved transportation has resulted in population shifts in urban-suburban regions and how improved technology affects the age distribution in a population. Discuss the implications of such changes.
Readings, films, television and discussions can show the effects of over-population on society. Experiments of growing bacteria in closed environments will demonstrate what happens when population grows too fast. Discuss the 'harvesting' of wild deer to prevent over-grazing. Make calculations of per capita needs for energy, etc. Enable the development of models for 'Limits to Growth'.
Discussions and demonstrations on rate of filtration of sewage will show the effects of high population density on one facet of the environment.
Discussion and computer simulations of population control strategies will demonstrate the inertia involved in population growth and control.

While the suggested approaches to help students achieve the desired outcomes are stated very briefly, it is evident these are considerably different from the traditional classroom. The preparation of teachers to carry out these approaches must also vary from community to community and from class to class. Co-operative approaches among science and social science teachers in some cases is very beneficial, sometimes requiring the surrender of tradition as to who should teach what.

This brief description of some of the basic objectives of examples from a Science/Technology/ Society programme for secondary schools may serve to show how progress in this direction can be achieved. There are many more objectives and activities which might apply more directly in specific schools. Implementation of such a programme will depend on many factors and on the various components of the educational system. The following recommendations apply to each of those components. While it is not vital that each recommendation be carried out before some progress is made, it is obvious that unless some of the recommendations are followed very little will be accomplished in this most important area of education for the people who will spend most of their lives in the 21st century.

A science/technology/society curriculum: some recommendations

Schools (teachers, principals, curriculum committees and district level administrators) should encourage textbook publishers to include STS material in their texts in all areas of science.

Schools should encourage the development and use of special publications, films, etc., presenting specific STS situations such as automobile safety, fibre optics in communication, the connection between space exploration and the heart pacemaker.

Using knowledge gained from recent publications of new STS developments, individual teachers should be encouraged to develop their own curriculum materials to fit the teaching of the new development into their courses where appropriate.

A serious attempt should be made to introduce complete courses on STS into the school programme for all students at the secondary level. These courses should not be limited to either the fast learners or the slow learners of the school but rather should be directed to all citizens of a technologically-oriented society as general education.

Whether or not textbooks include STS material, teachers should be encouraged to include the teaching of STS at appropriate places in the courses they are teaching. For example, an explanation of radioactive decay could include a discussion and explanation of how the Optacon and Kurzweil machines aid the blind in reading directly from print or even from normal handwriting.

Science departments along with school administrators, should be encouraged to discuss with any other interested groups the question of what should go out of the curriculum as more STS material comes in or, if it is possible to include STS material so that little of the standard material needs to be eliminated.

Science departments, along with school administrators, should be encouraged to make more information regarding content of STS courses and potential careers in the STS area available to school counsellors so that they might more effectively guide students into appropriate courses and careers.

Many teachers are concerned that the inclusion of STS materials in their courses is not acceptable to state agencies and colleges. The state education department should make a special effort to assure teachers that the inclusion of such material is not only acceptable but is actually desirable at all levels.

One of the problems which crops up regarding STS issues is that in some areas of the school, there is much 'preaching' either for or against technology without the opportunity for students to make decisions which require a look at a number of alternative solutions to a specific problem. The energy crisis is one area in which social science and science teachers could work together to provide students with the opportunity to develop and examine all alternatives in the areas of education, legislation, and technology as potential solutions to the problem. They must then be encouraged to look at the secondary and even tertiary effects of each of the alternatives until they develop a real understanding of the statement: 'For every complex problem there is usually an answer that is forthright, simple, direct—and wrong.'

As clearinghouses are formed to include information and even curricular materials in the STS area, school teachers should be made aware of them through their administrators and be given encouragement and time to explore their contents for possible inclusion in their teaching.

State and local school systems should develop materials and systems for finding out what the students at various levels already know about technology as a basis for developing programmes for carrying out the above recommendations.

Existing courses of study should be evaluated, and material which is obsolete or not relevant should be deleted. This will provide 'space' to infuse into existing science programmes selected STS topics. Infusion of such topics into courses that are required (such as middle school science, general science, etc.) would ensure that the total spectrum of the student population would be exposed to this important area.

A wide range of materials should be developed supporting both formal courses of study as well as community information programmes. These would include such STS materials as:

learning activity packets; movies; slide-tapes; compendia of articles from magazines. Files of local field trips and community guest lectures should be established.

Pre-service and in-service teacher education programmes must contain systematic strategies to develop teacher awareness of the importance of including STS in their science courses as legitimate subject matter for study.

Since curricula for Grades 7 through 12 appear to reflect the disciplines as modelled in the universities and since teachers tend to teach as they were taught, it is important that new courses on STS and technology education be developed at the college level. Such courses would serve not only to educate students about appropriate issues and provide training in appropriate skills, but would serve as models for emulation to establish the credibility of STS in public education. These courses should be offered not only through the college or school of education, but also by the departments normally associated with arts, sciences, and engineering.

Because few people even know that technology education materials exist and because there is relatively little general knowledge regarding technological topics and issues themselves, it is suggested that large-scale national campaigns should be launched to increase the awareness of technology's impact on human lives. These campaigns would be directed to teachers and their supervisory counterparts, to teacher educators, and to those involved in curriculum development, especially authors and publishers of widely used textbook series.

Biweekly newsletters entitled something like 'Science, Technology and People' could be made widely available to teachers and others. They could include articles on the application of science principles (heavily valued by teachers) in technological developments and discussions of the positive and negative effects of these developments. Remembering from our data that teachers listen to other teachers more than anyone else for curriculum advice, there could be articles written by teachers about technology-related class activities, field trips, etc., and individual or classroom activities could be included.

Because of the dominance of textbooks in science education their selection becomes an extremely important decision at the local level. Criteria for textbook selection should be developed in such a way that they reflect science-technology-society concerns. Such criteria could be converted into checklists for use by states and localities in textbook selections. If such checklists had the credibility of endorsement by science teachers' organizations (e.g., NSTA) and organizations of scientists (e.g., AAAS), there would be a better chance of their use in the decision process.

Chapter 5

Primary science is integrated science

Jos Elstgeest, Netherlands

Children learn in their living-environment and they live in a learning-environment. School belongs to and is part of this environment. If it were not, school education would become alien to the children and lose its point.

Science education in the primary school, in the light of the statement above, is not to be identified with factual instruction, although factual information is a valuable part of it when given at the proper time. Neither is it only a teacher's activity, even though the teacher will be very active indeed. Primary education differs from 'teaching about scientific facts and discoveries' in as far as it educates children through the processes of science.

Science education, particularly in the primary school, is a three-way simultaneous interaction between children, their environment and their teacher. To be more specific: children do not interact with an abstract 'environment'; they work with specific and selected things, materials, features or events from within their environment. These may either occur in their natural environment and call for a spontaneous response, or they may be consciously made part of the children's environment in, for instance, the school or classroom. Here the response of the children may be spontaneous, but also be guided or even evoked by the teacher. Whichever, there should always be a relationship between the organized environment of the school and the children's own, wider, living-environment so that, in fact, the teacher uses and enriches the children's environment and catalyses their learning interaction.

As science is the interaction between the searching human mind and the universe in which mankind lives, so is primary science an interaction between the growing mind of children and their expanding environment.

Here we touch upon the two most significant integrating factors of primary science:

1. The natural environment which children undergo as a whole, although they explore it through its details. Children do not 'select' topics on a rational basis: they encounter and interact with whatever captures their immediate attention and holds their interest. Detailed experiences become more relevant within the totality of the children's conscious relations with their environment.
2. The developing mind of each child which assimilates and accommodates concepts, forged by experiences of personal encounter and interaction, into the whole of its intellectual structure.

Integrated science in the primary school locks into the daily experiences of children, and so becomes a special form of environmental science education by which the children learn to use their environment, and all that occurs in it, in a scientific way as a source of information.

Every child, as an individual, grows up within a unique, but very concrete environment. The child learns from it, belongs to it, contributes to it and exerts his own influence on it. Unique as it is, however, the child's environment is not isolated. It is interwoven with and related to, indeed it is part of, the environment of other children. All children share the school they attend together with its surroundings, which gives the school a central place and makes it play a most important role in our attempt at integrated environmental primary science education.

School or no school, there always is a continuous interaction between a child and his/her environment about which we ought to think in concrete and even colourful terms. Within it we find the child and everything he encounters when he explores and acquaints himself with the nettle that stings, the bird that catches the worm, the wind that bends the reed and sways the trees, the lights controlling the roar of traffic by turning green, amber and red, the bells that toll, and the lightning that splits a dark sky into two. Thousands of impressions intrude upon the child and try to occupy his mind. The child accommodates himself to this avalanche, attempts to make sense of it all, selects what impresses him most, and creates order in this chaos, at least somehow. This helps him to establish his own place in it. It is upon this natural ability that we build our environmental education when we consciously and positively influence, secure, encourage, enrich and guide the child's manifold interaction with his environment of which we, as teachers and educators, have now become an influential part.

Let us divert a little to a class of children working with soil. 'Soil', 'sand', 'dirt', 'dust', 'earth', it lives under various aliases among the children. Their own experiences count as they form the basis of further learning, and they should be made part of the learning process. Soil makes your clothes and hands dirty. It blows into your eyes in a strong wind. It hurts when you fall on it. It can be very hard, and sometimes loose and soft. It bears flowers and grass; it supports shrubs and trees. It gets sludgy and slippery when wet, and it sticks to your soles. You can play in it, dig in it, tunnel in it, build with it. Sometimes you can model things out of it. In science lessons it becomes an object of orderly encounter and interaction, but... there are many soils. It is, therefore, a variable object of investigation. Besides, any soil is composed of many things. The presence of soil components and their various proportions give different kinds of soil their own characteristics. A study of soils, however elementary, searches for the relations between these components and characteristics.

A scientific look at soil is a new experience for the children. The more or less superficial impressions they have about soil are to be bundled into the question: 'Soil, what is it?' And a closer look is called for. The first orderly attempt at getting to know more about soil is to get some soil, and preferably not one kind of soil, but different kinds of soil. One should not look for the predetermined kinds of soil which one finds only in books (sand, clay, loam), but for the real soils that are found in the environment: e.g. a sample of soil from the school garden and a sample from, say, the roadside. Choose soils which look different. Now various investigations become possible, for the first concrete, operational question is: 'What do you find in your soil?'. Foreseeing that the question 'what makes soils different?' will be important, as it relates closely to what can be found in the soil, the teacher would do well to let the children work in small groups of four so that pairs can work together, each pair taking a different soil. They will do the same activities, use the same skills, but they may well get different results, which makes immediate comparison possible. However, this is a matter of organisation to be left to the teacher.

On a sheet of (news)paper both soils can be analysed into their constituents. A wet finger dipped into the soil and then smeared upon paper, shows the characteristic colour of the soil. It is a first record which can be preserved by putting a strip of cellotape over it. Fine and coarse particles, pebbles and organic remains are readily identified and even crudely quantified. The presence of water and air usually escapes the attention of the children here. No matter, a logical step is to shake up the soils in water and let things settle out separately. The suggestion to do this comes from the teacher, as children seldom think of this technique. If the teacher sees to it — and (s)he should discuss this with the children — that equal volumes of soil are used in vessels of the same size, then finer quantitative comparison becomes possible. An interesting added question would be: 'should we use equal volumes of water?'

Adding water to the soils reveals the presence of air, as it escapes in bubbles. Apart from a better answer to the question 'what are soils made of?', the children are now also faced with a new set of problems:

• How much air is there in the soil?
• How can we measure it?
• How fast does water percolate through (sink into) the soil?

- How do you measure that?
- How much water is retained by a soil (or: how much runs out of it again?)
- Do we get different answers for different soils? How come?
- Would that have anything to do with, for instance, the size of particles in the soil?

These problems can be tackled by the older primary children. They call for creative experimentation. The question: 'should we use equal volumes of water (in equal vessels to shake up equal volumes of soils)' now attains a special meaning in connection with the first two problems about air in the soil. As the air escapes being replaced by water creeping between the soil particles, the sum of the volumes of water and soil may be measurably more than the resulting total volume, the difference being the volume of escaped air.

Questions on soil fertility are much more difficult to answer by classroom experiments. The question is bound to come up; and the children always insist on planting seeds in their different soils 'to see which one is more fertile'. Let them. The results are always unreliable: seeds germinate in almost anything that is kept moist. Besides, the variables are so many that the children overlook most of them, and 'fertility' is by itself a rather vague concept. However, it is good to discuss this with the children in connection with their work for, when they are occupied, busy and interested, they show that they really want to know more. They are then ripe and ready to absorb information by other means: by word of mouth, by reading or, even more so, by pictorial and graphic explanation about things unseen, but which may be (at least partly) verifiable in the soils they handle:

The presence of minerals.

The effect of particle size on water retention or capillarity and related adaptations of root systems of plants. (A collection of roots from their own different soils may be made).

The use of manure and fertilizers. (Photographs of the results of experiments in agricultural research may now take on meaning for the children).

The effect of prevailing kinds of soil on the occupations and lives of people and on agricultural products in various regions of the country or the world.

The obvious variations in the vegetation in areas around the school and homes of the children may well be related to visible differences in soil. While the children occupy themselves with soils from various locations, they should be given an opportunity to take a closer look at these locations and become involved with whatever lives therein and on the soil. They may want to follow the dung beetle they come across rolling its treasure to its larder (or nursery, whichever may be the case). They may want to study the behaviour of worms, or watch how the blackbird finds and pulls the worm out of the ground. They may be struck by the occurrence of erosion and be fascinated by the patterns it makes. All these, and many others, are valuable lines of investigation and learning worth pursuing.

Integrated science allows for a certain amount of open-endedness because the questions of the children are a criterion to planning, too. The teacher should, therefore, feel free to divert with the children from the strict and straight path of her own curricular planning, provided the investigations enrich the topic at hand, reveal new relationships, increase the children's understanding, satisfy their curiosity, and give scope to practising and strengthening scientific process skills.

Now we have arrived at the third integrating principle of primary science: the practice and mastering of fundamental scientific process skills, which implies and emphasizes the doing of science.

In primary science education the young child is encouraged to orient himself in his world. 'His world' is still pretty close by. It is not the whole big world of mankind, but the surrounding world of his immediate experience. In this the child is shown a way, given a direction, provided with information where appropriate or given means to find information. So the child is given the keys to disclose his world. The educator — the teacher — holds a powerful influence over the children's world, for (s)he can enrich and embellish it. By giving it order and system (s)he adds meaning and greater relevancy. Within this orienting endeavour skills are learned and practised which render the child's self-reliance effective, for they increase the child's aptitude to reap knowledge and understanding. We can circumscribe this process as problem-posing science education which leads to problem-solving learning.

The learning activity occurs between a question and its answer, between the problem posed and its solution found. When an answer is obtained, as soon as a problem is solved, the quest is at its end and the learning activity ceases. However, a new question usually arises from it, which calls for renewed action and fresh learning, and so the scientific process continues. Wonder, constant questioning, and the development of curiosity, inquisitiveness, studiousness, together with the practice of the skills required to satisfy these urges, are conditions as well as objectives of science education.

It is important to remember that no one can practice learning skills without learning something. You cannot practice knowledge-making skills in a vacuum. As the example of the study of soils shows, the learning activity is always directed at something real, something the children can handle, with which they have entered into a dialogue, an interaction. The soils are placed in the hands of the children, and their involvement brings learning and knowing together. Soils were only one example; anything, no matter what, as long as it is part of their experienced surrounding world, available in or around the school, can be the object of attention and scientific interest on which the children can sharpen their intellectual skills.

The continuous practice of scientific process skills make independent and self-reliant learning possible. They are the skills of the scientist. We teach the children clear questioning, for he who formulates a question well has already made a decisive step towards its solution, for he knows what he is after. Observation is required in the first place and the sharp use of all senses is applied to notice what is relevant. The observation may be organized into what is called 'experimentation', from the simple attempt to solve a 'what happens if...' problem to the more sophisticated planned experiment by which a supposition, or hypothesis, is verified. This calls for creativity, foresight, prediction, use of relationships recognized in the past, manipulative skill, accuracy, control of variables and honesty in drawing conclusions on the basis of genuine evidence.

This seems a tall order for a primary child, and so it is. It is obvious that children need time and continuous guided practice to become proficient in doing science, and the primary school is none too early to begin.

Chapter 6

Teacher behaviours which facilitate integrated science teaching

Ronald J. Bonnstetter,
University of Nebraska, United States

Introduction

A colleague recently shared a list of teacher generated student outcomes in response to the question: 'As a science teacher, how would you go about teaching integrated science?' The list could easily have been created by a group of top science educators flown in for a special task force report. It included all the current philosophical directions and goals for science education. The punch line of this story is that the teachers generating the list had been identified by a local university as unusable as cooperating teachers because of their poor classroom model.

We appear to have a number of teachers who understand the goals of science education, but have no idea what these goals look like in the classroom. What are the teaching behaviours that facilitate teaching every science every day? What is the role of a teacher who sincerely wants his/ her students to develop higher order thinking. Are there any special attributes for teaching integrated science?

The role of the teacher: a rationale

Helping each student develop to the fullest

For many students, the challenges of maintaining skills of inquiry while learning to operate within an independent study mode are tested to the limit during junior and senior high school. In the junior high school years students begin to explore career choices and are able to handle greater intellectual freedom. Far too often secondary education has taken a very limited view of learning by placing too much emphasis on low cognitive level achievement and by measuring that achievement with standardized tests. Students need to be given the opportunity to go beyond recall and fact memorization. The successful teacher, especially one who is teaching integrated science, provides students with an understanding of the thought processes which are necessary throughout life: synthesis, comprehension, analysis, organization, and self evaluation skills.

Teaching research over the years indicates that the vast majority of effective teaching techniques previously described for the gifted are both fitting and extremely advantageous for all students (Costa, 1985). For learning in a classroom to be maximized, the intellectual gap between the top students and the bottom students may be much greater at the end of the year than it was at the beginning. This does not suggest that any one group of students has been hampered in their learning, but rather that each individual was challenged in an appropriate manner, resulting in individual growth.

The teacher as facilitator

Consider the differences between a director and a facilitator of learning. The director establishes course requirements, imposes student activities, and is solely responsible for evaluating outcomes. The facilitator takes on the role of encouraging the students' self- or cooperatively-initiated learning goals and is responsible for providing appropriate feedback for self-evaluation. To be an effective facilitator the teacher must thoroughly understand the philosophy behind the teaching strategies and model chosen and be committed to this new set of goals. The teacher who understands the nature of integrated science and holds fast to the goals of processing and using content versus merely knowing facts will be far more likely to feel comfortable in the facilitator role.

Time to explore in an open access educational environment

The arrangement of the classroom should allow for maximum student access to resources. Upon entering a room attuned to this philosophy you would find a wide range of objects available to students and class time provided for students to explore with them.

David Hawkins (1965) was one of the first to recognize the importance of allowing children time for 'messing about' in science. In response to Hawkins, a number of elementary programmes in integrated science, including the Elementary Science Study (ESS) and Science Curriculum Improvement Study (SCIS), provided elementary schools with activities built around this 'messing about' concept. Although historically some of the best 'serious science' has been derived from unfocussed messing about, the concept has for the most part disappeared from the secondary schools. For some reason, we have failed to recognize that students learn more effectively and rapidly when they are interested in a topic and motivated to learn it. We are, however, far too often faced with the opposite scenario; that of moving rapidly through material presented inappropriately; thus creating a lack of time to develop student interest and leading to boredom. Romey (1980), suggests that many secondary and university science courses fail to recognize the importance of pre-exploration to stimulate student interest and establish mental structures before presenting an underlying concept. Romey goes on to say that teachers often falsely assume that their students are already motivated and prepared to work at or near their potential.

A student in such an environment feels free to explore new fields, to experiment with new techniques, to share, to respect differing ideas, make mistakes and learn from them, and learn to define difficult problems. These students feel comfortable with revealing their feelings, ultimately, reaching the point where they feel at ease with themselves.

Teacher characteristics and behaviours

A general overview of desirable teacher characteristic for integrated science include: the use of individual teaching strategies, capitalizing on strategies which promote critical thinking skills, the ability to develop individualized and cooperative curriculum, extensive subject-matter knowledge, and the ability to view and handle the dynamics of a classroom. In other words, integrated science as a goal must employ integrated and varied approaches. These characteristics appear to work best when coupled with personal characteristics of enthusiasm for teaching, self confidence, and being a model of active inquiry. (Brandwein, 1959; Witty, 1971; and Costa, 1985). The teacher characteristics found in exemplary science programmes and described by Bonnstetter, Penick, and Yager (1984) reinforces this statement.

Desirable Characteristics

Teacher and teaching traits that aid in the development of creativity and critical thinking skills among high ability students means being a facilitator rather than a director of learning. In acting as a facilitator for learning rather than the dominant source of information, teachers must:

Value and encourage creativity and accept student ideas.

Show interest in developing personal creative potential and outwardly model this interest for students.

Recognize personal limitations.

Provide a stimulating and accepting environment.

Have high expectations of themselves and students.

Not view classroom walls as boundaries.

Be concerned with developing effective communication skills.

Want students to apply knowledge.

Recognize the need for maximizing individual potential.

Place more emphasis on process of learning than on the products.

Stimulate students to go as far and as deep into a subject as they can.

Provide for activities allowing pursuit of a variety of extensions, thus letting students decide the point of closure.

Create in students a sense of ownership for learning.

Allow for student choices and decisions concerning the organization and planning of activities.

Design learning experiences around the student's natural curiosity by dealing with problems relevant to personal needs, purposes and interests.

Keep programmes flexible enough to encourage initiative, inquiry, risk taking and a questioning attitude.

Reduce the level of anxiety.

Encourage divergent thinking in problem-solving settings.

Allow students to make mistakes and formulate corrections.

Encourage frequent self-evaluation by students.

Provide enough structure for students to understand goals and limitations, but not enough to stifle creative responses.

Model the nature of science in all science activities.

Showing students the role of science and science-related careers in everyday experiences.

Provide each student with an awareness of the inter-relationships of science, technology, and societal issues.

These characteristics apply to all levels and aspects of teaching, but they are particularly important in teaching integrated science.

A repertoire of teaching strategies and teacher behaviour

Appropriate use of some of these teaching strategies varies with the cognitive development of the student. In the primary grades a greater emphasis is generally placed on interdependent learning and greater teacher direction. As students develop their self concepts, the learning environment must be enriched with more independent activities, thus decreasing teacher dependence and enhancing the potential for developing self- motivated students. The use of these strategies results in greater expression of creativity and development of critical thinking skills.

The following teaching techniques, methods, situations and teacher behaviours are applicable to the teaching of all students, but may have a more dramatic effect on the teaching of integrated science. Generic examples for many of these teaching techniques are described by Williams (1982).

Ask provocative questions

These questions, more commonly referred to as 'open-ended' or 'extended answer' questions, are intended to stimulate the development of critical thinking skills and to get children mentally excited about inquiry, exploration, and the discovery of new knowledge. The teacher's thoughtful use of questions can be particularly useful for gifted children in providing insight into challenging situations. These questions should go beyond the 'what' and 'when' and pursue the 'why', 'how', 'to what extent', 'for what reason' and 'for what purpose'. Through the use of these questions students can be asked to think of science as a whole and not simply view the lesson in isolation.

Example: The age old question of 'why is the sky blue?' is a rather limited example of this strategy. To answer 'why' requires knowing the right answer. Looking at other possibilities allows exploration. Thought provoking extensions of the initial question might include: 'Why isn't the sky red?'; 'How could you make the sky red?'; 'Why, at times, does the sky appear to be red?'; or 'How would a different coloured sky affect your environment?'

Taking full advantage of appropriate wait time

Research has shown (Rowe, 1978) that the effect of even the most provocative question is negated by teachers not waiting for answers. The amount of time required depends on many variables, not the least of which is the level of difficulty implied by the question. In general, 'why' questions require greater wait time than 'how' or 'what' questions which, in turn, require more time then simple recall questions.

Focus on the 'search' for the answers

Content knowledge is the means for developing an understanding of science processes, not an end unto itself. Richard Feynman once defined science as 'a belief in the ignorance of experts.' If science is taught as a set of known quantities, a great injustice is done to the student's ability to understand the true nature of science. Far too often teachers assume that the processes are obvious and dwell on only the outcomes.

Example: Ask students to create a model of a living cell using common household objects. After students have had an opportunity to share their models and explain the role played by various objects, expand the discussion to include the role models play in our understanding of science. Teacher initiated questions might include: 'What are examples of other models used in science?' or 'What are some of the reasons for using models in science?' By approaching an activity in this manner the student not only gains an insight into the form and function of a cell, but sees the importance of modelling as a process of improving our understanding of science.

Presenting paradoxical situations

A paradox is a true situation that seems contradictory, unbelievable or absurd; but may in fact be true. It is an observation that is inconsistent with common experience.

Example: Discrepant events lend themselves well to creating a paradoxical situation. The interaction of wood and water as an activity is an example. After students generate a list of expected outcomes about the interaction, they set about testing their hypotheses. The introduction of lignum vita, a type of wood with a specific gravity greater than water, provides a discrepant event as it sinks and creates a contradiction between many expected outcomes and actual observations.

Introducing the role of modelling and assumptions in science

Science is full of gaps in knowledge, missing information, and unknown facts that force scientists to draw logical assumptions concerning phenomena and to generate models that portray these assumptions.

Example: Ask students to identify phenomena in science that we do not understand and have them generate ways that this information could be gained. The far-too-often inability of science to have direct access to needed information provides opportunities to introduce the role of assumptions and models in science.

Teaching the role of habits in our lives

One of the first steps in enhancing creativity is development of a sensitivity to the effect of habit-bound thinking, thus allowing students to examine the advantages and disadvantages of convergent versus divergent thinking.

Example: Hold up a waste paper basket and ask students to generate a list of uses. Mentally keep track of the number of uses that involve putting objects 'in' the basket (this being a rather conventional usage). After discussing your findings concerning their responses, continue the collection of ideas in a new less habit-bound, more divergent setting. Consider the rationale for having automobile engines in the front or stop-lights being red.

Develop skills in visualization/perceptions

Help students visualize and describe objects or situations from different viewpoints allowing greater awareness of these differing perceptions and trusting personal intuitions.

Example: Students focus on how different people might feel and react to the same event. Write an essay on how a geologist might feel about an extremely destructive Californian earthquake. How would the people directly affected by the disaster feel?

Libel by label

Once an object has been named or for some other reason becomes familiar, students stop looking at it carefully and assume that they know about it. Often a student approaches a teacher with an object and asks for information. Many times, once naming has taken place, the student moves on to something else.

Pablo Piccaso once said, 'An answer is a lie that makes us feel that we've heard the truth'. Most science classes focus on attaining answers, not providing questions. When we move our emphasis from the acquisition of knowledge to the study of the processes of science, we are better able to see the value of questioning as a strategy.

An understanding of the nature of science forces us to realize that the truths of today, the explanations we find so familiar and comfortable and which are the basis for regurgitation tests, are nothing more than scientific answers that happen to be in vogue at this time. In this way, the truths of today are no different from the truths of two-thousand years ago. Carrying this scenario to its fullest, one can picture a lesson plan from years past stressing the flat earth concept and expounding on the universal centricity of our planet. Once students realize that there are no final answers, they are free to question and to wonder.

Making the familiar strange and the strange familiar

Most of science is involved with familiarizing the student with the unknown, yet this goal can many times be better served by backing up and taking a closer look at what is already assumed to be known. Instead of providing names, a series of questions may lead to greater depth of knowledge. In the case of discovering an aquatic insect, the teacher could apply the strategy by asking some of these questions: Where did you find it? What was it doing? How is it similar to others we have found? How is it different? What do you think it eats? What leads you to believe that your assumptions are true?

Others ways of making the familiar strange include a refocusing of attention. This can be accomplished by examining only a small portion of the object, magnifying a section or removing the object from its familiar environment. Perhaps this is why creativity is sometimes described as 'looking at one thing and seeing another.'

Focus on problem identification — not merely problem solving or doing

This strategy provides the student with the opportunity to grapple with the difficult task of identifying a problem and the process involved in searching for causality.

Example: Students design their own experiment by identifying a researchable problem, describing a logical path of investigation, and formulating expected or potential outcomes. The last step is the testing of their hypothesis and reporting their findings.

Allowing for organized random investigations

This strategy encompasses the philosophy of messing about within boundaries or ground rules established for the student's exploration. Such activities focus on the process of investigation and develop skills of inquiry and search.

Example: Open-ended laboratory activities and experiments that lend themselves to extensions allow for this strategy to develop. Even batteries and bulbs can start with the simple task of lighting a bulb using one wire and one battery and expand in numerous directions, including the design and testing of circuits, motors, generators, and experimentation with voltage and amperage.

Looking for attributes

Attributes are the characteristics, qualities or properties of an object or concept.

Example: After providing students with opportunities to experiment with magnets, and only after this open-ended encounter, ask students to develop a list of attributes or qualities of those items that were attracted by magnets. A separate list could be generated for those items lacking magnetic qualities.

Harry Wong has a fascinating classification activity that fits this strategy. He asks each student to remove their right shoe and place it in the middle of the classroom. He proceeds by having his students identify progressively smaller sub-groupings of shoes based on observable characteristics. This branching taxonomic key is created on the black-board and ends with each shoe having a separate entry and corresponding student name. In keeping with the dramatic, and with only ten minutes left in class, he explains how he has 25 children with only one shoe and asks for help in returning the missing footwear.

Model a tolerance for ambiguity

Provide situations that allow greater student control over variables and hypothesis formulation. Create open-ended situations that do not force closure or final answers. Such activities leave the door open for the student to continue thinking, developing, and testing long after the formal class activity has ended. This strategy forces the student into situations where there is no single right answer and more accurately portrays the nature of science; that ultimate answers do not always exist.

Example: Students build a machine that is powered by the wind from a hair drier and which will lift or move a weight. Combine this strategy with the use of open-ended questions. How much weight will your machine lift? How could you improve your machine? Make up an explanation for how it works.

Develop the concept of fate control

Through the use of this strategy, first described by Mary Budd Rowe (1978), students can personally experience models of how a person develops or changes reality rather than simply adjusting what ever comes their way.

Examples: A Focus On Excellence monograph is filled with examples of students taking charge of their own destiny: from Connecticut where students are saving hundreds of thousands of dollars with their energy audits to a 9th grade class in Missouri taking the city council to court.

Teaching through analogies

An analogy describes similarities between things when they are otherwise entirely different. In biology an analogy could be used to show the similarity in function between two body parts which are dissimilar in origin and structure.

Examples: Students identify man-made objects that exhibit similar characteristics or qualities depicted by various parts of the human body.

Develop skills in creative writing and reading

With this approach students are taught to express their ideas and feelings clearly and concisely. In the same manner, students are taught to read for meaning and to search for implications.

Examples: Students examine newspapers, television, and magazines for colloquial statements and paradoxical situations. The teacher helps them to differentiate between verifiable information and assumptions or editorial assertions. Also, students develop a tentative position on a science-related issue, report and examine data relative to the issue, and express their conclusions and implications based on their assessment. To maximize the potential of these activities, the student must work in a classroom environment that permits risk taking.

Encourage cooperative learning

Romey (1980) describes the dire results of over emphasizing the role of competition. He also expands on the negative impact that this competitive model has on the advancement of science in our society and stresses the importance of presenting science as a cooperative venture. The use of cooperative groupings and teamwork allows the teacher the opportunity to demonstrate how today's science and technological problems require the combined efforts of many specialists working together.

Examples: Establish independent study project contracts for student pairs or triads. The product of their efforts must be the combined efforts of all team members.

Encourage self evaluation

Whenever possible, students must be given the opportunity to self-evaluate and sense the intrinsic value of learning. This strategy helps students dare to be themselves by providing a classroom environment free from premature external evaluation by the teacher.

Examples: The culminating activity to a topographic mapping lesson might be the assigning of a different plot of land to each student or group of students. From a regional map, request students to tell as much as possible about their land and to give reasons for their responses. Such an assignment enhances student creativity and allows the student to assess the final results. After a class presentation of findings, students assess the degree of task completion by responding to several questions. Are there any other conclusions you could have drawn from your topographic land plot? If so, describe your new findings and offer reasons for these conclusions.

Conclusions

The skills of a teacher of integrated science today are probably much the same as they were ten years ago, although with more emphasis on Education for All, and thematic topics related to the environment and science and society. They do, however, need to be re-emphasised to show their importance.

A careful assessment of student needs and a balanced blend of teaching strategies are necessary for maximizing learning for any child. The final decision as to what should be done by a teacher on any given day should include:

a. an understanding of what the students are like and the kinds of experiences they bring with them;

b. a knowledge of the overlying science concept and how that concept can be applied to each subject area; and

c. ultimately, the decision of what teacher behaviours will best tie together the curriculum and the students.

We as teachers have a responsibility to develop the kind of individuals that can best mould the 21st century. The development of a scientifically literate society with enhanced creativity and heightened critical thinking skills is a necessity. But at the same time we must help our students integrate this knowledge and see the application and implications in new settings. Imagine a world in which human behaviour is characterized by the collection of evidence, a synthesis of that evidence and logical conclusions formulated after careful consideration and comparison against personal values and morals. Teacher behaviour plays a key role in the development of such people.

References

BONNSTETTER, R.J., PENICK, J. E., and YAGER, R. E. (1984). *Teachers in Exemplary Programs: how do they compare?* Monograph of the National Science Teachers Association, 1742 Connecticut Avenue, N. W., Washington, D. C., 20009.

BRANDWEIN, P. F. (1984). A plan for action [Summary]. *Proceedings of the Annual Curriculum Update Conference*, Iowa City, Iowa.

BRANDWEIN, P. F. (1959). *Teaching Gifted Children sSience in Grades Seven Through Twelve.* California State Department of Education, The Center for the Study of Instruction, San Francisco, California.

COSTA, A. L. (ed.) (1985). *Developing Minds: a resource book for teaching thinking.* Association for Supervision and Curriculum Development. Alexandria, VA.

HAWKINS, D. (1965). Messing about in science. *Science and Children*, 2, (5), 5-9.

ROMEY, W. D. (1980). *Teaching the Gifted and Talented in the Science Classroom.* National Education Association, Washington, D. C. (ISBN-O-8166-07360)

ROWE, W. B. (1974). Wait time and rewards as instructional variables: their influence on language, logic and fate control. *Journal of Research in Science Teaching*, 11, 81-94.

ROWE, M. B. (1978, March). Wait, wait, wait... *School Science and Mathematics*, 78, (3), 207-16.

WILLIAMS, F. E. (1982). Teaching strategies for thinking and feeling. In C. J. MAKER (Ed.), *Teaching Models in Education of the Gifted*, pp. 371-412. Aspen Systems Corporation, 1982.

WITTY, P. A. Ed. (1971). *Reading for the Gifted and the Creative Student.* International Reading Association, Neward, Delaware, (ERIC Document Reproduction Service ED 070044).

WONG, H. K. (1983). *How You Can Be a Super Successful Teacher: a cassette tape program.* 1536 Queenstown, Sunnyvale, California.

Chapter 7

Integrated science teaching needs integrated science teacher education

John E. Penick, University of Iowa and Ronald Bonnstetter, University of Nebraska, USA

Introduction

Integrated science implies coordination of scope and sequence not often found in the traditional classroom. Not only must teachers in the integrated classroom know science as a broad field, they must be alert for opportunities which promote integrated teaching. Such opportunities include natural phenomena (earthquakes, typhoons, drought) and societal issues (family planning, dams, water quality).

Since one goal of integrated science is for students to see and understand the nature of science, such issues and phenomena are ideal and teachable moments. By studying current events, students apply knowledge, seek evidence, see the tentative nature of science, and strive to learn more. But, this does not happen in the standard lecture/laboratory format.

An integrated curriculum requires teachers who know how to structure debates, discussions, controversy, and action. They must see new connections between bits of knowledge. Effective teachers of an integrated curriculum must be prepared with new goals, skills, strategies, and evaluation systems. And, they must competently defend their unusual goals and teaching with more than hearsay and personal opinion. An appropriate preservice teacher education programme for integrated science could be structured to provide desired attitudes and competencies, all supported by a teacher developed, research-based rationale.

An effective teacher of integrated science (and, thus, teacher education) must continuously consider three primary factors:
1. What are my goals for students?
2. How do my students learn and what should they be doing if they are moving toward those goals?
3. If I know what students should be doing, what should teachers be doing to facilitate their activities?

At the same time, the total classroom climate must reflect the nature of science. This highly integrated system of goals and behaviours is far from intuitive for most teachers and usually requires considerable nurturing, practice, and understanding as well as concrete examples to follow.

Commonly expressed goals for students

In more than 200 workshops with science teachers we have asked for their goals for students. While there is some variation, teachers of all grade levels invariably say they want students to:
1. Use their knowledge in identifying and solving problems.
2. Be more creative.
3. Communicate effectively.
4. Feel knowledge is useful and take action based on their knowledge.
5. Know how to learn.

While there are certainly many more possible goals, few would say these five are not valuable and useful. Many would go further and say that without these particular goals, an integrated science curriculum would be lacking its prime elements of learning through research, debate, and resolution.

These goals imply considerable student activity. Yet, as Goodlad (1983) pointed out, 'In our visits to schools, we received an overwhelming impression of student passivity.' (p. 554). Others (Yager and Penick, 1983) have pointed out clearly that what little action students take is often oriented toward more traditional and limiting goals reflecting no more than memorizing content knowledge. Overall, our students are generally not even working towards, much less achieving the goals we want and they need. Much of this failure can be traced to the classroom climate established by the teacher. Although we find teachers stressing these five goals, rare is a teacher who is aware of how to achieve them and, thus, they continue teaching in the same manner as they, themselves, were taught.

Yet, not all teachers fail in their attempts. We all know of teachers who seem instinctively to do the right thing and their students respond in kind. Teachers do make exemplary integrated science programmes (Penick et al., 1986). While we can admire such teaching, we must not be content to rely on merely waiting for good teachers to be born; we must make them. Professional teachers must recognize that students tend to learn along lines they find most rewarding (Torrance and Myers, 1970) and that they must be given appropriate opportunities if they are to achieve such lofty goals. At the same time Weiss (1977) reported that science teachers, in particular, are not very current in their formal education, the various United States National Assessments of Educational Progress were showing students becoming disenchanted by school as they progressed through it. Students also indicated clearly that they saw little value or application for their knowledge. Bonnstetter's study of exemplary science programmes (1983), on the other hand, demonstrated that teachers in identified outstanding programmes are current, energetic, innovative, and produce students who are as well. These teachers produce students who, using the affective portion of the 1977 United States National Assessment, like science and science teachers and feel science is useful. The 1986 United States National Assessment in Science (Mullis and Jenkins, 1988) showed a high positive correlation between students with the highest achievement scores and their perceptions of their classrooms as innovative, valuable, stressing application, and focusing on the use of equipment and applications.

Only a truly master teacher of integrated science can arrange teaching while remembering goals, applying knowledge of research on teaching and learning, and integrating subject matter. To do so, a teacher must be very aware of teacher influences. Unfortunately, most teachers do not seem to be aware of their classroom behaviour (Good and Brophy, 1987). But, evidence exists that we can educate them to do so. Krajcik and Penick (in press) in a study of graduates of an innovative secondary teacher education programme, found that recent graduates (averaging only three years experience) produce students who are every bit as positive as the students from Bonnstetter's study of teachers in exemplary programmes.

These relatively young science teachers (as well as Bonnstetter's very experienced ones) relate goals to action in a very systematic manner. For each student goal in integrated science, they see a particular set of student behaviours which enhance achievement of that goal. For example, a teacher wishing to enhance effective communication will determine what students must be doing to develop such skills. Then, knowing the relationship between student behaviour and teacher behaviour, this teacher can design appropriate teaching behaviours and strategies which will facilitate students. All of this, obviously, requires either a 'born teacher' or someone who has systematically learned appropriate actions and, at the same time, learned to control their own behaviour. Such must be the preservice curriculum for an issues-oriented teacher.

Needs in teacher education

To create purposely a relationship between goals and teacher behaviours, teachers must consciously structure their classrooms and personal behaviours. A teacher education programme attempting to do this must provide a model of the behaviours desired, resources needed to understand the model, and opportunities to develop their own concepts of the model. We will discuss each within the traditional United States framework of an introductory practicum, a foundations course in educational psychology, a subject methods course, and student teaching.

An ideal preservice teacher education programme proceeds from a sound foundation. For us, this foundation rests on six basic assumptions:

1. There is a large body of knowledge about effectiveness and the teaching/learning process.
2. Most people need to change aspects of their behaviour in order to use the research and be most effective.
3. Behaviour change takes time, intensive effort, and feedback.
4. Feedback based on early, continual, and broad school experiences leads to the most adequate teaching competence.
5. School experiences are more optimal when accompanied by seminars and direct supervision.
6. Teachers need to be able to place their content knowledge in a school learning context (Penick and Yager, 1989).

Thus, each component of an ideal programme must consider, use, and build on this foundation.

The introductory practicum

Usually offered as an introductory course, giving real-world, recent experience to students before more theoretical courses, the practicum should be more than mere observation. Here is a time to not only observe but to investigate, analyze, test, and discuss issues with colleagues. Providing a seminar of a few hours each week allows this to be as much a methods course as practicum.

In such an early methods course students can study students, noting how they react and when, what activities they prefer, their learning patterns, and begin formulating a notion of 'who is the child?' This is a time to assess student cognitive level via simple Piaget-type tasks, teach simple activities to small groups of students, and begin a systematic study of their own teaching behaviour.

To facilitate this requires structured opportunities to discuss events in the school and learn techniques such as the Piaget tasks. At the same time, a regular seminar puts emphasis on reflective thinking, the kind that teachers rarely find time for. Such reflective thinking is the beginning of teacher self-evaluation and behaviour change. And, if seminar discussions model effective discussion practice, preservice teachers will learn how to discuss, a vital skill in an integrated curriculum.

Supervision of the early practicum student focuses on feedback and questioning from the supervisor. This feedback and questioning should move the teacher in the direction of being more analytical in his/her approach to teaching. By raising questions and seeking solutions, a preservice teacher begins to see teaching as understandable, a series of problems amenable to solutions, action, and resolution. Through this approach, teachers can, as they need it, be introduced to the literature on effective teaching. By the end of the first practicum, teachers should be able to work with a small group, asking appropriate questions while providing time and encouragement for student discussion.

Educational psychology

Perhaps taken at the same time as the Introductory Practicum, Educational Psychology should provide teachers with a rational basis for observing and analyzing student learning behaviours. Focusing heavily on the child's cognitive and affective development, this course should give teachers an understanding of what to expect from students, how they approach and think about phenomena, and a solid concept of motivation and encouragement. Obviously, this educational psychology course should model desired approaches with the instructor being concerned with understanding, attitude, motivation, and appropriate evaluation.

Subject methods course

A methods course should be just that: how to 'do' teaching. And, as we well know, knowing requires doing and the doing must be physical as well as mental (Piaget, 1964). The doing in a methods course should begin with preservice teachers defining and developing a well-thought set of goals, goals they can justify, support, and work toward. This would be their own goal set, not a set imposed on them.

With goals in hand, the class would focus on identifying research on child development and learning which relates to the goals. While working toward the 'communicate effectively' goal for example, we would want students to be questioning and responding with their peers since logical thinking requires not just verbal learning but action (Piaget, 1964). In addition, since this goal reflects long-term learning, we expect to see students personally involved, initiating, discovering, and self-evaluating (Rogers, 1969).

With each piece of research related to what a child is doing when working towards a goal, preservice teachers would then seek evidence as to what teacher behaviour, strategy, and classroom climate will structure the setting so students will behave appropriately. In this case, 'appropriately' means in a manner which will, ultimately, lead to the desired goal. For instance, to achieve the student behaviours listed above, the teacher must model aspects of effective communication continuously, not just as an example. Students do copy their teacher's behaviour patterns (Anderson and Brewer, 1946). Teachers would also find that, since they are seeking self-initiation on the part of students, they must not use praise since praise reduces motivation when the learner has previously been performing the behaviour for intrinsic reasons (Deci, 1975). And, since communication requires conceptual understanding and confidence, teachers must avoid overly directive behaviours and teacher-oriented instruction since these behaviours increase anxiety and reduce conceptual learning (Flanders, 1951, Brophy, 1979). Evaluation, rather than being a teacher or student decision, becomes contingent on cause or consequence. In seeking consequences of ideas or actions, students must continually analyze. In the process they enhance their thinking ability as well as creativity (Torrance, 1965). This same pattern can be duplicated with dozens of research supported ideas associated with each goal.

Since most of this study and analysis of research during the methods seminar will be in a discussion mode, preservice teachers will have considerable opportunity to see and experience a well-run discussion. And, since students model their teachers' behaviour, effective modelling on the part of the methods instructor is required.

Combining this methods course with a well-supervised practicum would give teachers considerable opportunity to test their ideas and behavioural skills with students. Seeing and analyzing the effect (perhaps via video tape) serves to reinforce since they are actively involved and are evaluating via consequences of student behaviour and reaction.

Student teaching

An apprenticeship with a master teacher, while a marvellous idea, rarely happens. Instead, student teachers are more likely to be with a reasonably competent teacher with modest skills. But, if education is to improve, each generation of teachers must be better than, not just as good as, the preceding generation. Thus, our student teachers need to continue looking at the science as well as the art of teaching.

By 'science of teaching' we mean approaching it logically, orderly, and with analysis in mind. Observing, seeking patterns, evidence, and explanation characterise science. So, too, should teachers look at their own teaching as a scientist would. In this way, they will come to see what they do (assessment) and compare that with what they wish to do (evaluation).

To assume that the cooperating teacher knows educational research and is an adept supervisor and teacher educator goes well beyond our six assumptions. So, this defines the role of the student teacher supervisor. While the classroom teacher can compare the student teacher to other student teachers and teachers, the supervisor helps the student teacher to assess personally, self- evaluate, and plan new actions. These are the mark of a truly professional person. Again, since supervision in this case implies indirect teaching, helping the learner to self-evaluate, ask appropriate questions and, in general, to be analytical, so we would expect the student teacher to develop skill in these areas as well as in supervisory skills. Such skills are a key element in indirect teaching, the type most effective in learning to think (Costa, 1985). Again, students learn and teachers teach as they've been taught.

Some final notions

Integrated science in a classroom implies discussion of ideas, relating new thoughts to old. Students must deal with connections among the disciplines if they are to see and value them. The classroom setting must be appropriate if this is to occur. Facilitating such settings involves far more than mandating them. Few teachers or students have experienced such teaching. As a result, we, as teacher educators, must specifically teach for these roles. The key elements for integrated science teachers to remember and model are:

1. Provide stimulating settings, issues, and opportunities to make connections.
2. Ask questions which require thought but which allow a broad range of students to make suggestions and raise new questions.
3. Wait patiently and with interest for responses. Do not interrupt or act impatiently.
4. Accept all responses without evaluation. Evaluation is a separate task and must be contingent on cause and consequences.
5. Use student ideas for new questions, suggestions, or action.
6. Ask students for clarification: don't clarify for them.
7. Approach ideas scientifically, observing, seeking evidence and patterns. Do not rush to judgement and closure when the fun (and learning) is usually in the search.
8. Design classroom and curriculum so 'science', not a single discipline, is evident.
9. Be personally involved in the science and issues which evolve.

Teacher educators, seeking to develop teachers as above, must follow the same rules. Practice, not preaching, is still the guideline.

A teacher education programme kept faithful to this idea will produce teachers who can both do and teach (Krajcik and Penick, in press). These are the teachers we must have to proceed toward our most powerful goals of the future. Remember, teacher education students copy their university teacher's behaviour. Would you want yours to copy you?

References

ANDERSON, HAROLD H. and BREWER, Joseph E. (1946). Studies of Classroom Personalities, II: Effects of Teachers' Dominative and Integrative Contacts on Children's Classroom Behavior. *Applied Psychology Monographs*, No. 8.

BONNSTETTER, R., PENICK, J. E., and YAGER, R. E. (1983). *Teachers in Exemplary Programs: How Do They Compare?* National Science Teachers Association, Washington, D. C.

BROPHY, Jere. (1979). *Teacher Praise: A Functional Analysis.* Occasional Paper No.28, Institute for Research on Teaching, Michigan State University.

COSTA, A. L. (1985). Teaching for, of, and about Teaching. In: COSTA, A.L. (Ed) *Developing Minds*, Association for Supervision and Curriculum Development, Alexandria, VA.

DECI, E. (1975). *Intrinsic Motivation.* New York: Plenum.

FLANDERS, Ned A. (October, 1951). Personal-Social Anxieties as a Factor in Experimental Learning Situation. *Journal of Educational Research*, 45.

GOODLAD, John. (April, 1983). A study of schooling: Some implications for school improvement. *Phi Delta Kappan*, 64 (8).

KRAJCIK, J. S. and PENICK, J. E. (in press). Evaluation of a model science teacher education program. *Journal of Research in Science Teaching.*

MULLIS, Ina, and JENKINS, Lynn. (1988). *The Science Report Card: Elements of Risk and Recovery.* Educational Testing Service, Princeton, N. J.

PIAGET, Jean. (1964). Development and learning, Part 1 of Cognitive development in children. *Journal of Research in Science Teaching,* 2 (3).

PENICK, J. E. and YAGER, R. E. (Winter 1988-89). A model school-based program for science education majors. *Action In Teacher Education.* 10 (4).

PENICK, J. E., YAGER, R. E., and BONNSTETTER, R. (October, 1986). Teachers make exemplary programs. *Educational Leadership.*

ROGERS, Carl. (1969). *Freedom to Learn.* Columbus, Ohio: Charles E. Merrill Publishing Company.

THOMAS, GOOD, and BROPHY, J. (1987). *Looking In Classrooms.* Harper and Row, New York.

TORRANCE, E. P. (1965). *Rewarding Creative Behavior.* Englewood Cliffs: Prentice Hall, Inc.

TORRANCE, E. P. and MYERS, R. E. (1970). *Creative Learning and Teaching.* New York: Dodd, Mead and Company.

YAGER, R. E. and PENICK, J. E. (August, 1983). School science in crisis. *Curriculum Review,* 22 (3), 67-70.

Chapter 8

Curriculum emphasis in integrated science teaching

Jack B. Holbrook, Executive Secretary, ICASE
and Malcolm Rosier, ACER, Australia

Introduction

An examination of curricula can give some indication of the trends in the teaching of Integrated Science. Is it integrated by the compilation of Biology, Chemistry and Physics with a firm balance between them, is it integrated thematically with perhaps emphasis on interdisciplinary areas such as Energy, or is it integrated on local societal lines such as rural science, or environmental considerations?

This paper reports on a global review of curriculum emphasis from data obtained as part of an international science study conducted in the early 1980's. The curriculum emphasis was initiated so that it could be used as a basis for the selection of test items for an international measure of science achievement. An earlier study (Comber and Keeves, 1973) had shown that curricula were academic in nature and tended to be factually orientated. They showed that a content area grid could be usefully used to designate most science curricula at that time.

Integrated science gained its prominence in many countries by a consideration of the junior secondary science curriculum at grade levels approximating to 7-9. The curriculum emphasis considered in this paper refers to this level corresponding to Population 2 as defined for the Second International Science Study (SISS). The data given in this paper reflect curricula at grade levels 8 or 9.

In all countries, students at the Year 8/9 level study science curricula which include aspects of biology, chemistry and physics, and generally also of earth science. In some countries the curriculum has widened to include topics from other areas of science, as illustrated in the results later in this paper. The extent to which these aspects are fully integrated into a single 'integrated' science curriculum can only be established by systematic classroom observation. However, a study of the emphasis on topics within the following content area grids can indicate whether trends away from a fundamental content-driven approach have taken place. The results in this paper cannot thus demonstrate the extent or even the meaning of integration, but only provide an indication of the range of content covered and the extent of emphasis across the various topics, or of concentration in some areas. Patterns of emphases across countries can show whether trends are taking place in integrated science curricula.

Meaning of curriculum

The first stage in an examination of a curriculum sequence is the *intended curriculum*. This is the curriculum that is expected to be covered by schools in the teaching of integrated science and is specified in most countries at the level of the central agency responsible for education, such as the Ministry of Education. In other countries, where responsibility for decisions about the curriculum has been given to individual schools, the intended curriculum may be defined in terms of an average measure collated from the curriculum of individual schools.

It does not follow that the intended currciulum is actually taught. The *implemented curriculum* represents the interpretation of the intended curriculum by the teachers in the classrooms, who must develop the range of activities to present to the students. In the SISS, the implemented curriculum is measured by means of ratings supplied by the teachers, who indicate the extent to which the concepts underlying each item in the science tests has been covered by the students in that class.

The *achieved curriculum* indicates the extent to which students have internalized the curriculum as intended by the system and as implemented by the teachers. The measure of the achieved curriculum is the students' performance on the science tests developed for the SISS.

Classification of the curriculum

A classification system was developed with three components.

The first component covered traditional science content areas: earth science, biology, chemistry and physics. The 58 content areas in this component were defined in terms of a list of the kinds of topics covered.

A second component was topics grouped under other topic area which allowed for more locally relevant areas, such as environmental science and rural science.

The third area was a measure of the process skills emphasised during the course and would indicate emphasis on such areas as practical skills, decision making skills and communication skills.

Rating system

The next stage in the curriculum analysis involved assigning ratings to each content or objectives area on a 3, 2, 1, 0 scale.

    3 : the topic is given a major emphasis and is taught to all or most students
    2 : the topic is given a minor emphasis and is taught to only some students
    1 : the topic is given a low emphasis and is taught to only a few students
    0 : the topic is not included in the curriculum

Results

The remainder of the paper presents the results of the curriculum analysis.

Each table shows the mean and standard deviation (SD) of the country content ratings. The standard deviation is provided to indicate the variability across the country ratings. For this report, a 'significant difference' may be considered to exist where the difference between the country rating and the mean is greater than two standard deviations.

Each table shows a summary mean score for the set of curriculum ratings for each country. For example, the summary mean score for Earth Science is based on the six content areas for earth science. This gives an indication of the overall emphasis placed on earth science by the country, irrespective of whether the curriculum is integrated or taught as separate components. This row of the table also gives the mean of the country ratings and the standard deviation of these scores.

The calculation of the mean value of the set of curriculum ratings is based on the assumption that the content areas in the set have equal value, which may not be the case. In addition, comparisons of the mean scores for earth science across countries are necessarily based on the assumption that the relative weight given to each content area is the same in each country, and this assumption may not be valid. The same considerations apply to comparisons of mean scores for biology, chemistry and so on.

Caution is also needed in making precise comparisons of summary mean scores between the four groups (Earth Science, Biology, Chemistry and Physics), although general patterns of high or low ratings may readily be noted.

This paper includes only a few general comments on the results in the tables, with an emphasis on areas where there is a high level of coverage of the curriculum. It was not the purpose of this paper to make comments about specific countries; the results for a range of countries are included primarily to illustrate the classification system and the trends in curricula.

Science content areas (Tables 1-4) [1]

The tables enable the identification of content areas that generally have high mean curriculum ratings across all countries. Similarly it is possible to show content areas that generally have low mean curriculum ratings across countries.

At Year 8/9 the higher mean ratings for *earth science* are for the categories Solar System, Meteorology and Constitution of the Earth (Categories 1, 3 and 4).

The emphasis at this level for *biology* is on Cell Structure and Function, Cell Metabolism, and Metabolism of the Organism (Categories 7, 9 and 13). There is also a high coverage of Human Biology (Category 18).

In all countries, Introductory Chemistry (Category 24) received the maximum rating for *chemistry*. Other high ratings were given to Chemical Processes and Chemical Structure (Categories 27 and 33). On the other hand, content areas dealing with descriptive aspects of chemistry were not well-covered.

The content area with the highest mean rating for *physics* was Measurement (Category 39). Forces and Energy (Categories 41 and 43a) receive high mean ratings. Another group with high ratings have topics related to heat: Introductory Heat and Change of State (Categories 45 and 46). A third group with high mean ratings focussed on electricity: Current Electricity and Electro-magnetism/Alternating Currents (Categories 53 and 54).

It is obvious that some science content areas are given very weak coverage at the Year 8/9 level. In particular, little attention is paid to science topics of a more applied nature. A similar picture was obtained in the first science study conducted in 1970. Especially in developing countries, many students will leave school or otherwise discontinue the study of science after Year 8/9. It is inevitable that these students will take with them into adult life a lower understanding of the practical role of science in modern society than if their science courses had offered more exposure to applied science content areas.

Other Science Content Areas (Table 5)

The second component covered 'Other Content Areas'. These were included to enable countries to indicate where there were science activities beyond the traditional areas. The other content areas were arranged under the headings History and Philosophy of Science, Environmental Science, Technical and Engineering Science, Rural Science and Health Science.

Within the History and Philosophy of Science group, the Nature of Science received medium ratings across all countries, although some attention was also given to Historical Development of Science. The mean ratings for the content areas in the Environmental Science group and the Health Science group were generally at a medium level. The zero ratings for Hong Kong was largely due to the analysis being undertaken at the Year 8 level, whilst the Integrated Science course was designed to continue for a further year. Although still low, a higher level of coverage occurred in Year 9, the terminal year for the junior secondary science course.

Curriculum Objectives (Table 6)

The final component dealt with Objectives Areas, arranged under the headings Processes, Application, Manual Skills, Attitudes and Orientations.

The seven topics in the processes group represent a hierachy of stages of 'scienctific method'. The mean results across countries support the idea of a hierachy as shown by the sequence of decreasing mean values. The mean ratings for Application were usually lower than for other objectives.

The mean ratings for Manual Skills, and for Attitudes, Interests and Values were generally at a medium level.

At grade levels 8/9, the Orientations group received low ratings, indicating little concern for the place of science in the wider world.

Conclusion

The information presented in this paper is intended to introduce a system used for the analysis of science curricula across countries in the Second International Science Study (SISS). In addition to its use for describing curricula at one point in time, the system may be used to monitor changes in curricula which develop over time.

In order to reflect the structure of curricula as they existed in most of the countries in the SISS, the classification system was mainly based on the traditional areas of earth science, biology, chemistry and physics. There was little evidence that the countries had extended their curricula beyond these traditional areas into the 'other science content' areas which were also examined. There is also little evidence that an integrated science curriculum differs substantially in content or curriculum objectives from those offered as separate disciplines at the Year 8/9 level.

One challenge for those interested in integrated science is to modify the classification system cited in this paper so that it more adequately represents the coverage of content and objectives of integrated science curricula, and then to systematically map integrated science curricula across the world so that more comprehensive comparisons may be made.

References

COMBER L.C. and KEEVES J.P. *Science Education in Nineteen Countries*, Almqvist and Wiksell, Stockholm, 1973.

Note 1: The following abbreviations for country names have been used in tables 1-6.

AUS = Australia, CAE = Canada (English-speaking), CAF = Canada (French-speaking), CHN = Peoples Republic of China, ENG = England, FIN = Finland, GHA = Ghana, HKO = Hong Kong, HUN = Hungary, ISR = Israel, ITA = Italy, JAP = Japan, KOR = Republic of Korea, NET = The Netherlands, NIG = Nigeria, NOR = Norway, PAP = Papua New Guinea, SIN = Singapore, SWE = Sweden, THA = Thailand, USA = United States of America.

Table 1 Earth Science: Population 2

Content Area	AUS	CAE	CAF	CHN	ENG	FIN	GHA	HKO	HUN	ISR	ITA	JAP	KOR	NET	NIG	NOR	PAP	PHI	POL	SIN	SWE	THA	USA	Mean	SD
1 Solar System	2	2	0	3	1	2	1	2	3	2	1	3	3	2	0	0	3	1	3	0	3	3	3	1.9	1.1
2 Stellar System	1	1	0	2	1	1	1	0	1	2	1	3	3	0	0	0	2	1	2	0	2	0	3	1.1	0.9
3 Meteorology	2	1	1	3	2	2	0	2	2	1	2	3	0	3	0	0	3	2	3	0	3	3	3	1.8	1.1
4 Constitution of the Earth	2	0	2	2	1	2	0	2	3	2	2	0	2	3	0	0	3	2	3	1	0	3	2	1.7	1.1
5 Physical Geography	2	0	1	3	1	2	0	2	3	1	2	0	3	3	0	0	3	1	3	0	0	3	2	1.5	1.2
6 Soil Science	1	0	0	0	2	2	1	2	2	1	1	0	0	3	0	0	3	1	3	0	1	3	1	1.2	1.1
Mean: Earth Science	1.7	0.7	0.7	2.3	1.3	1.8	0.5	1.7	2.3	1.5	1.5	1.5	1.8	2.3	0.0	0.0	2.8	1.3	2.8	0.2	1.7	2.5	2.2	1.5	0.8

Table 2 Biology: Population 2

Content Area	AUS	CAE	CAF	CHN	ENG	FIN	GHA	HKO	HUN	ISR	ITA	JAP	KOR	NET	NIG	NOR	PAP	PHI	POL	SIN	SWE	THA	USA	Mean	SD
7 Cell Structure and Function	2	3	2	3	3	2	3	2	3	3	3	3	0	3	3	3	3	2	3	3	3	3	2	2.7	0.7
8 Transport of Cellular Material	1	3	3	1	1	2	1	0	2	3	3	0	0	2	0	0	0	2	1	2	2	3	2	1.6	1.1
9 Cell Metabolism	2	3	3	1	2	3	3	3	3	3	3	0	3	3	1	1	3	2	3	1	3	3	2	2.4	0.9
10 Cell Responses	1	1	1	1	1	1	0	0	2	2	2	2	0	2	2	2	0	0	2	1	3	0	2	1.3	1.0
11 Concept of the Gene	0	3	3	0	1	1	0	0	1	2	2	2	2	1	0	0	2	1	0	0	3	0	2	1.1	1.1
12 Diversity of Life	2	3	0	3	3	2	3	3	3	3	2	3	3	3	3	3	3	2	3	2	3	0	2	2.3	1.0
13 Metabolism of the Organism	2	3	3	3	3	3	3	3	3	3	3	3	3	3	2	2	3	1	3	2	3	3	2	2.7	0.5
14 Regulation of the Organism	1	2	1	2	2	1	0	2	2	2	3	3	0	3	1	1	3	0	2	0	3	0	2	1.7	1.1
15 Co-ordination/Behaviour of the Organism	1	2	3	2	2	2	0	2	2	1	1	2	0	3	3	3	2	0	3	1	3	0	2	1.7	1.0
16 Reproduction and Development of Plants	2	3	0	3	3	2	3	3	3	2	3	3	3	3	3	3	3	1	3	2	3	3	2	2.6	0.8
17 Reproduction and Development of Animals	2	3	3	1	3	1	0	3	2	2	3	0	3	3	3	3	3	3	3	2	3	3	2	2.3	1.0
18 Human Biology	2	3	3	3	3	1	2	3	3	2	2	3	3	3	3	3	3	3	3	1	3	3	2	2.5	0.7
19 Natural Environment	2	3	0	3	2	3	2	2	3	2	3	0	0	2	2	2	3	1	3	2	3	3	2	2.0	1.1
20 Cycles in Nature	2	3	0	0	2	3	3	0	2	2	3	0	0	0	3	3	3	1	3	3	3	3	2	1.9	1.2
21 Natural Groups and their Segregation	0	1	0	1	1	0	0	0	0	0	1	0	0	3	0	0	0	0	0	0	0	0	1	0.3	0.7
22 Population Genetics	0	1	0	0	0	1	0	0	0	0	0	0	0	2	0	0	0	0	0	0	3	0	1	0.3	0.8
23 Evolution	1	1	0	3	1	1	0	0	3	2	3	3	3	2	2	3	0	0	1	2	3	0	1	1.5	1.2
Mean: Biology	1.4	2.5	1.5	1.8	2.0	1.8	1.4	1.7	2.3	2.1	2.4	1.7	1.3	2.6	2.1	2.1	2.2	0.9	2.3	1.5	2.9	1.7	1.8	1.8	0.5

Table 3 Chemistry: Population 2

Content Area	AUS	CAE	CAF	CHN	ENG	FIN	GHA	HKO	HUN	ISR	ITA	JAP	KOR	NET	NIG	NOR	PAP	PHI	POL	SIN	SWE	THA	USA	Mean	SD
24 Introductory Chemistry	3	0	3	2	3	3	3	3	3	3	3	3	3	2	3	3	3	3	3	3	3	3	2	2.7	0.7
25 Electro-Chemistry	1	1	0	1	1	3	2	2	0	3	2	2	3	2	3	3	2	2	1	0	2	3	1	1.7	1.0
26 Chemical Laws	1	0	0	3	1	2	1	0	2	3	1	3	0	1	3	0	0	3	2	0	2	3	2	1.4	1.2
27 Chemical Processes	2	0	0	3	2	3	2	0	3	3	1	3	3	1	2	3	3	2	3	1	3	3	2	2.1	1.1
28 Periodic System	1	0	2	0	2	2	3	0	3	2	0	0	0	1	3	3	0	3	1	0	3	0	2	1.3	1.2
29 Energy Relationships in Chemical Systems	1	0	0	2	1	1	0	0	1	3	1	3	3	1	2	0	0	3	0	1	1	2	1	1.2	1.0
30 Rate of Reactions	0	0	0	0	1	0	0	0	0	3	0	2	0	0	3	0	0	3	0	0	1	3	0	0.8	1.1
31 Chemical Equilibrium	1	0	0	0	1	0	0	0	0	0	1	0	0	0	3	0	0	0	0	0	0	0	0	0.2	0.7
32 Chemistry in Industry	2	0	2	0	2	2	0	0	0	0	1	0	0	2	3	2	3	1	0	0	2	0	1	1.1	1.1
33 Chemical Structure	2	0	2	3	2	3	3	2	3	3	1	3	0	2	3	3	3	2	1	1	3	3	2	2.2	1.0
34 Descriptive Inorganic	2	0	0	3	2	3	3	2	3	3	0	3	0	2	2	0	0	2	3	1	3	3	1	1.7	1.2
35 Organic Chemistry	1	1	1	0	2	2	0	0	3	1	0	0	0	1	1	3	3	1	1	0	3	0	1	1.1	1.1
36 Environmental Chemistry	1	1	2	0	1	2	0	3	2	2	0	0	0	1	0	2	3	2	0	1	3	3	1	1.3	1.1
37 Chemistry of Life Processes	1	1	2	0	2	1	1	2	0	2	0	2	3	1	1	1	3	2	0	1	3	3	1	1.4	1.0
38 Nuclear Chemistry	0	1	0	0	0	0	0	0	0	0	0	0	0	0	0	1	0	1	0	0	0	0	1	0.2	0.4
Mean: Chemistry	1.4	0.3	1.1	1.3	1.7	2.2	1.4	1.1	2.0	2.3	0.8	1.8	1.2	1.3	2.2	2.0	1.8	2.2	1.2	0.7	2.5	2.0	1.4	1.5	0.5

Table 4 Physics: Population 2

Content Area	AUS	CAE	CAF	CHN	ENG	FIN	GHA	HKO	HUN	ISR	ITA	JAP	KOR	NET	NIG	NOR	PAP	PHI	POL	SIN	SWE	THA	USA	Mean	SD
39 Measurement	2	3	3	3	3	3	2	3	3	3	2	3	0	3	2	3	3	3	3	3	3	3	3	2.7	0.7
40 Time and Movement	1	2	0	3	2	3	1	2	3	3	2	3	3	2	2	0	0	2	3	1	3	3	2	2.0	1.0
41 Forces	2	3	3	3	3	3	1	2	3	3	3	3	3	3	3	3	3	2	3	3	2	3	1	2.7	0.6
42 Dynamics	1	2	3	1	1	3	1	2	3	3	3	0	2	2	3	2	0	1	3	0	3	3	2	1.9	1.0
43a Energy	2	3	3	3	2	3	1	2	3	3	2	3	3	3	3	2	3	2	3	2	2	3	2	2.6	0.6
43b Machines	1	2	3	3	2	2	1	0	1	2	1	2	2	0	3	1	0	1	3	1	2	3	1	1.9	0.8
44 Mechanics of Fluids	2	1	3	3	2	2	1	0	3	3	3	3	0	3	3	2	3	1	3	0	1	3	1	1.8	1.1
45 Introductory Heat	2	3	3	3	3	3	3	3	3	3	3	2	1	3	3	1	3	2	3	3	3	3	2	2.7	0.6
46 Change of State	2	3	2	3	3	3	1	3	2	3	3	3	0	3	3	3	3	2	2	1	1	3	2	2.4	0.8
47 Kinetic Theory	2	3	0	3	2	2	1	2	2	2	0	0	0	3	2	1	3	2	3	0	3	3	2	1.8	1.2
48 Light	2	1	2	3	2	2	2	2	3	2	3	3	0	3	3	3	3	1	3	3	2	3	2	2.3	0.8
49 Vibration and Sound	0	1	1	1	1	3	1	0	1	2	2	3	0	2	3	3	0	1	2	0	1	0	1	1.8	0.9
50 Wave Phenomena	1	1	0	0	1	2	0	0	0	2	1	0	1	0	3	0	3	1	0	0	1	0	2	0.5	0.8
51 Spectra	2	1	2	0	2	2	0	2	1	2	0	0	1	2	3	2	0	1	2	1	2	0	2	1.1	1.0
52 Static Electricity	2	2	2	3	2	2	3	2	2	3	3	2	0	2	3	3	3	2	3	2	2	0	2	2.0	1.0
53 Current Electricity	2	1	3	3	3	2	3	3	3	3	2	3	0	3	3	3	3	2	3	2	3	2	2	2.5	0.8
54 Electromagnetism/ Alternating Currents	2	1	3	3	2	2	1	0	3	3	2	3	0	3	3	3	3	1	3	1	2	2	2	2.1	1.0
55 Electronics	0	1	0	0	1	0	1	0	3	2	0	3	0	2	1	3	0	1	3	0	2	0	1	1.0	1.1
56 Molecular/ Nuclear Physics	0	0	0	0	0	2	0	0	0	1	0	0	0	0	2	3	0	0	0	0	3	0	1	0.5	1.0
57 Theoretical Physics																									
Mean: Physics	1.6	1.9	2.2	2.4	2.1	2.4	1.4	1.8	2.5	2.6	2.0	2.3	0.9	2.5	2.7	2.1	2.1	1.5	2.8	1.2	2.3	2.3	1.9	2.1	0.5

Table 5   Other Content Areas: Population 2

Content Area	AUS	CAF	CHN	ENG	FIN	HKO	HUN	ISR	JAP	KOR	PAP	PHI	POL	SIN	SWE	THA	USA	Mean	SD
History and Philosophy of Science																			
1 Historical Development of Science	1	3	1	1	0	0	0	2	2	2	2	1	3	1	1	0	1	1.2	0.9
2 Nature of Science	2	3	0	1	1	0	2	3	2	1	3	3	2	0	1	3	2	1.7	1.1
Mean: History and Philosophy	1.5	3.0	0.5	1.0	0.5	0.0	1.0	2.5	2.0	1.5	2.5	2.0	2.5	0.5	1.0	1.5	1.5	1.5	0.8
Environmental Science																			
3 Energy Resources	1	1	1	2	2	0	2	2	0	2	3	2	3	2	3	2	2	1.8	0.9
4 Energy Use	1	3	1	1	2	0	0	2	0	1	2	1	3	2	2	2	2	1.5	---0.9
5 Environmental Impact	1	3	1	1	2	0	2	2	0	2	3	2	3	1	3	3	2	1.8	1.0
6 Habitats	1	0	1	2	2	0	3	2	2	0	3	1	3	2	3	2	2	1.7	1.0
Mean: Environmental Science	1.0	1.8	1.0	1.5	2.0	0.0	1.8	2.0	0.5	1.3	2.8	1.5	3.0	1.8	2.8	2.3	2.0	1.7	0.8
Technical and Engineering Science																			
7 Transport	1	3	0	1	1	0	2	1	0	0	3	0	3	0	2	3	1	1.2	1.2
8 Manufacturing Processes	1	2	0	1	1	0	1	1	0	0	3	1	2	1	2	0	1	1.0	0.8
9 Computers and Microprocessors	1	0	0	1	0	0	0	0	0	0	0	0	0	0	1	0	1	0.2	0.4
Mean: Technical/Engineering Science	1.0	1.7	0.0	1.0	0.7	0.0	1.0	0.7	0.0	0.0	2.0	0.3	1.7	0.3	1.7	1.0	1.0	0.8	0.6
Rural Science																			
10 Animal Husbandry	0	0	0	1	1	0	2	1	0	0	0	0	2	0	2	2	1	0.7	0.8
11 Plant Husbandry	0	0	0	1	1	0	3	1	0	0	3	1	3	0	2	2	1	1.1	1.1
12 Housing and Rural Amenities	0	2	0	1	1	0	2	1	0	0	3	1	3	0	1	2	1	1.1	1.0
Mean: Rural Science	0.0	0.7	0.0	1.0	1.0	0.0	2.3	1.0	0.0	0.0	2.0	0.7	2.7	0.0	1.7	2.0	1.0	0.9	0.9
Health Science																			
13 Personal Health	2	3	2	2	1	0	3	2	0	3	3	2	3	0	3	3	2	2.0	1.1
14 Inter-Personal Relationships	1	3	2	2	1	0	3	1	0	3	3	1	3	0	3	3	2	1.8	1.1
15 Community Health	1	3	2	1	1	0	0	0	0	0	3	1	0	0	3	3	0	1.1	1.2
Mean: Health Science	1.3	3.0	2.0	1.7	1.0	0.0	2.0	1.0	0.0	2.0	3.0	1.3	2.0	0.0	3.0	3.0	1.3	1.6	1.0

Table 6 Objectives Areas: Population 2

Objectives Area	AUS	CAF	CHN	ENG	FIN	HKO	HUN	ISR	JAP	KOR	PAP	PHI	POL	SIN	SWE	THA	USA	Mean	SD
Processes																			
1 Knowledge and Understanding	3	3	3	3	2	3	3	2	3	3	3	3	2	3	3	3	2	2.8	0.4
2 Observation	3	3	3	3	2	3	3	3	3	3	3	3	3	3	3	3	3	2.9	0.2
3 Measurement	2	3	3	3	2	2	3	3	2	2	3	3	2	3	1	3	3	2.5	0.6
4 Problem Solving	2	3	3	2	1	2	2	2	3	3	3	2	1	1	2	3	2	2.2	0.7
5 Interpretation of Data	2	3	2	2	1	3	2	2	3	2	3	3	1	1	2	3	2	2.2	0.7
6 Formulation of Generalizations	2	1	1	2	0	2	2	2	3	1	3	3	3	0	1	3	2	1.8	0.9
7 Model Building	1	1	0	2	0	1	0	1	2	0	0	2	0	0	1	1	1	0.8	0.7
Mean: Processes	2.1	2.4	2.1	2.4	1.1	2.3	2.1	2.1	2.6	2.0	2.6	2.7	1.7	1.6	1.9	2.7	2.1	2.2	0.4
Application																			
8 Application	2	3	2	2	1	2	2	2	2	2	3	2	2	1	2	3	1	2.0	0.6
Manual Skills																			
9 Manual Skills	3	3	3	3	3	3	3	2	3	3	3	2	3	3	3	3	2	2.8	0.4
Attitudes																			
10 Attitudes, Interests and Values	2	3	2	2	3	2	3	2	3	3	3	2	3	1	3	3	2	2.5	0.6
Orientations																			
11 Historical Background	1	3	0	1	0	0	2	1	2	1	0	1	1	1	2	1	1	1.1	0.8
12 Science and Technology	1	3	1	1	1	0	2	1	0	2	3	2	2	2	2	3	1	1.6	0.9
13 Social and Moral Implications	1	1	1	1	1	0	2	1	0	1	0	1	1	1	3	3	1	1.1	0.8
14 Limitations of Science	1	1	1	0	0	0	1	1	0	1	0	1	1	0	2	1	1	0.7	0.6
Mean: Orientations	1.0	2.0	0.8	0.8	0.5	0.0	1.8	1.0	0.5	1.3	0.8	1.3	1.3	1.0	2.3	2.0	1.0	1.1	0.6

Part 2

Regional and national trends in integrated science teaching

Chapter 9

Africa

General

Primary level

Science is now included on the timetable for all primary-level classes in most African countries. But the time allocated to it varies widely — from forty minutes per week in Sierra Leone to two or three hours per week in some other countries (e.g. Lesotho).

The approach is, invariably, an integrated one, most often based on the environment, and in many countries reflects the philosophy and practice of the Science Education Programme for Africa (SEPA) which was originally introduced as the African Primary Science Programme twenty-five years ago. Some of the original units and teaching materials are still in use as part of the primary-school courses in some countries. But in many cases new curricula have been developed within the last few years. One such example is Lesotho where the new primary science syllabus comprises eighteen units spread over seven years (see Table 1). Another notable example is the Nigerian Primary Science Project for the northern states which is a pupil-centred approach based on topics, including the environment and applications of science (technology).

In the Gambia the primary science syllabus has recently been revised so that teaching and learning are more activity, oriented with additional reading material for primary-school students. The Science Teachers' Association of Gambia (STAG), the Book Production and Materials Resources Unit and the Curriculum Development Centre jointly organized writers' workshops to produce and print supplementary science books for children which were to be provided free of charge to schools in 1988/89.

Secondary level

Most African countries have introduced a two-, three-, or four-year junior secondary school course in integrated or general science, but the extent of integration varies considerably. General science courses include biology, chemistry and physics topics but often these topics are taught as separate subjects with no real attempt to integrate or even co-ordinate the teaching. In a historical survey of integrated science in many developing countries, Bajah, 1982 traced the origin of published integrated science textbooks to the Scottish *Science for the Seventies*, published in 1971.

The pattern of development of integrated science in many African countries follows a straight forward modality. In the first place, science educators in many of the African countries spent a good deal of time trying to understand and accept the inherent philosophy of integrated science.

While, on the one hand, many traditional classroom science teachers saw integrated science as a body of knowledge consisting of parts of the established sciences, science curriculum developers, on the other hand, continued to stress the process nature of integrated science — integrated science is a way of teaching science. It was not until the second half of the last decade that the underlying philosophy of teaching science as unity became accepted as possible by a majority of practising science teachers with an initial training in one of the basic sciences.

Because many of the African countries operated a tight examination system, and because many of the countries operate a central education system, considerable effort was put into the development of an accepted and approved core curriculum or syllabus for a country. Subject specialists from universities, colleges of education and secondary schools put together a certain amount of subject matter drawn from the sciences. When subjected to a critique group, the initial draft was updated to show integration of not only science subjects but also important issues in the environment. A document on integrated science with the approved government stamp on it thus evolved.

It is one thing to prescribe *what* to teach as content for integrated science but it is another thing to show *how* the approved content can be effectively transmitted in a typical African classroom. Immediately there was need to write corresponding textbooks that followed the approved syllabus almost to the letter. Two patterns of producing the relevant books emerged: (a) groups of authors got together to produce the texts; (b) the professional science teachers association assembled some members to produce books with the approved stamp of the association.

A further step in the development trend involved the provision of resources — both human and material — for the teaching of integrated science. It is this step that has presented the greatest obstacle to many of the Ministries of Education and to classroom interaction.

Key issues in integrated science

Several issues have arisen since the adoption of integrated science into many school systems in Africa. For the purpose of this paper, five key issues are discussed:

1. *Non-acceptance of integrated science as a university option.* Over three-quarters of the federal universities in Nigeria have refused to accept integrated science either as entry qualification in science or as an academic discipline in these universities. Physics, chemistry, biology and agricultural science are accepted as basic science courses. The result is that many academically able students at the secondary-school level or in colleges of education who aspire to proceed to the university shun integrated science.

2. *Training teachers of integrated science.* There is strong disagreement among university faculties of education whether to train specialist integrated science teachers or to produce traditional science graduates with some exposure to integrated science. Since integrated science is, at present, taught only at the primary and lower secondary levels, specialist integrated science teachers may find themselves perpetually relegated to work at those levels, thus raising the issue of prestige.

3. *Integrated science examinations at the national level.* A major issue has arisen with regard to the scope and depth of integration in the national examination questions. At present, an integrated science test paper could easily be classified into sections of the traditional sciences. The opponents of integrated science see this situation as an inherent weakness in the whole philosophy of integrated science.

4. *Crisis in the classrooms.* A large majority of science teachers in the classrooms still teach their traditional specialist science when not under strict supervision. An integrated science teacher with a strong background in the biological sciences has a hard time with subject-matter involving a knowledge of the physical sciences. And besides, the traditional 'chalk and talk' approach is still prevalent in many of the schools. The question now is 'Should there be an integrated science laboratory?' Can African countries afford this?

5. *Need for continued research in integrated science.* There is need to organize, fund and continuously carry out research in classrooms across countries where integrated science is taught in schools. A cross-cultural study is suggested.

Southern Africa

In the southern Africa states of Botswana, Lesotho and Swaziland, the original Boleswa integrated science — leading to a regional junior certificate examination — is currently under revision since the three countries are no longer linked by a Regional Examinations Board and each now has its own autonomous university. The revision to Boleswa science in Lesotho, undertaken by the National Curriculum Development Centre (CDC) in 1985, has produced a new five-year syllabus leading to the Cambridge Overseas General Certificate of Education Examination, in which each of the separate sciences is clearly defined. Thus although the course is designated 'Science and Integrated Science' the extent of integration is now *less* than it was in the original Boleswa scheme, reported in 1978. For the time being, Swaziland is still using the original Boleswa approach.

Table 1   Arrangement of units for class 1 to class 7

UNITS \ CLASS	1	2	3	4	5	6	7
1.	EXPLORING THE ENVIRONMENT	—	—	LIVING AND NON-LIVING THINGS	—	—	—
2.	SIMPLE TOYS	—	—				
3.	SOIL	—	—	—	—	—	—
4.	WATER	—	—	—	—	—	—
5.	ANIMALS	—	—	—	—	—	—
6.	PLANTS	—	—	—	—	—	—
7.	MEASUREMENT	COMMON SUBSTANCES	—	—	—	—	—
8.		MEASUREMENT	CHANGES	—	—	—	—
9.			AIR	—	—	—	—
10.			BALANCING	—	—	SIMPLE MACHINES	—
11.			MEASUREMENT	TIME	—		
12.				SENSES	—		
13.						FRICTION	—
14						HEAT & FIRE	—
15.						LIGHT ENERGY	—
16.							ELECTRICITY
17.							MAGNETISM
18.							SOLAR SYSTEM

By contrast, the revisions in Botswana, which are still under development, are leading towards new syllabuses with the title 'Science by Investigation'.

These syllabuses have three main themes: health, environment and social relevance. There are twelve units spread over three years. The syllabuses are supported by teachers' guides and pupils' worksheets for each unit. Kits of equipment — based on those developed in Zimbabwe (ZIMSCI project) — have been introduced for the new community schools. The emphasis of the new syllabuses is on social relevance and local environment; and the syllabuses are intended to provide considerable depth of integration — much more than in the original Boleswa science.

The syllabus themes or topics are as follows:

Theme or topic	Approximate time
Basic science skills	6 weeks (x 6 periods/ week)
Cells, reproduction and family life	4 weeks
Water for living	6 weeks
Air and gases	6 weeks
Detecting the environment	6 weeks
The human body and plants	6 weeks
Electricity and its uses	7 weeks
Chemicals in the household	5 weeks
Natural resources and environmental awareness	7 weeks
The house	3 weeks
Transportation	4 weeks
How to keep healthy	2 weeks

The unit on water is probably the most important of the syllabus. Botswana is a hot and dry country, the average annual rainfall varies from 250 mm in the south to 650 mm in the extreme north, the country often experiences longer periods of drought, and there is always a shortage of water. It is therefore essential that pupils be made aware that '*water is an important natural resource*', that they know how to conserve water and how to prevent its contamination.

The general and specific objectives for this section of the syllabus and some examples of teaching modules are given in Chapter 14 of this book.

This section of the syllabus is preceded by laboratory work on water which includes observing the different states of water and the changes of state, determining the boiling and melting points of water, plotting heating curves and measuring rate of evaporation for different conditions.

Many of the activities in this section lend themselves best to field trips and project work, such as working out the best position for a rain-water tank for the school. Where do you place it to collect maximum amount of rain-water? How much will it collect? Is this water safe to drink? How do you prevent contamination of this water?

Rather than make a laboratory model of a water filtration bed, a usable size of filtration bed is made using a drum, which can be directly copied for home use. Booklets prepared by the Water Hygiene Project are sent to schools as resource material for such projects.

Although the primary health care programme has dramatically improved the health of children in the country, infectious intestinal diseases, mostly diarrhoeal , are still the main cause of illness and death in early childhood. Science teachers have a responsibility to assist in this area. Pupils prepare milk formulae using water from different sources (tap water, river water, boiled river water etc.) and observe the effect of harmful micro-organisms. They discuss the advantages of breast-feeding and the precautions to be taken when bottle- feeding. Pupils should be able to recognize the symptoms of dehydration and they prepare an oral rehydration drink in class.

In choosing technology topics for the new syllabus, examples that are appropriate for the present needs of the country have been given priority. They will also make pupils aware of and adaptable to new technological developments which may change their way of life.

Solar appliances are becoming increasingly common in Botswana, in particular solar water heaters. Photovoltaic panels are used to provide electricity for telecommunication transmitters in rural areas and also to provide lighting in some remote area schools. For a country with an average of 320 cloudless days per year, solar technology is very relevant and it is included in several sections of the syllabus. The Botswana Technology Centre has assisted by developing solar kits with instructions for all schools.

In Botswana, most people build their own traditional houses. These are increasingly being replaced or complemented by 'modern' houses, the simplest type consisting of a cement floor, brick walls and a 'zinc' roof for which a builder is contracted. The customer buys the building materials and the builder (usually someone who has been employed as a worker at a large construction firm) builds the house to the customer's specifications. Architects are usually only engaged in larger villages and towns for medium- or high-cost buildings. Hence it is appropriate that students should investigate *factors to be considered when designing and building a home'*.

For this purpose support material and practical advice have been obtained from the Botswana Renewable Energy Technology Project, which has built a 'solar home' to demonstrate how a house can be kept cool in summer and warm in winter through appropriate building design.

A typical activity in this section is to measure, record and compare temperatures in model houses made from small cardboard boxes (chalk boxes) and using transparent plastic sheeting for windows.

In Zambia the basic education system (Grades 1 to 9) is adopting an integrated science course. The aim of education in Zambian society is 'to develop the potential of each citizen to the full for his own well being as well as that of society and for selfless service to his fellow man' (Education Reform Document, 1977). In order to accomplish this goal, the party and its government recommended a new structure in 1977 as follows:
1. Basic education in grades 1 to 9
2. Second stage education — secondary school (three years) - vocational training
3. Third stage education

The government aims to provide equal opportunity for children of all socio-economic groups in the nation, but the magnitude and complexity of the task of equality of educational opportunity is gigantic. It requires vast amounts of financial, material and human resources. In this context, equal opportunity can be interpreted as providing a minimum of 'universal basic education'. The basic education stage 'will aim at providing some practical skills and a strong foundation for further full time or part time education' (Reform Document, 1977). For the vast majority of the school going population, it is the end of their formal education. The nine years of basic education should give the pupil enough skills to lead a useful life in society.

The primary and junior secondary school will finally merge and form a nine-year basic education programme. Already the junior secondary school is reduced to two years and the secondary school is now from grades 10 to 12.

The educational reforms identified a number of subject areas to be studied during basic education. Science is selected as one of the subjects and the reasons given form the rationale for the new syllabus. 'Pupils should be able to master useful practical skills which they would apply in life in various ways: they should adopt a scientific approach and attitude; they should observe, collect information, draw conclusions and apply what they know'. (Reform, Document 1977).

A new environmental science syllabus which forms an integrated course of science was proposed for grades 1 to 9 to replace the old syllabuses of primary science and junior secondary science. The content of this syllabus is written in behavioural objectives concerned with allowing the pupil to gain in knowledge and skills as appropriate to the material being taught. While the teacher is primarily concerned with the cognitive development of pupils, other areas, such as the affective domain, are not ignored. The course aims generally to develop in the pupil:
1. an attitude of scientific curiosity and enquiry
2. the skills necessary to investigate a situation in a scientific manner
3. a critical approach to evidence
4. the ability to generate new ideas
5. a willingness to work with others and share knowledge
6. an understanding of man as a living organism and his place in nature
7. an understanding of major aspects of the physical environment

8. an increased awareness of the variety of life and of the relationship of living things to their environment
9. an increased awareness of the importance of science and technology in everyday life and in expanding the boundaries of human knowledge
10. the ability to productivity skills and knowledge gained during the course.

(Proposed Syllabus for Basic Education, Science, 1982).

The subject matter is divided into eighty-two units. Each unit has aims, content and then specific behavioural objectives. The approach to teaching these topics is spiral or concentric, and so the topics recur in succeeding years, taught in greater depth in higher grades. It allows the development of abilities (such as observation, experimentation, description, deduction, etc) to take place at a reasonable pace geared to the level the pupil has reached. The material for the syllabus has been selected from all major disciplines of science and an integrated approach is expected in teaching it. There are seventeen topics altogether, namely : matter, animals, weather, light, water, ecology, universe, broadcasting, forces, energy, sound, farming, plants, man, gases, heat and electricity. The time allocation is one hour a week in grades 1 to 4, to 160 minutes in grades 5 to 7 and 240 minutes in the higher grades. Pupils are assessed by a public examination consisting of a multiple choice paper (40 per cent weighting) and structured questions (60 per cent).

The main problems identified so far include:

a. The behavioural objectives given in the syllabus are an indication of what changes in behaviour the teaching is supposed to bring about in the pupils. But they give no guidance as to how such changes are to be achieved. There are no handbooks or guides for teachers prepared by the Ministry or the CDC.
b. The curricula have been implemented at the grade 8 level — but the pupils have not learned the grade 1 to 7 syllabus and find it difficult to follow the topics. Teaching has to be adjusted to include some topics form grades 1 to 7.
c. Many of the primary schools have now become basic schools and go up to grade 9. But the teachers at the primary school are not trained to teach this science syllabus. So a retraining programme is required. Even the teachers at the junior secondary schools need in-service training to teach this new syllabus.

Possible solutions to these problems are:

a. The CDC and the Ministry of Education are getting funds from the Finnida and Norad agencies to prepare textbooks and teacher guides. Meanwhile the Zambian Association for Science Education (ZASE) has written handbooks for teachers at the grades 8 and 9 levels.
b. In-service courses and retraining will take a long time to plan. ZASE is now conducting small workshops and seminars for primary, and secondary, school teachers to give them some guidance in teaching the new syllabus.
c. ZASE regional groups have prepared schemes of work including topics which they feel are not yet covered by the pupils at primary level. (The syllabus is not adopted grades 1 to 7 and so it will take another seven to eight years before the first batch of pupils who have covered the entire syllabus sit for this examination.)

West Africa

In West Africa the West African Examinations Council School Certificate and General Certificate of Education Syllabuses dominate the secondary school syllabuses throughout the region. The examination syllabuses offer general science and additional general science as well as the traditional separate sciences of biology, chemistry and physics. Nevertheless, there are several schemes or projects at the junior secondary level that have been developed to provide two-year courses in integrated science.

The Science Teachers' Association of Nigeria (STAN) has continued to be partners in progress with the Federal Ministry of Education and other educational agencies in continuing the search and efforts for the most viable and appropriate means of delivering quality education to as many people as possible using indigenous expertise and resources and where possible that of other parts of the world. The relationship between education, the individual and society has long been established as being not only intricate but also continuous. Education has implications for the survival of the individual and society and consequently is a strong determinant of the quality of life. STAN also recognizes the enormous challenge which integrated science poses for science educators and curriculum planners.

In 1968, STAN was asked by the West African Examinations Council to make recommendations on the review and improvement of the then GCE 'O' level science syllabuses. A revision was deemed necessary in the light of developments in science education all over the world. In response to this request, the STAN National Executive Committee created four curriculum development committees, one each in biology, chemistry, physics and mathematics. A generous offer of financial support was received from the Ford Foundation through the Comparative Education Study and Adaption Centre (CESAC). Additional support was received from the Curriculum Renewal and Educational Development Overseas (CREDO) through the British Council. Support in the form of curriculum materials was received from Unesco and from the Longman Publishing Company.

In 1970 Heinemann published the pupil's textbooks I and II, accompanying workbooks and teachers guide all produced by the STAN writing team. Other STAN members produced textbooks that went side by side with the STAN integrated science textbooks and for a decade, beginning in 1971, four parallel textbooks on integrated science were written for Nigerian students almost entirely by Nigerian authors, all members of STAN.

The new 6-3-3-4 education system encompasses three years of junior secondary education which is pre-vocational and academic and cover all the basic subjects which enable pupils to acquire further knowledge and develop skills. The curriculum developers thus recognize the need for integration of related subjects so as to accommodate all subject areas in the school timetable. Such basic subjects taught using the integrated approach include English, integrated science, social studies, business studies, introductory technology, home economics.

The Federal Ministry of Education organized in September 1980 a national curriculum workshop to design a new three-year integrated science project for Nigerian junior secondary schools (JSS). Nearly all members of the national writing team were STAN members. The JSS Integrated Science Project adopted a thematic approach. It was structured in six themes:

• You as a living thing
• You and your home
• Living components of the environment
• Non-living components of the environment
• Saving your energy
• Controlling the environment

A spiral arrangement is adopted for each theme.

Immediately following the approval of the three year JSS integrated science curriculum, STAN mounted a series of writing workshops to enable writing teams to complete manuscripts for books I,II and III to correspond with the three year programme. By August 1985, all student texts, accompanying workbooks and teachers guides were published. All STAN books are comprehensive, simple and readable and very relevant to the Nigerian child.

Other publishers are also producing their own texts for JSS integrated science. As the number of young persons is extremely large the population of Nigeria is about 100 millions, the market is large and can accommodate many good and well-produced JSS integrated science textbooks.

In addition to the production of textual materials, STAN places a high premium on teacher education and preparation for greater effectiveness. The entire STAN body is subdivided into subject panels for thorough, relevant and meaningful activities. One such panel is the integrated science panel which has been consistent in mounting every year in-service education and training courses/workshops for teachers of the subject. At least one panel workshop on a national level is organised yearly on a rotational venue basis. Each of the various twenty-two state branches including the federal capital, also mounts courses/workshops for members of the state branches of STAN. Some states have even been divided into five or more zones and workshops are organized for teachers in these zones. This is one way by which STAN activities have reached the grassroots.

The Federal Ministry of Education and the various State Ministries of Education organize Teacher Vacation Courses (TVC) always in collaboration with STAN. Distinguished STAN members are involved as resource persons and many of the participating teachers are members of STAN. Integrated science is always one of the areas to be considered because of the challenge it has continued to pose to educators and curriculum planners.

The Federal Ministry of Education and the various State Ministries of Education in close collaboration with STAN have been producing instructional materials and developing resources for the teaching of integrated science in Nigerian schools. Science Production Centres have been established by the Federal Ministry of Education and many of the State Ministries of Education. Several workshops, some lasting for two weeks or more, have been organized to help teachers acquire teaching skills as well as that of improvisation of instructional materials for teaching integrated science. For instance, four zonal workshops, each of two-weeks duration, were mounted by the Federal Ministry of Education between March 1982 and September 1983. Each workshop focussed primarily on acquisition of effective teaching skills and that of improvisation by the teachers. Furthermore, in September 1986, the Federal Ministry of Education organized in each state of the Federation a four-week TVC including the three-year JSS integrated science. Again teacher-made instructional material was an essential component of the four-week course. Many members of STAN also participated as resource persons or trainers.

STAN recognizes the importance of project work and out-of-school science activities and their role in encouraging learners to participate in the construction (or reconstruction) of knowledge. STAN has a national science fair co-ordinator, and state science fair co-ordinators. These science fair co-ordinators meet twice a year and ensure that the standard of science fairs and exhibitions is continually improved.

Science fairs and STAN members, exhibitions mounted during the annual conference are most attractive and remarkable features. All science teachers including those of integrated science are encouraged to display instructional materials they have improvised using locally available materials. This activity is usually made an award-winning competition to encourage keen participation. Very many new and 'how-to-go-about-it' ideas useful to the teacher have been generated and communicated to other colleagues.

For the past two decades, the development and promotion of integrated science education in Nigerian schools have continued to fascinate STAN. This is because of the enormous challenge which the integrated science paradigm has continued to pose. A flourishing and influential body such as STAN has, as a deliberate policy, accepted this challenge and has been making determined efforts to see that integrated science is taught effectively and accepted nationwide.

The struggle to deliver good quality integrated science education that could improve the quality of life particularly those of the rural dwellers is, however, not an easy one. Schools are constrained by inadequate teacher supply, defective pre-service teacher education and training, and non-availability of facilities and instructional materials. Nonetheless, STAN continues the struggle.

In Sierra Leone the Core Course Integrated Science (CCIS) is still available as an indigenously developed integrated science for the first two years of the secondary school but there are no textbooks for the course and difficulties are reported with respect to local printing of workbooks for the student and teachers' guides. This is resulting in some schools abandoning the CCIS approach. The topics of CCIS are given in Appendix xx. As conceived and originally taught it represents a good example of an integrated approach to science, developed by an indigenous team of science educators, with a considerable intensity of integration.

Chapter 10

Arab States

A comparative study of science teaching at the lower secondary level (grades 7 to 9) in four Arab States — the Arab Republic of Egypt, Jordan, Qatar and Saudi Arabia — was undertaken during 1987/88 by the Science Education Center, Ain Shams University, Cairo. This survey revealed that in Egypt and Qatar integrated courses of science were taught at the lower secondary level; in Saudi Arabia and Jordan combined science was taught.

In Egypt, an environmental approach was adopted. The themes 'Man and His Local Environment' (grade 7) 'Man and Natural Resources' (grade 8) and 'Man and the Universe' (grade 9) provided the basis for the programme development. Elements of physics, chemistry, biology, health, geology and astronomy were included in these programmes, as well as technology. While the curriculum also made provision for related laboratory work and other practical activities, the large number of students in classrooms (around sixty students per class) has meant that such work is mainly of a demonstration kind. A major problem in the teaching of integrated science in Egypt is that the teachers themselves have usually been taught science as separate disciplines. Attempts are being made, through in-service training, to help the teachers cope with this problem.

In Qatar, a similar environmental approach is followed, using comparable integrated themes. The number of students in classes is relatively small and some practical work is carried out by the pupils themselves. The problem of teacher training is similar to that in Egypt, i.e. the teachers have been trained to teach the separate science disciplines. In-service courses are being conducted.

In Saudi Arabia, a 'unit' approach is taken to the teaching of science. Most of the units are based on a single science subject but some integration is attempted in units dealing with the environment and genetics. Because of relatively small class size, some individual practical work is possible.

In Jordan, the curriculum in grades 7 to 9 follows a similar 'unit' pattern and practical work is mainly of the demonstration type. The teachers are prepared to teach the individual science subjects and, at present, there is little attempt at integration.

Integrated science education in Kuwait

R. Al Hamed

The Ministry of Education in Kuwait has interpreted 'integration' to mean the strict sense of bringing together several subjects in a single course in which scientific concepts are approached uniformly in spirit and method, in such a way as to express the fundamental unity of scientific thought. It is believed that integrated science is better than separate subjects in teaching science for children for many reasons (such as the nature of knowledge, the study of interdisciplinary subjects, economic use of time and resources).

Models of integrated science teaching in Kuwait

Primary stage

Primary education in Kuwait covers from grades 1 to 4 (6 to 10 years old). Science education at the primary level has been integrated for more than twelve years and courses are completely integrated. The topic approach to integrated science is promoted, combined with the concept and process approach, in which major concepts of science are not studied in their entirety at once, but each is spread out over the length of the course, leading to the slow development of an idea as the age of the student advances.

At each grade level a balanced coverage of content from the life, earth, and physical sciences gives students a unified view of their environment.

The content is designed to meet the interests and needs of the children, and give them a realistic, full-dimensioned view of the world around them and an awareness of the many ways which science affects their lives. Students' books and science laboratories interact to help students discover concepts for themselves through active investigation.

Recent changes

In the school year (1987/88), Arab Gulf countries introduced a newly developed, experimental and unified science course with textbooks, and preparations are now being made to generalize it in the first and second primary grades for all Gulf Arab States in 1988/89. The new science unified course takes a fully topic-integrated approach, combined with a concept and process approach e.g.
- our home and school
- our bodies
- animals and plants around us
- air and water around us
- tools which help us
- our health and safety
- our clothes
- transportation.

Intermediate stage

The intermediate stage in Kuwait includes grades 5 to 8. The integrated science teaching approach which starts in grades 1 to 4 in the primary stage, continues through the intermediate school with the same approach but with variations in the type of integration and the content of the course. Besides the topic-concept-process approach, another interesting type of integration is incorporated centring around real local issues in the life and environment of students, such as water, air, noise, pollution, and world-wide problems such as over-population, food production, conservation of natural and human resources and world health problems. Again, as at the primary stage, students' books and science laboratories interact to help students develop concepts for themselves through active investigation.

The secondary stage

The secondary stage in Kuwait includes grades 9 to 12. In grade 9, science is taught using an integrated science approach. The type of integration centres on the so-called 'pattern approach', which may be regarded as a combination of the concept and process models and represents the search for patterns in the sciences and the use of these patterns in solving problems. A pattern may be regarded as an important generalization or explanation in science.

Again, as in the intermediate and primary stages, students' books and science laboratories interact to help students develop concepts for themselves through active investigation. In grades 10, 11, 12 general education science is taught as separate subjects (physics, chemistry, biology and geology). Although science subjects at higher levels in the secondary school are taught separately, there is unity inside the course of each subject, by making various parts of the syllabus relevant to each other. By internal relevance we mean the connections between and the interdependence of different parts of the subject.

The new science curriculum projects have themselves illustrated integration within the discipline. For example, physics courses are no longer a mixture of light, heat, sound, dynamics, electricity and magnetism. Physics itself is unified through major concepts such as fields, conservation laws and waves. Biology is no longer divided into botany and zoology. There are attempts now to make some partial integration between science subjects in the last grades of secondary school using the interdisciplinary subjects, such as astrophysics, bio-physics, biochemistry, microbiology and also human and economic science.

Teachers of integrated science

Again and again the trials of integrated courses in various parts of the world have confirmed the lack of enthusiasm of teachers teaching outside their usual scientific discipline. This problems is tackled through in-service training for science teachers and by using fully instructional teacher guides. Furthermore, there is now an attempt between the Ministry of Education and the Faculty of Education in Kuwait University to specifically prepare integrated science teachers for intermediate and first class secondary schools.

Chapter 11

Asia and the South Pacific

Section 1: Asia

Integrated science education in South East Asia

C.R. Netto

Introduction

The main inspiration to introduce integrated science as a science subject at the lower secondary level in Brunei Darussalam, Singapore, Malaysia and Hong Kong was the publication of the Scottish *Integrated Science Scheme*. The switch from the traditional science in forms I, II and III (grades 7 to 9) to integrated science started in the 1970s.

The new approach in science teaching is to change from chalk and talk to an inquiry/ practical method, rote memory in the learning of science no longer being encouraged but rather the spirit of discovery and scientific thinking is advocated. Less emphasis is given to theory and factual knowledge, and more to the understanding of basic scientific concepts and the relevance of science to daily life, industry and society.

In the integrated science syllabus the various disciplines of science, mainly biology, chemistry, and physics are integrated into a single course, although the extent of integration is dependent on the understanding of integration.

Changes

From the mid-70s several changes have taken place in integrated science syllabuses. Brunei Darussalam is the third largest producer of oil in South East Asia (after Indonesia and Malaysia) and the world's fourth largest producer of liquified natural gas (LNG). Thus, 'Earth and its Resources' (including oil and gas) is retained in the integrated science syllabus in Brunei and more relevance is given to the learning of these topics. Freshwater biology is included as a new section helping students to know their environment and to acquire an interest in nature and its conservation.

In Hong Kong, the integrated science syllabus has undergone several noteworthy changes to meet the local needs. Electronics is slowly being introduced and some attempts to provide for the less able pupils are being made.

In the Singapore system, the lower secondary science syllabus is based on energy as the linking theme, boosted by the basic concepts needed for any science course, like units and measurements and classification. Attempts have been made to introduce a more appropriate science programme at the junior and lower-secondary level related to the local environment and the science processes.

At the lower secondary level, Malaysian integrated science is offered to all the pupils. The pupils are exposed to various aspects of scientific investigation, apparatus and the method used in carrying out the experiment as well as the scientific process in obtaining the conclusion.

Integrated science has become an interface subject linking primary science with 'O'-level science subjects. With the advent of a new science syllabus at the lower-secondary level, suitable changes were brought about in the primary science syllabus to include environmental studies so that the pupils would be familiar with nature and the language of science. The innovators of the new primary science programme believe that the children should gain as much first-hand experience of things around them as they can. Textbooks have simple content, are lavishly illustrated and encourage a programme of seeing and doing science activities — both in school and at home.

For pupils who are not following science subjects at 'O' level, integrated science course is terminal. To others who pursue a course in science subjects, the integrated science course gives an introduction to examination courses leading to 'O' grade in the various science disciplines.

Problems of implementation

Syllabus content and teaching approach

The key to interest and achievement in science lies in experimentation. The topics studied should be experienced at first hand. There is often the complaint from ntegrated science teachers that the syllabus is full that they have no time to give all the required experiments to the pupils. The syllabus content is in need of reduction or adjustment so that there will be sufficient time to enact the 'discovery method' of teaching and learning.

In-service courses

Many teachers express feelings of inadequacy and incompetency in teaching science. They feel inept at doing science experiments, some of which often fail to work. In-service courses need to be regularly organized to update teachers' knowledge and teaching skills. A massive effort is required, especially as motivation, is low, particularly at the junior level.

Laboratory facilities and lab staff

Laboratory facilities need to be augmented to cope with the activity-oriented teaching-learning programme. Trained laboratory technicians and laboratory assistants are needed to form a vital thrust in running integrated science classes.

Out-of-school science education

At present the majority of the schools in many Asian countries are double-session schools. Moving to single-session schools will facilitate informal study or out-of-school activities to supplement/complement academic work. Students could be encouraged to engage in project work, research or surveys in their own environment.

Science teachers' association can play a vital role in organizing extracurricular science activities for students and teachers. BASE, STAS, HKASME etc. are a few of the well known science and maths associations of the region which organize co-curricular activities for students and teachers.

Audio-visual aids

The use of audio-visual aids — such as charts, models, slides, transparencies, films etc. in science teaching, have not been fully exploited by science teachers. Television sets, video cassette recorders etc. have become modern tools in presenting science lessons. Television science programmes are being produced in Singapore, Malaysia, Hong Kong, Brunei Darussalam, etc. in accordance with the topics in the syllabus. Perhaps a mutual exchange of the tapes could be beneficial to all.

Integrated science education in Brunei Darussalam

C.R.Netto

Science curriculum

The importance of science and technology in the development of a country has long been accepted. Like many other developing countries Brunei Darussalam imports most of the scientific and technical know-how from the industrialized countries. It is believed that the economic advancement can only be achieved by the ability of the country to absorb ideas and methods of modern science and technology.

The emphasis on science education in Brunei Darussalam has inevitably brought several changes in the science curriculum — both at primary level and secondary level. Under the new science curriculum developed by the Curriculum Development Centre (CDC), science is incorporated in general studies at the lower-primary level and primary science which includes health science at the upper-primary level. Compulsory integrated science is taught at the lower-secondary level and three separate sciences (physics, chemistry and biology) are taught at the upper-secondary level as well as at the advanced level.

Integrated science

The impact of the changes in science education in the West and neighbouring countries like Malaysia had brought constant review of the science curriculum in Brunei Darussalam both at primary level and secondary level by the CDC. One such step taken by the CDC was the adaptation of the Scottish integrated science to suit Brunei Darussalam's needs in 1969. The first trial of integrated science was conducted at two schools — one in Malay Medium (SMJA) and the other in English Medium (SOASC) in 1970. By 1972, all government schools had replaced general science with integrated science.

Definition of integrated science

Integrated science in the Brunei Darussalam context is the unification of various science subjects whereby concepts found in each science subject are presented in such a way as to minimize if not eliminate the distinction between these subjects. For example, concepts that are found in physics, chemistry, biology, mathematics, geography and social studies are unified in integrated science.

Rationale of integrated science

It is hoped that the introduction of integrated science will satisfy the need:
1.   to improve the methods of approach and effective teaching of science;

2. to give science education to all to suit the needs of the country after leaving lower-secondary schools;
3. to give a strong foundation in science to enable children to pursue pure science at upper secondary level as well as at advanced level;
4. to ensure continuation of the integrated approach of science teaching from primary level.

Teaching staff

Beforeintegrated science was tried out in 1970, teachers who were responsible for the running of the course were sent to Malaysia to attend courses in the method of teaching integrated science in Malaysia. Thus in 1969, seven local teachers were sent to Malayan Teacher's College, Johor Bahru, to take up the short course. On their return to Brunei, some of these teachers were responsible for running courses for teachers to teach integrated science while others were sent to schools to teach integrated science. In 1970 and 1971, local teachers were sent to attend the same course in Malaysia. At the same time, there were also courses organized by the Education Department in Brunei for teachers involved in integrated science.

At present, the teaching staff of integrated science falls into the following categories:
1. Graduate science teachers with post-graduate certificate of education (PGCE) or diploma in education. These teachers are not trained to teach integrated science.
2. Graduate science teachers without PGCE or diploma in education. They are not trained to teach integrated science.
3. Non-graduate teachers who have been trained to teach TT integrated science. These teachers are produced by the TT Institute of Education.

Curriculum materials

When integrated science was tried out in 1970, both the syllabus and worksheets were adapted from Scottish integrated science. By 1972, a Malaysian version of the Integrated Science Worksheets was used in all schools. In 1975, this version was revised and the revised edition was used in all schools at lower-secondary level in 1977. These worksheets called 'Integrated Science Worksheets for Brunei' and come in sets of three i.e., Forms I, II and III. The present integrated science is set by the CDC as a result of a series of meetings of CDC officials with members of the secondary science committee, secondary school principals, the heads of science departments and teachers as well as visits to schools. The syllabus consists of sixteen topics whereby most of the topics are covered in the first year and second year of the lower-secondary schools. Table 1 shows the topics in the integrated science syllabus.

Teaching approach

Although the syllabus set by the CDC shows flexibility and with no teacher's guide to rely on, much of the methods of approach are rigid as teachers tend to depend heavily on worksheets for science activities. The methods of teaching employed by teachers include expository method, demonstration method, stationary method and class practicals.

Table 1

CONTENT

FORM ONE	—	SECTION 1	—	INTRODUCING SCIENCE
		SECTION 2	—	INTRODUCING LIVING THINGS
		SECTION 3	—	ENERGY
		SECTION 4	—	MATTER AS PARTICLES
		SECTION 5	—	GASES IN THE AIR
		SECTION 6	—	CELLS, REPRODUCTION & GROWTH

FORM TWO   —   SECTION 7   —   MAKING HEAT FLOW
                      SECTION 8   —   ELECTRICITY
                      SECTION 9   —   HYDROGEN, ACIDS & BASES
                      SECTION 10   —   THE SENSES
                      SECTION 11   —   WATER & OTHER SOLVENTS
                      SECTION 12   —   TRANSPORT SYSTEM

FORM THREE   —   SECTION 13   —   ELECTRICITY
                      SECTION 14   —   SUPPORT & MOVEMENT
                      SECTION 15   —   EARTH & ITS RESOURCES
                      SECTION 16   —   FRESH WATER BIOLOGY

Bibliography

Curriculum Development Centre, Education Department, Ministry of Education and Health, Negara Brunei Darussalam; The Education System of Negara Brunei Darussalam; 1985.

Science and Mathematics Education in SEAMEO countries; RECSAM, Educational System in Brunei Darussalam.

Curriculum Development Centre, Negara Brunei Darussalam; Integrated Science Syllabus for Lower Secondary Schools 1984.

BASE; Science Education in the Development of Brunei Darussalam.

Pusat Perkembangan Kurikulum Kementerian Pelajaran Malaysia; Kaedah dalam pendidikan Sains — Pengajaran Sains Paduan di Malaysia; 1980.

Integrated science education in China

Mi Zi Hong

Introduction

In China, primary schools offer a course in the study of nature, which is followed by physics, chemistry and biology at the junior middle-school level. If China is to face the developing trends in world science and technology, the branches of science must develop transversally and permeate each other. New research in one specialist field of science is used increasingly in another. There is a demand for a sound science base so that the surrounding material world can be introduced to students enabling them to become aware of world science development and assist in the modernizing of China.

Difficulties

For this, however, there are many difficulties:

There are no textbooks to introduce integrated science education relevant to the special needs of the country. Some textbooks have been published in several provinces and cities, but they are far from sufficient. It is also important to consider the guiding ideology to establish courses in integrated science. There will be many difficulties since the natural sciences such as physics, chemistry, biology, astronomy and geography, have been developed for so many years, accumulating knowledge and forming their own specialist structure. Integrated science books have to not only embody a synthesis of the sciences, but also reflect the knowledge of each separate system. The relation between these two aspects must be carefully balanced.

Teachers for integrated science education do not exist. Teachers have their own majors in present-day China. They will need a long time to become familiar with integrated science teaching. Generally speaking, teachers are interested in teaching the traditional courses and lack a strong desire to change the present situation. This is probably the most important drawback in China.

The lack of financial support and experimental apparatus. In order to launch a course in integrated science, the availability of experimental apparatus must be increased. It will be necessary to buy new equipment, even though physics and chemistry instruments can be still useful. It will be a large financial burden to schools.

Teaching evaluation and examinations. The second subordinate middle school of East China Normal University has conducted a trial to launch integrated science teaching. A special class has been organized there. Students in the class did not drop physics and chemistry courses but received an integrated science course of two hours a week in addition. If the school offered the integrated science course only, it would need to ask for permission of the authority concerned. The point is, if only integrated science is taught, how can one be sure that students are able to cope with the senior middle school entrance examination, before the nation-wide examination system has been reformed.

There are thus many problems to overcome in China. Since integrated science education would be a new trend in junior middle schools, it should have a long transition trial period before dissemination. It is important to gain from experiences in foreign countries at first, then produce a series of textbooks, teachers' guide books and student reading books for such a course. During this trial period, teachers must be re-educated and schools selected suitable to conduct the trials. The trial region should not be vast (East China, for example, would suffice), because the larger the region, the more regional educational differences emerge. At present, trials have begun in Shanghai and in North-East China and it is hoped to strengthen co-operation and exchanges with foreign countries thus gaining more support and useful ideas.

Integrated science teaching in India

B.B. Ganguly

Introduction

Integrated science was first introduced by the National Council of Educational Research and Training (NCERT) at the upper primary level (age 11+ to 13+) along the lines of recommendations made in the approach paper, 'Ten Years Curriculum' (NCERT, 1975). The curriculum package included an introductory paper, textbooks, teachers' guides, kit with kit guide, activity books and various audio-visual aids. In the same period, i.e. 1975-78, environment-based science curriculum was introduced at the lower primary level (age 5+ to 10+) and the package included textbooks (for III, IV, V), teachers' guide (I -V), low-cost kits and audio- visual items. The contents of both lower and upper primary level were selected from daily life experience and presented according to the learning ability of the child. Besides creating interest and awareness about scientific phenomena, efforts were made to strengthen the power of observation, decision-making ability and certain desired values. Certain skills which are important in daily life situations were also emphasized. The science curriculum at the secondary level (age 14+ to 16+) continued to be organized according to various disciplines.

The materials for integrated science developed by NCERT at the national level were implemented by schools affiliated to the Central Board of Secondary Education without adequate orientation of teachers. A few states and union territories followed this material. But most states introduced their own materials, which were environment-based at the lower primary but continued to be organized according to various disciplines at the upper primary level.

Neither discipline-oriented science nor integrated science could in fact make much of an impact on the classroom, for the latter has always been ill-equipped and the proceedings therein conducted by teachers whose predilection for traditional methods and devotion to disseminating information outweighed their ability to adapt to the changing trends. It would be unfair to put all the blame on the teacher, however. In spite of all their efforts and enthusiasm, the curriculum developer, the textbook writer and the teacher trainer did not always succeed in integrating the concepts of science and perceiving its holistic nature.

A number of voluntary agencies such as Kerala Sashtra Parishad, Homi Bhabha Centre for Science Education, Vikram Sarabhai Community Science Centre, Eklavya and Kishore Bharati, worked at the grass-roots level to implement integrated science materials developed by them. Results of such micro-experiments have been quite encouraging.

Current trends

A discussion on current trends in integrated science teaching will remain incomplete if it is not preceded by an account of thinking that has been generated recently in the field of education.

In order to give a complete picture, this section is divided into the following components: (a) emergency of a new national policy on education, 1986; (b) present position of science education; (c) Recommendations pertaining to science in the national policy on education; and (d) recommended steps for improving science education.

National policy on education (1986)

The period between 1984 and 1986 will be long remembered in the history of Indian education. Innumerable activities in the form of conferences, seminars and group meetings were held to review the existing state of the art in education; all this led to the formulation of the National Policy on Education (1986). But while all these debates were going on, two very important documents, (namely, (i) Challenge of Education (1985) and (ii) National Curriculum for Primary and Secondary Education — A Framework (1985)) were brought out. The former document was the outcome of in-depth studies which candidly presented the problems of the Indian educational scene and suggested some of the tasks to be undertaken. This document was placed before the country for national debate. The 'National Curriculum for Primary and Secondary Education — A Framework' acted as forerunner of the new education policy and held the promises of revolutionalizing the content and processes of school education.

Ten core areas were identified: history of India's freedom movement; constitutional obligations; content essential to nurture national identity; India's common cultural heritage; egalitarianism, democracy and secularism; equality of sexes; protection of the environment; removal of social barriers; observation of small family norm and inculcation of the scientific mentality. It was suggested that these should be strengthened immediately through education.

Present position of science education

Various in-depth studies have revealed that all the efforts made by government and voluntary organizations towards the implementation of science education have failed to produce much impact. The most important objective of science in general education, i.e. development of scientific mentality, has remained unfulfilled. All the functionaries such as teachers, method masters, science educators and subject experts, who were connected with the development and implementation of science curricula, studied science only to pass examinations. The materials developed by them and the method adopted by them helped the students to pass examinations in their turn. A self-perpetuating and self-propagating retrogressive system has generated and extended from universities to primary schools. The objectives like creation of interest and curiosity, inculcation of an enquiring mind, promotion of problem-solving attitudes and decision-making powers, development of courage to question, and growth of concern for other people and

Primary science, Bombay

consequences have been talked about but never implemented. On the pretext of knowledge explosion, the child has been loaded with content information while learning of concepts has been ignored. No serious efforts have been made to stress the unified principles of science and the development of scientific literacy. The entire planning of science education has been urban-oriented and directed at the traditional learners who constitute less than 3 per cent. This has been done on the presumption that all the students are going to undertake higher studies in science (actually less than 5 per cent of the students continue higher studies in science after completing class X).

105

Immediate steps are now needed to provide minimum threshold facilities for teaching science both in the formal as well as the non-formal system and essential learning outcomes of science and mathematics (in terms of knowledge, competencies and skills) must conform with the environment in which the child lives, areas of national development and the world of work.

Recommendations pertaining to science in the National Policy on Education

Science and mathematics will remain as core subjects in the first ten years of school education. Specific recommendations on science as a school subject in the National Policy of Education are:

The new policy will lay special emphasis on the removal of disparities and to equalise educational opportunity by attending to the specific needs of those who have been denied equality so far.

In the areas of research and development, and education in science and technology, special measures will be taken to establish network arrangements between different institutions in the country to pool their resources and participate in projects of national importance.

The new thrust in elementary education will emphasise two aspects (i) universal enrolment and universal retention of children up to 14 years of age, and (ii) a substantial improvement in the quality of education.

Teachers' training programmes will be reoriented, in particular for teachers of primary classes.

Secondary education begins to expose students to the differentiated roles of science, the humanities and social sciences. This is also an appropriate stage to provide children with a sense of history and national perspective and give them opportunities to understand their constitutional duties and rights as citizens. Conscious internalisation of a healthy work ethos and of the values of a humane and composite culture will be brought about through appropriately formulated curricula.

Vocationalization through specialised institutions or through the refashioning of secondary education can, at this stage, provide valuable manpower for economic growth. Access to secondary education will be widened to cover areas unserved by it at present. In other areas, the main emphasis will be on consolidation...

There is a paramount need to create a consciousness of the environment. It must permeate all ages and all sections of society, beginning with the child. Environmental consciousness should inform teaching in schools and colleges. This aspect will be integrated in the entire educational process...

Mathematics should be visualised as the vehicle to train a child to think, reason, analyse and to articulate logically. Apart from being a specific subject, it should be treated as a concomitant to any subject involving analysis and reasoning...

With the recent introduction of computers in schools, educational computing and the emergence of learning through the understanding of cause-effect relationships and the interplay of variables, the teaching of mathematics will be suitably redesigned to bring it in line with modern technological devices...

Science education will be strengthened so as to develop in the child well defined abilities and values such as the spirit of inquiry, creativity, objectivity, the courage to question and an aesthetic sensibility...

Science education programmes will be designed to enable the learner to acquire problem-solving and decision-making skills and to discover the relationship of science with health, agriculture, industry, and other aspects of daily life. Every effort will be made to extend science education to the vast numbers who have remained outside the trawl of formal education...

Non-government and voluntary effort including social activist groups will be encouraged, subject to proper management, and financial assistance provided. At the same time, steps will be taken to prevent the establishment of institutions set up to commercialise education.

Local communities, through appropriate bodies, will be assigned a major role in programmes of school improvement.

Recommended steps for improving science education

Both before and after the development of the National Policy on Education, a series of meetings, seminars and workshops were held for identifying the steps to be taken for improving science education. The following important actions were recommended:

Up to class X, science should be treated as 'one' area of human endeavour and not as compartmentalized disciplines. Learning of concepts should be emphasized rather than stressing content information. The most important purpose of science in general education would be to fulfil the seven dimensions of scientific literacy. The presentation of content should not be contrived. It must be need-based and relevant to life and teaching/learning situations are to be selected from both rural and urban areas. Linking of science with the constitutional commitments, different priority areas of national development (agriculture, communication, transport, textile, chemicals, etc.) and certain thrust areas (energy, environment, social forestry, wildlife management, industry). Learning ability of the child, specially the communication skills of the first generation learners should be taken into consideration in writing the instructional materials.

The pre-service teachers' training programme should be oriented towards the teaching of integrated science. Future teachers are to be acquainted with actual teaching/learning situations which can be created to attain different domains of scientific literacy and their evaluation. Activities must be done during the training programme to understand the linking of science with constitutional commitments, areas of national development and special thrust areas. The in-service teachers' training programmes need to be designed along the same lines. Resource centres or centres for continuing education should remain functional to meet the requirements of the teachers.

Many effective innovations and improvisations have been made at the grass-roots level by various government and non-government agencies. Proper dissemination of these innovations to all teachers and actual implementation of teacher performance need to be changed accordingly.

Like-minded workers and agencies need to be brought closer for working together.

The advantage of communication systems, electronic and educational technology should be fully utilised in the training of teachers and also to carry the messages of science to the masses. The latter effort will reduce the gap between the school and the community and help in the dissemination of the message of science. This is urgently required for making 'science for all' a meaningful reality.

Development of new curriculum and instructional materials

Immediately after the National Policy on Education was published, the Government of India set up twenty-two task forces to draw up strategies of implementation. The report of the task forces has been released under the title 'Programme of Action' (POA). According to the POA, instructional packages have been developed in the following phases:

March 1987 — classes I, II, III and VI
1988 — classes IV, VII, IX and XII
1989 — classes V, VIII, X and XII.

Each instructional package will include textbooks (for III and above), teachers' guide, laboratory manual, sample materials, kits, kit guides, audio-visual aids and computer softwares.

NCERT has developed guidelines and syllabuses for classes I to X. The expected learning outcome for each class has been spelt out. This was developed with the help of classroom teachers, subject experts, voluntary agencies, and teachers' associations. The draft syllabuses were circulated to all the states/union territories for their comments and it has been finalized on the basis of the comments received. Steps have already been taken to develop the instructional packages classes I to III and VI. Voluntary agencies like Vikram A. Sarabhai Community Science Centre Ahmedabad, Centre for Environment Ahmedabad, Tata Institute of Fundamental Research Bombay, Kerala Sashtra Parishad, Kerala, Delhi Science Teachers Forum are involved with the Department of Education in Science and Mathematics of NCERT in the writing of the class VI book.

Training of teachers for integrated science teaching

The Department of Education in Science and Mathematics in collaboration with the Department of Teacher Education of NCERT, is emphasizing the in-service training of teachers, which is important for the implementation of an integrated science curriculum. Various training modules have been developed to help teachers to create teaching/learning situations. Such activities are meant to be related to the thrust areas of national development, linking science with technology and keeping in view the development of values which underlie science. In the in-service training programmes participants review the course content, and discuss with fellow participants and resource persons about each other's constraints and remedial measures to be adopted. Because most of the teachers have had a training in discipline-oriented science, they are required to be familiar with activities which are interdisciplinary in nature and which have social relevance. The use of hand tools, organization of out-of-school activities, preparation of projects, use of micro-computers and use of new-generation teaching aids in the teaching/learning situation are the important components of the training programmes. Special training programmes are organized for the educationally backward areas and physically handicapped groups.

Besides the training of teachers, the in-service training programmes are directed to create a number of resource persons and resource centres, where teachers may come at any time for solving their problems.

Integrated science teaching in Indonesia

Definition of integrated science

Integrated science in Indonesia is the integration and also the combination of science concepts with emphasis on those that are related to environment, technological needs and everyday life. It also incorporates social values.

The level of integrated science taught

According to the programme structure of teaching-learning in Indonesia, integrated science is mainly taught in primary schools in grades 4 to 6. The main aim is to encourage pupils' curiosity, and to develop a basic knowledge and understanding of the phenomena and processes which they find in their environment.

Although integrated science is not taught in secondary school it can be said that there is a certain amount of integration in many of the topics taught.

Because of the policy of the Ministry of Education and Culture, integrated science is now taught in the upper-secondary school (in grade 3). The aim of this is to prepare the students for the entrance test into university which covers various disciplines including biology, physics, chemistry and integrated science.

Who teaches integrated science ?

Integrated science teachers in primary schools come from SPG (Sekolah Pendidikan Guru/Teaching Training Colleges). In this school/college each trainee teacher is trained to teach in each field of study. The training course lasts for six semesters.

In fact, each teacher in the primary schools not only teaches in one field of study, but often they teach all the subjects in each class. We call them 'guru kelas'.

Most integrated science teachers are graduates of lower-secondary schools. To help them improve, they usually follow a pre-service training course which is organized by one division in the Ministry of Education in a certain region. This usually happens in distant areas for instance in Irian Jaya, transmigration area, etc.

In the upper-secondary schools, integrated science teaching is conducted by the teachers who are experienced. For instance, senior teachers who are qualified in the fields of biology, physics or chemistry.

Facilities

Generally, integrated science teachers do not use much equipment in primary school. This is because there is no provision due to the lack of funds. Although equipment is sometimes provided, the teachers cannot use it, especially teachers who have different non-integrated science backgrounds.

In secondary schools, teachers commonly use teaching models and other environmental resources.

Curriculum materials

In order to achieve the objectives, many items have been provided such as:

GBPP (syllabus). It helps to guide the teacher in the teaching-learning process. It covers components, such as
- objectives (general, instructional);
- curriculum content/topic;
- teaching-learning strategies which include teaching methods, learning materials, etc.;
- facilities in integrated science teaching;
- time-allocation.

The production of the syllabus by the CDC involved not only subject-matter specialists but also curriculum developers, and teachers.

The syllabus is centrally developed and the implementation of this syllabus in schools is not very rigid but rather flexible.

Teacher guide. To help teachers to deliver the topics/content which are stated in the GBPP, and to make teaching-learning more effective so that the objectives of teaching could be achieved some teachers' guides have been produced, such as:
- Teachers' guide for teaching-learning process;
- Teachers' guide for evaluation;
- Teachers' guide for counselling;
- Teachers' guide for using facilities in teaching-learning activities;
- Teachers' guide for field-work.

Approaches

The former approach was the lecture method. The weakness of this method is that the teacher is only concerned with giving information, without giving due attention to the pupils' understanding of the subject matter. The pupils were not given a chance to express their ideas.

However, a new system/approach called CBSA (Active Student Learning) has ncw been introduced. With this system, pupils can express their ideas and are able to retain more of what has been taught.

Problems in integrated science teaching

- Lack of integrated science teachers.
- Some teachers are unfamiliar with the apparatus.
- Inadequate facilities.
- Low teacher-pupils ratio (in class).
- Some teachers still use lecture method .
- Some teachers do not make teaching-plan.
- Some teachers have different background.
- Official policy → not our responsibility/duty.
- Some service-training courses are ineffective.

Current trends in integrated science

• Change in the approach to make more use of environment resources.
• Curriculum changes to avoid the overlap of context and topics and adjustment of time allocation .
• More emphasis on the child-centred approach.

Integrated Sscience syllabus

Broad topics covered especially in primary school are:
• Concepts of science
• Living things and environment
• Matter and changes
• Natural resources and management
• Pollution and prevention
• Systems in man, animals and plants
• Hygiene and cleanliness

Some of the topics taught in upper-secondary schools, which are usually treated in greater depth and with more relevance to environment and everyday life are:
• Living things and environment
• Physics and chemical process in man, animals and plants
• Energy
• Solar system
• Matter and changes
• Natural resources.

Integrated science education in Malaysia

Abdullah b. Ibrahim and Zaini bt. Hussain

Introduction

Malaysian integrated science is offered to all pupils at the lower-secondary level. The content of the integrated science is designed specifically to fulfil the needs of the nation in the field of science and technology. At the end of the course, pupils should have acquired an appropriate degree of knowledge and understanding of science as well as some basic principles, a favourable attitude towards science and some practical skills.

Integrated science is the integration of biology, chemistry and physics, which were previously taught separately in the subject called 'general science'. The eighteen topic syllabus was adapted from the Scottish integrated science and originally tried out in twenty-two schools in 1969.

The integrated science teaching approach encourages:
• a move from teacher-centered to student-centered learning, and
• from expository-method to discovery-method teaching.

Through integrated science it is desired that pupils are exposed to various aspects of scientific investigation, apparatus and methods used in carrying out the experiment as well as the scientific thinking process in obtaining the conclusions.

Objectives of integrated science

The objectives are divided into three aspects:
• knowledge, understanding and capability
• attitude
• practical skills.
Related to aspects of knowledge, understanding and TT capability, the students are expected to:
• acquire knowledge of some facts and concepts concerning the environment
• know the use of appropriate instruments in scientific experiments
• have an adequate scientific vocabulary
• be able to communicate using the vocabulary
• comprehend some basic concepts in science so that they can be used according to the situation
• be able to apply knowledge in various situations
• be able to analyse data and draw conclusions
• be able to think and act creatively
• be able to evaluate in terms of suitable criteria.
Expected attitudinal outcomes would be for the student to:
• be aware of inter-relationship of the various concepts in different disciplines of science
• be aware of inter-relationship of the various fundamental concepts in science
• be aware of the relationship of science to other aspects of the curriculum
• be aware of the contribution of science to the economic and social life of the community in the nation
• have an interest in science
• be able to observe and evaluate results objectively.
From the aspect of practical skills, the students would:
• acquire some simple scientific skills
• acquire some knowledge in experimental techniques which require several skills.

Teacher training

When integrated science was introduced in Malaysia there were no qualified teachers available, so the Ministry of Education had to set up in-service courses for science teachers to encourage them to change their methods of teaching from traditional to the integrated science methods and approaches. At the beginning a few science teachers from each state in Malaysia were trained in Kuala Lumpur at the federal level. Later on, these qualified teachers ran in-service courses in their own state until all the science teachers teaching in lower-secondary schools had the opportunity to attend.

At present student teachers in the Teachers Training College are trained to teach integrated science. Despite all the training there is still a shortage of integrated science teachers in the rural schools. Some schools had to employ untrained teachers. The minimum qualification for an integrated science teacher is college trained with S.P.M. (M.C.E.) or STPM (HSC).

How is integrated science taught ?

The syllabus has been designed in such a way that there will be an equal proportion of practice and theory. The class is still under the control of the teacher as the teacher is required to introduce the activities in the worksheets, to carry out all demonstrations and then lead the discussion in forming the concepts investigated.

There are five periods per week, each period consists of forty minutes. As there are five periods a week there should be two double periods and one single period. The two double periods are called lab-periods because teaching and learning are done in the laboratory. Most of the schools have three integrated science laboratories for forms 1 to 3.

In the laboratory the students in each class are divided into groups consisting of three to five students per group. Activities in the laboratory are grouped into:
'P' - Activity by pupil or group using simple apparatus.
'S' - Station methods where experiments requiring expensive and bulky apparatus are placed at various strategic areas so that groups of students can carry them out following specific procedures, e.g. using energy conversion kits.

'D' - Experiments demonstrated by teacher because they are considered dangerous such as :
the burning of hydrogen in air;
the use of discharged tube, Maltese cross tube.

Curriculum material

In Malaysia the worksheets used are published by two publishers approved by the Ministry of Education. They are Heinemann and the Dewan Bahasa dan Pustaka (D.B.P.). The syllabus centrally developed by the CDC with the co-operation of D.B.P. is supplied to every school. Teachers' guides are also provided by the publisher. Although there are many textbooks published by different publishers, most schools use the textbooks supplied by the government book-loan scheme known as (S.P.B.T.). The Ministry of Education, with the co-operation of T.V. Malaysia, produces television programmes for school children. Every school is provided with at least one colour television and one video tape set.

Topics taught for the three years consists of fifteen sections:

Form 1	Section 1:	Introducing science
	Section 2:	Introducing living things
	Section 3:	Energy
	Section 4:	Matter as particles
	Section 5:	Gases in air
	Section 6:	Cells and reproduction
Form 2	Section 7:	Heat
	Section 8:	Electricity.
	Section 9:	Hydrogen, acids and bases
	Section 10:	Detecting the environment
	Section 11:	Solvent and solutions
	Section 12:	Transport system
Form 3.	Section 13:	More about electricity
	Section 14:	Support and movement
	Section 15:	Earth

Integrated science education in the Philippines

Introduction

Integrated science in the Philippines is taught both at the elementary and secondary level. The subject is first introduced in the third grade of the elementary level, then onward to the four years of secondary education. The diagram below shows the system of education in the Philippines and the levels where integrated science is implemented:

Philippine educational system
and integrated science:

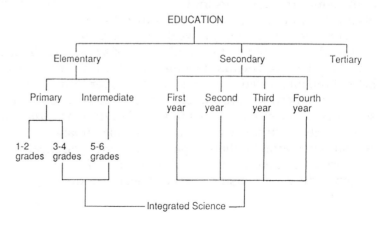

Integrated science at the elementary level

From grade 3 to grade 4, 'Science and Health' within the theme of 'Man and His Environment', is based on the following:

Man and his environment

Man is a biological being with certain needs for quality.
Man grows and develops as he lives.
Man needs many things in order grow and develop into a healthy and productive citizen/agent.

Environment is composed of living and non-living components.
There are elements from his environment which man uses to meet his basic needs.
There are elements in man's environment that change.

Interaction between and among these components brings about changes

In using these elements from his environment for his growth and development, man creates, changes, searches and studies continuously to be more productive and also minimize the negative effects on himself and his environment and in so doing maximize use and conservation of the environment.

The 'Handbook on Minimum Learning Competencies' (DECS, Manila, 1988) describes the science programme as follows: 'Science and Health' aims to develop an understanding of how science relates to everyday life and at the acquisition of scientific skills, at attitudes and values necessary in solving everyday problems. On the other hand, its goal as a health program is the development and promotion of knowledge, attitudes, values and behaviour essential to individual family and community health'.

The approach in the development of competencies, skills and attitudes for elementary grade pupils spirals from the more basic simple ones for grade 3 to the more detailed and complex in the higher grade levels. Science and health are not taught as separate disciplines but as one learning area where science complements health and health reinforces science.

Integrated science at the secondary level

A series of consultations were carried out among those involved in the improvement of science education at the secondary level, particularly the regional and division science supervisors, science education specialists and science teachers. Based on the consultative meetings, the 1989 secondary science curriculum aims to achieve the following goals of secondary science education:
to be more responsive to the needs of Philippine society and to national development goals;
to strengthen the scientific knowledge, processes, and values acquired in the elementary grades
    for scientific literacy and the improvement of the quality of life;
to communicate the excitement of scientific endeavours and stimulate students with an aptitude
    in scientific and allied careers for the development of high-level scientific manpower of the
    country.

The programmes proposed for the four years are:

1st year — Science and Technology I
2nd year — Science and Technology II (Biology)
3rd year — Science and Technology III (Chemistry)
4th year — Science and Technology IV (Physics)

The integrated approach to the S & T courses are as follows:

Science and Technology I. The subject is exploratory in nature and builds on science taught in grade 4. However, basic concepts in physics, chemistry, biology and earth science are presented in preparation for the higher S & T courses. Specific topics include:
Scientific process
Matter
Force, work and energy
The earth in the universe
Science in the living world

Science and Technology II. The subject emphasis is biology, and the topics included are:
Nature of biology
The chemical and cellular basis of life
Energy transformation
The organ systems
Reproduction
Heredity, variation and population
Evolution
Diversity and adaptive forms of living things
Ecological systems

Science and Technology III. The subject emphasis is chemistry, and the topics included are:
Chemistry around us
Patterns in any forms
Patterns of change
Kinetic molecular theory
The atom
Elements and their relations
What atoms hold together
Time of change
Solutions at work
Colloids
Life and carbon compounds

Science and Technology IV. The subject emphasis is physics, and the topics included are:
Nature and importance of physics
Motion and force
Force and energy
Energy and wave motion
Electrical energy
Nuclear energy
Frontiers of physics

In the Science and Technology II to IV courses, technology applications of science are emphasized. Focus is on useful technologies at home, in the community and country. Also stressed are the implications of science and technology to Philippine society. Furthermore, the skills to be developed include:
finding reliable information;
decision-making;
communication
critical and creative thinking.

The scope and selection of topics were based on the needs, interests and abilities of the students; availability of learning materials in the school and community; and national and community concerns.

Teacher qualifications

Elementary school teachers are holders of the Bachelor of Science degree in elementary education. The teachers do not have a subject specialization.

Secondary school science teaches are holders of the Bachelor of Science in Education degree with subject area specialization (general science, biology, chemistry or physics).

In-service programmes for teachers

Agencies co-operate with each other or co-ordinate efforts to upgrade competencies of science teachers. These are through science summer institutes, short-term competency-based courses, through seminars and workshops.

These agencies are: the Department of Education Culture, and Sports; Department of Science and Technology, Science Education Institute; the University of the Philippines Institute for Science and Mathematics Education Development (UPISMED). The Philippine Normal College and other state colleges and private universities also conduct programmes for science teachers to upgrade their teaching competencies.

Teacher's associations' activities are for the professional development of teachers and include the Biology Teachers' Association of the Philippines, the Philippine Association of Chemistry Teachers, and the Philippine Association of Physics Teachers.

International agencies have also shown concern in improving the science education programmes of the country. Operational in April 1990 is the National Learning Resource Center for Teacher Training in Science and Mathematics Education, a JIC-funded project to be implemented by UPISMED. The Philippine Australian Science and Mathematics Education Program trains secondary science and mathematics teachers — in Australia and in the country.

The in-service programmes are on new developments in content, methods, equipment, technology, research and evaluation in science and mathematics education.

Books and teaching aids and equipment

Curriculum materials in the form of teacher's guides, textbooks and laboratory manuals are prepared mostly by the national curriculum development centre in science and mathematics, the UP Institute for Science and Mathematics Education Development, in co-operation with the DECS, and some private organizations.

The teaching aids and equipment to be used in teaching are also described in the curriculum materials provided to the schools. Prototype equipment and audio-visual equipment are prepared, samples of which can be found at UPISMED.

Supplemental materials are available in the market, a contribution of the private sector to the science education programme. Titles such as 'Salaguinto' (for elementary level), 'Bato Balan'i (for secondary level), 'Science Math and Technology Magazine' (for teachers), and 'Parents' (magazine for parents) are available at the Diwa Learning Systems.

Conclusion

The implementation of the science education programmes in the country will hopefully prepare the youth of the Philippines to live for the year 2000 — to be more creative, to solve logical problems and, most of all, to be scientifically and technologically literate. The integrated approach to science education is not only in terms of subject areas, but also in terms of knowledge, values and skills.

Integrated science education in Singapore

Lee Sik Hui

Science education in Singapore

Science in primary schools

Science is first introduced into primary school at Primary 3. At the primary level, the emphasis of science education has been on the pupils and their general educational needs and interests. It revolves around the conceptual framework of 'man in his environment'. It stresses:
the characteristics of life and interdependence of living things;
the interactions among the various components of the environment.
changes in matter and energy.

The themes of the science content at each grade level are:
Primary 3: Looking at the environment;
Primary 4: The value of the various components of the environment;
Primary 5: The interaction with various components of the environment;
Primary 6: The effects on the environment as the result of interactions.

The curriculum time recommended for the various levels is as follows:
3 periods (or 1 hour 45 minutes) for Primary 3 science;
5 periods (or 2 hours 55 minutes) for Primary 4 to 6 science.

Science in secondary schools

At the lower-secondary level (secondary 1 & 2) science courses are designed to:
develop science concepts and an understanding of our physical and biological environment;
develop ability to use the methods of science;
provide the pupils with the essential scientific knowledge and skills that are both relevant and
    meaningful in the technological environment of today and that will meet their educational
    and vocational needs;
enable pupils to appreciate the humanistic aspects of science.

The lower-secondary science course embodies not only the fundamental principles of physics, chemistry, biology but also some environmental and ecological concepts. It is a confirmation of science education from the primary and serves as a link towards science education at higher levels. The concepts found in various disciplines are integrated into unified themes which require an integrated approach to the teaching of the basic components of science.

Science courses for the upper secondary, to a great extent, are still being influenced by the needs and requirements set by the higher educational institutions. Brighter pupils in school are streamed into what is commonly known as the 'science classes' and they offer two or three of the available science options. All upper-secondary pupils must take at least one science subject. These science subjects are taken from the following list :
biology/human and social biology chemistry
physics
science (physics, chemistry)
science (physics, biology)
science (chemistry, biology)
combined science
science (physics, chemistry, biology)
integrated science

Integrated science course in Singapore

The content of primary science is arranged along four lines, namely, animals, plants, matter and energy. The topics however are not to be viewed as independent, compartmentalized blocks of knowledge. Rather they are to be perceived as coherent and interrelated conceptual schemes. In short it is an integrated science in nature.

Integrated science teachers

Primary science is taught by teachers who have undergone science course training in the Institute of Education in Singapore. Courses of short duration (about three to six months) on the teaching approaches, methodology and philosophy of teaching integrated science have also been organized by the Institute of Education for in-service science teachers to upgrade their teaching skills.

In most secondary schools in Singapore, science graduates as well as non-graduate science teachers may be asked to teach lower secondary science. Courses and seminars on the teaching of lower secondary integrated science have been organized for in-service science teachers to help them acquire special skills, knowledge and insight to the subject.

Curriculum materials

The Curriculum Development Institute of Singapore (CDIS) has prepared a curriculum package to improve the teaching of science at the primary levels. The package for each level comprises:
a pupil's text book;
two workbooks;
set of audio-visual teaching materials;
a teacher's guide.

This series of primary science books (3 to 6) is adopted by all primary schools in Singapore.

The lower-secondary science is a scheme of integrated science, a combination of physics, chemistry, biology with the inclusion of environmental studies. CDIS has also developed a series of two books for secondary one and two.

These comprise:
The pupil's book 'Exploring Science 1 and 2', a text-book which provides scientific information, useful background reading for science experiments for secondary one and two.
The workbooks (A, B, C, D) 1 and 2 are guides to the science experiments. Each of the workbooks corresponds to a unit in the pupil's text.
The teacher's guide which is a guide to the workbook experiments and provides a link to the pupil's text.
Set of audio-visual teaching materials.

The series of books caters for students of varied ability and for various courses, namely express, special and normal courses. The books have been recommended to schools by the Ministry of Education of Singapore and are accepted as pupils' text books in all secondary schools in Singapore.

Some problems in secondary integrated science teaching

The teaching of integrated science is never a simple task. A teacher who is deemed capable of fulfilling his objectives of teaching the subject must be equipped with a working knowledge of various disciplines of science, and must be familiar with appropriate teaching approaches, and be supported by sufficient science apparatus, equipment and facilities.

Problems will inevitably arise from all related sectors and areas such as teaching materials, syllabus, apparatus and equipment, the attitude and aptitude of teachers, the general ability of pupils in school as well as the school administration.

Teaching materials

The recommended text books and workbooks for the lower-secondary pupils, 'Exploring Science' were developed for pupils of different courses, namely, special, express, and normal. There are some basic exercises for all pupils and optional projects, assignments and materials of more challenging nature for the express and special streams. It is found, however, that even in a streamed class, pupils' interests and abilities are varied. But, because of the time, syllabus, tests, facilities and other constraints, pupils in the same class are usually given the same worksheets for experiments which are done during the lesson periods. It is, in practice, difficult to have flexibility in the selection of topics experiments and assignments that would suit the ability and need of each and every pupil in class.

Methodology in teaching integrated science

A significant change found in the syllabus of integrated science is that a new approach of teaching is adopted, a move from what is seen to be purely fact-centred to an enquiry-based science. This means that the course needs to be activities-centred and whenever possible, lessons conducted in laboratories with active participation of pupils. Process skills, such as observing, classifying, communicating, measuring, inferring, predicting, forming hypotheses and so forth are emphasized.

In Singapore, the lower science course is planned and worked on a tight schedule within a given time frame. Coverage of the syllabus is perhaps one of the problems that a teacher faces. When teachers are hard pressed for time, traditional teaching techniques dominate, i.e. lecturing; and teachers treat the subject as a mere body of knowledge. The attainment of the objectives of teaching integrated science has thus become doubtful and questionable.

Integrated science syllabus

What is integrated science in Singapore ? The tables that follow will give some idea of content and approach.

Concepts are selected for primary as well as lower-secondary science. It is expected that each concept is developed slowly, looked at in many contexts, enriched in meaning as pupils explore the idea in class and in the laboratory. 'Man in his environment' in primary science; 'energy' in the lower-secondary science are some of the examples.

Problem solving activities are also used in the course. In some cases processes of science are emphasized when pupils develop the skill of how to ask fruitful questions, develop working hypotheses, collect relevant data, analyse this data and make sensible judgements.

Integrated science is thus suggested as the science teaching materials in which the concepts of science are presented through a unified approach.

Conclusion

In Singapore, integrated science courses are perhaps the best vehicle for the development of an understanding of the nature of science. However, the importance of specialization for effective work in science must also be emphasized. Specialized science is still deemed to be specially effective for preparing pupils for scientific and technological occupations and professions.

PRIMARY SCIENCE SYLLABUS   ANNEX1

THEME	PRIMARY 3	PRIMARY 4	PRIMARY 5	PRIMARY 6
I. ANIMALS	a. Variety b. Characteristics c. Similarities and difference among animals	a. Animals need food b. Animals and their food c. Useful animals d. Harmful animals	a. Population and communities b. An artificial habitat The aquarium c. Factors affecting survival of living things in the aquarium	a. Food and energy b. Food relationships c. Decomposers d. Preservation of food
II. PLANTS	a. Parts of a plant b. Variety c. Similarities and differences among plants d. Characteristics of plants	a. Plant parts and their functions b. Life Cycle c. Usefulness of plants d. Some plants are harmful e. Trees	a. Reproduction b. Seed dispersal c. Growing plants from parts other than seeds.	a. Plants make food b. Plants exchange matter with the environment
III. MATTER	a. Variety b. Differences between living and non-living things d. Man uses materials	a. States of matter b. Properties of the states of matter c. Simple lessons on air d. Expansion of matter caused by heat	a. Changes in the environment b. Energy and Change c. Water and change of state d. The water cycle	a. Causes of Pollution b. Prevention of pollution

IV. ENERGY	a. Objects in the sky
	b. The sun gives us heat and light
	c. Shadows
		a. Heat and temperature
		  i) the sun
		  ii) simple properties of heat
		  iii) measuring temperature
		b. Batteries and bulbs
		c. Magnets
			a. Forms of energy
			b. Energy conversion
			c. Man uses energy
			d. Fuels
				a. Force
				b. Force and work
				c. Machines

Lower-secondary science syllabus

Secondary One   Unit 1   Introduction
                   Unit 2   Looking at matter
                             Study of air
                   Unit 3   Energy and life
                   Unit 4   Science of life

Secondary Two   Unit 1   Water and solution
                   Unit 2   Life and ecology
                   Unit 3   More about energy
                   Unit 4   Molecules and atoms

Integrated science education in Thailand

The new educational system of 6:3:3 in Thailand provides for six years of primary, three years of lower-secondary and three years of upper-secondary education. Higher education follows upper-secondary education.

Science in the primary school

In the primary level, science education is geared towards solving social problems. Social studies, health education and science are integrated into one subject called 'Life Experience'.

Science in the secondary school

Science courses in the lower-secondary school or from Mathayom 1 to 3 (M.1 to M.3) are to develop an understanding of the basic principles and theories of science and to promote good attitudes towards science. Science courses at this level are integrated. The time allocation for learning in lower-secondary school is 20 per cent.

In the upper-secondary level, students are guided to concentrated on areas of specialization needed for their chosen career or occupation. All science courses at this level are electives. There are three main categories of science course:

1. for science students;
2. for vocational students;
3. for non-science students.

Although all courses are electives, all students have to select at least twelve periods of science.

For science students, they must select physics, chemistry and biology. For non-science students, they must select physical and biological science.

Physics is presented as a single unified course containing mechanics, heat, light, sound, electricity, magnetism and nuclear physics. Chemistry is an integration of theory with practice. Biology adopts an activity-oriented approach. Materials are adapted from foreign texts.

What is integrated science ?

In Thailand, integrated science is divided into two levels:

1. *Primary level.* There is integration within science subjects and other subjects. Science is integrated with health and social studies within the life experience area. The aims of 'Life Experience' are to emphasize the problem-solving process and the various aspects of human/ societal needs and problems, for the purpose of survival and leading a good life.

2. *Science in the lower-secondary school.* Science is compulsory for all children at the lower-secondary level. Science is the integration of chemistry, biology and physics. Throughout the curriculum, chemistry, biology and physics are integrated and interwoven with development of skills and science attitudes.

This means the integration of science content and science process.

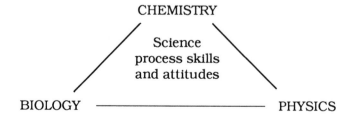

In the lower-secondary schools there is the final grouping of topics around the three major themes and the interrelationship of the topics are shown in the conceptual scheme of the Institute for the Promotion of Teaching Science and Technology (IPST).

Who teaches integrated science ?

There are two institutions which produce teachers: the teachers' college and the university. Every person who will become a teacher has to be trained how to teach in every subject in the primary school, while for secondary school teachers, they can choose chemistry, biology, physics or general science. In other words, they are trained to teach a particular subject. There are three grades of science teachers: diploma, bachelor degree and master degree.

If a new science curriculum or new science programme is introduced, public institute, IPST, Education Department must conduct in-service training for teachers in order to familiarize them with the new system.

Curriculum materials for integrated science

In Thailand, the science and mathematics curriculum for primary and secondary school levels was developed by IPST.

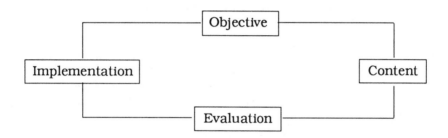

Circle of curriculum development

IPST also designs and produces science equipment, which isthen tried out in the schools. Evaluation of the curriculum materials is also done by IPST but implementation is up to the Ministry of Education. The Ministry of Education produces student's texts, teacher's guides and science equipment for sale throughout Thailand. There are some private publishing companies producing resource books. The individual schools normally provide teacher's guides and science equipment but students have to buy their own texts.

Section 2: Australia and the South Pacific

Integrated science education in Australia

Ruth Dirks

Whereas the concept of integrated science can vary from country to country, in Australia it varies from classroom to classroom.

Across the states and territories, Australia has a curious mix of conformity and non-conformity and this is demonstrated by the primary school situation. Some states talk about P–6, where 'P' stands for pre-school, while others say K-7, where 'K' stands for kindergarten. In most states primary schooling ends with year 6, but a few go on in primary school to the end of year 7.

And yet, in spite of the different names and years, all states and territories have similar problems with the teaching of science in primary schools. In some schools science is very well taught, based on process skills and related to the students' lifestyles and environment. In most schools, however, there is a heavy emphasis on natural history and in a few, science is hardly mentioned or, worse still, is taught only as the academic content of science.

At the junior secondary level, the first integrated science courses originated over twenty-five years ago, and there has been integrated science in all states and territories for many years. There are varying degrees of support to help teachers with the difficulties associated with devising appropriate programmes, ranging from extensive notes on an integrated science syllabus in the early 1960s through the 'Do it Yourself Curriculum Guide' in the late 1970s to the just published 'The Science Framework P- 10', which for teachers in Victoria crosses the primary-secondary interface.

Again the biggest variation is within states, ranging from excellent programmes which are built around the philosophies of science for all and with a science technology and society approach — or better still society, science and technology. Some states have fairly specific syllabus statements, but there is still the problem of a mismatch between the intention of the course designers and what actually happens in the classroom.

In Australia there are some integrated science courses in years 11 and 12. In some states there are a few senior colleges for years 11 and 12, but in the Australian Capital Territory (ACT) the whole system has junior-secondary schools and then separate senior colleges. This structure combined with the fact that there are no external examinations at the end of year 12 in the ACT, means that teachers devise their own units of work — many of which are integrated science units.

In addition to the traditional courses in physics, chemistry, biology and to a lesser extent geology, some states (e.g. Western Australia, Queensland and Victoria) have integrated science courses in years 11 and 12, designed for those students who do not have aptitudes and interests in the separate science disciplines. New South Wales is unusual in that it has two different integrated science courses. One originated over ten years ago and was designed to raise awareness of science and its impact on our lives, in able students who are not going on to science-based careers. It was hoped that this course would lead to scientifically literate lawyers, politicians, economists, business managers, etc. This course has not achieved these aims mainly because there was no appropriate course for the less able students. Once the course was used for the weaker students the better students avoided it.

The second integrated science course in New South Wales (NSW) is designed for the most able students of science. It is a demanding course which shows the interconnections and interdependence of the science disciplines and also prepares students for science at the tertiary level. The next exciting step may well be taken in NSW, where course designers are now working on an integrated science curriculum for all those students who want to take science in years 11 and 12. So far it is at the exploratory stage, with the possibility of differences in the students' needs and interests being catered for by a variety of electives.

Integrated science education in New Zealand

E. Lalas

Core curriculum review

What students should study in New Zealand schools is under review. The report on curriculum review identifies eight areas of knowledge as well as skills and attitudes.

One of the eight areas of knowledge is: helping students to learn about and make sense of their biological, physical and technological world.

Science education is clearly seen as having a particular contribution to make in this area of knowledge. So what form does science education take in New Zealand?

Primary science infants to standard IV (K to 5) or 5 to 10 year-olds — national syllabus

The science syllabus for this group emphasizes student experiences. There are science advisers in each geographic region who support teachers with equipment, resources and in-service training. Teaching is often thematic and integrated with other areas of learning, e.g., language. The teaching approach is interactive. (Interactive is the name given to the approach developed during research carried out on learning in science at the University of Waikato).

Secondary science from 1 to 4 (years 6 to 10) or 11 to 16 year-olds

The existing syllabus for secondary schools is being reviewed and it is expected that a new syllabus will emerge soon.

A quote from the aims statement of this syllabus, entitled 'Science for All', will give something of the flavour of this course.

Science and technology are a part of the lives of all students. There is science and technology in understanding Cyclone Bola; the Edgecumbe earthquake; the mining debates in the Coromandel; the recent cervical cancer inquiry; in building and flying kites; repairing a surfboard; growing vegetables; first aid; caring for pets; using household cleaners; microwave ovens; compact discs — to name a few. Science and technology are part of the lives of all New Zealanders — at home, work, in leisure activities, and the environment around them.

Science curricula in New Zealand have always aimed to cater for all students. However, it has often been on the basis that a science education for future scientists and technicians is suitable for all students and syllabuses have been constructed around educating all students as if they were going to be scientists. This has not been entirely successful as indicated by the research of the Learning in Science Projects: the numbers of girls, Maori, and Polynesian students choosing not to study science in the senior school; and the negative feeling of many adults to science.

Rather than taking students to the world of the scientist, we need to bring science to the world of the students, to help them better understand the science and technology in their own lives. This is one of the emphases in the current review of the F1-5 science syllabus. All students, whether they will continue to a tertiary science education and a science career or not, can benefit and enjoy from learning about the science and technology in their own lives. Instead of a separate and different course for future scientists and technologists, there can be opportunities within this kind of curriculum to nurture scientific talent and interest.

Science education in F1-5 can be seen as successful if students finish their fifth form year having found science and technology interesting, useful and relevant to their lives and that as adults they want to learn more about science and technology: in the home, for example, as a home handy person, in caring for a sick child: in the community, for example, taking part in environmental decisions such as sewage disposal, and supporting community health initiatives such as hepatitis immunisation; at work, for example, DNA fingerprinting and the law; satellites and the telecommunications industry; fertilisers and agriculture; making concrete and the construction industry; in leisure time, for example, keeping bees, growing orchids, electronics, dyeing and weaving wool; and understanding the environment, for example, preventing erosion, understanding weather patterns.

Eight development groups have been set up around the country to produce teachers'-guide materials for the syllabus in those areas which have been identified as issues by the syllabus committee:

Science Aotearoa — the Maori perspective in science and technology

Girls in science

Planning a local science curriculum

Learning in science teaching

Learning strategies role of practical work.

These groups involving sixty practising teachers will also be involved in in-service and professional development of other teachers.

Senior science years 11 to 12 (16 to 18 year-olds)

The courses in this area are predominantly the separate sciences — biology, chemistry, physics, agricultural science. These are national courses. However, there are opportunities for individual schools to develop new courses and have them registered for study in year 11. This enables schools to better cater for their own students who are staying on at school in larger numbers but who do not want the traditional academic subjects.

A number of school-based integrated science courses in year 11 have been developed in this way and one school has developed an even more broadly integrated course on motoring studies. This course integrates economics, history, physics, design technology and personal driving skills.

Integrated science education in Papua New Guinea

M. Wilson

Formal schooling was introduced into what is now Papua New Guinea in the 1870s by a number of Christian missionary groups. It was not until after 1945 that the Australian colonial administration took a direct responsibility in school provision with the long term goal of universal primary education in English. In the 1960s the prospect of early independence pushed policy towards emphasis on secondary and tertiary education. Secondary education began in the late 1950s and the first tertiary courses were offered in 1967. The first upper-secondary school offering grades 11 and 12 was established as late as 1969. The Papua New Guinea education system has thus developed very recently — even by Third World standards.

The structural pattern of primary, lower-secondary and upper-secondary education in Papua New Guinea is 6-4-2. There is a major exit point between each of these three levels and at each a proportion of students are forced to leave the system. The medium of instruction throughout all three levels is English. About 85 per cent of the age cohort enter grade 1 but only about 50 per cent normally complete grade 6. A medium-term aim is universal primary education before the year 2000.

The next level, lower secondary, is of four years-duration (grades 7 to 10) and was offered in 111 provincial high schools in 1983. Approximately one-third of grade 6 children were selected by means of a competitive examination for grades 7 and just 18 per cent of the age cohort in 1983 entered provincial high schools.

Upper-secondary education (grades 11 and 12) is conducted almost entirely in just four national high schools with a total enrolment of about 1,600 (less than 2 per cent of the age cohort). Approximately 15 per cent of grade 10 graduates are selected on the basis of their grade 10 school certificate results to enter these schools. The schools have as their primary function the provision of an academic preparation for tertiary education.

Science is a compulsory subject in grades 1 to 11 through the national education system using a common nationally prescribed integrated curriculum for all students. Aims are broad in an attempt to meet the needs both of the majority at each level who will not proceed to the next level but rather return to their communities, and the needs of those going on to further study or science related employment. Thus community-school science is based on science-related experiences which stress the immediate environment (but also go beyond it). However, science is very limited in extent at this level, receiving a total time allocation of only forty minutes per week on average from grades 1 to 6. At the same time there is also a health programme in community schools and students undertake practical work in agriculture.

At the provincial-high-school level, science is taught as an integrated subject for five forty, minute lessons each week and is based on a philosophy of 'science for all' rather than traditional academic science. The result is a broadly based curriculum with stress on qualitative science related to applications and the environment.

At the upper-secondary level there is a radical change in science curriculum orientation as the national high schools have as their main function the preparation of students for tertiary study in science and other areas. The curriculum in science becomes academic and quantitative for the first time and specialization by student choice, in either 'arts' or 'science', occurs also for the first time in grade 12.

The compulsory grade 11 science course and the optional grade 12 major science courses both contain separate strands of physics, chemistry and biology each usually taught by a different teacher. At grade 11 each strand is allocated two fifty minute lessons per week and at Grade 12, three. Students who do not choose to study major Science in Grade 12 (about 40 per cent) may choose minor science, a science and society course of three lessons per week for students not planning further science-based study. The main components of this course are human biology, evolution and technology.

Grade 12 major courses are separate courses in biology and physics.

Chapter 12

Europe and North America

Section 1: Europe

There is considerable variety in the teaching of science throughout Europe. Even the pattern of school systems varies widely. But all countries now offer some science at the primary-school level, often as part of environmental studies. In some countries projects for development of primary-school science are currently under way. In the United Kingdom, the Association for Science Education, the non-governmental science teachers' association, has recently established a primary science section with its own membership and journal, in response to the growing interest in the introduction of primary science courses throughout the country.

In the Netherlands, science at primary level has been part of the curriculum for more than a century but has not been effectively taught until quite recently. In 1978 the Dutch Institute for Curriculum Development (SLO) launched a new project for primary science for trial in selected schools based on materials, organisms and phenomena with emphasis on experimental work. It was given wider implementation throughout the Netherlands in 1988, with attainment targets formulated for the end of primary education (age 12 pupils).

At the secondary level many countries have now introduced integrated science at least for the first two or three years of secondary education. In the Netherlands, for example, this innovation was introduced in 1983 as a direct result of the Nijmegen Conference in 1978. The Dutch course also typifies trends in other European countries by offering a curriculum that integrates the traditional disciplines of science as well as providing for the whole ability range. For this purpose the topics of the course have been chosen from the everyday world of the student viz:
- my clothes
- pets
- your home
- soil
- milk
- maize
- weather report.

A description of the unit 'my clothes', for the 12-year-old students, is given in the Bangalore Conference Paper No. 54, Industry and Technology Theme, by J.G. Hondebrink.

The course is adapted for mixed-ability teaching by using the core and options model. The core is studied by all students, in about seven lessons and then there is a choice of options (in the case of 'my clothes', there are ten options), ranging widely in difficulty and lasting about four lessons.

The Dutch science teachers' association, NVON, has established (in 1987) a special section, within NVON, for the stimulation and development of integrated science in the Netherlands, including vocational schools as well as general secondary schools.

In Norway, new curriculum guidelines are currently being introduced. At the primary level they provide for an interesting integration of science and social studies, as shown by the sections for the grades 1 to 6 syllabus:
• exploration of the surroundings
• children's everyday life
• collaboration between human beings
• man and society
• the Sami people
• Norway and Scandinavia
• the human body and health
• life and foundations of life in nature
• resources and trade and industry
• materials, tools and techniques
• the world that surrounds us
•communication, drama, pictures and media.

The new curricula in Norway also typify the importance that many European countries are giving to computer technology. A four-year programme of action was launched in 1984 to introduce computer technology in selected schools. The evaluation of this programme will determine the basis for extending the case for computers and the study of computer technology in all schools.

In Belgium, an experimental integrated science course has been introduced in the last two years of senior high schools (grades 10, 11) within the stream known as 'human sciences'. This project was launched, in 1978, as part of a Flemish Television series. It comprises twelve sections which are supported by books. Since 1980 the course is no longer compulsory for the human science stream; and it became an optional course for all non-science streams in general education, with two periods per week. It is decreasing in interest.

The United Kingdom was among the first countries to introduce courses in integrated science (e.g. Nuffield Combined Science, Scottish Integrated Science) in the 1960s and 1970s. Many of these courses were described and analysed at the Nijmegen Conference 1978. During the last ten years the number of courses in integrated or combined science has increased considerably, but the trend has been towards local or sub-regional development rather than through large, national initiatives. A recent checklist of integrated science courses in the United Kingdom, compiled by David Hitchcock, shows forty-three separately available courses at the secondary level. Many of the more recent courses include aspects of social relevance which are reflected in titles such as 'Science and Society', 'Science for Life'. The original integrated science courses, reported at Nijmegen, have been revised and now include social aspects of science as well as computer or information technology. (See Chapter 4B for a more detailed description of science and society courses in the United Kingdom; and Section 3, Chapter 14 for examples of teaching modules)

Nevertheless, there are still many students in the United Kingdom who do not study all the sciences, especially at the senior-secondary level, and there are some who do not study any science at the grade 9, 10 level. A survey (in 1984) of students in England showed that:
12 per cent studied biology, chemistry, physics at grades 9, 10;
8 per cent studied biology, chemistry;
6 per cent studied biology, physics;
9 per cent studied chemistry, physics;
19 per cent studied biology only;
3 per cent studied chemistry only;
10 per cent studied physics only;
21 per cent studied no science.

This reflects the decentralized nature of the British system, but the recently published National Curriculum for Science which has been implemented in 1989, has established a 'balanced' science in all secondary schools with a minimum of 10 per cent of available time in grades 6, 7, rising to 15 per cent or 20 per cent in grades 8, 9, 10. This will inevitably increase the number and range of integrated science courses, leading to the new General Certificate of Secondary Education (GCSE) at grade-10 level.

For teacher training courses in the United Kingdom there are very few which are designated as integrated science, but the majority of post-graduate certificate of education courses offer a basic course in science, usually taught in cross-disciplinary groups, to prepare students for teaching general or integrated science at the junior-secondary level. Most students also specialisze in a single subject science to prepare them for teaching at the upper-secondary level.

Many older teachers trained only in a single science discipline find integrated science a threat. They are reluctant to leave the security of their preferred discipline. Hence the need for in-service training courses.

Section 2: North America

Introduction

The United States and Canada were among the first countries to introduce integrated science courses in schools. Many of these early projects were reported and analysed at the Nijmegen Conference in 1978. There was even a Federation of Unified Science Education (FUSE) in the 1960s and 1970s acting as a clearing house for ideas and projects and providing some in-service training on the philosophy and practice of integrated or unified science teaching.

It is not surprising, therefore, to report that there are now literally hundreds of projects or courses at primary or secondary level available for students throughout North America. Some of these, e.g. the Atlantic Science Curriculum Project, administered by the University of New Brunswick, Canada, and initiated by the Educators of Atlantic Science Teachers (EAST), are quite new (1986, 1987). Others are revisions of well-known earlier projects (e.g. SCIS). Many are based on commercially published textbooks. The National Science Teachers' Association (NSTA) provides a valuable service by listing all the suppliers of books and equipment, with the titles of the courses for which the materials are supplied, in a catalogue revised annually. The 1987 list contains an extensive list of computers and computer software.

In 1981 the NSTA began a systematic search for excellence throughout the United States. Using criteria developed by twenty-three leading science educators, they identified fifty school science programmes most closely meeting these criteria.

These fifty programmes, representing elementary science, biology, physical science, science as inquiry, and science/technology/society, were studied to determine how they came about, what they do, and how they are maintained. Descriptions of the programmes were published in a series of monographs, *Focus On Excellence*, available from NSTA.

One example of the curriculum goals, rationale, and planning of an integrated science programme for junior-secondary science — in British Columbia, Canada — is given in the following section. Further analysis of the fifty United States programmes and a general review of developments in the United Staes are given in the final section of this chapter.

Junior-secondary science in British Columbia, Canada

The 'Curriculum Guide and Resource Book' is in four parts:

Part I: Junior Secondary Science Rationale, Curriculum Goals and General Learning Outcomes.
Part I outlines the framework of the curriculum. This framework consists of a rationale, four goals and general learning outcomes. The rationale is the major statement of intent and the basis from which all other curriculum components were derived. The goals are statements, developed from the rationale, which more clearly identify the intents of the curriculum. These goals are further

clarified by including a set of general learning outcomes. Part I enables teachers to visualize the type of course which must be designed to achieve the curriculum intents.

Part II: Junior-Secondary Science Curriculum Model Organizers, Learning Outcomes and Possible Activities. Part II introduces a model which shows the relationship between the intents, outlined in Part I, and the content outlined under 6 organizers: Astronomy and Space Science; Changes in Matter; Changes in the Environment; Ecology and Resource Management; Energy; and Life Functions. This relationship is clearly established through the identification of specific learning outcomes for each grade. The scope of each grade is defined through the designation of essential and optional learning outcomes. A number of activities have been suggested under each organizer to assist teachers in planning how they will teach towards each of the specified learning outcomes. For teachers wishing to teach in an integrated fashion or to identify relationships between organizers, a section of suggestions for integration has been developed. The learning outcomes, activities and suggestions for integration complete Part II. Teachers should read this section in its entirely to obtain an overview of the grade 8 to 10 programme. Following this, they can concentrate on the specific grade they are to teach, examining the essential and optional learning outcomes and the activities they will use to fulfill these learning outcomes.

Part III: Planning an Integrated Science Programme. Part III is introduced with a rationale for teaching junior secondary science in an integrated manner. A number of overview plans, appropriate to each grade level, are provided to illustrate some possible organizations of content in an integrated manner. A single overview has been selected for expansion at each grade level. After studying the examples provided, teachers can select, modify or develop an integrated sequence of instruction to satisfactorily achieve the learning outcomes.

Part IV: Resources for Junior-Secondary Science. This part of the guide contains some resources which may be helpful in the planning and teaching of junior secondary science. These resources include: teaching strategies; evaluation suggestions; references and provincial educational media centre audio-visual aids.

Junior-secondary science curriculum goals and general learning outcomes

The following goals are listed arbitrarily and do not indicate any priority. All four goals should receive equal emphasis throughout the junior science programme. Following each goal are general learning outcomes which have been included to assist teachers in further defining the goal.

Goal A: *The junior secondary science programme should provide opportunities for students to develop positive science attitudes.*
    Opportunities should be provided to:
develop curiosity about natural events and an interest in trying to understand them;
show how science can be helpful solving many everyday problems;
discuss how scientific endeavour is important to our society;
foster an appreciation of the impact of technology on the world;
develop a more responsible attitude towards self and society through the examination of social and environmental issues;
use scientific knowledge and skills to help clarify personal values and beliefs;
discuss some science-related activities which could be done during leisure time;
gain an appreciation of the benefits and responsibilities of working co-operatively as well as independently;
develop a concern for safety;
deal with problems in an open-minded manner.

Goal B: *The junior secondary science programme should provide opportunities for students to develop the skills and processes of science.* Opportunities should be provided to develop the psychomotor skills necessary for proper laboratory techniques and for the appropriate and safe handling of equipment and materials.

Opportunities should be provided for:

observing - the training of the senses to gain information both qualitative and quantitative (Note: the student should be able to distinguish between observations, inferences and interpretation);

classifying - the organization of materials, events, and phenomena into logical groupings;

quantifying - the comparison of objects or events to S1 standards of length, mass, temperature and time, including the estimation of these quantities;

communicating - the presentation and explanation to others of objects or events, using various media;

inferring - the logical extension of specific data or observations based on past experience;

predicting - the use of existing data, information, perceptual patterns, and trends to suggest non-observed or future outcomes and occurrences;

interpreting data - the identification of trends from data which allow for predicting and formulating hypotheses;

formulating hypotheses - the formulation of generalized statements based on the processes of science. Further investigation may be required to test and revise such hypotheses;

controlling variables - the identification of possible variables influencing the outcome of an investigation;

experimenting - the testing of predictions and hypotheses by designing and carrying out appropriate procedures;

defining operationally - to describe an object or event in terms of observable or measurable characteristics ;

formulating models - the creation of analogies to demonstrate or explain an idea.

Goal C: *The junior-secondary science programme should increase the students' scientific knowledge.* Opportunities should be provided to:

apply and demonstrate the knowledge of major concepts, basic principles, laws and supporting facts;

recognize the existence of interrelationships between the various disciplines of science and between science and other subject areas;

develop an understanding of the history, nature, and philosophy of science to further:
  (a) understand the processes of science by seeing science in action through historical perspectives;
  (b) understand how discovery has changed scientific outlook in the past and how these changes have affected society;
  (c) recognize the pursuit of science as a human endeavour which involves chance discovery and human fallibility;
  (d) understand that science is one way of searching for truth and that the present understanding of science is tentative pending further research;

develop knowledge of past and present technologies to further:
  (a) understand the difference between science and technology;
  (b) understand that technology can solve some, but not all, present and future problems;
  (c) recognize future implications for society as a result of technology .

Goal D: *The junior secondary science programme should provide opportunities for students to develop creative, critical and formal (i.e. abstract) thinking abilities.* Opportunities should be provided to:

recognize a problem, identifying its central issues and underlying assumptions ;

integrate learning from different areas in order to solve a problem;

develop alternate solutions to a given problem;

transfer concepts and principles to new situations;

evaluate evidence or authority to:
- (a) judge the consistency of print and non-print materials;
- (b) recognize stereotypes, cliches, bias, and emotional factors;
- (c) identify essential, relevant and verifiable data;
- (d) judge the validity of conclusions;

reason abstractly, including:
- (a) the application of reasoning patterns to relationships and properties that are not directly observable; solve abstract problems by manipulating words and/or symbols;
- (b) a recognition and understanding of proportionality;
- (c) understanding probability;
- (d) the development of a plan for systematically considering all combinations.

Junior-Secondary Science Scope of Topics Chart   (Essential in UPPER CASE. Optional in lower.)

	ASTRONOMY AND SPACE SCIENCE	CHANGES IN MATTER ENVIRONMENT	CHANGES IN THE MANAGEMENT	ECOLOGY AND RESOURCE	ENERGY	LIFE FUNCTIONS
GRADE EIGHT	A. Position and Motion of Earth in Space	A. PROPERTIES OF MATTER B. ELEMENTS AND COMPOUNDS C. MIXTURES D. Personal E. Textiles	A. EARTH MATERIALS B. WEATHERING AND EROSION C. GEOLOGICAL TIME	A. COMMUNITY RELATION-SHIPS B. A Topic in C. BIOCIDES D. Weather	A. SUN B. HEAT C. INSULATION D. Light E. Sound	A. SENSES B. NERVOUS SYSTEM C. EFFECTS OF DRUGS ON THE BODY
GRADE NINE	A. SOLAR SYSTEM B. UNIVERSE	A. REACTIONS B. SYMBOLS C. Rate of Reaction D. Household Chemicals	A. EARTH FORCES B. FOSSIL FUELS	A. A TOPIC IN RESOURCES B. Soil Science C. Biomes D. Fertilizer	A. RENEWABLE AND NON-RENEWABLE ENERGY SOURCES B. TRANS-FORMATIONS OF ENERGY C. ENERGY CALCULATIONS D. Heat Curve E. Simple Machines	A. BODY SYSTEMS B. NUTRITION
GRADE TEN	A. Space Technology B. Space Travel	A. CHEMICAL FORMULAS B. PERIODIC TABLE C. SIMPLE REACTIONS D. IONIC COMPOUNDS E. Industrial Processes	A. Radioactive Dating B. Seismology and Interior of the Earth C. Prospecting and Explora-tion Geology	A. POPULATION GROWTH B. A TOPIC IN RESOURCES C. POLLUTION AND CONTROL	A. ELECTRICITY MAGNETISM B. HOME ENERGY USE C. HOUSEHOLD CIRCUITRY D. NUCLEAR E. Computers	A. SIMPLE CELLULAR PROCESSES B. REPRODUCTION C. EUGENICS D. INHERITANCE OF CHARAC-TERISTICS E. Disease Identification and Treatment

A rationale for teaching integrated science

The rationale of this curriculum suggests that the material contained in this guide be taught in an integrated fashion. An integrated approach is one in which the disciplines of science (i.e. biology, chemistry, physics, earth and space science) are united around several themes, phenomena, or topics. Other names often used in place of the term integrated are interdisciplinary, holistic, unified and multidisciplinary.

The decision to encourage an integrated approach was based upon a number of reasons including:

The natural world is a unified whole and examining it through distinct disciplines can lead to a fragmented understanding of it.

Students are interested in the real world about them and do not view it from the perspective of discrete disciplines.

The major issues facing society today, like disease, overpopulation and resource depletion, cannot be completely understood through one discipline of science. Science needs to be understood broadly and in the context of other disciplines.

In schools that have taught students in an integrated manner there is evidence to indicate:
An increase in the elective enrolment in science.
A great proportion of students going to college choosing science as a major.
Students also have grades as good as or better than their peers who have studied science as separate disciplines.
Students achieve higher scores on scientific literacy tests.

In the initial stages of the development of this curriculum many teachers remarked that they have attempted to draw upon the many disciplines of science whenever possible to enhance student learning. This curriculum is designed to further this endeavour. It should also be noted that teaching in an integrated fashion can include more material than other approaches since, in fact, topics do overlap. By expanding topics to include a range of science disciplines a holistic view of science is easier to attain.

The viewing of science as a unified whole appears to be an international trend of increasing significance and impact. This approach, if carefully planned, has the potential of improving the scientific literacy of all students.

Bibliography

Cox, D. 1980. *Unified Science Education and the Paradigms of Science.* World Trends in Science Education. C.P. McFadden, Editor.

Showalter, V. 1978. *The Case for Teaching Science as a Unity.* Integrated Science Education Worldwide. International Conference, Nijmegen, Netherlands.

Integrated science programme models

In developing integrated science programmes, work in small groups is an effective means of generating ideas, identifying resources and gaining a good working knowledge of the curriculum. It is recommended that several teachers, perhaps teaching the same grade level, engage in the development of integrated programmes. Alternatively, whole science departments and/or district science committees working on sequences of instruction would provide a clear perspective of the grade 8 to 10 science programme and pave the way to an excellent continuity between each grade.

Based on the rationale for teaching science in an integrated fashion, it is hoped that teachers will work toward utilizing this approach to develop all or part of their junior secondary science programme. The previous curriculum emphasized learning of science through the individual disciplines of biology, chemistry, physics, earth science and space science. Despite this, many teachers do integrate the disciplines of science at various points in their teaching. In order to promote the integrated approach and to illustrate how the new curriculum facilitates this approach, examples of year-long plans have been developed. It is hoped that these concrete examples will encourage teachers to try the integrated approach. It should be stressed that each of these plans represent only one of many possible sequences. There is no 'right' way to integrate a set of topics. Teachers are encouraged to develop their own integrated plans. If individuals or groups develop their own model, rather than choosing one that is illustrated, they may find the process useful in gaining a greater understanding of the integrated approach. Part of the design of this guide has been that teachers (or departments or districts) should examine the topics to determine what emphasis is important for their locale and is compatible with their student group and own expertise.

The following integrated plans for science 8, 9, and 10 consist of several overview models, each outlining a sequence of topics organized under one or more themes. These themes have not been presented in any particular sequence. The final overview model at each grade level has been expanded into a more detailed sequence of topics, suitable for developing individual units and lessons to cover a year's science programme. The process is used to generate the components for the following plans.

Selecting themes

The topics chart was examined in conjunction with the learning outcomes to ascertain one or more themes which could bring together the learning outcomes in a logical fashion. The use of local issues involving science and applications of science was felt to be a particularly good source of themes to build integrated science plans. In some cases it was found that one theme could tie together a year, in other cases, two or more themes were used.

Developing models

Using the themes selected, models were developed to outline the general sequence of study. While most topics from the topics chart were included, other pertinent information linking topics was also included.

Developing an expanded model

The overview models were further developed by providing information that would allow more detailed (i.e. lesson) planning to be completed by the individual teacher. This information includes cross-referencing to learning outcomes. Each model covers all essential and some optional learning outcomes. Teachers may refer to the curriculum guide and the textbook in order to identify activities designed to fulfill the learning outcomes listed in the model. Learning outcomes may appear more than once in a theme and throughout a year plan.

In the development of a model of integration there is a hazard in trying to integrate all topics even if the 'threads' that tie them together are somewhat tenuous. If a connection between 'The Effect of Drugs on the Body' and 'Insulation' at Grade 8 seems hazy to teachers then it will certainly be difficult for students. Some topics may be better introduced as tools that are needed to study other topics (e.g. an understanding of joules is necessary to examine the 'Medical Applications' of 'Nutrition' on the body). Finally, the optional topics should not be overlooked as they are an important part of this programme and may provide some of the integrating links necessary between essential topics.

Science 8 yearly plan: Model C

Theme 1: A topic in resources (forestry)
Theme 2: Sensing

bold indicates topics from the Topics Chart.
BOLD indicates essential topics

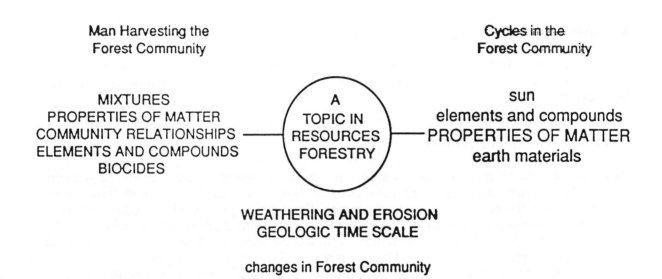

Man Harvesting the
Forest Community

Cycles in the
Forest Community

MIXTURES
PROPERTIES OF MATTER
COMMUNITY RELATIONSHIPS
ELEMENTS AND COMPOUNDS
BIOCIDES

A
TOPIC IN
RESOURCES
FORESTRY

sun
elements and compounds
PROPERTIES OF MATTER
earth materials

WEATHERING AND EROSION
GEOLOGIC TIME SCALE

changes in Forest Community

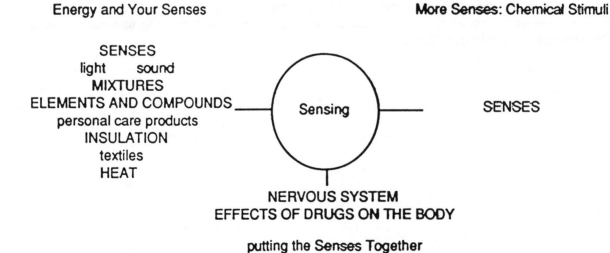

Energy and Your Senses

More Senses: Chemical Stimuli

SENSES
light   sound
MIXTURES
ELEMENTS AND COMPOUNDS
personal care products
INSULATION
textiles
HEAT

Sensing

SENSES

NERVOUS SYSTEM
EFFECTS OF DRUGS ON THE BODY

putting the Senses Together

Expansion of Grade 8 Model C

Lower case indicate topics from the topics chart. UPPER CASE indicates essential topics

AS - Astronomy and Space Science	EN - Energy
CE - Changes in Environment	ER - Ecology and Resource Management
CM - Changes in Matter	LF - Life Functions

POSSIBLE SEQUENCE	LEARNING OUTCOMES (All essential and some optional learning outcomes are included in this plan. Learning outcomes may be repeated several times throughout this sequence.)

Theme 1: A TOPIC IN RESOURCES: Forestry
Man Harvesting the Forest Community
Starter issue such as biocide spraying: e.g. control of spruce bud worm; spraying in populated areas (Captain in Kitsilano); spraying 2, 4-D in forests (to kill deciduous growth) would provide an appropriate introduction to this theme.
  The Forest as a Community
    COMMUNITY RELATIONSHIPS
    - forest ecosystems
    - populations in the forest
    - communities in the forest
    - habitats and niches
    - food chains and webs in the forest
        predation
        parasitism
        commensualism
        mutualism
    - abiotic and biotic environments
 	
  Ecological pyramids
  - trophic levels
       producers, consumers,
       decomposers
  - biomass pyramid
       trace route and accumulation
       of BIOCIDES
  - energy pyramid
  - effects of consumption of foods
   high on energy pyramid
The Forest as a Resource
A TOPIC IN RESOURCES: Forestry
The forests of B.C.
  - climax forest
  - classification of trees
      properties of wood
      - strength
      - rigidity
      - weathering resistance
      - fire resistance
      - predator resistance
  - mapping forest regions of B.C.
	1 (E) - DEVELOP A SENSITIVITY FOR THE DELICATE BALANCE IN THE ENVIRONMENT AND THE INTERDEPENDENCY OF POPULATIONS. (ER)
	1 (E) - USE THE PROCESSES OF SCIENCE TO INVESTIGATE EXAMPLES OF FOOD CHAINS AND FOOD WEBS FOUND IN THEIR LOCALE. (ER)
	1 (E) - UNDERSTAND THE INTER-RELATIONSHIPS OF LIVING ORGANISMS AND THEIR ENVIRONMENT. (ER)
	
	2.(E) - USE THE PROCESSES OF SCIENCE TO INVESTIGATE A LOCAL RESOURCE.(ER)
	2 (E) - APPROACH THE ISSUES SURROUND ING LAND AND WATER USE IN AN OPEN-MINDED MANNER. (ER)
	3 (E) - DEVELOP A MORE RESPONSIBLE ATTITUDE TOWARD SELF AND SOCIETY THROUGH A STUDY OF RESOURCES. (ER)

Exemplary integrated elementary science programmes in the United States

John E. Penick

Introduction

The studies of the fifty programmes identified by the NSTA search for excellence referred to at the beginning of this chapter show that all these programmes were designed to be excellent, to use a locally developed curriculum, and not to place textbooks in a central position. Teachers of these programmes have had several years of focussed, intensive in-service training, with emphasis on team teaching, and they have close ties with higher education. Usually, there is strong central and building administration support and often a science supervisor playing a key role. These teachers are more current in their science education than teachers in general, have strong community involvement and support, and feel they and their programmes are still evolving. Their positive influence in the science curriculum has also had impact on other aspects of the school curriculum.

Learning from excellence

'Teachers of the future may become facilitators of learning, rather than dispensers of new knowledge.' - A United States National Science Foundation Commission, 1983.

While there is much wrong with science education and many classrooms are as dismal as John Goodlad reports in his *A Place Called School*, most of us have known for sometime that many excellent teachers, outstanding school science programmes, and good student achievement were evident and working well. Many have sought to describe schools and programmes. But, as we have read more and more case studies and ethnographic reports of school settings, we have become convinced that they are of little use in bringing about innovation in science education. Enlightening as these studies may be, they afford little assurance that the practices they describe will be more successful than the usual trial-and-error process. As Thomas Edison once said, there is some merit in knowing a lot of things that will not work. However, knowing what *does* work is a considerably more direct route to success.

We wanted to identify outstanding school science programmes and study systematically how these programmes arose, what was their inspiration, how they were supported, what it is they do, and how they are maintained and might evolve. In organizing our search throughout the United States we used criteria developed by Project Synthesis, a funded effort in five focus areas; elementary science, biology, physical science, science-technology-society, and science as inquiry (Harms and Yager, 1981). The criteria for Project Synthesis were developed over a two year period after critical reading of societal indicators, foundation reports, philosophical arguments, and a number of status study reports (Helgeson, et. al., 1977; Stake and Easley, 1978; Weiss, 1978).

Project Synthesis goals provide far more than an arbitrary description of excellent science programmes, they describe programmes leading to science literacy for the general public; they describe the sort of learning that most scholars agree we need both now and in the future. These goals strongly reflect disturbing trends from the third United States National Assessment of Educational Progress where it appeared that the more American students studied science in school the less likely they would find it interesting, fun, or useful. Also, the longer students studied science in their school career, the more likely they were to think that teachers were not interested in them and did not value their opinions.

The synthesis goals also rise from the realization by many science educators that there is a strong mismatch between the science curriculum found in schools and that which ninety percent of students want and need. For instance, nearly all science teachers emphasize goals for school science that are directed toward preparing students for the next academic level, are oriented towards a specific discipline of science, and emphasize the production of scientists rather than science-literate citizens. A key part of the synthesis goals is attaining direct experience in science as well, rather than merely reading about science.

In essence, the science researchers with Project Synthesis were looking at a total curriculum not just a text; not just activities, but a curriculum consisting of students, goals, learning materials, teacher behaviour, and an appropriate classroom atmosphere.

The search for programmes most closely meeting the synthesis criteria was begun when leading science educators (generally state science consultants) in each state were identified as chairs of committees charged with identifying and nominating outstanding science programmes in their own states. Programmes were not considered as being the best in the nation but merely the ones that best fit the criteria. It was arbitrarily decided that ten science programmes in each focus area would be selected, the ten that best fit the criteria.

Teachers from these programmes submitted extensive data about their preparation, their outlooks, their experience, and their views of the nature of science. These programmes, all judged as exemplary by a national panel, have some most interesting similarities and lead to fascinating generalizations about both teachers and programmes. (For more detailed information, see the *Focus On Excellence* monographs available from NSTA, 1742 Connecticut Avenue, N. W., Washington, D. C., 20009.)

Some generalizations

Without exception, these programmes were designed to be excellent. While many schools were seeking 'the better textbook' on the usual five year cycle these exemplary science programmes were after something else. After trying a variety of textbooks they gave up the search for 'the text that would solve all their problems,' deciding instead that they must develop their own programme. Not surprisingly, they see process as more basic than content. But, rather than uniformly developing a programme to replace the text they decided to develop programmes with a focus on excellence. Generally, they recognized that this would take time and considerable effort but, because of strong individual commitment and administrative support, these schools and districts found the time to develop excellent programmes.

Some generalizations from the exemplars

Excellent science programmes:
- were designed to be excellent
- emphasize integrated science
- involve several years of focused intensive in-service training
- use a locally developed non-text curriculum
- have a science supervisor who plays a key role and who is active in professional societies
- followed well-organized plans for development and implementation
- have close ties with higher education
- have strong community involvement and support
- have teachers who are extremely active professionally
- have unique features which provide observable local ownership and pride.

The Porter-Gaud School in North Carolina had a functioning elementary science programme but nothing that would be considered outstanding. In search of an outstanding programme they hired Margaret Harrison, a teacher experienced with innovation and change. In a matter of some six years she instituted a new curriculum, based upon elementary science study materials, made science the show piece of the school, brought them national recognition, and caused students to rank science as the number one subject at almost every grade level (Penick, 1983).

Almost without exception these programmes have developed their own curriculum. In almost all instances, textbooks are not in a central position. Teachers feel a locally developed curriculum is more relevant, responsive, and reliable. In fact, many teachers spoke of textbooks as 'supplementing the curriculum.' When we asked, 'What would cause your programme to fail?', the most common answer was, 'Adopt a textbook for science.' This does not mean they use no printed materials. But, most either write their own or use portions of commercial materials.

For example, in Jefferson County, Colorado, teachers felt a need for a junior high school course where students could apply science to environmental problems. All the textbooks they could find had the classical examples but none had examples totally relevant to where they lived. So, that school district sponsored a writing conference to develop activities in environmental science which would take advantage of their mountains, the rainfall patterns throughout the state, and the unusual distribution of population. The end result? A curriculum which leads students to understand what is happening in their own state while giving them an adequate content base to discuss issues affecting their own environment (Penick and Lunetta, 1984). While many school districts have developed such materials, few have taken the next step. Jefferson County, to make their activities seem more substantial and to overcome critics who demand a textbook in every child's hand, bound their materials into a hard cover book which is very respectable.

In Mesa, Arizona they took another approach. There, when they wanted a textbook, they could find none that met their needs. But, they found many books that had portions that seemed suitable. They took a chapter from here and a chapter from there, inserted a few pages of their own, and rebound them as hard cover books (Penick, 1983). This is not the usual, passive, approach to textbook selection which we tend to see in most schools in the United States.

Larger districts with many elementary teachers (some with as many as 41,000 K-6 students) were not content merely to develop curriculum materials. They saw that the curriculum was more than the printed materials and more than science kits; they needed to ensure that the teachers knew how to use materials and could manage a science classroom. These programmes relied on intensive and long-term in-service efforts as well. Although every Jefferson County elementary teacher has had at least three days of in-service training using the elementary materials for their grade level, when teachers change grade level they get an additional three days in-service training for materials at the new grade. This in-service time is provided during regular contract days with substitutes replacing teachers in the classrooms. While this is a relatively expensive effort it does promote excellence.

Most of the elementary exemplars, ranging in size from 3,000 to 41,000 elementary students, have developed a central science kit distribution system sending complete science kits to schools on a scheduled, rotating basis. While the kits and in-service training do not guarantee excellent science teaching they do eliminate many excuses for not teaching science. Teacher efficiency improves when you reduce the amount of preparation time required to teach science. And, the in-service training with these kits frequently focuses on the notion that you can teach science even if you do not understand all the concepts related to it. Once elementary teachers understand this, they find science is fun, and interesting, and they feel less guilty than when they did not teach science at all. There also seems to be some evidence from our exemplary programmes that even poorly taught hands-on science is more interesting to students than the typical textbook-based programmes. These programmes provide the unusual — many field trips, hands-on science, community speaking, activism, and a chance to do and use science. This allows students an active participatory role and they love it.

In addition to being designed to be excellent, these programmes were designed in an atmosphere of strong central and building administration support. Frequently, it was a central office administrator who initiated the innovation. Other times, hiring of a science supervisor provided an initial impetus to develop a new and outstanding programme. Their inspiration was most often a college or in-service course or involvement with professional organizations and journals. These leaders all seem to possess large quantities of energy, great optimism, and a reluctance to accept 'no' for an answer. They are organized people with well developed plans for development and implementation. Frequently this development is tied in with faculty members in universities and leaders of professional organizations. And, they all agree on one thing: their programmes are still evolving.

The teachers in these programmes are different as well. The typical teachers in exemplary programmes have more experience, are nearly twice as likely to have an advanced degree, are more recent in college credit, and feel themselves to be more qualified to teach than do teachers in general. These elementary teachers also spend more time teaching science, mathematics, and social studies and less time teaching reading. The differences between teachers in the 'search for excellence' sample and teachers in general also show up in what they do in the classroom. These teachers at every grade level are eight times more likely to provide students with hands-on material and they lecture less while discussing more with students. They are more likely to find in-service training useful and twice as likely to read a professional journal related to science teaching. These teachers are also four times as likely to have attended a recent in-service training course and are much more enthusiastic about science teaching in general than their colleagues nationally. These teachers do make a difference.

Teachers do make a difference by:
• providing a stimulating environment
• stressing integrated science, not a single discipline
• creating an accepting atmosphere
• putting in far more than minimal time
• having high expectations of themselves
• being models of active inquiry
• not viewing classroom walls as boundary walls
• using societal issues as a focus
• being extremely flexible in their time, schedule, curriculum, expectation, and view of themselves
• requiring considerable student self-assessment
• asking questions requiring new and unknown answers
• expecting students to question facts, teachers, authority, and knowledge
• stressing scientific literacy
• wanting students to apply knowledge

Teachers do make a difference and the differences show in what they have done, in what they are doing, and in what they expect to do. Many of these are very unique and innovative. Green Acres School in Santa Cruz, California, for example, provides students with two hours a week in a curriculum centred around a three acre garden. This garden, once a parking lot, now is filled with greenhouses, livestock barns, chicken coops, storage sheds, a pond, solar energy devices, and garden plots. In addition they have a grape arbour and a fruit orchard. Each classroom has two garden plots and must make decisions on what to plant, how to care for it, and when to harvest. Students spend about half of their time indoors working on nutrition and activities relating to gardening and the other of their time actually working in the garden itself (Penick, 1983).

Much of the total school curriculum revolves around the garden as students read about the care of tools, preparation of soils, and maintenance of vegetables. Then, students study the nutritional aspects of what they raise, learn how to prepare them for eating, and look at the cost of gardening in general. Green Acres also is an excellent example of one more generalization which can be made about these exemplary programmes: they have outstanding community support. In fact, in Santa Cruz, this community support led to organizing a non-profit corporation, Friends of the Harvest, as a support mechanism for the total school programme.

These schools and districts recognized early that science is a basic part of their curriculum. In doing so, they also took advantage of the fact that children seem naturally to enjoy science and that science is easily related to all aspects of the school curriculum. As a result, their excellent science programmes are having visible impact on other school programmes as well as on other schools. They are finding that students, teachers, and parents are coming to expect science to be interesting, fun, and relevant now and in the future. In the process, they are gaining support to continue and upgrade their programmes while allowing for a positive evolution.

In these exemplary programmes, students are experiencing more school science that closely mirrors the nature of science itself; a condition that must enhance scientific literacy, attitudes toward science, and an awareness of careers in science and science-related fields. Teachers are feeling more professional and competent because, for the first time for many of them, they are finding they can do a good job with science while enjoying it.

Criteria for excellence

Criteria for excellence in elementary science

In an exemplary elementary school science programme students will:
be able to exhibit effective consumer behaviour by evaluating the quality of products, the accuracy of advertising, and personal needs for the product;
use effective personal health practices; be able to learn when presented with new ideas and data;
recognize that their lives influence their environment and are influenced by it;
recognize and accept ways in which each individual is unique; recognize that the solution to one problem can create new problems;
recognize that some data can be interpreted differently by people depending on their values and experiences;
possess a sense of custodianship (collective responsibility for the environment over a period of time);
recognize that science will not provide 'magic' solutions or easy answers — instead, the use of hard work and the processes of science are required to 'resolve' rather than 'solve' many problems;
develop an understanding of information and concepts from a wide variety of topics selected from the life, earth, and physical sciences; (Variation in topics may be used to help develop the skills in generating, categorizing, quantifying, and interpreting information from an environment. Variation in topics may also be used for the sole reason that they are interesting to students at a particular age.)
recognize that scientists and technicians are people with personal and human characteristics; (Teachers should use biographical sketches, personal knowledge, etc.)
illustrate persons with different life-styles, socio-economic status, ethnicity, and sex who are participating fully in the scientific enterprise.

Programme characteristics which are viewed as desirable to produce student outcomes outlined above should include the following suggestions:
Genuine alternatives should exist so that real decisions can be made, real problems solved, and the consequences known or experienced.
The problems presented to students should be definable, possible to accomplish, and should grow out of first-hand experience.
Students should be actively involved in gathering data.
Information that is presented should be clearly articulated through alternative modes; i.e., books, films, 'hands-on' experience, etc.
Information transmitted should be as appropriate as possible for the age level of the student and should reflect how it was developed
Science programmes should be interdisciplinary in nature (involving areas other than science).
Students must use information and values to make decisions and evaluate the consequences for others in their community.

Criteria for excellence in biology

The biology programme defined as excellent focuses on helping students use biological knowledge to enhance their understanding of themselves and to benefit the quality of life and living for human beings. The study of the human organism in its natural, cultural, and psycho-social environments is essential — this includes a focus on human adaptation and future perspectives for human welfare. Biology taught for these purposes involves questions of ethics, values, morals, and aesthetics. Student goals in such programmes include the following:
to understand human beings as a distinctive organism;
to appreciate the universal human need to be in touch with our nature, and all of nature;
to learn to live in harmony with nature and to minimize the dissonance between the social and natural environments.

The biological knowledge for achieving these objectives is not unlike that found in most standard textbooks. However, the use of this knowledge in teaching and living is very different. The biology programme:

Focuses on environmental or ecological studies including current issues requiring a biology knowledge-base. Health — particularly those aspects dealing with topics such as alcohol, drugs, tobacco — and disease is included. The quality of life in the future is stressed.

Requires no changes in time allotments in schools. It is a course to be required of all students because the subject matter is primarily directed to improving human adaptation on both an individual and a social basis. To require the programme of all students would mean about a 15 per cent increase in biology enrolment over the current number of students taking biology.

Includes the following foci for evaluation: the ability of the student to use a knowledge of biology to interpret personal problems and social issues and a demonstrated ability to formulate rational decisions in the context of personal problems and social issues.

Criteria for excellence in physical science

The characteristics of a physical science programme considered excellent obviously are a function of specific goals and will vary accordingly. However, such programmes will generally have many of the following characteristics:

Opportunities should be provided to pursue individual needs, goals, and interests; e.g., provisions could be made for modularity, a project approach, or time periods for investigating individual topics;

Opportunities should be provided to apply physical science content and processes to real-world problems that have no 'pat' solutions but require trade-offs;

Basic concepts of physical science should be dealt with in a discipline-organized pattern at some point in the total programme;

Basic concepts of physical science should be dealt with in the context of socially relevant problems at some point in the total programme;

Personal needs, societal issues, and career preparation should be considered intrinsic to all facets of the science programme;

Opportunities should be provided to interact with people working in science including scientists, technicians, and others in science-related fields;

Emphasis should be placed on the means by which scientific knowledge is generated;

Within the total programme, learning experiences should be included which provide:
    (a) laboratory experiences, including opportunities to acquire information inductively;
    (b) out-of-school experiences;
    (c) illustrations of different problem-solving styles;
    (d) exploratory activities that involve such features as risk-taking, guessing, hypothesizing;
    (e) opportunities to participate in actual or simulated research activities;
    (f) opportunities to develop more advanced mathematical techniques as applied to science matters;
    (g) opportunities to develop reporting and writing techniques; and
    (h) opportunities to develop ability to read science materials.

Criteria for excellence in enquiry

Excellence for inquiry is defined in the context in which effective enquiry teaching occurs by considering teacher characteristics, the classroom, and the curriculum:

The *teacher* is critical in achieving a desired state consistent with enquiry teaching. Effective teachers value enquiry, encourage an enquiry orientation in others, and possess skills enabling others to use enquiry as a way of knowing.

Enquiry classrooms have science objects and events that are obviously in use. Equipment and supplies are organized and available in such ways as to stimulate student investigations. The physical arrangement of the classroom is flexible enough to allow engaging in activities of various kinds without undue problems or loss of time.

Curricula for all students include explicit statements of desired student outcomes that give attention to science process skills, the nature of scientific enquiry, and to attitudes and value while considering individual needs and goals.

Instruction in enquiry classrooms may reflect a variety of methods, i.e., discussions, investigative laboratories, student- initiated enquiries, lectures, or debates. Teachers serve as role models in debating issues, examining values, admitting error, and confronting areas of their own ignorance. The classroom atmosphere is conducive for students to ask questions and take action. The classroom climate stimulates a thorough, thoughtful exploration of objects, ideas, and events, rather than a need to finish the text. Techniques and instruments for evaluation are selected and used in such a way that student outcomes which reflect enquiry learning are assessed.

Criteria for excellence in science/technology/society (STS)

Excellence in the area of science/technology/society is found in programmes which:
prepare individuals to use science for improving their own lives and for coping with an increasingly technological world;
prepare students to deal responsibly with technology/society issues;
identify a body of fundamental knowledge which students may need to master in order to deal intelligently with STS;
provide studens with an accurate picture of the requirements and opportunities involved in the multitude of careers available in the STS area.

Programmes which have these features will have the following programme characteristics:
Opportunity to learn about the energy involved in a variety of areas — from taking long, hot showers; to potential indoor pollution resulting from sealing houses too tightly against drafts; to the world impact of increasingly rapid growth of energy use throughout the world.
Opportunity to discuss natural control of populations, the effect of technologies on population growth, and the impact of rapid changes of population growth on specific subsets of the world society.
Student awareness of the effects of personal and societal decisions on all aspects of the environment — from papers and food on the floor of the cafeteria, to the balance of gases in the atmosphere, to the 'noise' of home stereo systems.
Students in a position to question the apparent waste in various technological programmes as well as the potential benefits.
Focus on the complexity of day to day decisions related to science and technology. For example, while it can be demonstrated that 45 mph is a more energy-efficient speed at which to drive most autos, the national speed limit is 55 mph. The sociology behind such regulations should be understood along with the technology. The automation of supermarkets has been technologically feasible for many years. The sociology involved in gaining public acceptance for this system has slowed down its implentation.
Opportunity to consider such issues as weather control, test tube babies, genetic engineering, space shuttles, nuclear energy, and a myriad of technological developments require an education which enable individuals and groups to make intelligent decisions on support or opposition to such technologies.

The future

As excellence comes to be recognized as an attainable goal, we hope that parents will demand it, that school administrators will support excellent programmes and teachers, and that teachers will strive to provide conditions essential for excellence. As consumers raise their expectations for science classrooms, we hope that curriculum developers will produce materials that better suit the general goals, structures, and conditions that characterize the exemplary programmes. When students experience school science that more closely approaches real science, it is likely that more of them will study science and more will seek careers in science and science teaching than ever before. Excellence does not come about by chance; it must be nurtured.

We feel that these examples from the 'search for excellence' will motivate and inspire schools and school districts seeking innovation and science literacy for their students. At the same time, we might also influence colleges and universities preparing teachers for elementary schools. All of these influences should ultimately affect students and lead to excellence for our educational enterprise in general.

Finally, we hope that the example of the NSTA 'search for excellence' might spread to colleges and universities and to other disciplines. Eventually, we can all hope that all decisions affecting students will be made in light of the answer to the question: how will this lead to excellence for our learners?

References

HARMS, N. and YAGER, R.E. (1981). *What Research Says to the Science Teachers*, Vol. II, Washington, D.C.: National Science Teachers Association.

HELGESON, S.L., BLOSSER, P.E., and HOWE, R.W. (177). *The Status of Pre-College Science, Mathematics, and Social Science Education: 1955-57*, Columbus: Center for Science and Mathematics Education, Ohio State University.

PENICK, J.E. (ed.) 1983. *Focus on Excellence: Elementary Science, 1 (2)*. National Science Teachers Association, 1742 Connecticut Avenue, N.W., Washington, D.C. 20009.

PENICK, J.E. and LUNETTA, V.N. (eds.) 1984. *Focus on Excellence: Physical Science, 1 (4)*. National Science Teachers Association, 1742 Connecticut Avenue, N.W., Washington, D.C., 200009.

STAKE, R.E. and EASLEY, J. (1978). *Case Studies in Science Education*, Vols. I and II. Urbana: Center for Instructional Research and Curriculum Evaluation, University of Illinois.

WEISS, I.R. (1978). *Report of the National Survey of Science, Mathematics, and Social Studies Education*, Research Triangle Park, N.C.: Center for Educational Research and Evaluation.

Chapter 13

Latin America and the Caribbean

Integrated science education in Latin America

Introduction

This brief report applies particularly to recent developments in the Andean countries of South America, where some trends in integrated science are regional and others are limited to one or a few countries.

Several regional and subregional meetings sponsored by Unesco and by regional organizations and institutions have been held in Latin America during the last ten years, but even so, the development of integrated science teaching is not very great in the region. This is probably due to the fact that most educational systems have been under the influence of European curricula dating back to the 1930s. Universities changed rapidly during the 1960s but general education changed more slowly. The traditional curricula favoured separate courses in natural sciences, biology and in the upper-secondary school, physics and chemistry. Mathematics has been and continues to be a separate subject matter in all or most of the curricula.

The resistance of some teachers to change has also been a factor in the lack of more integration in the teaching of science. Some teachers trained in a given discipline (biology, for instance) resist the introduction of physics, chemistry and earth science, because of the amount of time and effort needed to learn about these other sciences.

Education systems have expanded rapidly to cover significant percentages of the population in school age. This has meant large investments, usually involving long-term loans from multilateral organizations (World Bank and Inter-American Bank, for example). These loans have been used to build new schools, many in far out places, and to give them basic facilities such as furnishings and teaching equipment.

National budgets had to assume, besides the payment of the loans, the increased payrolls for new teachers and the improvement of salaries and fringe benefits for all teachers. In the last decade the burden of the foreign debt and the cost of inflation have put educational systems in very difficult situations. Just keeping salaries at a constant level of purchasing power has implied using all extra money to pay salary increases but, even so, salaries have lagged behind the rampant inflation of many countries in the region. New investments have been abandoned and the number of teachers in some countries has decreased.

Under these conditions it is very difficult to begin or to continue programmes aimed at the improvement of the quality of education and through that to help improving the quality of life. To push ahead in integrated science teaching programmes implies huge programmes of in-service training for teachers for which ministries of education do not have the resources. They have a hard time paying salaries to avoid teacher's strikes when salaries are not paid in time.

Field work in Peru

Curriculum reform

Despite all the difficulties, several countries in the region have undertaken the task of changing curricula. This is the case of Colombia, where the Ministry of Education has recently changed the curriculum from five years of primary school and six years of secondary school to a general school lasting nine years, after the kindergarten, followed by two years of vocational training in a diversified upper-secondary school (grades 10 and 11, ages 16 to 18).

Initially this curriculum reform was planned to include a strong integrated science component, but after experimenting in some schools, the 'integration' was abandoned, because it ran into difficulties from a lack of teacher training and also a lack of sufficient funds to implement this very ambitious reform.

The new curriculum includes topics mainly in biology, chemistry and physics, with relatively minor contributions from astronomy and the health and earth sciences. The topics are presented sequentially but in recommendations to teachers, curriculum developers seem to insist on the same processes in the teaching of the separate topics. From grades 1 through 9, the science curriculum is presented in a sequence of topics: biology, chemistry, physics and astronomy and there is a real danger that teachers will take this literally and go through the sequence. Then, since they do not teach all periods due to strikes, local festivals and the like, pupils will get a lot of biology, a little of chemistry and no physics, because this last discipline is the one the teachers are least comfortable with.

In principle the new curriculum is not rigidly fixed, as was the case in the past, and leaves open the possibility that teachers may make adaptations, using a different selection of topics and approaches in the rural areas from those in the cities. But the crucial questions to pose are: Are teachers prepared to do this kind of adaptation? Will they have the time and the minimum of

145

resources to attempt experimenting with the curriculum? In some cases there will be teachers with the right background, the enthusiasm and the dedication to do a good job, but in general teachers will show reluctance to undertake the adaptation of the new curriculum. Very few universities and higher education institutions are involved in any way with providing teachers with a minimum of support or training to face these new challenges.

In other Latin American countries similar reforms are in the process of being implemented or are in an advanced stage of planning and will be adopted soon by ministries of education. The problems to implement new curricula are similar, but the lack of adequate training of the teachers is perhaps the most difficult one to solve in the short run. The numbers of teachers to be given in-service training are very large, and resources are scarce.

Teacher training

Primary-school teachers have been traditionally trained by the so-called 'normal' schools, where young people go instead of attending a regular secondary school. These schools have usually less hours dedicated to science than the regular secondary schools, thus they produce teachers with poor science backgrounds. The result is that normal schools graduate teachers at 17 or even younger with less science background and they are then asked to teach a new curriculum that pretends to be more demanding of scientific and technological knowledge from the teachers. The new curriculum had initially the inclusion of significant in-service training of the teachers, but that part of the plan was severely cut down because of lack of enough money to do it.

Recently, in Colombia, the Ministry of Education has introduced a ranking system that pays the same salary to a teacher according to his/her qualifications, regardless of what level they teach. Thus secondary-school teachers, having four years of university training, are now teaching in some primary schools. This helps in the maturity problem and in the science background, but not in the familiarization with the primary science teaching problems.

In-service training of teachers has also been divided. Primary school teachers are offered courses and activities by special centres of the Ministry of Education while secondary-school teachers take in-service training in the universities.

In the last ten years a favourable change has taken place. The Ministry of Education has established a ranking system for all teachers (primary and secondary). In order to go up in the ranks, teachers have to take in-service training every few years, and to reach the top of the ranks they need a post-graduate programme leading to a degree. In this reform the teachers are paid according to their place in the ranking system and not according to where they teach, as was done before, thus people with university training, if they teach primary school get the same salary as a secondary-school teacher with the same academic credentials and experience. The trend now is towards a university-level training for primary-school teachers and universities are now offering programmes particularly structured for primary-school teaching. Teachers already in the system can take part-time programmes that allow them to progress toward a university degree and then to get a higher salary. The system has then created significant stimuli and economic rewards for the improvement of the teachers, but the programmes offered by some universities are of poor quality and do not include much science, because those universities lack the facilities of laboratories and equipment. Nevertheless the trend is a positive one and has the potential of helping greatly in the efforts to improve the quality of our educational system.

Concluding remarks

Very briefly one could summarize the situation of science teaching in Latin America as follows:
(a) During the last ten years some favourable changes have taken place: new curricula are being implemented, the ranking system for the teachers, in, for example, Colombia, stimulates more training and some written materials of somewhat better quality have been produced.
(b) The teaching of science is centred, to some extent, in the processes of science, but integration is not very great.

(c) More pre- and in-service training of teachers is needed and rationalization of current efforts is urgent. There is a favourable trend towards having post-secondary training for primary-school teachers.

(d) Very little research has been done in science teaching, but this situation is changing with the establishment of several groups that are active in this field and that are proposing post-graduate programmes in several universities to further train secondary-school teachers and enrol them in an effort to do more research.

(e) The economic limitations of many countries with the high costs of inflation and devaluation place severe restrictions on budgets for expansion and improvement of the educational system in general.

Integrated science education in the Caribbean

W. King

Introduction

The history of the development of science education in the Caribbean shows a struggle for its acceptance in the school curriculum.

Many factors are related to this. Some are socio-economic and political. Science education and its related areas still do not enjoy the status of some of the more popular professions.

It is true that governments speak glibly of the importance of science and technology education in national development, but few put into action their beliefs, possibly hamstrung by lack of resources and a deep political will. If one is to judge by political utterings it seems that the areas of technical education and vocational training are the ones to which priority is accorded at the moment.

Integrated science from its very inception was destined to meet with scepticism and disapproval. Some doubts were understandable, but others flow from ignorance and a type of reaction that borders on mild hysteria. It is not uncommon to hear science educators dismiss integration out of hand without even knowing what is involved. The pride of being a biologist, chemist or physicist often overrides any claim of efficiency and effectiveness of an integrated approach.

Despite all the problems, integrated science has found a niche for itself in Caribbean education, to which a study of the various programmes will attest. It seems that in the years to come it will grow slowly but steadily as Caribbean peoples attempt to provide a broad-based education for learners.

Overview of science education in the education system

The teaching of science in most Caribbean countries begins officially at the first level (age 5 years). For the whole of that first level science is integrated, with heavy emphasis on the processes of science. Integrating themes such as energy and the environment form the threads which run throughout the course.

Integrated science continues into the first stage of the second level (11+ to 14 years). At the second stage of the second level (14+), students opt to follow one of two pathways to science up to age 16. They either continue with integrated science or they follow the three separate sciences. Further work in science continues as biology, chemistry, physics through the first and second stages of sixth form and university. In the case of teacher training colleges, science is integrated for prospective first level, first stage second level and some second stage second level teachers.

At the end of the second level students sit externally set examinations. Up to the recent past these examinations were set in the United Kingdom. With the establishment of the Caribbean Examinations Council (CXC) in 1979, most students now sit local examinations.

At the end of the sixth-form level students sit external examinations set by examining boards in the United Kingdom. These examinations provide entry into the university level.

The development of integrated science at the junior secondary and secondary levels

Junior-secondary level

In 1968 the Scottish Integrated Science Programme was adapted to produce the West Indian Science Curriculum Innovation Project (WISCIP) for the 11 to 14 age range.

An amended version, now called WISC, is used in some form in the age range 11-14 in most countries. The curriculum materials have long disappeared but certain ideas and textbooks written for the programme remain.

Senior secondary (14+ to 16+): CXC Integrated Science (double award)

Many Caribbean science educators still express surprise at the choice of CXC in offering integrated science as one of its first examination subjects.

Lambert (1979) conjectures that it was probably influenced by the relative success of the CEDO/Unesco Integrated Science Teacher Education Workshop held in Barbados in 1973. One of the main outcomes of this workshop was a set of topic statements called CARISO (Caribbean Integrated Science to 'O' level).

It is interesting to note the inclusion of school-based assessment as an integral part of the pupil's final assessment grade. This school-based assessment is carried out by the teachers themselves, including the practical work required by the syllabus sections along with the project. The course-work is moderated by examiners.

The syllabus defines a project as 'an exercise executed by the student demonstrating his/her ability to apply scientific principles and processes to the following situations:
(i)   Investigation of a problem.
(ii) Technology in which the student constructs or modifies devices.
(iii) Displays resulting from student research in an area of interest.'

The method of certification is in many respects new and innovative. The certificate will show a single grade, which later counts as two general proficiency grades. In addition, there is a profile report consisting of four three-point scales. The four 'profile points' are, in keeping with the aims: knowledge, enquiry skills, social awareness and practical skills. These are calculated both on the examination and the school-based assessment.

The issuing of a profile report is indeed a progressive step. With proper explanation of what the certificate means, employers would find themselves in a position to choose precisely what skills they require in a would-be employee. An overall grade does not allow this fine discrimination.

CXC integrated science (single award)

After many years and beset by many barriers the double award has progressed very disappointingly. The candidate population has decreased significantly but the Council still continues to offer the subject.

Mainly because of the problems encountered by the double award, partly in an effort to produce a syllabus for persons offering technical/vocational areas, nursing and such professions, the single award was developed in 1983. It is not intended for persons wishing to pursue careers in science.

The main thrust of the syllabus is to attempt to have an impact on the daily lives of students and the society at large. The syllabus adapts some of the themes from the IUBS/CBE programme for non- biologists. The four themes are: the home, the workplace, recreation and transport — chosen because they represent adequately the common areas of human activity and experience. (See Part 3 for details of the syllabus.)

Some barriers to implementation

There are many factors which are curtailing effective implementation: teacher re-orientation, lack of proper facilities and resources, teaching/learning problems, lack of proper innovation climate, lack of text books and background reference materials.

Teacher re-orientation

The majority of science teachers in the Caribbean are specialists, in the sense that their training has been in one, or maybe two subject areas in science. For meaningful implementation teachers must be trained to handle the new innovation. Many science educators are ready and willing to help in the training, but finances dictate that efforts will be only on a limited basis. Some of the problems, of course, stem from the need to change attitudes towards science and science education.

Lack of proper resources and facilities

In many cases schools find difficulty in properly implementing integrated science courses because of insufficient facilities and equipment. The problem is compounded by the fact that the so-called better grammar schools do not choose integrated science.

The choice of schools, and students to a certain extent, is somewhat strange. Countries seem to lack a philosophy of science education which is in keeping with their stages of development. The whole question of the purpose of science education must be squarely faced. The region must decide whether in the light of the dire need for 'technician type' personnel resulting from the spurt of industrial/technological development, it would continue to produce specialists; or whether there is a case for a broad education for as long as possible.

Teaching/learning problems

The CXC syllabus represents an improvement on the 'traditional' ones by the inclusion of general and specific objective and in giving more guidance and direction than do mere topic statements.

Teachers experience problems of scarcity of information related to school-based assessment and assessment of projects. The Council has been working feverishly to alleviate this.

Many teachers are experiencing difficulty in achieving the myriad objectives in a meaningful way. The main problem here is the large volume of work that is to be covered in a short time. The problem is further compounded by the fact that schools tend to put their weakest students into integrated science. Remedial activities help to slow the pace even further.

Lack of proper innovation climate

It seems that innovations flourish best in an atmosphere that is conducive to change. This holding on to the known and tried, even if not serving one's purposes at the present time, is probably one of the major obstacles to the success of integrated science in the Caribbean. Not only are most teachers lacking in expertise to teach the subject, but the majority do not even want to hear. They are physicists, biologists, and chemists, and will never teach anything else, even though they may receive relevant training.

In a sense, the reluctance to change, or even to contemplate it, may have been brought about by experiences from previous attempts at curriculum innovation and development. The region has seen many 'modern' curriculum materials with 'new' methods of teaching and instruction. These have come on the scene, created some stir while external funding agencies have maintained them, and with equal speed they have disappeared. They now adorn the most infrequently-used shelf in someone's office. The teachers in the field are cautious that all the apparent upheaval in the system, caused by the new innovation is not just another passing fancy.

It may be that the Council did not advance the cause of integrated science when they announced that in the near future they will be examining in the separate sciences. Whatever market ability that there was dissipated immediately.

The lack of effective and agents of change is a problem somewhat tied up with the lack of a climate of innovation. The 'word' which is to be spread needs dedicated channels for its transmission. As in so many other innovations, the teachers who have been involved in the development and pilot phases are 'fired' with a fervour towards integrated science that in some cases is almost evangelical. They have made significant efforts. To change attitudes, however, requires long and frequent effort, along with showing good example. The relative few teachers have neither the time nor the financial support to sustain such an attack.

Lack of textbooks and reference materials

Another factor which has tremendous impact on implementation of integrated science courses is the lack of adequate text and reference materials.

Teachers of integrated science come from a variety of backgrounds and so their needs are different. What most of them need is some information which would at least give them a slightly deeper knowledge than those whom they teach. To demand such is not unreasonable. Not to answer such demand is to open the door to frustration and lack of confidence. Both states are inimical to the success of this innovation.

Part 3

Examples of integrated science teaching

Examples of integrated science teaching

Introduction

This final section provides some examples of syllabuses and teaching modules in integrated science from a few selected countries. These range from the grade 10 syllabuses available in the Caribbean for integrated science as an examination syllabus for 16 year old school leavers of the Caribbean Examinations Council (CXC), to the integrated science syllabuses in Botswana and Sierra Leone in Africa and the Philippines in Asia. The Botswana approach is illustrated by teaching modules from units of the new textbooks for junior secondary science. The approach in the Philippines syllabuses is illustrated by some specimen teaching units issued to help teachers understand how to interpret the syllabuses. Trends in Europe are illustrated by examples from textbooks and teachers' guides from the Netherlands and the UK.

Botswana

The new syllabuses for junior secondary level in Botswana are entitled 'Science by Investigation'. They are issued with objectives — general and specific. Two units from the syllabuses — given below — illustrate the nature of these objectives.

Selected objectives from the topic 'Water for Living'

General objectives: *Pupils should be able to:*	Lesson objectives: *Pupils should be able to:*
Discuss the sources of water available in Botswana.	-Explain the water cycle. -Identify and describe the two main water sources in Botswana. -Explain how ground water is replaced. -List the main uses of water both nationally and in their own area. -Appreciate the value of water.
Describe methods of conserving water and how to prevent contamination of water.	-State why it is essential to conserve water. -List ways of conserving water. -Describe three methods of collecting and storing rain-water. -State how stored water can be contaminated. -Suggest methods to prevent contamination during storage. -List several contaminants of rivers and dams. -Understand and properly use the word 'contamination'. -Describe at least three ways of preventing stored water in the home from becoming contaminated. -Explain how latrines reduce water contamination.
Identify water-related diseases common in Botswana and suggest ways of preventing them.	-Recall and explain the bilharzia life-cycle. -Describe the symptoms, prevention and cure of bilharzia. -Explain how intestinal infectious diseases are contracted, list the symptoms, and suggest how to prevent them. -Explain the use of an oral rehydration drink and be able to mix it. -Explain how malaria is spread. -State the cause of malaria and suggest methods of prevention. -Recall and explain the life cycle of a mosquito.

Use and describe methods of making water safe to drink.	-Clean water using
	  (i) sedimentation, (ii) a filter bed
	  (iii) a cloth (iv) boiling
	  (v) a solar still (vi) chemicals
	-State why or why not each of the above provide drinking water.
	-Explain how groundwater is purified by natural filtration.
	-Describe how a town water purification system cleans water.

Objectives related to housebuilding

General objectives: *Pupils should be able to:*	Lesson objectives: *Pupils should be able to:*
Identify locally available building materials and discuss their properties and uses.	-Make a list of different building materials. -State the properties of the different building materials. -State the advantages and disadvantages of both a modern house and a traditional house. -Mould a brick.
Describe the three ways in which heat is transferred.	-Demonstrate heat transfer by conduction, convection and radiation. -Explain how heat is transferred by these three ways. -Apply these three ways of heat transfer.
Investigate how the insulation of a house can be improved.	-State the meaning of insulation. -Investigate the insulating properties of different building materials. -Plot a temperature/time graph using the results from the investigation. -Give examples of good and bad insulating materials used for building houses.
Investigate how the ventilation of a house can be improved.	-State the meaning of ventilation. -Use ventilation methods in building both the traditional and the modern house. -Describe the role played by a fan in ventilation.
Investigate ways of controlling the heat radiation from the sun.	-State how heat moves into a house. -Put windows in the right direction for making a house warm in winter. -Determine the size of roof overhang to make a house cool in summer. -State that light colours absorb less heat radiation from the sun while dark colours absorb more heat radiation.

The actual approach to the teaching of this syllabus is illustrated by selections from some of the units of the text in the Water for Living module.

Reproduced from *Science by Investigation*, pp. 96-100, 105-106, 109-114, Heinemann Educational Books Ltd., with permission of the Ministry of Education, Botswana.

3.4 Using and storing water

Can you imagine what a day would be like without water? Every day you use water for washing and drinking. There are many other uses of water. In this section you will learn more about the value and uses of water. You will also learn about ways of storing water and about keeping water safe to drink.

The Value of Water

fig 3.4.1 photo person washing car using hose pipe	fig 3.4.2 photo people queuing with buckets at a standpipe
The good years....	... and the bad years

All animals and plants need water to live. Without water there is no life. In years when water is plentiful we often don't think of its importance. In dry years, when some water sources dry up, we realise how valuable water is. In dry years many people have to walk long distances to collect a bucket full of water. Why is water so valuable? The next activity will help you to think about this.

▲ | **ACTIVITY   Water in my home**

Think of the different uses of water in your home. Estimate how much water each person uses in a day.

❏ Make a table like the one here to help you estimate.
❏ Assume that all people in Botswana use the same amount of water as you do. The population of Botswana is about 1 200 000.

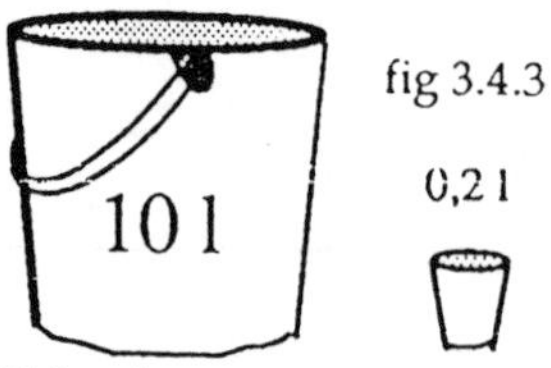

fig 3.4.3

10 l   0,2 l

(1 bucket = 10 litres; 1 glass = 0,2 litres)

a) How much water will be needed for the whole population each day?
b) Compare your answer with the bar chart on the next page.

Use of water	Amount needed for one person
Total:	

▲	EXTENSION
▲	**ACTIVITY Reading a water meter**

Many homes and institutions have water meters installed by the Water Utilities Corporation.

❑ Record the reading on the water meter at your home or in the school.

❑ Return exactly one week later to read the meter again.

a) Why are water meters installed?

b) How much water has been used in one week?

Not only people use water. Cattle also require water. Where else is water needed?

Look at the bar chart showing the water usage in Botswana. Each column shows the amount of water used each day for different purposes. The unit is cubic metres, m³. 1 m³ = 1000 litres = 100 buckets of water.

a) Who is the largest consumer of water?

b) Who is the smallest consumer of water?

c) How much water does Selebi-Phikwe mine consume in <u>one day</u>?

Add up all the figures in the bar chart. This gives the total amount of water required every day in Botswana. This is the total **water demand** in Botswana. Do you think that this figure is likely to get bigger, get smaller or remain constant over the next few years?

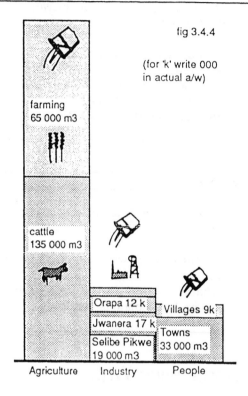

fig 3.4.4

(for 'k' write 000 in actual a/w)

farming
65 000 m3

cattle
135 000 m3

Orapa 12 k

Jwanera 17 k

Selibe Pikwe
19 000 m3

Villages 9k

Towns
33 000 m3

Agriculture   Industry   People

157

▲ | ACTIVITY   The increasing demand for water.

Look at the graph here. It shows that the demand for water in Botswana is expected to increase very sharply over the next 20 years.

❑ In your group, discuss the questions below.
❑ After 10 minutes one group member should present your group answer to the whole class.

a) Why do you think the demand for water is increasing?
b) Is the water available in the country enough for this increasing demand? If not, how should we solve this problem?

fig 3.4.5 a/w
Graph showing projected water demand in Eastern Botswana 1986 - 2011

● | EXERCISE

Use the graph above to answer these questions:

1. List three things which require a lot of water.
2. What is the annual water demand in Eastern Botswana this year?
3. What is expected to be the annual water demand in 10 years time?
4. By how much will the water demand increase over this 10 year period?
5. If the rainfall remains at its present level, where are we going to get the extra water from?

Conserving Water

Water supplies can sometimes be unreliable. In a dry year the **surface water** evaporates quickly. Rivers and dams dry up. We then have to rely on **underground water** for our daily needs.

If it does not rain for a long time, the water we pump up from the ground is not replaced. This means that we are slowly using up the groundwater. To prevent this it is important that we collect, store and use water with care. keeping water and preventing it from being wasted is called **water conservation**.

Two methods can be used to conserve water. One is to collect rainwater. Can you think of some ways of collecting rainwater? The other is to use water with care, without wasting it. Can you think of some ways in which people waste water?

Many homes have rainwater tanks. The rain that falls on the roof flows through the gutter to a storage tank. The amount of rain that is collected depends on the area of the roof. You can calculate the volume of water collected by multiplying the area of the roof by the amount of rainfall.

Area of roof x rainfall = volume of water

From the figure, you can calculate the roof area:

9 m x 4 m = 36 m²

Suppose 10 mm of rain falls. We must convert this to metres. 10 mm = 0,01 m Then the volume of rain that can be collected from the roof is:

36 m² x 0,01 m = 0,36 m³

This is the same as 360 litres of water or 36 buckets of water. You see that even from a small rainfall a useful amount of water can be collected.

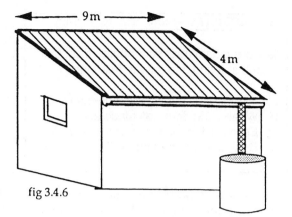

fig 3.4.6

▲ ACTIVITY   Collecting rainwater

You are going to calculate how much rainwater can be collected from the roof of your science room. You will need a long measuring tape.

☐ Use the tape to measure the length of the roof of the science block.
☐ Estimate the width of the roof.
☐ Calculate the total area of the roof. Remember that there are two sides.
☐ Use the rainfall map on page .... to find the annual rainfall in your area.
☐ Calculate how much water could be collected in one year from the roof of the science block.

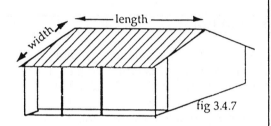

fig 3.4.7

On a larger scale water can be collected in dams. Gaborone and Shashe dams are very large and serve both people and industry in the towns. There are also many smaller dams around the country.

A dam is made by building a wall across a river bed. This holds the water after a rain. The wall must be strong enough to hold a great weight of water. In large dams the wall is made of cement and reinforced with large rocks on the sides.

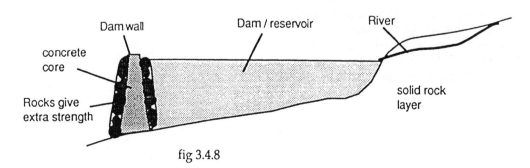

fig 3.4.8

⚠ ACTIVITY Field trip to a dam	fig 3.4.9 photo Gaborone or Shashe dam
Is there a dam near your home? If so, take a look at it and find out the following: a) Where does the water come from? b) What is the dam wall made of? c) Estimate the thickness of the wall. d) Draw the shape of the wall.	

People who farm far from any dam or borehole sometimes catch rainwater in a **ground storage tank**. The tank is built into the ground and lined with cement. The water runs off the ground and collects in the tank. Why is the ground storage tank cemented?

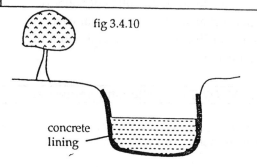

fig 3.4.10

concrete lining

● EXERCISE	
1. Rra Molefi wants to buid a ground storage tank on his farm. To meet his needs, the tank must hold 12 m³ of water. a) Suggest suitable measurements for a rectangular tank.	EXTENSION b) Suggest suitable measurements for a round tank.

Getting the water home

When you turn on the water tap in the science room water flows out of it. How is this possible?

The water we use in our homes may come from a dam, a borehole or a well. This water is pumped into a large storage tank placed on a hill or high structure. Pipes run from the tank to the taps at the standpipes or in the houses. Why is the tank placed high above the ground?

fig 3.4.11 photo
Village water tank on small hill , elevated above ground.

Diarrhoea

The most common water-related disease is infection of the intestine. This usually causes **diarrhoea**. Diarrhoea is very common amongst young children in Botswana. It is one of the main killers in early childhood.

Intestinal infections are often caused by **bacteria**. Water or food may be infected with bacteria. If we use such water or food, bacteria enter the body.

Why does diarrhoea kill? About two thirds of the human body consists of water. This body water contains salts and is essential to life. A person with diarrhoea passes out loose or watery faeces several times a day. A lot of water and salts are lost with the faeces. If this salty water is not replaced the body will dry out. This is called **dehydration**.

fig 3.5.1 a/w
dehydrated child with signs of dehydration labelled

Look at the picture a dehydrated child. What are the signs of dehydration?

Dehydration can quickly cause death, especially in young children. Many deaths could be prevented by giving enough liquid t o drink. If someone in your family gets dehydrated, give them plenty of boiled water, tea, soup , or other wholesome liquid.

An **Oral Rehydration Drink** is a special drink for someone who is dehydrated.

▲ | **ACTIVITY   Making an oral rehydration drink**

You need a 1 litre bottle, a cup, a teaspoon, a container for mixing, and salt and sugar.

fig 3.5.2

- ❏ Boil a pan of water for 15 minutes. This kills any bacteria in the water. Cover the boiled water and let it cool. (This step may have been done for you before the lesson).
- ❏ Put 5 cups of the boiled water into a container.
- ❏ Add 1 level teaspoon of salt and 8 level teaspoons of sugar. (How do you make the teaspoon level?)
- ❏ Stir until the salt and sugar have dissolved. The rehydration drink is now ready. Pour it into the bottle.

(better to show with children)
a) Why do you think salt is added to the drink?
b) Why do think sugar is added to the drink?

Warning: Do not taste the drink if you have been using laboratory equipment. To make a rehydration drink at home, make sure you use only clean utensils.

As you can see, it is easy to make the rehydration drink. If you remember this, you may be able to save the life of a child.

The rehydration drink should be started as soon as the diarrhoea starts. Do not wait for signs of dehydration - that may be too late. The patient should drink as much rehydration drink as possible - at least one cup after each watery faeces.

▲ | **EXTENSION**
▲ | **ACTIVITY   Getting information from the clinic**

You can get first-hand information about water-related diseases from a clinic. Try to arrange to visit a clinic to talk to a health worker.

fig 3.5.3 photo
village clinic

- ❏ Find out if diseases which cause diarrhoea are common in your area.
- ❏ Ask how many children are brought to the clinic with diarrhoea every week. What treatment do they receive?
- ❏ Think of some other questions about diarrhoea.
- ❏ Write a short report on the information you collect.

3.6 Making water safe to drink

In section 3.4 you saw how water could become contaminated. In the last section you read about diseases which can be caught from contaminated water. In this section you will investigate how water can be made safe to drink.

Water can be contaminated by urine and faeces from humans or animals. Washing powder and other chemicals also can contaminate water.

Not everything that is in water is harmful. For instance, some water is salty. Salt is not harmful, but if water is very salty it may not taste nice. Carbonate salts in hard water are harmless. Some salts are good for us. For instance, water rich in **fluoride** helps to protect our teeth.

Cleaning water at home

Sometimes we have to use river or well water for drinking. Before we drink the water we have to clean it. To make it safe we need to remove harmful substances.

Sand and other solid particles can be removed by using a cloth. What is this method called?

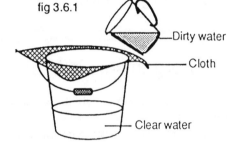

fig 3.6.1

Dirty water

Cloth

Clear water

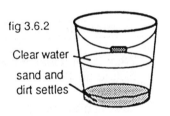

fig 3.6.2

Clear water

sand and dirt settles

Another method is to allow the sand and dirt to settle at the bottom. The solid which settles to the bottom is called a **sediment**. You can then carefully transfer the clear water at the top to a different container. This method is called **sedimentation**.

A Larger Filter

A filter made of cloth is all right for small quantities of water. But sometimes you want larger quantities of water, for instance for washing clothes or yourself.

Then you can use a **sand filter**. As the water moves through the filter, dirt particles stick to the sand and stones.

163

▲ | **ACTIVITY   Make your own sand filter**

You will need a drum, the larger the better, for the filter. You will also need a second drum or a bucket to collect the clean water.

❑ Cut the bottom out of the drum and place it upside down on a support.
❑ Place stones inside the drum. Start with large stones, then small ones, then course sand. At the top put fine sand.

Your filter bed is now ready. Pour dirty water at the top. Cover the drum. Observe the water coming out at the bottom.

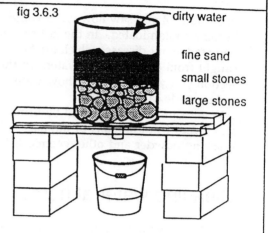

fig 3.6.3

dirty water

fine sand

small stones

large stones

Micro-organisms in Water

Do you think that water which has been filtered is safe to drink?

After filtration or sedimentation the water may look clean, but it could still contain harmful micro-organisms. It is not safe to drink.

▲ | **ACTIVITY   Using a bioviewer to look at micro-organisms**

You will need a bioviewer, and strip no. 2 named "Pond life".

❑ Place the bioviewer next to a window so that lights falls on the stage.
❑ Put the strip in the slot. Adjust the eye-piece until you get a sharp picture.
❑ Find picture no. 4. Draw a diagram of this organism and label its parts.

a) What is the name of the organism in picture no.4?

❑ Look at pictures 2,3, and 5. Draw these organisms, name them and label them.
❑ Pictures 6,7 and 8 show larger organisms which you may have seen in ponds. Select one, study it, draw it and write down its name.

▲ | EXTENSION
▲ | **ACTIVITY   Looking at pond water with a microscope**

You will need some pond water, a microscope, and a microscope slide.

❑ Put a drop of pond water on a micro-scope slide. Cover it with a cover slip.

❑ Observe the pond water through the microscope.
❑ Daw any oprganism that you see.

Compare what you draw with the pictures on the next page. Can you recognise any of the organisms?

The photographs below show some organisms that you may have seen in ponds. Record the ones you have seen before.

figs 3.6.4a, b, c a/w
Paramecium, Euglena, Chilomonas.

figs 3.6.5a, b, c microphotos
mosquito larva, daphnia, and a nemotode worm

(many from BLS I p.69)

Micro-organisms in water

We cannot see the harmful micro-organisms in water, but we know that they are there because of what they do to us. They give us pain and diarrhoea. To make the water safe to drink, the micro-organisms must be killed.

It is possible to destroy micro-organisms by using heat, or chemicals, or radiation. This process is called **sterilisation**.

In the next activity you are going to investigate different ways of sterilising water from a river or open well. You will use the water to make milk.

▲ | ACTIVITY   Preparing milk using river water

You will need three bottles with stoppers, some milk powder, and some sterilising solution. You will also need apparatus for boiling water, unless your teacher has already prepared some boiled water.

The bottles must be sterilised. This can be done by leaving them overnight in sterilising liquid. This may have been done for you already.
Prepare three bottles of milk as shown in the diagrams .

Bottle A
Water sterilised by boiling

figs 3.6.6
a,b,c

milk made
with boiled
water

Bottle B
Water sterilised with sterilising liquid

milk made
with unboiled
water and
sterilising liquid

Bottle C
Water not sterilised

milk made
with unboiled
water

- ❏ Boil some water for about 15 minutes. Let it cool.
- ❏ Pour 100 cm3 of this water into bottle A.
- ❏ Add 5 cm3 of milk powder and stir or shake well.

- ❏ Pour 100 cm3 water into bottle B. Add 2 cm3 of sterilising liquid.
- ❏ Add 5 cm3 of milk powder and stir or shake well.

- ❏ Pour 100 cm3 water into bottle C.
- ❏ Add 5 cm3 of milk powder and stir or shake well.

- ❏ Leave the bottles until the next day. Describe the look and the smell of the milk in each bottle.

a. Which bottle of milk is unsafe to drink? Explain why you think so.
b. Which two methods can be used to kill harmful micro-organisms?

c. If you were to prepare a bottle of milk for a baby using milk powder, which method would you use? Give reasons.
d. Why were the bottles sterilised before use?

Boiling water for 15 minutes kills harmful micro-organisms. Whenever you use water from open wells and rivers make sure you boil it before drinking.

For very young babies **all** water must be boiled before they use it.
Sterilising liquids are not usually used in homes, except for cleaning baby bottles.

Making pure water

Filtering water removes solid matter. Boiling water kills micro-organisms. But even after these processes, the water will contain dissolved salts. Sometimes we want to remove **all** impurities from the water, including the dissolved salts.

Water with nothing else in it is **pure water.**

Pure water is needed for car batteries, steam irons and in steam engines used in industry.

● | EXERCISE

1. To get pure water we can use **distillation.** Look back to the activity you did on distillation (p.00). Write a paragraph, in your own words, describing what happens when a solution is distilled.

During boiling only water turns into steam. Dissolved and undissolved impurities are left behind. The steam moves through the side-arm, is cooled, and condenses back to pure water. A distillation apparatus is often called a **still.**

Pure water can be bought in shops in bottles labelled 'Distilled Water'. Using distillation to get pure water is costly.

Why do you think is it costly?

Scientists are now developing more economic stills using heat from the Sun. Some of these experimental **solar stills** are used in the Kgalagadi and Gantsi Districts to remove the salty taste from the water in the area. The process is called **desalination.**

fig 3.6.7 photo
Communal stills at Khawa

Communal stills at Khawa

▲ | ACTIVITY Make your own solar still

You will need a plastic bowl, a sheet of plastic, a beaker, and some tape or elastic to tie the plastic sheet to the bowl.

❏ Set up your solar still like the one shown here. Note that the plastic sheet is pressed down by a stone. Place the beaker directly under this stone.
❏ Place your still in the sunlight for 3 hours or more.

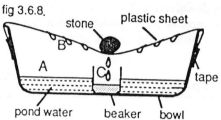

fig 3.6.8.

a) Explain what is happening at each of the places labelled A, B, and C on the diagram.
b) Does the solar still produce water that is safe to drink? Explain your answer.
c) What would happen if you did not place the stone on the plastic sheet?

d) You could also make a solar still by digging a hole in the ground. Think how this could be done. Make a drawing to show what you would do.

The drawing here shows a solar still like the ones used in Khawa and other Kgalagadi settlements. The water there is very salty. The stills are used to make water without salt. This is called desalinated water.

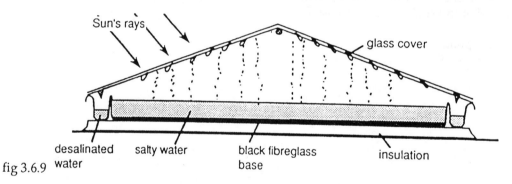

fig 3.6.9

● | EXERCISE

2. Why is the fibreglass base painted black?
3. Where does condensation take place?
4. Where does the desalinated water collect?
5. What happens to the salt?

Each solar still can purify 4 litres of water per day.

6. How many stills will be needed to desalinate 20 litres of water per day?
7. Suppose there are 25 families in a village. If each family needs 20 litres of desalinated water per day, how many stills will be needed?

The Caribbean

The Caribbean Examinations Council (CXC) syllabuses for integrated science as an examination subject at the grade 10 level are in four parts as follows:

Part 1

SCIENCE IN THE HOME

the structure of living organisms
asexual reproduction
sexual reproduction in higher plants
formation of fruits and seeds
parts of a seed
germination and growth
puberty and adolescence
sexual reproduction in mammals
population control
sexually transmitted diseases
nutrition in man
types of food
a balanced diet
teeth
nutrition in green plants
diffusion and osmosis
transport in plants
circulation and the blood
respiration
air and breathing
excretion
heat transfer
nervous and endocrine systems
parasitic diseases
pests and pesticides
micro-organisms
water for life
using water in the home
hard and soft water
water pollution
when is electricity dangerous?
materials that conduct electricity
measuring electricity
resistance and power
Mrs Singh's electricity bill
fuses, plugs, flexes and transformers
electric lighting
using electricity to communicate
oil is important
from oil to plastics
the sun has the power, we need the
energy metals and us
rusting and its prevention
pH, acids, bases and salts
analysis - what is there and how much?
using chemicals with care

Part 2

SCIENCE IN THE WORKPLACE

ventilation
how hot is it?
air-borne diseases
smoking and respiratory tract diseases
sanitation
easing our daily chores
using simple machines
soil - its formation and components
food chains and ecosystems
our aquatic environment

Part 3

SCIENCE IN SPORT

physical activity and body functions
drugs and athlete
leisure and recreation
projectiles
materials used in sport
the camera and the eye
colour
making the light bend
bouncing light off surfaces
light and shadow
making music
how we hear sounds

Part 4

SCIENCE IN TRANSPORT

defence, repair, damage and infection
maintaining balance
floating and sinking
moving through water
forces and motion
the carbon, nitrogen and water cycles
air masses and their effects
tides and their effects
volcanoes and earthquakes
energy changes that make things happen
stored energy and energy in motion
wave motion

The Netherlands

Two examples from the integrated science project for 12-16 year olds and one example from the primary science project are given below:

One of the functions of your clothes is to absorb moisture from your skin. Clothes do this without really getting wet themselves.
The moisture they absorb is then given out to the atmosphere.

In the next experiment we are going to measure how much water different types of cloth absorb. We are going to do this by measuring the maximum amount absorbed. So the cloth is going to get very wet.

Task 4.4 You are going to measure how much water different types of texiles can absorb.

 You will need:
- Strips of cloth from different types of textiles, 2 cm. broad and 50 cm. long
- a pair of tweezers, a pair of scissors and a ruler
- a beaker and a measuring jug
- something on which you can leave the pieces to dry

a. Fill the measuring jug with exactly 100 ml. of water and pour this into the beaker.
b. With the help of the tweezers, soak one of the strips of cloth in the water for about half a minute.
c. Take the strip out and let the water in it drain into the beaker.
d. When it has almost stopped dripping, hang it up or leave it to dry.
e. Pour the water from the beaker back into the measuring jug and take a reading of how much water there is.
f. Calculate how much water is left in the strip of cloth.
g. Note down your results in the format given below.
h. Repeat steps a to g for different types of textiles. Remember that if you want to make a fair comparison all your strips of cloth must have the same length and the same breadth.

Type of Material	Amount of water absorbed in ml.
	100 - = ml.

Figure 1 Fragment   from the theme "My Clothes" (second version), project Integrated Science 12-16

Figure 3 "What belongs to which shadow?"
        Fragment from "Natural Science in lessons",
        project Natural Science at primary level

Reproduced from the unit *Milk* of the project Integrated Science 12-16, by permission of the National Institute for Curriculum Development of the Dutch Ministry of Education.

A part of the food we eat is called "building materials". These "building materials" look after growth, maintenance and repair in our bodies.

Task 3.7 Who needs more "building materials" - a calf or a fully grown cow? Why?

_____

_____

Milk contains "building materials": milk proteins and calcium.

A part of the food we eat is called "energy producing materials". These "energy producing materials" give our bodies energy.

Task 3.8 Who needs more "energy producing material" - a calf left loose in a meadow or a calf that is tied up in a stall? Why?

_____

Milk contains energy producing materials: Milk fat and milk sugar.

A part of the food we eat is called "protective materials". These materials protect us from diseases and infection.

Task 3.9 In the first milk that a calf drinks from its mother, there is extra protective material. Can you think of reasons why this is so?

_____

The protective materials in milk are vitamins.

Because milk contains building materials, energy producing materials and protective materials, we say that milk is a complete food. It has a high nutritional value.

Figure 2 Fragment from the theme "Milk" (first version), project Integrated Science 12-16

The Philippines

Sample lessons in integrated science have been issued by the Department of Education, Culture and Sports in the Philippines as guides to teachers. Some pages from these lessons are given below:

Reproduced from *Science - Technology - Society*, Diwa Learning systems Inc., by permission of the Department of Education, Culture and Sports of the Philippines.

SAMPLE LESSONS IN INTEGRATED SCIENCE

By ERLINDA Y. BASA

Researcher, Enviromental Science Workgroup,
Institute for Science and Mathematics Education Development
University of the Philippines

TOPIC: Water: Its Use and Conservation

I. **Objectives:** After finishing the lesson, the students should be able to do the following with at least 75% success:

1. list all the ways in which they use water in their homes;
2. estimate by counting the number of litres of water their family consume in one day;
3. infer from data the amount of water used by certain activities and water consumed per family;
4. distinguish the types of faucets;
5. identify the parts of a faucet;
6. summarize the steps involved in fixing a leaking faucet;
7. explain the information indicated by the entries on a water bill
8. make accurate water meter readings registered in different water meter diagrams;
9. compute for the amount of water used in a month and the cost of water consumed.

II. **Pre-requisite** Concepts / Skills:
Your students should possess the following mental / process skills before taking up this lesson:

1. Measure volumes of liquids;
2. Identify the mL, cm³ , and litre   as the units used in measuring volumes;
3. Make estimations on the volume of liquids;
4. State some physical and chemical properties of water;
5. Explain the water cycle with the use of a diagram; and
6. Distinguish surface water from ground water.

III. **Lesson Proper**

A. **Motivation:**

    Ask your students to give all the ways they and their families use water.
them classify the uses of water in their homes into two groups: the necessary ι
water (drinking, cooking, bathing, etc.) and luxury use (swimming pools,
sprinklers, air conditioners, etc. If no luxury use is given, ask them to give examples.
Ask them in which of the activities they mentioned, did they use the greatest amount
of water; the least amount of water.

B. **Activity 1** - How Much Water Does Your Family Use?
    Preliminary Activity: Before doing Activity 1, have students observe for 2 or 3
days water consumption in their homes   so they can more accurately estimate
consumption later.

10

Distribute *Worksheet #1*. Have them find out how much water they use in one day. Tell them to make a list of the activities that require the use of water in the homes. Remind them that they should concentrate their listing on the use of water in the home. If you see that some have difficulty making estimations, give them the following measurements:

1 teaspoon	-	5 mL	- 12000 mL or 12 litres
1 cup	-	250 mL	- 1000 mL
1 glass	-	330 mL	
1 pail	-	1 litre	

While they are doing the activity, make Table A on the board

Table A

Activities	F_1	F_2	F_3	....Ave.
1.				
2.				
Total amount of water consumed				

Legend: F = family

Post Activity Discussion:

Have them examine Table A and ask them to rank the activities from the greatest to the least user of water. Then ask the following questions:

Which activity uses the greatest amount of water?
Which activity uses the least amount of water?
Is the given amount of water used in each activity by each family the same, or is it different?
If they differ, what could have contributed to the difference?
(Show data about amount of water used in a given activity)
Could the families use less water for the same purpose? How?
Would the time of day or month affect the amount of water you used for each activity? Cite examples.
Which attitudes are important? needs conservation?

Ask them to make generalizations from their analysis of Table A. Their generalizations should include the relation between amount used and number of members in a family, between lifestyle and amount used.

Brainstorming:

Present the following situation: (This situation emphasizes the need for all to conserve water.)

Eduardo and his family use up a great amount of water. As head of the family, Eduardo says their use of much water is all right because they can afford to pay for the water even if it costs 100 times as much. How would you react to this?

Tell them to form groups and discuss among themselves. After about 5-10 minutes, ask one member of each group to report about their discussions.

11

Ask the students from which of these sources do they get their water supply and how do they obtain their water from these source. Review them on the water cycle to show how surface water, ground water and rain water are formed. Refer to ISMED module on *Ground Water and Surface Water* for more information about them.

Show illustrations of the different types of faucet. Ask them to point out the type of faucet they are using at home and the different parts of the faucet. Let them explain how the faucets in their home work. It would be better if you show them actual samples of faucets particularly the screw type. Have at least one working (actual) model.

Find out how often they use their faucets each day and what happens to their faucet with constant use. This will lead them to answer that sometimes their faucets leak. Follow up your questioning as to the causes of a leaking faucet and what is to be done about it.

Ask how many have leaking faucets at home or once, have a leaking faucet. Have them find out how much water is wasted from a leaking faucet. Assign those with leaking faucets at home to measure water lost from a leaking faucet. Tell them to set a container under a leaking faucet for one hour. Measure the amount of water they collected. Then multiply the amount by 24 to obtain the amount of water wasted in one day.

Give some data about water being wasted from a leaking faucet.

Kinds of flow	Amount of water wasted
slow drip stream of water	3 Kerosene cans of water a day or 67.5 litres daily 80 Kerosene cans of water a day
0.8 mm diameter hole (as big as a ballpen point)	as much as 900 litres daily
3.2 mm diameter hole (as big as a mongo bean)	as much as 14,000 litres daily

C. **Activity 2** - Repairing a Leaking Faucet

Have the students find out how much water is lost in one day from the data you gave them about the kinds of leak from a faucet, e.g. How much water is lost in one day from a faucet that drips slowly?

Ask them how can they stop this loss of water. Students should suggest fixing the faucet. If nobody can give the correct answer, give a hint on what must be done with the faucet. Ask them if they know how to repair a leaking faucet. Tell them that they will be doing this in the next activity.

Distribute *Worksheet #2* and have them to do the activity in groups. After the activity, discuss with the students their answers to the questions given in the worksheet. Point out that with a leaky faucet, they do not only waste water. They also waste

12

175

money. Ask them why. It should come out from their answers that water flowing from their faucet is being measured with a water meter. The measured water is what they are billed for, which they have to pay.

Find out what they know about a water bill. Show them copies of a water bill and ask them what a water bill contains. Tell them that the amount of water consumed is actually measured by their water meter.

Show drawing of a water meter and explain how it works. Discuss how water consumption is measured by the 2 types of water meter. Give some exercises. Let them locate and read the school's watermeter. Determine consumption over a period of time, say one month.

Activity 3 - Computing water consumption in a month. Distribute *Worksheet #3* and instruct them to do the activity individually. You should go around to see that the students are doing the activity correctly.

Post-lab discussion:

Ask them the procedure for computing monthly consumption of water. Find out their answers on the questions on the worksheet.

Give them the MWSS metered rates per month and have them compute for the cost of water that was consumed in one month. Tell them to use the amount of water they computed in the worksheet.

D. Evaluation:

Choose the best answer and write the letter of your answer on the space provided before each number.

1. Suppose each member of a family of six drinks 8 glasses of water and one glass of milk daily, how many litres of drinking water would the family consume? (1 glass - 300 mL)
   - a. 2.0 litres
   - b. 2.3 litres
   - c. 2.5 litres
   - d. 2.7 litres

Questions 2-4 refer to the table which shows the amount of water consumed in litres by 4 families when doing the given activities.

Activity	F_2	F_3	F_6	F_{12}
1. washing clothes	48	120	100	130
2. cooking	24	40	36	24
3. bathing	48	300	80	100
4. drinking	4	6	9	20

2. Which activity in the Table showed a great increase in the amount of water consumed as a result of an increase in the number of members in the family?
   - a. washing clothes
   - b. cooking
   - c. bathing
   - d. drinking

3. Which family consumed the greatest amount of water?
   - a. F_2
   - *b. F_3
   - c. F_6
   - *d. F_{12}

13

4. Suppose a water shortage occurs in the community, which of the activities can be minimized by the families?
   - A. cooking food
   - B. drinking
   - C. washing clothes
   - D. bathing
   - a. A and B
   - *b. C and D
   - c. A and C
   - d. B and D

5. Which of the following measures the amount of water consumed in a certain period?
   - a. faucet
   - b. well
   - c. water bil
   - * d. water meter

6. A faucet is a device that
   - a. stops the flow of water.
   - b. allows the water to flow out.
   - c. increases the flow of water.
   - * d. controls the flow of water.

Questions 7 and 8 refer to the following meters.

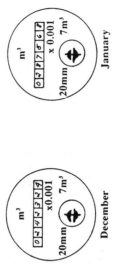

December   January

7. How much water was consumed in January?
   - a. 4.524 m³
   - b. 45.000 m³
   - *c. 45.244 m³
   - d. 452.440 m³

8. How much will you pay for your water that you consumed in January if the cost per m³ is P 4.50?
   - *a. P202.50
   - b. P203.40
   - c. P302.75
   - d. P450.00

L. Assignment:

For those who did not reach the 75% score, find out by asking them to raise their hands which part of the test they missed/have incorrect answers. Assign them to review on the topics they failed to answer correctly.

For those who reach the 75%, give them the following questions:

1. How does water from rivers reach the users?
2. What processes are involved in making water safe to drink? Explain each process.

14

Appendix A

Worksheet #1

How Much Water Does Your Family Use?

Water is used in the homes for a variety of purposes. It is used in keeping our homes and things clean. It is also necessary in the preparation and cooking of food. Have you ever thought how much water is used in each activity in the home?

In this activity you will estimate the amount of water you use in the home.

Procedure:

Recall all the activities in which you and your family use water. Estimate the approximate number of cups you use in each activity. Then convert the number of cups to litres. There are about four and a half cups of water in one litre.

Make estimates on the number of cups of water your family used in cooking breakfast, lunch, supper, snack. Give the approximate number of cups of water you and the other members of your family drink for one day. This includes the milk, soup, softdrinks, etc. you take. Repeat the same procedure in estimating the amount of water you use in the other activities you listed down. Record your answers in Table 1.

Table 1 Amount of Water Consumed in the Home

Activities	Approximate amount of water consumed . (litres)
1. drinking	
2.	
3.	
TOTAL	

Questions:

1. How many litres of water did your family used in one day?
2. Which activity in the home required a large amount of water? the least amount of water?
3. Which of these activities do you consider important? needs conservation?
4. Whenever the number of people in a family increases, the amount of water that they use also increases. How would you explain the observation that some families with fewer members use much more water than families with more members?

Appendix B

Worksheet #2   Repairing a Leaky Faucet

The most common leak that usually happens in your home is the leak from your faucet. The main cause of leaks in the faucet is a worn-out washer or "zapatilla." It is easy to fix a leaking faucet especially if it is the screw type. Anybody can do it. You can do it. In this activity you will be given the procedure on how to repair a leaking faucet.

Materials: faucet, screw driver, monkey wrench or pliers, washer

Procedure:

1. Turn off the main valve to shut off all water coming into your house.
2. Unscrew the cap screw using a monkey wrench. The cap screw is found just below the handle of the faucet.
3. Remove the entire valve system and cap screw by turning the handle of the faucet.
4. Use the screw driver to remove the small screw which holds the washer in place.
5. Take out the worn washer and replace it with a new one of the same size. Make sure it is held firmly by putting back the small screw.
6. Now, set the valve system in the faucet and turn it in the direction to shut off water. Do not turn it all the way down.
7. Screw on the cap screw and tighten it with the monkey wrench. Now turn the handle all the way down.
8. Turn on the water at the main valve. Try turning the water on and off several times. Does the faucet still leak?

Questions:

1. Why must you know how to repair a leaky faucet?
2. Suppose you see a leaky faucet at home but there was no extra washer to use in replacing the worn out washer, what will you do? Explain your answer.
3. Many people rinse the clothes they are washing with water flowing continuously from the faucet. If you see your mother or sister doing it what will you do?
4. You noticed that a leaky faucet from your neighbor's house has not been fix for se days, which of the following will you do and why?
   a. tell them to call a plumber and have it fixed
   b. volunteer to fix it if you know that nobody knows how to fix it
   c. do nothing since it's none of your business
5. Think of other ways you/your family consume less water.

Appendix C

Worksheet #3

Computing Water Consumption in a Month

Many homes in the cities and towns have faucets. It is very likely that they have water meters too. A water meter is an instrument used to measure the amount of water flowing through the pipe. It registers the amount of water consumed during a period of time. The cubic meter (m^3) is the common unit for measuring the amount of water consumed. Below are drawings of the two types of water meters. What are the readings on the two meters?

Round Reading Meter

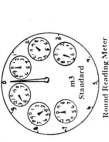

Straight Reading Meter

The correct readings are 0430.960 m³ and 0672.625 m³ for the round reading meter and the straight reading meter, respectively. Did you get the correct answer? If you did, skip the following exercise and proceed to the computation of water consumption. If you did not get the correct answer in one or both meters, then do the following exercise.

Study the dials in the water meter. Then complete the following statements.

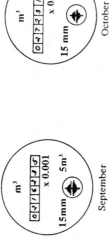

A.
1. The first dial at the right of the center sweep hand shows the water consumed is 40 litres
2. The second dial on the right is 300 litres.
3. The third dial is 2 cubic metres.
4. The fourth dial is 80 cubic metres.
5. The fifth dial is 500 cubic metres.
6. The sixth dial is 0 cubic metres.
7. The meter reading is 582.340 cubic metres.

B. Study the reading registered on the water meter
1. The first number on the right is 2 litres.
2. The second number is 50 litres.
3. The third number is 100 litres.
4. The fourth number is 4 cubic metres.
5. The fifth number is 20 cubic metres.
6. The sixth number is 300 cubic metres.
7. The seventh number is 0 cubic metres.
8. The meter reading is 0324.152 cubic metres.

Now, you are ready to compute for the water consumption in a month. When you compute the amount of water you consume in a month, the number of litres of water you used is not included. This amount is carried or added to the amount of water used the following month. Suppose the water meter reading for May is 0739.146 m³ and 0775.285 m³ in June, how many cubic metres of water was consumed in June? First consider only the m readings. Second, you get the difference between the readings, by subtracting the previous readings from the present readings, which is done as follows:

Reading in June	-	0775 m³
Reading in May	-	0739 m³
Water consumed in June	-	0036 m³

The difference between the number of liters of water used in May which is 0.146 litres, and 0.285 m³ in June will be added to the computation for July.

Now, you know how to read your water meter and to measure the amount of water you use. Read your water meter everyday and know your daily consumption. (You can try reducing the water you use daily so that you can save on your water bill. At the same time you help others who can not get enough water.)

17

Read and answer what is asked for in the following:
1. How much water was used by the Reyes family in one month if the previous monthly reading is 0498 m³ and the present reading is 0519 m³?
2. The meter readings in Mrs. Bueno's house for September, October, and November are shown below. Find the amount of water they consumed in October and in November.
3. How can you reduce your daily water consumption? Why is it important to decrease our water consumption?

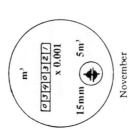

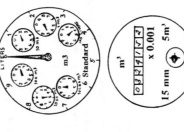

September

October

November

References:
MECS-LWUA. PROJECT WATER: Module 1-Measuring water consumption
MWSS. 1978. The MWSS Story.
Science Education Center. 1980. Keeping Water Safe to Drink. Diliman, Quezon City: University of the Philippines.
ISMED. 1984. Water in Your Community. Diliman, Quezon City: University of the Philippines.
_____. 1984. Water and Health. Diliman, Quezon City: University of the Philippines. Science Education Center 1980. Surface Water. Diliman Quezon City: U.P., Science Education Center
1980. Ground Water. Diliman Quezon City: U.P., Science Education Center

18

Sierra Leone

The core course integrated science syllabus for Sierra Leone is designed for the junior secondary level. The key topics from this syllabus are as follows:

Core course integrated science syllabus in Sierra Leone

Year 1

WATER	recognition of water
	water as a major component of living things
	water as a solvent
	water content of organisms
	water as a home for living things
	evaporation, condensation and the water cycle
	making water good to drink
	leaching and drainage
AIR	the nature of air
	where air found
	the importance of air
	air movement and pressure measuring winds
	using air pressure
	some things found in air
	air and living things
SOUND AND HEARING	investigating our own hearing
	the production and nature of sound
	the transmission of sound
	structure and care of the human ear
	sound and hearing in animals
	making simple musical instruments
VISION	judging distance, size and shape
	designing spectacles
	illumination
	colour and colour contrasts
	movement
	guessing distances - the advantages of binocular vision
	seeing in animals
	the inside of the eye
	making images
	prisms and colour
GROWTH	animate and inanimate growth
	measurement of growth
	growth zones and differentiation
	factors affecting growth

Year 2

MATERIALS AND MEASUREMENT	materials in the environment
	properties of materials
	what, how and why we measure
	making more measurements
	uses of materials
	investigation of building materials
ROCKS, STONES AND SOIL	classification of soils and soil profile
	formation and properties of soils
	rocks
	minerals
	soil ecosystem
	soil fertility
EARTH AND ITS TRUNKING	the movement of earth and moon around the sun
	the solar system
	the night sky
	observing the sky - the telescope
	space travel
PUSHES AND PULLS	field forces
	the effects of forces
	forces at work
	balancing forces
	forces and structures
FOOD	why do we need food ?
	what food do we need ?
	how do we get our food ?
	preparation and preservation of food digestion
	production of food

United Kingdom

1. Three pages from the SATIS project materials are given below to illustrate the science, technology and society approach to integrated science as suggested in this particular project in the UK.

DAM PROBLEMS

General Briefing

1 Introduction

Electricity generated from water is known as hydroelectric power, or HEP. HEP usually involves building huge dams and creating large reservoirs. This can seriously affect the environment. In this unit you will be looking at this problem.

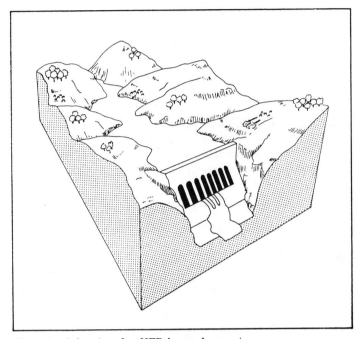

Figure 1   A drawing of an HEP dam and reservoir

Working in groups, you will be looking at the possible effect on the environment of three different HEP schemes. You will be making what is known as an **Environmental Impact Assessment**, or **EIA**. The purpose of an EIA is to give the decision-makers (politicians, industrialists and others) advice. The EIA gives advice on the likely environmental impact of different schemes. This advice is used when deciding which scheme to go ahead with.

There are four people in your EIA team. There are three scientists from the country's biggest university, and a politician. They are:

1   An **ecologist** who will look at the impact of the three HEP schemes on forests and fisheries

2   A **land use consultant** who will look at impacts on the way land is used, and soil erosion problems of the three schemes

3   A **sociologist** who will look at impacts on people's health and homes.

4   A **politician** (the Minister of Energy) who will make the final decision about which scheme should get the go-ahead.

THE LIMESTONE INQUIRY

General Briefing

You are going to take part in an imaginary Public Inquiry concerning a limestone quarry.

Limeco Ltd have a large limestone quarry set in beautiful country in the Peak District National Park in Derbyshire. Limeco have asked the National Park Authority for planning permission to extend the quarry. They want to double the amount of limestone produced. The Authority has refused permission. Limeco have appealed against the decision, and now there is to be a Public Inquiry.

You will be playing a part in the Inquiry, and later you will have to read a special briefing about that part. But first you should read the rest of this General Briefing.

What is limestone?

Limestone is calcium carbonate, $CaCO_3$. It is formed from the remains of organisms that lived in ancient seas 300 million years ago. The limestone that occurs in the Peak District is especially pure, so it very useful, particularly for the chemical industry.

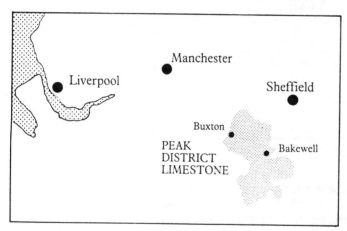

Figure 1 Map showing the Peak District

What happens in a limestone quarry?

Over a million tonnes of limestone are taken from the Limeco quarry every year. Explosives are used to blast the rock from the quarry face (Figure 2). The quarry face is 2 km long and 30m high.

The rock is loaded onto huge lorries and taken for sorting into pieces of different size. Part of the limestone is processed on the quarry site. It is used to make other things such as cement and quicklime. Part is carried away by rail or road to customers who use limestone itself. A lot of limestone is used for aggregate. Aggregate is lumps of rock or stone used to make concrete or in road-building.

Figure 2 Blasting limestone.
60 000 tonnes are blasted at a time

Part 2 The Story of Lin Xian

Lin Xian is a remote valley in China. Cancer of the gullet (oesophagus) is about one hundred times more common among the people who live in this valley than in the surrounding areas of China. This seems to have been the case for many centuries.

Why? It needed a team of scientists to find out the reason. You will see why as you look at the evidence and the deductions.

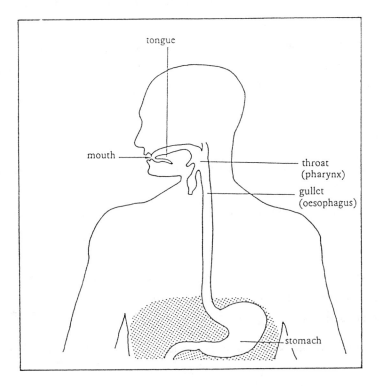

Figure 3

Evidence

- Analysis showed that the soil in the Lin Xian valley is short of the element molybdenum.

- The water supply in the valley was found to be high in chemicals called nitrites.

- The people of Lin Xian liked mouldy food. They ate mouldy bread, pickled cabbage rotted in water, and persimmon (a fruit) preserved in a crust of dried wheat husk.

- Wherever the people of Lin Xian valley had a high rate of cancer, so too did their chickens.

- The people in Lin Xian had a high level of nitrites in their bodies and a low level of vitamin C.

'A Study of Paper'

SCIENCE ACTIVITIES

STARTING POINT -

Collection of as many different kinds of paper as possible.

Have children sort these into different categories according to different criteria e.g. texture, size, colour, use, thickness, how easy it is to write on, smell, sound it makes when crumpled, how easily it tears etc.

From the above starting point can arise a great variety of practical activities. The activities suggested below are not in a hierarchical order, the actual choice and sequence is left to the teacher. She is in the best position to decide the stages of development of her pupils.

1. Size of paper -

    Ask children to measure the length and breadths of the whole sheets of paper from the collection.

    Are any of them standard sizes? (link with A4, A5, broadsheet, tabloid etc.)

2. Colour of paper -

    Ask the children to find out what happens to the coloured paper when it is submerged in water overnight. Is the colour 'fast'?

    Does adding detergent to the water have any effect?

    Children could try dyeing white paper using dyes made from natural substances such as lichens, onions, fruits etc.

    Investigate ways of making their dyes 'fast'.

3. Thickness of paper -

    Children could measure the thickness of different kinds of paper by taking 10, 20, 30 sheets and measuring the thickness of these in order to calculate the thickness of one sheet. They could make their own calipers for this purpose.

4. Uses of paper -

    Ask the children to write down as many uses as possible for paper.

    (writing, wrapping, tracing, drawing, typing, carrying articles as in paper bags etc.)

    Ask them to devise tests to find out the best paper for each use and to look for patterns.

Reproduced from *Document Series 19* (pp. 51-58) Unesco Division of Science, Technical and Environmental Education.

5. <u>Tearability of paper</u> –

Ask children to find out which paper is the easiest to tear. (It is advisable to limit the number of different kinds of paper to be tested in order to avoid confusion)

Normally children will initially do this by hand and it may be that the teacher will have to suggest that fairer methods should be used. A discussion on variables will arise at this point and time must be devoted to this most important aspect of scientific investigations.

The children should be encouraged to devise their own tests.

Here are a few suggestions :

At the start of each ask the children to predict which one they think will tear most easily.

(i) Cut strips 1 cm by 10 cm from each sample paper to be tested.

Fold the strip over an elastic band and hold the loose ends at the end of a ruler.

Gently but steadily pull the elastic band until the paper tears. Note the reading on the ruler. Repeat and take average result.

Repeat for the other strips, remembering to use the same elastic band. Why?

Compare results with predictions.

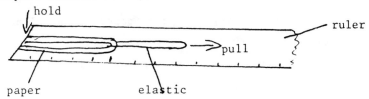

(ii) Cut strips of paper 5 cm by 10 cm from each sample to be tested.

Fold the strip over a loop of string and pin the loose ends to the edge of a table.

Add weight to the string until the paper tears. Repeat and find the average weight needed to tear the paper.

Repeat for the other strips and compare results.

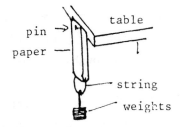

(iii) Cut strips of paper 2 cm by 10 cm from each sample to be tested.
Fold one end of the strip over a pencil and hold it in a bulldog
clip. Attach clip to a hook and fold other end round a pencil and
hold using another clip.
Add weights to the lower clip until the paper tears. Repeat and
find the average weight required to tear paper.
Repeat using other papers and compare results.

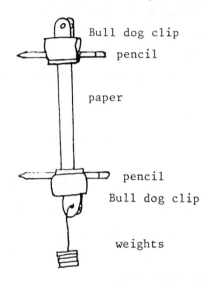

(iv) Try (i), (ii) and (iii) using strips of paper of same length but
different widths. Does this affect tearability?

(v) Try (i), (ii), and (iii) using strips of same width but different
lengths. Does this affect tearability?

6. Absorbency of paper -
   (i) Cut strips of paper 3 cm by 10 cm from each sample to be tested.
   Pin one end of each to a long piece of wood and lay the wood across
   the top of a clear plastic tank. Add water to the tank until it is
   about 1 cm up each of the strips of paper. Compare the height that
   the water rises up each strip.
   (ii) Lay 10 cm square pieces of paper across the top of a clear jar.
   Using a straw or dropper add water one drop at a time to the centre
   of the paper until the water drips through. Compare results.

The children could be asked to devise tests to find the strength of the
wet paper. This could be further extended by drying the paper and testing
its strength. Is there any difference between this and the original paper?

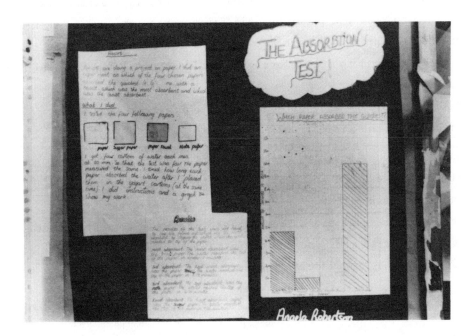

Example of child's chart on absorbency

7. <u>Newspapers</u> –

   (i) Survey of pupils in class to find out what daily newspapers are read in their houses. Graph results. Could extend this to other classes.

   (ii) Apply tearability tests from 5., but note take one newspaper only to begin with and compare its tearability across the print with up and down the print. Children will find that there is a difference.
   Ask them to tear the paper by hand, first across the print, then up and down the print. Ask them to examine the direction of the tear in each case and to look closely at the torn edge using a magnifier. What do they notice?
   Children should be able to see the fibres that make up paper.
   Which way do the fibres run?

   (iii) Apply absorbency tests to the newspaper.
      a) Drip ink or coloured water onto the surface of the paper.
         What shape is the blot? Is it circular or oval? Why?
      b) Cut strips of equal sizes from across and up and down the print.
         Suspend these so that one end is in coloured water or ink.
         How far up does the water / ink travel?
         Is it the same in both cases? Why?

Tests (ii) and (iii) can lead on to how paper is made and the way the fibres run.

   (iv) Try test (i) and (ii) with different newspapers. Are the results similar?
   If samples of tabloid and broadsheet papers are used the children will discover that the results are reversed.
   This again ties in with how the paper is made and then how it is used in the printing of the particular newspaper.
   Ask the children to fold the broadsheet newspaper in half and they will see it is the same size as the tabloid newspaper.

8. <u>Paper making</u> –
   This is a natural follow on to previous lesson.
   There are many books and pupil cards that give details of how to make paper from different scraps of paper torn into strips and left to soak or put in a liquidiser, before laying on a grid and pressed with felt.
   Children can compare their recycled papers using a variety of methods.

Stages in paper making.

Making paper from scrap paper   Pupil Sheet

1. Tear the scrap paper into strips.

2. Steep the torn strips in water overnight.

3. Stir the pulp mixture thoroughly.

4. Add some Kaolin, so as to give the mixture a milky consistency.

5. Place the sieve and the frame in the dish as shown.

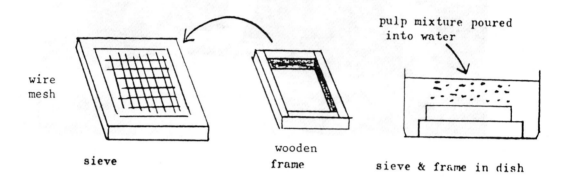

wire mesh

sieve

wooden frame

pulp mixture poured into water

sieve & frame in dish

6. Pour the pulp mixture into the frame, trying to distribute it as evenly as possible.

7. Keeping the frame in position, lift the sieve out of the dish, and place it on the newspaper.

8. Remove the frame.

9. Place the felt on top of the pulp which is spread out on the frame, and then roll the felt firmly.

10. Lift the felt carefully. The pulp should adhere to it as a wet sheet.

11. Place the felt, with the pulp sheet uppermost, on the newspaper.

12. Carefully lift a corner of the pulp sheet from the felt, and peel off the whole sheet.

13. Lay the sheet out to dry.

Try writing, drawing on your paper using different types of pens and inks.

Which give the best results?

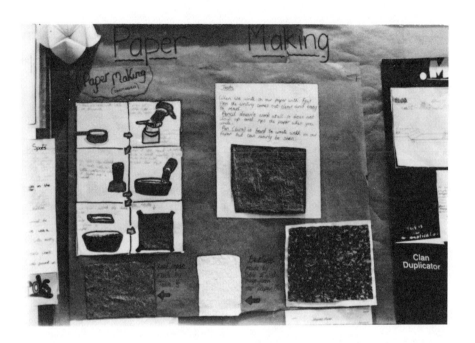

Paper making chart.

Part IV

Bibliography

Annotated bibliography of integrated science teaching

Judith Reay

Introduction

This annotated bibliography samples publications from 1978 to 1988.

The term 'integrated science' teaching is used in a broad sense here, covering such topics as science, society and technology and a variety of matters of concern to any science educator. Levels include primary, secondary, higher, vocational and teacher education. It has been necessary to limit coverage to items dealing with integration across the whole curriculum, such as primary education in a general sense, as well as environmental education. Also excluded are teaching materials sold by commercial organizations, which have their own means of dissemination.

Otherwise, this is not a selective bibliography in the sense of being evaluative. In an attempt to meet the needs and resources of educators worldwide, the sample aims to represent as many local publications as possible, together with a selection of internationally-known items. Only English language publications have been perused.

The literature over the decade since the bibliography prepared by Benning et al. in *New Trends in Integrated Science Teaching*, Vol. V, reveals an evolution in science education more or less in accordance with the trends identified by Haggis and Adey in 1978 in the same *New Trends*. There is also now more opportunity for educators to find a medium in which to publish their work and views, and it is those professionals who have made this bibliography possible.

The bibliography contains more than 370 entries which are arranged chronologically by year. Within each year the entries are arranged alphabetically by title.

Each entry has a master file number, which is a sequential number assigned by Unesco's Computerised Documentation System (CDS/ISIS). The bibliographical entries section is followed by indexes for subject, author, meetings and corporate bodies, and title and series. Each bibliographical entry contains an annotated description of the subject and a set of key words used in the subject index.

BIBLIOGRAPHY : MAIN ENTRIES

00001 - **The Activity approach in school science learning: foundations, theory and practice, with special reference to Science 5-13 Project and Nuffield 'O' Level Physics Programme.** Mwakyembe, Genesis R.A. London, Centre for Science Education, Chelsea College, University of London, 1978. 155 p. (eng). (Unpublished M.ED. (Science Education) dissertation). // University of London. Chelsea College

The concern of the author, a Tanzanian teacher trainer, is a science teaching and learning approach to meet the goals of Tanzania's Education for Self Reliance in the face of entrenched content-centred practice. Chapter V (90-114) includes a review of the methods of Science 5-13 and its strengths. Drawbacks identified include problems of communication between teacher and child, unreasonable expectations of teachers' work, and societal resistance.

Keywords: primary school curriculum; teaching methods; learning methods; activity learning; Tanzania UR – teacher student relationship; teacher role; pressure groups; physics education; upper secondary education.

Identifiers: "Education for Self-reliance" (Tanzania UR) // Schools Council Science 5-13 Project (UK) // Nuffield 0-level Physics Programme (UK) //

00002 - **The Analysis of science curricula for Piagetian level of demand.** Shayer, Michael. Leeds, UK, Leeds University Centre for Studies in Science Education, 1978. p. 115-130. (Studies in science education; 5) (eng). // Leeds University (UK). Centre for Studies in Science Education

Describes a study based on the analysis of the Nuffield Combined Science curriculum together with the results of tests on a sample of first year pupils who had followed the course for a term. The conclusion is that, given an adequate exposure to a science course, pupils' performance is mostly determined by the level of thinking that pupils have attained. The author reflects on the origin of Nuffield Combined Science (for a selective school population) and considers the implications for comprehensive school pupils. He suggests an approach to arriving at a course suitable for a particular class.

Keywords: lower secondary education; educational psychology; child development; academic achievement; curriculum evaluation; UK – ability grouping; comprehensive schools.

Identifiers: Nuffield Combined Science (UK) //

00003 - **Consumer science and comparison shopping: a short interdisciplinary course.** Zipko, Stephen J. Washington, Heldref, 1978. p. 29-36. (Science activities; 15, 2) (eng).

A ten-day minicourse in consumerism is described which utilizes outside speakers, experiments, audiovisual material, and field trips to local stores. This is a junior high school course but is adaptable to elementary, secondary or college level.

Keywords: consumer education; learning modules; activity learning; short courses; USA – home economics education; lower secondary education.

00004 - **Curriculum and language: an investigation of a science curriculum in two cultural settings.** Isa, A.M. Norwich, UK, University of East Anglia, 1978. (1 v. in various pagings). (eng). (Unpublished Ph.D. thesis). // University of East Anglia (UK)

This study in the context of Scottish Integrated Science was carried out with Scottish and Malaysian children aged 13+. The former responded in English and the latter in Malay. Scientific terms had more everyday meaning for the Scottish children than for the Malaysian, and the learning materials were found to be related to the Scottish culture but not to the Malaysian.

Keywords: education and culture; language barriers; language of instruction; comparative education; UK; Malaysia – teaching materials; educational relevance.

Identifiers: Scottish Integrated Science Project (UK) //

00005 - **Curriculum development for astronomy and earth sciences in Japan.** Inamori, Jun. Tokyo, Japan Society of Science Education, 1978. p. 209-213. (Journal of science education in Japan; II, 4) (eng). // Japan Society of Science Education

Explains that Earth Sciences is a course of study for senior secondary schools in Japan, an integrated science course including astronomy, meteorology, geophysics, geochemistry and geology. Describes the history of the curriculum and summarises it.

Keywords: curriculum development; earth sciences; astronomy; physical sciences; upper secondary education; Japan.

00006 - **A Detailed teaching scheme for integrated science.** Hong Kong, HKASME, 1978. p. 46-96. (Journal of the Hong Kong Association for Science and Mathematics Education; VI, 2) (eng). //

Hong Kong Association for Science and Mathematics Education. Integrated Science Sub-committee

Seeing the need to help teachers, the Association set up a working party. The outcome, presented here, is a sample set of detailed notes for the teacher (including options for less able and more able pupils). Even without the official scheme to which these notes relate, they are of interest as one attempt to provide aid to teachers who have the usual problems.

Keywords: curriculum guides; teaching guides; classroom techniques; Hong Kong – ability grouping.

00007 - **Elementary school science.** Karplus, Robert; Hall, William C.; Elstgeest, Jos; Morris, Robert W.; Dyasi, Hubert M.; Warren, Keith; Herandez, Dolores F.; Alabi, Rufus. Paris, Unesco, 1978. p. 47-109. (Prospects: quarterly review of education; VIII, 1) (eng; also in ara, fre, spa). // Unesco

This dossier consists of eight short papers giving inputs from USA, Asia and the Pacific and Africa. Reference is made to science programmes in these regions in the context of aims and strategies of science education, problems of mathematics and language of instruction, resources and teacher education.

Keywords: primary school curriculum; educational aims; teaching strategies – concepts; language of instruction; child development; mathematics education; teacher education; USA; Australia; Africa; Asia; Philippines; Nigeria.

00008 - **Geology, earth science and the core curriculum: geology and the Nuffield Combined Science course.** Fleming, D.A.; Sidley, M.J. Keele, UK, Association of Teachers of Geology, 1978. p. 35-37. (Geology teaching; III, 1) (eng). // Association of Teachers of Geology (UK)

Nuffield Combined Science has no geology, so the school has put some in. The modified scheme is outlined.

Keywords: earth sciences; geology education; lower secondary education; secondary school curriculum; UK.

Identifiers: Nuffield Combined Science (UK) //

00009 - **Geology, earth science and the core curriculum: geology in the Schools Council Integrated Science Project (SCISP).** Weaver, Rosemary. Keele, UK, Association of Teachers of Geology, 1978. p. 37-42. (Geology teaching; III, 1) (eng). // Association of Teachers of Geology (UK)

The author outlines practice in her school, together with some problems. Earth science integrates physics, chemistry and biological sciences as well. The pupils have been enthusiastic.

Keywords: earth sciences; geology education; upper secondary education; secondary school curriculum; student attitudes; UK.

Identifiers: Schools Council Integrated Science Project (UK) //

00010 - **History, science and technology.** Hennessey, R.A.S. London, HMSO, 1978. p. 20-25. (Trends in education; 1, Spring1978) (eng). // UK. Dept of Education and Science

The author, a history educator, argues that history has a clear and central role to play in developing a curriculum to prepare young people for life in a technology-based society. He develops working definitions of science, technology and history. In fact, he seems to advocate the injection of science and technology into history courses, but one should beware of pitfalls.

Keywords: science and technology; history education; general education; educational relevance.

00011 - **Integrated science.** Hall, William C. Paris, Unesco, 1978. p. 58-65. (Prospects: quarterly review of education; VIII, 1) (eng; also in fre, spa). // Unesco

The writer summarises changes in primary and elementary science in the previous decade and proposes a model (concepts-processes-content) which can be used to characterise all methods of teaching science. He illustrates with curricula in a variety of countries. Trends include change from content to process emphasis, discovery, increasing relevance, environmental science, use of objectives and learning theories, links to other subjects, and curriculum development. He stresses the need to improve the science background of teachers, especially if they are to teach integrated science, and encouraging them to produce their own courses.

Keywords: primary school curriculum; educational trends; teaching method innovations – primary school teachers; primary teacher education; educational aims; concepts; educational relevance; environmental education; learning processes; skill development; educational psychology.

00012 - **Integrated science at all levels.** Adey, Philip S. Tokyo, Japan Society of Science Education, 1978. p. 203-209. (Journal of science education in Japan; II, 4) (eng). // Japan Society of Science Education

Outlines the better-known integrated science curricula of the UK and shows that there is great variety. There is an attempt to convey what is meant by integrated science and a brief mention of some of its advantages.

Keywords: curriculum; UK.

00013 - **Integrated science education worldwide.** Chisman, Dennis. London, ICASE, 1978. 122 p. (eng). // International Council of Associations for Science Education // International Conference on Integrated Science Education Worldwide, Nijmegen, Netherlands, 1978

Includes summaries of the working group discussions (which formed the basis of the chapters in "New Trends in Integrated Science Teaching", v.5) as well as a list of papers submitted to the groups. Of special value is the full text of the plenary lectures.

Keywords: curriculum development – teacher education; primary school curriculum; secondary school curriculum; university curriculum; environmental education; health education; nutrition education.

00014 - **Integrated science for the less able.** Kellington, Steuart H.; Mitchell, Alison C. Harlow, UK, Longman Journals Divisons, 1978. p. 129-134. (Remedial education; XIII, 3) (eng).

The article was written shortly after the revision of Scottish Integrated Science to improve its suitability for pupils over the whole ability range, special attention being paid to the needs and problems of the less able. It outlines the procedure for the revision, and improved flexibility. It also outlines the various procedures for evaluating the revision, and the broad findings, which were encouraging.

Keywords: lower secondary education; low achievers; ability grouping – curriculum development; curriculum evaluation.

Identifiers: Scottish Integrated Science Project (UK) //

00015 - **Integrated science: reasons and constraints.** Fox, M.; Oliver, P.M. Hatfield, UK, ASE, 1978. p. 16-19. (Education in science; 79) (eng). // Association for Science Education (UK)

In their secondary school the authors modified "Science for the 70s" for Years 1 and 2, Nuffield Secondary Science for Year 3 and SCISP for Years 3 to 5. They met difficulties including laboratory facilities, money, technician assistance, and resistance from colleagues and administrators.

Keywords: secondary school curriculum; project implementation – teacher attitudes; school laboratories; educational administrators; UK.

Identifiers: Scottish Integrated Science Project (UK) // Nuffield Secondary Science (UK) // Schools Council Integrated Science Project (UK) //

00016 - **Latest development in Scottish Integrated Science.** Kellington, Steuart H.; Mitchell, Alison C. Hatfield, UK, ASE, 1978. p. 725-733. (School science review; 209) (eng). // Association for Science Education (UK)

The article begins with a brief history of the Scottish Integrated Science Project and then explains why a revision was needed. It gives the aims and objectives of the revised course, the design of the course materials, and describes the trials and evaluation. Practising teachers were heavily involved. Notes that the work is part of a process of continuous development.

Keywords: lower secondary education; curriculum development; UK – curriculum evaluation; ability grouping.

Identifiers: Scottish Integrated Science Project (UK) //

00017 - **Nuffield Combined Science: do the pupils understand it?** Shayer, Michael. Hatfield, UK, ASE, 1978. p. 210-223. (School science review; 211) (eng). // Association for Science Education (UK)

This curriculum supposed to be suitable for children in all-ability schools, is the most used of all Nuffield curricula. The author, well known for his techniques of analysing Piagetian development, shows that the structured development of concepts leaves most children behind before the end-points are reached (e.g. density as a weight to volume/ratio concept, pressure as a force per unit area concept). He points out that curriculum development has been carried out by people from the experience of the (able) children they had taught and their own development, but that today's school population is not achieving mastery of the minimal objectives.

Keywords: physics education; lower secondary education; curriculum development; secondary school curriculum; UK – learning processes; student evaluation; academic achievement.

Identifiers: Nuffield Combined Science (UK) //

00018 - **On the Nuffield philosophy of science.** Stevens, Paul. Oxford, UK, Carfax Publishing, 1978. p. 99-111. (Journal of the Philosophy of Education Society of Great Britain; XII) (eng). // Philosophy of Education Society of Great Britain

Explores the terms heuristic method, hypothesis, discovery, direct observation and the Nuffield Spirit. Generally, he criticises some of the theory underlying modern science courses and the way it works in practice. He sees an important incompatibility between learning and discovering. The errors can give rise to psychological mistakes. We need a different balance between discovery methods and more traditional demonstration methods.

Keywords: curriculum; science philosophy; concepts; teaching method innovations; heuristic method (teaching); educational trends; educational psychology; activity learning; practicums; demonstrations (educational).

Identifiers: Nuffield Science Teaching Projects(UK) //

00019 - **The Role of science education in a developing country.** King, Winston K. Accra, Ghana, GAST, 1978. p. 20-24. (Journal of the Ghana Association of Science Teachers; XVII, 2) (eng). // Ghana Association of Science Teachers

With particular reference to the Caribbean, the author attempts to clarify the meanings and functions of science and technology and argues that science education leads to a way of life that is essential for citizens in developing countries.

Keywords: educational goals; developing countries; civic education; Caribbean.

00020 - **School science for the education of all.** Davison, A. Hatfield, UK, ASE, 1978. p. 343-344. (School science review; LX, 211) (eng). // Association for Science Education (UK)

The author judges that there is total confusion in the curriculum planning of science, as an element in the whole curriculum of British schools. He sees the need for debate.

Keywords: core curriculum; curriculum development; UK.

00021 - **Schools Council modular courses in technology.** Page, R.L. Hatfield, UK, ASE, 1978. p. 342-343. (School science review; LX, 211) (eng). // Association for Science Education (UK)

The curriculum development strategy is flexible, involves practising teachers, further education lecturers and industrialists and embraces inservice teacher education. The flexible approach should appeal to teachers.

Keywords: technology; curriculum development; learning modules; modular instruction; UK – inservice teacher education; higher education; industry and education.

Identifiers: UK. Schools Council // Modular Course in Technology (UK) //

00022 - **Science for the least able pupils, leading to a CSE qualification.** Peck, M.J.; Williams, I.P. Hatfield, UK, ASE, 1978. p. 353-357. (School science review; XL, 211) (eng). // Association for Science Education (UK)

The difficulties faced by non-academic pupils and the needs of an assessment procedure for these children are identified. Features of the course (which draws on a range of British resources) are outlined.

Keywords: ability grouping; slow learners; comprehensive schools; examinations; core curriculum; upper secondary education; UK – activity learning; reading ability.

00023 - **Science in general studies: has it a place?** West, R.W. Macclesfield, UK, General Studies Association, 1978. p. 8-11. (General studies; 31) (eng). // General Studies Association (UK)

The writer is concerned about the weakness of the three A-level curriculum in the 6th and 7th years of secondary school. Therefore the question is how can general studies become sufficiently general to include an appreciation of science and technology as well as literature, the arts and social sciences. He suggests strategies for such a curriculum.

Keywords: sixth forms; general education; upper secondary education; secondary school curriculum; specialization – science and technology; humanities education; social studies; UK; curriculum development.

00024 - **Should science be included as part of general studies courses?** Lyth, M. Macclesfied, UK, General Studies Association, 1978. p. 17-19. (General education; 31) (eng). // General Studies Association (UK)

Gives aims of a science component of a course for non-science specialists in the sixth form. Ends by advocating the SCISP Patterns scheme, seeing it as a useful resource for sixth form general studies. He provides a short list of other reading.

Keywords: sixth forms; general education; upper secondary education; UK.

Identifiers: Schools Council Integrated Science Project (UK) //

00025 - **The Social function of science education.** Williams, W.F.
London, HMSO, 1978. p. 32-35. (Trends in education; 1978,
1) (eng). // UK. Dept of Education and Science
*The author was one of the founders of the SISCON project for
university science students. He explains the rationale of the project
and outlines the materials produced.*
Keywords: sociology of science; university curriculum; curriculum
development; UK.
Identifiers: Science in a Social Context (UK) //

00026 - **Some implications of research conducted in mathematics
education, psychology and socio-linguistics in Papua New
Guinea.** Meek, C. Suva, Fiji Mathematics Association, 1978. p. 13-20.
(eng). // Fiji Mathematics Association // Fiji Mathematics
Association. Conference, Suva, 1978
*This significant article stresses the influence of culture and
language on Western-style problem-solving ability, and reminds us of
the implications for currriculum development.*
Keywords: education and culture; language barriers; mathematics
education; problem solving; curriculum development; Papua New
Guinea – sociolinguistics.

00027 - **The Sources of learning of young children.** Dyasi, Hubert M.
Accra, Ghana, GAST, 1978. p. 9-14. (Journal of the Ghana
Association of Science Teachers; XVII, 2) (eng). // Ghana Association
of Science Teachers
*The Program Director for the Science Education Program for
Africa (SEPA) outlines three distinct sources of learning which enter
into almost every SEPA lesson: tradition, experience and reflective
abstraction. An important article from an insightful, original and
experienced educator.*
Keywords: education and culture; learning processes; primary school
curriculum; cultural identity; Africa – reasoning.
Identifiers: Science Education Programme for Africa //

00028 - **Unified science and teacher's conceptual level.** Heikkinen,
Michael V.; Armstrong, Terry. Bowling Green, Ohio, School
Science and Mathematics Association, 1978. p. 513-516. (School science
and mathematics; LXXVIII, 6) (eng). // School Science and
Mathematics Association (USA)
*Teachers are seen as having attained differing conceptual levels,
this influencing the extent to which they can use data from multiple
sources and the level at which they can use knowledge. Thus the
teacher's approach to teaching the subject is affected, and only at the
higher conceptual levels will teachers be able to unify their teaching.*
Keywords: teacher effectiveness; educational psychology; teaching
methods.

00029 - **Ways of assessing how effectively a curricular innovation has
been implemented.** Brown, Sally. Penang, Malaysia, SEAMEO-
RECSAM, 1978. p. 25-37. (Journal of science and mathematics
education in Southeast Asia; 1, 1) (eng). // SEAMEO. Regional
Centre for Education in Science and Mathematics
*Discusses some of the ways in which interviews, questionnaires and
classroom observation may be used to explore the extent to which
curricular innovations are being implemented in schools. The focus is
on exploring the problems of implementation of the Scottish
Integrated Science Scheme used in Scotland.*
Keywords: curriculum evaluation; educational innovations; teacher
effectiveness; UK – interviews; questionnaires.
Identifiers: Scottish Integrated Science Project (UK) //

00030 - **"Acceptability Equations" and case studies of three major
disasters involving industrial chemicals.** Burton, W.H. Hatfield,
UK, ASE, 1979. p. 624-634. (School science review; LX, 213) (eng). //
Association for Science Education (UK)
*A description of an approach used in a sixth form General Studies
Science and Society course. The case studies are frightening.*
Keywords: upper secondary education; general education; social
problems; man-made disasters; UK – teaching strategies.
Identifiers: "Science in Society" (UK) //

00031 - **Alternative technology – non conventional renewable.** Richmond,
Peter E. London, Institute of Physics, 1979. p. 1. (Physics
education; xiv, 1) (eng). // Institute of Physics (UK)
*Well known for his interest in solar energy investigations in
schools, the author suggests that the time may now have come for
school physics to go 'applied'. Alternative technology uses basic
physics, and energy is a theme for integrated science if ever there was
one. No community in the world, he argues, can afford to neglect the
study of the capture of energy from renewable sources.*
Keywords: physics education; energy education; renewable energy
sources; solar energy.

00032 - **Alternatives for science education: a consultative document.**
Hatfield, UK, ASE, 1979. 61 p. (eng). // Association for
Science Education (UK)
*The document aimed to stimulate discussion which would lead to a
forward looking science education policy of the Association through
the 80s. Part 1 is a historical review attempting to identify elements
in the development of British education which account for the state
of education in the 70s. Part 2 broadly surveys the present. Part 3
presents options for the future, each covering three phases: (1) 5-11
years (2) 11-16 years (3) 16-18 years. Three models are presented in
order of increasing innovativeness.*
Keywords: primary school curriculum; secondary school curriculum;
upper secondary education; educational trends; UK – educational
history; educational innovations; curriculum development.
ISBN: 0-902-786-49-0.

00033 - **The Assessment of project work in science.** Lancaster, Colin
M. Cave Hill, Barbados, School of Education, Uniersity of
the West Indies, 1979. p. 19-26. (Caribbean journal of science
education; II,01) (eng). // University of the West Indies (Barbados).
School of Education
*Reviews the nature and aims of project work in science and
suggests an instrument for assessment of secondary school integrated
science projects.*
Keywords: student projects; evaluation methods; secondary school
curriculum; Caribbean.

00034 - **Bibliography on integrated science education.** Benning, Barbara;
Lockard, David; Showalter, Victor; Thomson, Barbara. Paris,
Unesco, 1979. p. 175-226. (New trends in integrated science teaching;
5) (eng; also in fre, spa). // Unesco // International Conference on
Integrated Science Education Worldwide , Nijmegen, Netherlands, 1978
*An annotated bibliography of 457 items covering work published
since volume III (1974) of this New Trends series, which also contains
a bibliography on integrated science education.*
Keywords: bibliographies.

00035 - **Bibliography on integrated science education.** Benning, Barbara;
Lockard, David; Showalter, Victor; Thomson, Barbara. Paris,
Unesco, 1979. p. 175-226. (New trends in integrated science teaching;
5) (eng; also in fre, spa). // International Conference on Integrated
Science Education Worldwide, Nijmegen, Netherlands, 1978
*An annotated bibliography of 457 items covering work published
since Volume III (1974) of this New Trends series, which also
contained a bibliography on integrated science education.*
Keywords: bibliographies.

00036 - **Chemistry for artists and art buffs.** Denio, Allen A. New
York, American Chemical Society, 1979. p. 30-33. (Journal of
chemical education; 66, 1) (eng). // American Chemical Society
*This course provides an attractive introduction to chemistry for a
group of students who would normally avoid traditional chemical
courses. Topics include color, pigments, metals, ceramics, glass, paints,
plastics, fibers, and dyes.*
Keywords: art education; chemistry education; interdisciplinary
approach – curriculum guides; higher education.

00037 - **Children's abilities in using seven of Piaget's logical operations
in problem solving.** Sintoovongse, K.; Wattanaseree, U.;
Tantriratana, K. Penang, Malaysia, SEAMEO-RECSAM, 1979. p. 5-15.
(Journal of science and mathematics education in Southeast Asia; II,
0202) (eng). // SEAMEO. Regional Centre for Education in Science
and Mathematics
*A report on research with Thai children. The results showed that
older children were able to outperform younger children in some of
the operations but not in others; and that the new Thai science
textbook had no influence on the performance of the older children.
Implications for the teaching of science are discussed.*
Keywords: mental development; problem solving; academic
achievement; teaching strategies; Thailand – age differences; textbooks.

00038 - **Cognitive development in some Caribbean secondary schools.**
Adey, Philip S. Kingston, Jamaica, University of the West
Indies, 1979. p. 197-220. (Caribbean journal of education; VI, 3) (eng).
// University of the West Indies (Jamaica). School of Education
*A report of a study of some 2300 children aged 11 to 15 in the
four largest Caribbean countries in four kinds of secondary school.
Cognitive levels, rates of development, and sex differences have
important implications for curriculum and teaching method.*
Keywords: secondary school students; secondary school curriculum;
Caribbean – teaching methods; sex role; cognition; child development.

00039 - **Co-operation between cousins: science and mathematics
educators look at what is possible and what has proved not
possible.** Fensham, Peter J. London, Taylor and Francis, 1979. p. 347-

352. (European journal of science education; I, 3) (eng).
This is a somewhat critical review of the outcomes of an ICSU/Unesco meeting. The author seems to feel that participants took a rather simplistic view of the issues, problems and challenges, and the article could lead to debate between science and mathematics teacher educators. The title of the article is not particularly informative.
Keywords: mathematics education; teacher education; teacher attitudes; educational coordination.
Identifiers: International Council of Scientific Unions // Unesco // Meeting on cooperation between science teachers and mathematics teachers, Bielefeld, Germany FR, 1978 //

00040 - **CXC and science: some issues about Basic and General Proficiency.** Brathwaite, Workeley E. Cave Hill, Barbados, University of the West Indies, 1979. p. 26.28. (Caribbean journal of science education; I, 1) (eng).
Examing the Caribbean Examinations Council Fact Sheet just before the first CXC examinations, the writer discusses the definitions of Basic and General Proficiency levels and their implications for science programmes. He shows that there are a number of issues which have not received attention.
Keywords: upper secondary education; Caribbean.
Identifiers: Caribbean Examinations Council //

00041 - **Do they teach physics abroad?** Vries, P.J. de. London, IoP, 1979. 65 p. (Physics education; XIV, 2) (eng). // Institute of Physics (UK)
A Dutch educator compares the number of physics periods in various countries, and concludes that in Britain there is time to link science in society compulsorily to physics, chemistry or biology if one of these is studied to A level. In Holland in 1980 about 10% of the examinations were linked to science in society for the schools that ask for it.
Keywords: upper secondary education; physics education; comparative education; Netherlands; UK – biology education; chemistry education; examinations.

00042 - **Do you really care?** Sandercock, Ted. Parkside, South Australian Science Teachers Association, 1979. p. 41-43. (South Australian Science Teachers Association journal; 792) (eng). // South Australian Science Teachers Association
Discusses the development of programs for Australian secondary school students of year 11 and 12. A modular science syllabus which has been developed in New Zealand and some examples of how some Australian schools have devised unified science programs are also discussed.
Keywords: learning modules; modular instruction; interdisciplinary approach; physical sciences; upper secondary education; Australia – curriculum development; New Zealand.
Identifiers: New Zealand Modular Science //

00043 - **Educational research and science teaching.** Whitfield, Richard C. Hatfield, UK, ASE, 1979. p. 411-430. (School science review; LX, 212) (eng). // Association for Science Education (UK)
The author observes that science educators have been as slow as any other kind of educators to base the process of teaching on research, but that the climate is changing considerably. Science teachers are increasingly coming to see the need to take research findings into account when executing their work. The article describes and comments on some results in science education.
Keywords: educational research; teacher attitudes; curriculum development; teaching methods; UK.

00044 - **Environmental approach: primary science curriculum, Belize.** Raymond, Ernest. London, International Council of Associations for Science Education, 1979. p. 40-45. (Science education for progress: a Caribbean perspective) (eng). // International Associations for Science Education
Outlines REAP, the Rural Education and Agriculture Project of Belize, which integrates rural environmental knowledge, skills and attitudes into a curriculum the aim of which is education relevant to the Belizean child.
Keywords: rural education; environmental education; agricultural education; educational relevance; rural environment; primary school curriculum; Belize.
Identifiers: Rural Education and Agriculture Project (Belize) //

00045 - **Facts or principles: directions in science education.** Malcolm, G.N. Wellington, New Zealand Science Teachers Association, 1979. p. 27-30, 35-38. (N Z science teacher; 21) (eng). // New Zealand Science Teachers Association
Briefly reviewing the ideologies of the waves of post-Sputnik curriculum developers, and views on the nature of science, a professor of physical chemistry concludes that school courses should contain both facts and principles. He challenges many of the beliefs of science educators of the day, and suggests that curriculum development has ended up not very far from its starting point.
Keywords: curriculum development; science philosophy; educational aims; educational trends.

00046 - **A Further look at some old myths.** Woolnough, Brian E. Hatfield, UK, ASE, 1979. p. 21-24. (Education in science; 81) (eng). // Association for Science Education (UK)
Some very interesting trends in O level, A level, CSE and university entries are given.
Keywords: educational trends; examinations; educational certificates; upper secondary education; UK.
Identifiers: General Certificate of Education (UK) // Certificate of Secondary Education (UK) //

00047 - **Home economics today and tomorrow.** Chambers, Judy. Dunedin, New Zealand, Association of Home Science Alumnae, 1979. p. 72-80. (Journal of the Association of Home Science Alumnae New Zealand; LXVIII) (eng). // Association of Home Science Alumnae (New Zealand)
This article will be of interest to those concerned about general issues of curriculum, and the relationship between science education and home economics education.
Keywords: home economics education; interdisciplinary approach; educational trends.

00048 - **The Implementation of curricula adapted from Scottish Integrated Science.** Williams, Iolo Wyn. Jerusalem, Israel Science Teaching Centre, Hebrew University, 1979. p. 295-299. (Curriculum implementation and its relationship to curriculum development in science) (eng). // Hebrew University (Israel). Science Teaching Centre // Seminar on Curriculum Implementation and its Relationship to Curriculum Development in Science, Jerusalem, 1978
Scottish Integrated Science formed the foundation of lower secondary science curricula in a number of different countries of the Commonwealth in the late 1960s and early 1970s. The advantages and disadvantages are identified.
Keywords: curriculum development; lower secondary education; educational cooperation; comparative education – UK; Trinidad and Tobago; Malaysia; Lesotho; Botswana; Swaziland; Hong Kong; Brunei; Israel.
Identifiers: Scottish Integrated Science Project (UK) // West Indies Science Curriculum (Trinidad and Tobago) // Malaysian Integrated Science // Boleswa Integrated Science (Africa) // Hong Kong Integrated Science // Brunei Integrated Science //

00049 - **The Implementation of curriculum change in school science in England and Wales.** Waring, M. London, Taylor and Francis, 1979. p. 257-275. (European journal of science education; I, 3) (eng; abstr. in fre, ger).
The limited evidence available suggests that, in the dissemination and diffusion of curricula, the project teams were not too successful in developing teachers' perceptions of the projects' messages. Accordingly, and also because more attention was paid to the materials than to the teachers, implementation has been less than expected. The writer concludes that innovation needs to arise from teachers working together (with some outside help) on classroom-based action research, reflecting on their own practice and building a body of theory rooted in the real world of the classroom.
Keywords: educational innovations; curriculum development; teacher effectiveness; inservice teacher education; UK – educational aims; teaching materials; curriculum research; teacher attitudes; classroom environment.

00050 - **Innovations in science and technology education, v.I.** Layton, David. Paris, Unesco, 1986. 188 p. (Innovations in science and technology education; 1) (eng; also in ara, fre, spa). // Unesco
Chapters from a variety of contributors cover teaching of the various scientific disciplines. Integrated and interdisciplinary science teaching, education in technology, nutrition and health, social relevance, teaching in relationship to the local environment and links with industry and agriculture are included. The book is addressed to science educators, ministry of education officials and practising teachers.
Keywords: teaching method innovations – primary education; secondary education; community development; biology education; biotechnology; chemistry education; teaching methods; physics education; mathematics education; computer assisted instruction; computer applications; calculating machines; educational cooperation; curriculum development.
ISBN: 92-3-102374-8(eng); 92-3-202374-1(fre); 92-3-302374-5(spa); 92-3-602374-6(ara).

00051 - **Integrated science education in primary schools in Rome: the research project of the university-school group.** Arca, M.; Vicentini-Missoni, M. London, Taylor and Francis, 1979. p. 125-129. (European journal of science education; I, 1) (eng).

Outlines the project of the University of Rome and its philosophy. Mentions the desired nature of educational research.

Keywords: primary school curriculum; Italy – teachers; curriculum development; educational research.

00052 - **Integrated science to 0-level: a case study.** Lambert, Ernos N. London, ICASE, 1979. p. 46-51. (Science education for progress: a Caribbean perspective) (eng). // International Council of Associations for Science Education // Conference on Science Education for Progress: a Regional Perspective, Bridgetown, 1979

As the first Caribbean Examinations Council examination in the core subject integrated science is imminent, the leader of the Syllabus Panel (a school teacher) discusses measures necessary to facilitate its implementation. These include enhanced 'marketing', increased flow of information to science teachers, the exploitation of a full range of strategies for teacher reorientation and for revision of the syllabus, clarification of the practical and project work elements, and the production of guides.

Keywords: examinations; core curriculum; upper secondary education; Caribbean – curriculum development; inservice teacher education; refresher courses; practicums; student projects; teaching guides.

Identifiers: Caribbean Examinations Council //

00053 - **The Introduction of integrated science teaching in Swaziland, 1972-1976.** Slimming, David. Accra, Ghana, GAST, 1979. p. 39-45. (Journal of the Ghana Association of Science Teachers; XIX, 1) (eng). // Ghana Association of Science Teachers

Describes the rationale and background of the Swaziland Integrated Science Project and its initial impetus from the Swaziland Science Teachers' Association. From five existing projects West Indies Science Curriculum Innovation Project was selected as the most suitable for adaptation to the Swaziland Integrated Science Project. Describes the development and trial procedures, which were concurrent and which were typical of that era. Includes a description of how the teachers were prepared and how examiners were controlled.

Keywords: curriculum development; lower secondary education; Swaziland; Caribbean.

Identifiers: Swaziland Science Teachers Association // Swaziland Integrated Science Project //

00054 - **Investigating the human environment: land use.** Hickman, F.M. Boulder, Colo., BSCS, 1979. p. 7-16. (Biological Sciences Curriculum Study journal; II, 1) (eng). // Biological Sciences Curriculum Study (USA)

An outline, with examples, of a curriculum emphasising problem-solving and decision-making. It is intended to be used in a variety of classes from social studies to advanced science.

Keywords: interdisciplinary approach; secondary education; problem solving; decision making; USA – land use; environmental education; social studies.

00055 - **Lifelong education: a new challenge.** Gestrelius, K. London, Taylor and Francis, 1979. p. 277-292. (European journal of science education; I, 3) (eng; abstr. in fre, ger).

The concept of lifelong education, recurrent education and lifelong learning are first explored. Necessary conditions for lifelong learning are outlined. A Unesco study developed a set of criteria for determining factors favourable to lifelong learning, the criteria being listed here. The author describes how these were applied in Sweden, and gives the results of the analysis. Deficiencies are identified. Science educators elsewhere could find this article of interest in judging whether what goes on in schools and in science teaching is conductive to lifelong development.

Keywords: lifelong education; recurrent education; learning processes; adult education; adult learning; Sweden.

Identifiers: Unesco //

00056 - **Mathematics modeling: a new approach to teaching applied mathematics.** Burghes, D.N.; Borrie, M.S. London, Institute of Physics, 1979. p. 82-86. (Physics education; XIV, 2) (eng). // Institute of Physics (UK)

Believing that applied mathematics is too idealised to interact with reality, the authors suggest a new approach, which they call applicable mathematics. The possible relationship with physics, chemistry, technology, economics, management, geography, demography, biology/medicine and sport are illustrated.

Keywords: mathematics education; interdisciplinary approach; teaching strategies.

00057 - **A Model of test development procedure for Nigerian Integrated Science: the construction and evaluation of a test to measure a unit on motion.** Oyebanji, P.K.; Lockard, David. Ibadan, Nigeria, STAN, 1979. p. 64-67. (Journal of the Science Teachers Association of Nigeria; XVIII, 1) (eng). // Science Teachers' Association of Nigeria

The development procedure, and evaluation of the test, are described. The test is not given.

Keywords: educational testing; curriculum evaluation; Nigeria.

Identifiers: Nigerian Integrated Science Project //

00058 - **The Modern trends of science education in primary schools.** Yeoh Oon Chye. Singapore, Science Teachers' Association of Singapore, 1979. p. 30-40. (Scientas; XIII, 2) (eng). // Science Teachers' Association of Singapore

Believes that school science education should leave students interested in science and prepared to cope with the future. Identifies five pedagogical elements of science education: pupil, teacher, objectives, content and the environment for science teaching and learning, and discusses these briefly. Diagrammatically summarizes the interpretations of inquiry by various authorities. Finally asks nine questions intended to help a teacher analyse whether her curriculum is in keeping with trends.

Keywords: primary school curriculum; educational aims; motivation – student attitudes; teacher attitudes; classroom environment; teacher effectiveness; activity learning; Singapore.

00059 - **Modular courses in technology at O Level and CSE.** Page, R.L. London, IoP, 1979. p. 255-261. (Physics education; XIV, 4) (eng). // Institute of Physics (UK)

A flexible approach to courses which can be taught by either science or craft teachers or both.

Keywords: technology; learning modules; modular instruction; upper secondary education; examinations; UK.

Identifiers: Modular course in Technology (UK) //

00060 - **The Need for a biosociology.** Wallace, B. Boulder, Colo., BSCS, 1979. p. 1-3. (Biological Sciences Curriculum Study journal; II, 1) (eng). // Biological Sciences Curriculum Study (USA)

Author of a book on social biology, and designer of a course called Biology and Society for non-majors at Cornell University, the author believes that the time has come for a new discipline, biosociology. Welding together sociologists and biologists, such a discipline should be introduced at once into the university curriculum. Goals, organisation and content are suggested.

Keywords: biology education; sociology; interdisciplinary approach; university curriculum; USA – life sciences.

00061 - **New trends in integrated science teaching, v.5.** Reay, Judith. Paris, Unesco, 1979. 238 p. (New trends in integrated science teaching) (eng; also in fre, spa). // Unesco // International Conference on Integrated Science Education Worldwide, Nijmegen, Netherlands, 1978

The book is the outcome of a conference which aimed to take stock of the development over the previous decade and to look forward to the 80s and beyond. A number of chapters are summaries of the plenary addresses. The rest reflect working group discussions and the experience of a variety of specialists. Appendices include a 457-item bibliography on integrated science education, guidelines on the introduction of integrated science, and information about the authors of these and other papers presented for discussion.

Keywords: educational trends – curriculum development; curriculum evaluation; educational levels; teacher education; educational relevance; teaching materials; teaching methods; general education; bibliographies.
ISBN: 92-3-101757-8.

00062 - **1979: progress and promise.** Mayer, W.V. Boulder, Colo., BSCS, 1979. p. 1-2. (Biological Sciences Curriculum Study journal; II, 3) (eng). // Biological Sciences Curriculum Study (USA)

BSCS claims to be transdisciplinary in concept but is frankly hard-sell. Those interested in issues of the social and human context of biology teaching, and in values and ethics, could find a critical examination of the article useful.

Keywords: biology education; life sciences; interdisciplinary approach; USA – social values; ethics of science; humanism.

00063 - **Piggy-in-the-Middle: a plea for cooperation between mathematics and science teachers in secondary schools.** Turner, Anthony D. Hatfield, UK, ASE, 1979. p. 773-778. (School science review; LX, 213) (eng). // Association for Science Education (UK)

There is a mismatch between the approach of teachers of science and mathematics. The article suggests some reasons for this, and some changes in approach which might help to solve the problem.

Keywords: mathematics education; teacher attitudes; teaching strategies.

00064 - **Presidential address: what next?** Booth, Norman. Hatfield, UK, ASE, 1979. p. 153-156. (School science review; LXI, 214) (eng). // Association for Science Education (UK)

From his long experience the ASE president urges teachers to remember how and why they are teaching science in an age of accelerated science and technology. He suggests that training courses may be turning teachers into slaves of educational technology, and asks teachers to loosen their bonds and become liberated. Teachers will recognize the wisdom and experience in this article.

Keywords: teacher attitudes; educational aims; technological change – teacher education; educational technology; teacher responsibility; teaching strategies.

00065 - **Problems in the organisation and implementation of a model integrated science course in Nigerian schools.** Oriaifo, S.O. Ibadan, Nigeria, STAN, 1979. p. 89-93. (Journal of the Science Teachers' Association of Nigeria; XVII, 3) (eng). // Science Teachers' Association of Nigeria

This was a background paper for a workshop to revise STAN's Nigerian Integrated Science Project. As such, it attempts to identify issues about the teacher, laboratory space and facilities, and the learner and his background. The paper also reports on an opinion poll taken of teachers and students, and makes recommendations for the workshop.

Keywords: curriculum development; curriculum evaluation; lower secondary education; Nigeria – teacher attitudes; student attitudes; school laboratories.

Identifiers: Nigerian Integrated Science Project //

00066 - **Pupils' attitudes to the social implications of science.** Ormerod, M.B. London, Taylor and Francis, 1979. p. 177-189. (European journal of science education; I, 2) (eng).

A follow-up on the author's earlier "attitudes to science" work through extension of the SOCATT (social implications) sub-scale. Links reported for SOCATT/Science Subject Preference, while weak, are of interest; so, too, are those with Teacher Liking. Useful background reading for science educators at all levels, especially teachers, teacher trainers and curriculum developers.

Keywords: student attitudes; social values; UK – teacher student relationship.

00067 - **Recommendations on the revision of junior secondary science based on observation in the classroom.** Wilson, James D. Victoria, B.C., BC Science Teachers Association, 1979. p. 24-26. (The BC science teacher; XXI, 2) (eng). // British Columbia Science Teachers' Association (Canada)

A practising teacher's views and suggestions related to scope and sequence in a ministry course. Worth reading by those evaluating similar programs.

Keywords: lower secondary education; classroom environment; curriculum development; curriculum evaluation; Canada.

00068 - **The Relevance of new science and related education in Bangladesh: some salient features.** Ullah, A.K.M. Obaid. Bombay, British High Commission, British Council Division, 1979. p. 5-9. (Bombay science and education newsletter; 70) (eng). // British Council

Identifies aspects of new draft national curricula. The emphasis on technology is outlined and justified as an aid to national development. In an attempt to end the isolation of educated people from the masses, human and social qualities are to be developed, and the new curriculum integrates the humanities and social sciences with science and technology. Vocational education has been introduced side by side with general education after primary level. An emphasis on work-oriented education as an integral part of general education is intended to ensure the all-round development of personality. Among the compulsory subjects is one which relates education to life and the environment, a combination of social sciences and physical and biological sciences. Finally, the curriculum is intended to stimulate originality and creativity (although the primary aim of education is to produce efficient and skilled manpower).

Keywords: general education; educational relevance; education and development; interdisciplinary approach; educational goals; Bangladesh – technical and vocational education; manpower needs; physical sciences; life sciences; social studies.

00069 - **A Review of integrated science education worldwide.** Haggis, Sheila M.; Adey, PhilipS. Leeds, UK, Leeds University Centre for Studies in Science Education, 1979. p. 69-89. (Studies in science education; 6) (eng). // Leeds University (UK). Centre for Studies in Science Education

Aims to provide an overall picture of the state of integrated science education today, and to identify worldwide trends in the development of teaching and learning in integrated science.

Keywords: curriculum; curriculum development; educational trends;

comparative education.

00070 - **Rural Education and Agricultural Project in Belize.** Raymond, Ernest. Cave Hill, Barbados, University of the West Indies, 1979. p. 29-30. (Caribbean journal of science education; I, 1) (eng). // University of the West Indies (Barbados)

REAP is designed for children remaining in primary school after the age of 11 years. Observing that REAP has much to offer in terms of educational and economic development, the writer outlines the education and development strategies used in the first phase of the project. Educators will recognise the significance of these strategies, and the article should be consulted by those interested in relevant development in education.

Keywords: rural education; agricultural education; lower secondary education; Belize – educational strategies; educational relevance.

Identifiers: Rural Education and Agriculture Project (Belize) //

00071 - **Science and society.** King, Winston K. Cave Hill, Barbados, School of Education, University of the West Indies, 1979. p. 4-7. (Caribbean journal of science education; I, 0101) (eng). // University of the West Indies (Barbados). School of Education

Society is seen as an essential concern in school science courses. A set of eleven topics are suggested, to ensure that Caribbean youth is trained, not only as scientists, but as responsible citizens.

Keywords: social responsibility; civic education; Caribbean – education and employment; educational relevance.

00072 - **Science curriculum and cognitive levels in the Caribbean.** Adey, Philip S. London, Chelsea College, University of London, 1979. 257 p. (eng). (PhD dissertation). // University of London. Chelsea College

The study contains an analysis of WISC in terms of cognitive demands and sets this against cognitive levels found in Caribbean children on the basis of Piagetian measures. In general, a mismatch was found, and there is discussion of the implications for science curriculum development.

Keywords: academic standards; academic achievement; curriculum development; curriculum evaluation; secondary school students; Caribbean – educational psychology.

Identifiers: Piaget, Jean // West Indies Science Curriculum (Trinidad and Tobago) //

00073 - **Science curriculum directions: purpose planning and perspective.** Ramsey, Gregor. Wellington, New Zealand Science Teachers Association, 1979. p. 40-45. (N Z science teacher; 21) (eng). // New Zealand Science Teachers Association

Aims in science teaching in the decades from the 1950s to the 1980s are compared. The interaction between science teaching and society is considered, and the writer predicts that teachers will face ever-increasing challenges in the future.

Keywords: educational trends; educational aims; social needs; teacher responsibility; New Zealand.

00074 - **Science education and national development.** Madras, India, ICSU-COSTED, 1979. p. 9. (COSTED newsletter; IV, 2) (eng). // International Council of Scientific Unions. Committee on Science and Technology in Developing Countries // Seminar on Science Education and National Development, Ibadan, Nigeria, 1979

The report focuses on the generation of public understanding of science and technology.

Keywords: education and development; science popularization; science and development – scientific literacy.

00075 - **Science education in Europe at secondary school level.** Gibb, M. Belgium, ICASE, 1979. p. 5-9. (ICASE newsletter; VI, 4) (eng). // International Council of Associations for Science Education

An article arising from a round-table discussion in Luxembourg, at which participants reported practices, attitudes and constraints in eight countries. Similarities and differences are of interest, and the article ends by pointing out the close relationship between science teachers associations and curricular reform.

Keywords: curriculum development; comparative education; Western Europe.

00076 - **A Science teaching project in the primary school in Norway.** Johansen, O.E. Geneva, Advisory Committee on Physics Education of the European Physical Society, 1979. p. 11-12. (Europhysics education news; 7) (eng). // European Physical Society. Advisory Committee on Physics Education

"Meet Nature" is an adaptation of SCIS. Important features of primary science curricula are summarised.

Keywords: primary school curriculum; Norway; USA.

Identifiers: "Meet Nature" (Norway) // Science Curriculum Improvement Study (USA) //

00077 - **SLIP kits.** Coombes, S.D. Hatfield, UK, ASE, 1979. p. 28-40. (School science review; LXI, 214) (eng). // Association for Science Education (UK)

The article describes how groups of teachers went about making teaching packages, with help from industries.

Keywords: technology; learning modules; teaching materials; industry and education; UK – teacher role.

Identifiers: "Science Lessons from Industrial Processes" (UK) //

00078 - **Soaps and detergents: a "social" treatment.** Rust, R.C. Hatfield, UK, Association for Science Education, 1979. p. 635-641. (School science review; 213) (eng). // Association for Science Education (UK)

Soap lends itself to a "social" treatment without disturbing the overall framework of any chemistry or integrated science course. This article provides a number of interesting facts and a teaching approach which should take only one or two periods.

Keywords: chemistry education; teaching materials; experiments (lessons); teaching methods; secondary school curriculum; UK.

00079 - **Spreading the message.** Harris, J. London, Institute of Physics, 1979. p. 432-433. (Physics bulletin; xxx, 10) (eng). // Institute of Physics (UK)

October 1979 was designated 'International Energy Conservation Month' and this issue of the Bulletin invited a number of articles on the matter. This article outlines a number of educational programmes developed in Britain, from primary to university and for the public.

Keywords: energy education; science popularization; energy conservation; UK – primary school curriculum; secondary school curriculum; higher education.

Identifiers: International Energy Conservation Month, October 1979 //

00080 - **A Survey of the teaching of integrated science in Kaduna State.** Aminu, Dorayi Mohammed. Ibadan, Nigeria, STAN, 1979. p. 88-96. (Journal of the Science Teachers' Association of Nigeria; XVIII, 1) (eng). // Science Teachers' Association of Nigeria

The survey was based on a questionnaire to teachers, and embraced teacher qualifications and experience, proportion of timetable allocated to integrated science and practical work, teaching methods and textbooks. The writer concluded that a pressing need was inservice and preservice teacher education programmes, as well as programmes for training of school laboratory attendants. The textbooks need revision.

Keywords: curriculum evaluation; Nigeria – teacher effectiveness; teacher education; inservice teacher education; activity learning; school laboratories; textbooks.

00081 - **Third international conference on integrated science education.** Becht, Paul A.; Gadsden, Thomas. London, Taylor and Francis, 1979. p. 109-112. (European journal of science education; I, 1) (eng).

. A summary of the proceedings of the 1978 Nijmegen Conference. There is a list of the working group papers and their authors. Comments on the problems of obtaining information on developments, these partly solved by conferences and Unesco's "New trends in integrated science teaching" series.

Keywords: international conferences; information sources; educational trends.

Identifiers: International Conference on Integrated Science Education Worldwide, Nijmegen, Netherlands, 1978 // "New trends in integrated science teaching" //

00082 - **UN Conference on Science and Technology for Development: the importance of education and training.** Malvern, UK, ICSU-CTS, 1979. p. 10-15. (ICSU-CTS newsletter; 3) (eng). // International Council of Scientific Unions. Committee on the Teaching of Science

The paper argues that the healthy growth of science and technology in any country depends critically on the availability of technically and scientifically trained manpower. Transfer of technology demands a scientifically literate public with self-reliance and understanding, and this in turn demands massive reappraisal of existing courses at schools and universities.

Keywords: science and development; scientific personnel training; technology transfer; manpower needs – scientific literacy; technical education; curriculum evaluation; university curriculum; vocational training; science popularization.

00083 - **Wildlife conservation: the need for expansion in education.** Horne, S.D. Hatfield, UK, ASE, 1979. p. 142-146. (School science review; LXI, 214) (eng). // Association for Science Education (UK)

If conservation discussions are to go beyond emotion, they should be associated with scientific knowledge. The first part of the article provides some information; it then goes on to present a powerful plea for more attention to wildlife conservation in classrooms and examination syllabi. Important reading for all science teachers.

Keywords: wildlife protection; conservation of nature; social responsibility; curriculum development; examinations.

00084 - **Applied science: a course for pupils of low educational achievement.** Clegg, A.S.; Morley, M. Hatfield, UK, ASE, 1980. p. 454-463. (School science review; 216) (eng). // Association for Science Education (UK)

A set of modules is outlined in an attempt to teach some science to those who normally stay away from class or exhibit disruptive behaviour. As a result, attendance rose to above 90% and some pupils gained CSE passes. Certainly worth trying in comprehensive schools.

Keywords: achievement motivation; low achievers; learning modules; teaching strategies; UK – educational attendance; comprehensive schools; modular instruction.

00085 - **The Assessment of pupils' performance in science education in Japan.** Nishinosono, H. Tokyo, Japan Society of Science Education, 1980. p. 149-161. (Journal of science education in Japan; IV, 4) (eng). // Japan Society of Science Education

The article outlines a variety of techniques for obtaining information about pupils' thinking. Some can be computer-processed, even in the classroom, some are open-ended, all appear to be innovative. This article is for researchers.

Keywords: student evaluation; academic achievement; evaluation methods; Japan.

00086 - **Balanced science approaches.** Winnerah, J. Hatfield, UK, ASE, 1980. p. 24-26. (Education in science; 86) (eng). // Association for Science Education (UK)

The author argues for balanced science courses for all if we are to have an adult population informed about science and technology, and scientists, engineers and technologists informed about all the sciences and educated in the humanities and the arts. Excellent reasons against early specialization are given.

Keywords: general education; scientific literacy; science popularization; specialization; core curriculum.

00087 - **Biomechanics in schools.** Vincent, J.F.V. Hatfield, UK, ASE, 1980. p. 648-663. (School science review; 217) (eng). // Association for Science Education (UK)

Most biological 'materials' are not at all, but structures. Investigation of these can be truly scientific, and therefore demand integration of biology with chemistry and physics. Possibly (and sadly), this article could prove more interesting to physical scientists than to life scientists. Recommended for any A-level or tertiary teacher attempting to make his teaching more scientific.

Keywords: activity learning; biology education; physics education; chemistry education; teaching method innovations; upper secondary education; higher education; UK.

00088 - **Committee on Science and Technology in Developing Countries.** Radhakrishna, R. York, UK, IUPAC Committee on the Teaching of Chemistry, 1980. p. 9-11. (International newsletter on chemical education; 14) (eng). // International Union of Pure and Applied Chemistry. Committee on the Teaching of Chemistry

The Scientific Secretary of COSTED outlines the terms of reference, aims and some of the programmes of the Committee. Although most of its activities seem so far to have been confined to Asia, there seems no reason why science educators elsewhere should not attempt to avail themselves of its help.

Keywords: educational assistance; science and technology; Asia; developing countries.

Identifiers: Committee on Science and Technology in Developing Countries //

00089 - **Constraint and autonomy in Australian secondary science education.** Fensham, Peter J. London, Taylor and Francis, 1980. p. 189-206. (Journal of curriculum studies; XII, 3) (eng).

The author claims that the Australian Science Education Project must be one of the most extensively studied curriculum projects in the world, describes the major studies and identifies lessons for further curriculum development in science education in Australia. He argues that curriculum developers have tended to concentrate on individual factors and to ignore social ones where the schooling system is an instrumentality in society as a whole. Further, science curriculum development has a time dimension which leads to gaps between intentions and implementations, as the social scene and schools undergo rapid change.

Keywords: curriculum development; curriculum evaluation; educational relevance; Australia – lower secondary education; educational trends.

Identifiers: Victorian Junior Secondary Science Project (Australia) // Australian Science Education Project //

00090 - **Continuity and diversity in the classroom.** Williams, Sandra E. Boulder, Colo., Mountainview Publishing, 1980. p. 9-19. (Outlook; 37) (eng).

Described is a teaching methodology which includes enrichment of the students' learning experiences through an integrated approach to curriculum development, using continuity of curriculum as the major objective. The teacher's responsibility in this approach is to point out patterns and explore and talk about patterns included in the students' experiences.

Keywords: educational aims; curriculum development; teaching strategies – primary school curriculum; USA.

00091 - **Designing an assessment system on the principles of criterion-referenced measurement.** Kellington, Steuart H.; Mitchell, Alison C. Hatfield, UK, ASE, 1980. p. 765-770. (School science review; LXI, 217) (eng). // Association for Science Education (UK)

Describes a Scottish system similar to that used by the Caribbean Examinations Council and, much later, by GCSE of England and Wales. The purposes and nature of criterion-referenced assessment are outlined, together with guidelines for carrying out the assessment and using the results.

Keywords: examinations; educational measurement; student evaluation; UK – educational aims.

Identifiers: Scottish Integrated Science Project (UK) //

00092 - **Enrolment trends in science during the 1970s.** Osborne, Roger. Wellington, New Zealand Science Teachers Association, 1980. p. 15-20. (N Z science teacher; 27) (eng). // New Zealand Science Teachers Association

Most of this paper consists of graphs of enrolments in New Zealand in various subjects in forms 5, 6 and 7 (of secondary education). As in other countries, physics and chemistry are low, especially for girls. Interestingly, at Form 5, biology is falling steadily, giving way to 'science', which by 1979 was taken by some 55% of children.

Keywords: upper secondary education; enrolment; elective courses; New Zealand – physics education; chemistry education; biology education; physical sciences; life sciences; girls education.

00093 - **Environmental education: a suggested strategy for Jamaica.** Dutton, R. Kingston, Jamaica, University of the West Indies, 1980. p. 43-63. (Caribbean journal of education; VII, 1) (eng). // University of the West Indies (Jamaica)

This article is introduced by an outline of the worldwide EE movement, followed by a more specific look at the Jamaican situation. The bulk of the article centres on a suggested map of EE in Jamaica, with four components: teacher education, primary and secondary education, adult education and information, and professional and vocational training. There is a bibliography of 87 items.

Keywords: environmental education; Jamaica – teacher education; primary school curriculum; secondary school curriculum; adult education; vocational training; bibliographies.

00094 - **Evaluation in a developing context: constraints on the evaluation of an integrated science course in Ghana.** Lutterodt, Sarah A. Hamburg, Germany FR, Unesco Institute for Education, 1980. p. 90-95. (International review of education; XXV, 1) (eng). // Unesco Institute for Education (Germany FR)

Hard-nosed evaluation was inhibited by many factors familiar to those with similar experiences elsewhere in the Third World. However, a wealth of useful information was obtained, and the author concludes that it is possible to carry out useful evaluation in spite of limited resources. Her experience reinforces arguments for evaluation of the illuminative variety.

Keywords: curriculum evaluation; developing countries; Ghana – secondary school curriculum; evaluation methods.

Identifiers: Project for Science Integration (Ghana) //

00095 - **Evaluation of science curriculum: some instruments.** Mallik, Uptal. New Delhi, NCERT, 1980. p. 17-25. (School science; XVIII, 3) (eng). // National Council of Research and Training (India)

Begins by clarifying some issues of evaluation and lists criteria for judging curricular materials. Goes on to describe how science curriculum analyses are used and carried out. Ends by suggesting a scheme for the Indian context.

Keywords: curriculum evaluation; evaluation methods – India.

00096 - **An Evolving policy for science curriculum.** Heaney, J.C. Hatfield, UK, ASE, 1980. p. 24-26. (Education in science; 90) (eng). // Association for Science Education (UK)

The article discusses the need for the ASE to respond clearly, quickly and authoritatively to initiatives and proposals from elsewhere. He describes progress towards arriving at a policy which reflects the views of the large membership, a process which began with the consulting document, "Alternatives for science education". Principles,

aims and concepts are already agreed upon, and are listed in this article.

Keywords: educational policy; educational aims; educational coordination; teacher associations; UK – curriculum development.

Identifiers: "Alternatives for science education: a consultative document" (UK) //

00097 - **Examinations for an integrated science degree programme.** Moss, G.D. London, IoP, 1980. p. 302-306. (Physics education; XV, 5) (eng). // Institute of Physics (UK)

Examinations at an Australian university are analysed for skills tested. Emphases appear to be idiosyncratic and anyway not well related to the skills needed by science graduates.

Keywords: examinations; university curriculum; educational aims; educational testing; higher education; Australia.

00098 - **An Experience in teaching integrated science.** Holbrook, J.B. Hong Kong, HKASME, 1980. p. 111-121. (Journal of the Hong Kong Association for Science and Mathematics Education; VIII, 2) (eng). // Hong Kong Association for Science and Mathematics Education

A non-Chinese speaker undertook a trial to teach science to Form 1 students with a minimal grasp of English. Well-illustrated worksheets were found to be very helpful. The investigation showed that it was possible to teach in English, but whether or not it is desirable is another question. The policy of the Hong Kong Educational Department is criticised. The article is of interest to those concerned with the problem of standard English as a medium of instruction in societies whose vernacular is different.

Keywords: language of instruction; language barriers; classroom techniques – teaching strategies; teaching materials; Hong Kong.

00099 - **Experiments of RECSAM in developing sciences and mathematics instructional materials.** Chin, P.S. Penang, Malaysia, SEAMEO-RECSAM, 1980. p. 15-26. (Journal of science and mathematics education in Southeast Asia; III, 1) (eng). // SEAMEO. Regional Centre for Education in Science and Mathematics

The project features a research base, a systems appoach, and science/mathematics orientation. The objectives of the teaching materials are listed. An example of a unit is given, and development strategies are outlined.

Keywords: mathematics education; primary school curriculum; curriculum development; teaching materials; South East Asia.

00100 - **Heads, hearts and hands: future alternatives for science education.** Fensham, Peter J. Wellington, New Zealand Science Teachers Association, 1980. p. 31-36. (N Z science teacher; 27) (eng). // New Zealand Science Teachers Association

Failure of the "heads" science curricula of the 60s and the "hearts" curricula of the 70s is explained by the fact that neither is like the "hands" or "doing" science that scientists practise. It is argued that once students acquire practical skills in science, in situations meaningful and relevant to them, the effects will be lasting and social responsibility will fall naturally into place. The article is worth reading by secondary and tertiary science educators who see the need to re-appraise curricula.

Keywords: activity learning; educational relevance; educational innovations – secondary school curriculum; curriculum evaluation; university curriculum; educational trends; New Zealand.

00101 - **Identification of science teacher competencies for implementing ISIS minicourse instruction.** Chiappetta, Eugene L.; Collette, Alfred T. New York, John Wiley, 1980. p. 53-58. (Science education; 64, 1) (eng).

Identified and ranked in this study are such teacher competencies for successful implementation of the ISIS program as: uses a variety of instructional strategies, promotes individual instruction, provides humanistic learning environment, controls the classroom, and organizes the classroom to facilitate instruction. The appendix lists affective competencies and personality characteristics.

Keywords: secondary school curriculum; teacher effectiveness; teacher qualifications; teacher behaviour; secondary school teachers; USA.

Identifiers: Integrated Science Instruction Study (USA) //

00102 - **In-service training of teachers including the retraining of teachers of other subjects.** Ramsey, Gregor. London, CASME, 1980. p. 45-57. (Teacher education for national development: the training of science and mathematics educators with special reference to the social context) (eng). // Commonwealth Association of Science, Technology and Mathematics Educators // Commonwealth Association of Science, Technology and Mathematics Educators. South Pacific Regional Seminar, Darwin, Australia, 1980

The paper attempts to clarify issues for discussion in the conference. It includes some research findings on the effectiveness of

in-service programmes. In discussion, the group advocated mass and on-going in-service training aims. Practicalities were also suggested.

Keywords: teacher education; retraining; evaluation of education; Oceania; inservice teacher education – education and development; educational aims; distance education.

00103 - **Integrated science unit.** Vella-Zarb, T.A. Waterloo, Ont., University of Waterloo, 1981. p. 11-14. (Chem 13 news; 118-118) (eng). // University of Waterloo (Canada)

The unit is a study of urine, integrates skills aquired in physics, concepts learned in chemistry, principles of health and topics learned in biology. Much of it can be carried out at home. Full details are given for the teacher, and there should be few logistic problems.

Keywords: secondary school curriculum; teaching strategies; experiments (lessons); Canada – student projects; practicums.

00104 - **International environmental education: the myth and the reality.** Aldrich, J.L. London, CASME, 1980. p. 32-39. (Commonwealth Association of Science, Technology and Mathematics Educators journal; I, 1) (eng). // Commonwealth Association of Science, Technology and Mathematics Educators

This article looks back to IEE over a decade, attempts to clarify the concept, and looks forward to a new philosophy of mankind in nature.

Keywords: environmental education; educational cooperation; science philosophy; educational trends – humanism; environmental perception.

00105 - **Marine education.** Washington, NSTA, 1980. 52 p. (Science and children; XVIII, 2) (eng). // National Science Teachers Association (USA)

The whole issue is devoted to marine education and is of interest to anyone teaching primary or junior secondary students.

Keywords: primary school curriculum; lower secondary education; oceanography education; marine education.

00106 - **Nuclear power and the science curriculum.** Scott, W. London, IoP, 1980. p. 286-288. (Physics education; XV, 5) (eng). // Institute of Physics (UK)

The argument is that school science curricula are out of step with technological change in society. While the facts of nuclear progress are taught, the technologies and possible social effects are not. An informed public is needed for decision-making, and a radical change in school science curricula may be needed.

Keywords: new technologies; secondary school curriculum; social responsibility; scientific literacy; UK – nuclear energy; educational relevance.

00107 - **Primary school science.** Douglass, Raphael; Durgadeen, Lucy. St. Augustine, Trinidad and Tobago, University of the West Indies, 1980. p. 10-13. (Social studies education; 17) (eng). // University of the West Indies (Trinidad and Tobago)

An outline of the early stages in the development of SAPATT is followed by a brief account of the preparations of teachers for the Common Entrance science examination. The article ends with six specimen questions, one for each of the Bloom cognitive levels, and an explanation of these levels. Tests specification and content are also given.

Keywords: primary school curriculum; curriculum development; primary teacher education; inservice teacher education; examinations; Trinidad and Tobago.

Identifiers: Science: a Process Approach for Trinidad and Tobago //

00108 - **Problems of innovation in the Japanese science curriculum.** Imahori, Kozo. Tokyo, Japan Society of Science Education, 1980. p. 139-148. (Journal of science education in Japan; IV, 4) (eng). // Japan Society of Science Education

Most of the article deals in general terms with science education in Japan, providing a fair amount of data. The last part of the article claims that interdisciplinary or multidisciplinary curricula are very effective in attaining the important objective of an understanding of nature or natural phenomena, as one's general culture. There is a brief outline of some Japanese integrated science curricula. Teachers' problems are identified.

Keywords: educational innovations; curriculum development; interdisciplinary approach; education and culture; Japan – conservation of nature; teachers.

00109 - **Qualified to teach?** Manuel, D. Hatfield, UK, ASE, 1980. p. 26-27. (Education in science; 86) (eng). // Association for Science Education (UK)

If science teachers are to provide appropriate science education for all, the demands on them require that they should have real intellectual ability and flexibility. This is more likely to be true in the case of biology teachers. Biology graduates are also more likely than

other science graduates to be teaching integrated science courses. Implications for the profession are discussed.

Keywords: teacher effectiveness; teacher qualifications; core curriculum – teacher education; biology education.

00110 - **Questions of primary science: important questions which have been asked by teachers, with some practical answers.** Ward, Alan. Hatfield, UK, ASE, 1980. p. 639-647. (School science review; 217) (eng). // Association for Science Education (UK)

The author attempts to describe primary science in a way which will convince teachers that they are capable of teaching it in a way that is faithful to science. Process is emphasised.

Keywords: primary school curriculum; teacher effectiveness; teacher attitudes; skill development – teaching methods; teaching strategies; UK.

00111 - **Science and education.** Renwick, W.L. New Zealand, New Zealand Science Teachers Association, 1980. p. 6-14. (N Z science teacher; 27) (eng). // New Zealand Science Teachers Association

The Director-General of Education reviews curriculum development in New Zealand since 1945, and identifies directions for the future. Blurring of the boundaries between disciplines is projected, and more attention to social responsibility. There is a useful appendix which analyses the contribution of science curricula at various levels to fifteen various aims of education.

Keywords: curriculum development; educational trends; educational relevance; educational aims; New Zealand.

00112 - **Science and society studies in the school curriculum.** Solomon, Joan. Hatfield, UK, ASE, 1980. p. 213-219. (School science review; LXII, 219) (eng). // Association for Science Education (UK)

The article comments on the ASE's consultative document. It considers how to bridge the gap between the schoolchild and his society by using the social dimensions of science. An outline of a proposed syllabus of the SISCON course is given, and a suggestion is made for teachers to implement some of the "Alternatives for science education" from their own experience and endeavours.

Keywords: educational relevance; social values; upper secondary education – teacher associations; teaching strategies; UK.

Identifiers: "Alternatives for science education: a consultative document" (UK) // Science in a Social Context (UK) //

00113 - **Science: breadth, balance and potential in the 11-16 curriculum.** Yeoman, G.D. Hatfield, UK, ASE, 1980. p. 147-152. (School science review; LXII, 218) (eng). // Association for Science Education (UK)

The author takes a critical look at the ASE's consultative document. He then produces a model of curriculum development for the 80s which contrasts with that of the 60s. He believes that the time has come for theory and research to be taken into account, and that teachers are now in a position to select, for their own pupils, from the large amount of curricular materials available.

Keywords: educational trends; secondary school curriculum; curriculum development; educational reform; teacher role; UK – curriculum research.

Identifiers: "Alternatives for science education: a consultative document" (UK) //

00114 - **Science education: further thoughts.** Prestt, Brenda M. Hatfield, UK, ASE, 1980. p. 31-33. (Education in science; 87) (eng). // Association for Science Education (UK)

Facing the problem of teachers, the writer proposes a simple division of science teaching into three stages, which separate out the processes of science. Her experience is that primary teachers will be quite comfortable with stage I, which incorporates just over half of the hierarchy of processes. It is the higher processes which frighten many teachers, and these would appropriately be left to the secondary level. For the 13-16 level, she proposes a core plus options, the A level syllabuses to be based on the core and nothing else, which would encourage freedom in the options at the earlier stage.

Keywords: teaching strategies; primary school curriculum; secondary school curriculum; teacher attitudes; UK – core curriculum; elective courses.

00115 - **Science for all on trial.** Lambert, E. Norman. Port-of-Spain, Association of Principals of Public Secondary Schools of Trinidad and Tobago, 1980. p. 25-28. (Education forum; I, 2) (eng). // Association of Principals of Public Secondary Schools of Trinidad and Tobago

The first part of this article presents arguments for the integration of science up to 16+. The second part identifies needs of science teachers and makes suggestions for their resolution.

Keywords: upper secondary education; secondary school teachers; secondary teacher education; Trinidad and Tobago.

00116 - **Science report.** McClenan, Vilma. Kingston, University of the West Indies, 1980. p. 5-10. (Science education newsletter; XI, 2) (eng). // University of the West Indies (Jamaica)

A participant at a meeting in Grenada outlines the OAS Project set up in 1974 but seeming to have kept a low profile ever since.

Keywords: science popularization; nonformal education; scientific literacy; educational assistance; Caribbean.

Identifiers: OAS // Multinational Project for the Development of Strategies to Achieve Scientific Literacy and Technology Awareness in Caribbean Countries //

00117 - **Science, society and trends in science education: some thoughts on the development of integrated science in the educational systems of the world.** Manzelli, Paolo. London, Taylor and Francis, 1980. p. 253-260. (European journal of science education; II, 3) (eng; abstr. in fre, ger).

The writer argues that the development of schooling policies, and a science curriculum, must recognise evolving socio-economic circumstances. The science curriculum should have a utilitarian accent on work. No longer should every society follow a science curriculum to produce students with a "specialized limited perspective" which prepares people for narrow roles in a hierarchical social structure. A research-oriented integrated curriculum is required.

Keywords: educational policy; curriculum; socio-economic factors; educational relevance; education and employment – career development; educational research; educational trends.

00118 - **Science-society mini-courses hit home.** Nalence, E.E. Washington, NSTA, 1980. p. 26-28. (Science teacher; XLVII, 6) (eng). // National Science Teachers Association (USA)

A discussion on the utilization of mini-courses to investigate relevant problems and expose students to issues of social concern.

Keywords: social responsibility; teaching strategies; educational relevance; short courses; USA.

00119 - **The Scottish Integrated Science course: a school based study.** Park, J. Stirling, UK, University of Stirling, 1980. (1 v. in various pagings). (eng). (Unpublished M.Ed. thesis). // University of Stirling (UK)

This study deals with an aspect of the revised SIS course: the use of worksheets intended to individualise tasks according to each pupil's ability.

Keywords: lower secondary education; individualized instruction; ability grouping; teaching materials; teaching method innovations; UK – curriculum guides; classroom techniques; curriculum evaluation.

Identifiers: Scottish Integrated Science Project (UK) //

00120 - **The Secondary survey and science.** Hatfield, UK, ASE, 1980. p. 15-22. (Education in science; 86) (eng). // Association for Science Education (UK)

A summary of the Science chapter of a report resulting from an exhaustive inquiry by the Inspectorate into aspects of secondary education in England. Its recommendations would be most useful to science educators anywhere.

Keywords: secondary school curriculum; curriculum evaluation; teaching methods; UK – educational advisers.

Identifiers: HMI Secondary Survey (UK) //

00121 - **The SISCON-in-schools project.** Solomon, Joan. London, IoP, 1980. p. 155-158. (Physics education; XV, 3) (eng). // Institute of Physics (UK)

SISCON was developed for higher education. This article outlines its adaptation for 6th forms, and helps to illuminate what is meant by science in a social context for 6th formers.

Keywords: curriculum development; social needs; sixth forms; upper secondary education; UK.

Identifiers: Science in a Social Context (UK) //

00122 - **Social and economic influences in curriculum change in Japan: case history of environmental education.** Shimazu, Y. Tokyo, Japan Society of Science Education, 1980. p. 167-173. (Journal of science education in Japan; IV, 4) (eng). // Japan Society of Science Education

The writer shows that the Japanese attitude to nature is distinctly different from that of the Western world. He goes on to describe the environmental pollution which has increased so much in Japan, and the environmental issues which have appeared in school social studies and science curricula. This article should interest curriculum developers, science teachers and 6th form general studies students.

Keywords: environmental education; environmental perception; interdisciplinary approach; education and culture; Japan – social studies; general education.

00123 - **Social goals and science education in Japan.** Oki, M. Tokyo, Japan Society of Science Education, 1980. p. 121-127. (Journal of science education in Japan; IV, 4) (eng). // Japan Society of Science Education

The author suggests approaches which could help the achievement of social goals. Deploring the common view that science is remote from the general public, he illustrates how science is based on human thinking, and relates fundamental concepts and daily life experiences. He then turns to memorisation/inquiry and induction/deduction. The article closes by observing that science majors as well as non-science majors need to consider the social implications of science.

Keywords: educational goals; social values; general education; Japan – teaching methods; science philosophy; learning processes; educational relevance.

00124 - **Studies of the cognitive abilities of science teachers in the Philippines.** Acuna, J.E.; Villavicencio, R.R. Penang, Malaysia, Regional Centre for Education in Science and Mathematics, 1980. p. 30-40. (Journal of science and mathematics education in Southeast Asia; III, 1) (eng). // SEAMEO. Regional Centre for Education in Science and Mathematics

An account of studies with teachers of elementary science, integrated science, biology and physics. Factors influencing the ability of teachers to operate at the higher formal level are discussed, and the conclusion is that this ability is affected by the adult's occupation. Some strategies for teacher education are discussed.

Keywords: teacher effectiveness; teacher evaluation; teacher education; Philippines – biology education; physics education.

00125 - **A Study of curriculum development and evaluation in integrated science.** Kirby, D.M. London, Centre for Science Education, Chelsea College, University of London, 1980. 366 p. (eng). (PhD thesis, University of London). // University of London. Chelsea College

A study describing a modular programme for non-matriculation students in Newfoundland. The major aims were to improve students attitudes to science and their science-processed skills, and the conclusion is that the project was successful within the limitations of the evaluation. Features include a topic-centered approach and the use of inexpensive equipment.

Keywords: curriculum development; curriculum evaluation; learning modules; modular instruction; secondary education; Canada – student attitudes; activity learning; educational equipment; curriculum research; academic achievement; learning processes; teaching materials; readability.

00126 - **"Tchirrip...tchichirrip...tseep": an alarm call for primary school science.** Bainbridge, J. Hatfield, UK, ASE, 1980. p. 623-638. (School science review; LXI, 217) (eng). // Association for Science Education (UK)

A heavily documented discussion which, though somewhat disjointed, recognises the problems of teachers rarely perceived by the planners. The fact that teachers do not readily turn to books is emphasised. Much of the article, as illustration, deals with bird studies and could provide ideas for teachers. Different parts of this article will be of interest to different levels of science educators.

Keywords: teacher attitudes; primary school curriculum; teacher education; teaching methods; teacher effectiveness – life sciences; teacher evaluation.

00127 - **The Testing of attitudes.** St. Augustine, Trinidad and Tobago, ASETT, 1980. p. 15-16. (Journal of education in science for Trinidad and Tobago; VIII, 1) (eng). // Association for Science Education of Trinidad and Tobago

A short transcript of part of a meeting discussing the assessment of attitudes in Caribbean Examinations Council Integrated Science. It does not answer questions of concern to teachers involved in attitude assessment.

Keywords: student attitudes; student evaluation; educational aims; upper secondary education; Caribbean.

Identifiers: Caribbean Examinations Council Integrated Science (Double Award) //

00128 - **They're only playing: the problem of primary science.** Whitter, M. Hatfield, UK, ASE, 1980. p. 556-560. (School science review; 216) (eng). // Association for Science Education (UK)

The problem with primary school science is seen to be the chasm between skill oriented curriculum developments for that level and the didactic, 'right answer' science experienced at secondary level by most people – a social perception problem. One solution would be for secondary teachers to join the primary teachers to look at children and pool strenghts.

Keywords: primary school curriculum; skill development; activity learning; educational coordination; secondary school teachers; primary school teachers.

00129 - **Thoughts on the style of primary science.** Ward, Alan. Hatfield, UK, ASE, 1980. p. 418-426. (School science review; 216) (eng). // Association for Science Education (UK)

Suggestions about ways of making primary science more fun for teacher and pupils, spontaneous, integrated with other subjects and awakening a sense of wondering open-mindedness. The article is essentially a random collection of ideas.

Keywords: primary school curriculum; interdisciplinary approach; teaching strategies – interest (learning); activity learning.

00130 - **Unesco handbook for science teachers.** Lockard, David; Lowe, Norman K.; Pearson, Robert E.; Reay, Judith; Thier, Herbert. Paris, Unesco; London, Heinemann, 1980. 199 p. (eng; also in fre, spa, jap, gre, mar). // Unesco

The book is a companion volume to the "New Unesco source book for science teachers". The target readership is teachers, education administrators, curriculum planners and teacher educators concerned with upper primary and lower secondary levels. It describes concepts and techniques for making science classes more meaningful and motivating. An appendix intended for debate in teacher education draws on integrated science worldwide.

Keywords: primary education; lower secondary education; teaching methods; teaching guides – science philosophy; history of science; child development; educational psychology; teaching strategies; student evaluation; classroom techniques; school laboratories; educational laboratory equipment; teaching materials; activity learning; evaluation of education; teacher education.

Identifiers: Aristoteles // Galilei, Galileo // Newton, John // Piaget, Jean //

ISBN: 92-3-101666-0 ; 0-435-57970-3.

00131 - **Why science in the primary schools?** Jacobson, Willard J. Kingston, Jamaica, ASTJ, 1980. p. 27-29. (Science journal; I, 1) (eng). // Association of Science Teachers of Jamaica

Giving examples from Jamaica, an American teachers' college professor gives cogent arguments for primary science. Very useful reading for primary teachers reluctant to teach science.

Keywords: primary school teachers; educational aims; general education; Jamaica.

00132 - **Agriculture as science for society – in rural and urban settings.** Blum, Abraham. Malvern, UK, ICSU-CTS, 1891. p. 16-20. (ICSU-CTS newsletter; 7) (eng). // International Council of Scientific Unions. Committee on the Teaching of Science

The article outlines the relationship between Israel's "Agriculture as Environmental Science" and science and society. A Science in Society programme tailor-made for one school system cannot be adopted into another; adapters will be more interested in criteria than in topics and activities, and the article lists some criteria found most useful for the societal facets of the AES.

Keywords: agricultural education; environmental education; curriculum development; Israel.

Identifiers: Agriculture as Environmental Science (Israel) //

00133 - **Aims of the science teacher.** Limerick, Ireland, Thomond College of Education, 1981. p. 21-22. (Chemistry in action!; 4) (eng). // Thomond College of Education (Ireland) // Irish Science Teachers Association

This concise list and justification is intended to guide the young teacher, to serve as a checklist for the older teacher and to help the Irish Science Teachers Association to ensure sound science education.

Keywords: educational aims; curriculum guides; Ireland.

00134 - **Astronomy as a vehicle for motivation in science education.** Stahl, Philip A. College Park, Md, International Astronomical Union, 1981. p. 7-10. (Astronomy newsletter; 9) (eng). // International Astronomical Union Commission

A teacher in Barbados describes how children responded much more enthusiastically than their teachers to approaches from the Barbados Astronomical Society and eventually formed a Student Astronomy Club. He also uses "the Father of Sciences" to motivate and integrate in his teaching for Caribbean Examinations Council integrated science. He observed that science educators tend to anticipate children's interests within our own frame of reference.

Keywords: astronomy; teaching strategies; interest (learning) – upper secondary education; out of school education; Barbados; Caribbean.

Identifiers: Barbados Astronomical Society // Caribbean Examinations Council Integrated Science (Double Award) //

00135 - **British science curriculum projects: how have they taken root in schools?** Tall, Graham. London, Taylor and Francis, 1981. p. 17-38. (European journal of science education; III, 1) (eng; abstr. in ger, fre).

Reviews the uptake of major curriculum development projects in

science from the Nuffield programmes of 1962 to 1980, and includes major Schools Council and some local projects. The writer advances the thesis that whilst dissemination and after-care are essential, they are not sufficient to ensure uptake. The prime factors are a positive atmosphere to innovation and the development of ideas and materials seen by the teachers to be both relevant and relatively inexpensive.

Keywords: curriculum development; curriculum evaluation; educational innovations; teacher role; UK.

Identifiers: Nuffield Junior Science (UK) // Schools Council Science 5-13 Project (UK) // Nuffield Combined Science (UK) // Nuffield Secondary Science (UK) // Schools Council Integrated Science Project (UK) //

00136 - **Changes in students' attitudes towards science in the transition between Australian elementary and secondary schools.** Power, Colin. New York, John Wiley, 1981. p. 33-39. (Journal of research in science teaching; XVIII, 1) (eng). // National Association for Research in Science Teaching (USA)

A study which measured 516 students' attitudes to science twice in their last year of primary schools and again after tansfer to secondary schools. The majority of students enjoyed science at both levels and there was no sharp drop-off in attitude as the secondary year progressed. It would appear, however, that students tranferring from primary schools where they had been actively involved in science activities into secondary schools with a non-involving programme suffered a drop-off in attitude.

Keywords: student attitudes; primary school students; secondary school students; Australia – activity learning; interest (learning).

00137 - **Children learning through science.** Richards, R. Hatfield, UK, ASE, 1981. p. 31-34. (Education in science; 92) (eng). // Association for Science Education (UK)

An outline of the strategies behind a Schools Council project for primary science. The main feature is flexibility, and the author claims that the materials have proved readily acceptable to teachers.

Keywords: primary school curriculum; curriculum guides; curriculum development; teacher attitudes; UK.

Identifiers: Schools Council Children Learning Through Science Project (UK) //

00138 - **Children's attitudes towards science.** Johnson, R.T. Washington, NSTA, 1981. p. 39-41. (Science and children; XVIII, 5) (eng). // National Science Teachers Association (USA)

Refers to a study which samples 72,000 students. This article examines the results obtained from the attitudes to science scale that was administered along with the achievement tests. The results are both surprising and depressing. The National Science Foundation funded programmes are used in so few schools that they have clearly had minimal impact. Some consideration is given to ways in which attitudes can be improved.

Keywords: student attitudes; achievement tests; USA – curriculum evaluation; teaching strategies; academic achievement.

Identifiers: National Science Foundation (USA) // National Assessment of Education Progress, 1976-1977 (USA) //

00139 - **The Cognitive demands of WISC: can the match be improved?** Adey, Philip S. Kingston, Jamaica, University of the West Indies, 1981. p. 1-25. (Caribbean journal of education; VIII, 1) (eng). // University of the West Indies (Jamaica)

The writer outlines how a method of analysing cognitive demands of curricula was validated, and summarises the demand levels. A mismatch between the West Indies Science Curriculum (WISC) and West Indian children was found. Possible required strategies are discussed.

Keywords: curriculum evaluation; academic achievement; Caribbean – teaching strategies; learning processes.

Identifiers: West Indies Science Curriculum (Trinidad and Tobago) //

00140 - **Cognitive style and developing attitudes in the SCIS classroom.** Waring, C. New York, John Wiley, 1980. p. 73-77. (Journal of research in science teaching; XVIII, 1) (eng). // National Association for Research in Science Teaching (USA)

An investigation into possible relationships between field-dependence-independence and scientific attitudes of 353 6th grade New England children who had used SCIS for four years. The Motz scale of attitude towards science and scientists and the Group Embedded Figures Test were used. No statistically significant relationships were found.

Keywords: primary school curriculum; student attitudes; psychological tests; educational psychology; USA.

Identifiers: Science Curriculum Improvement Study (USA) //

00141 - **A Common core in science? Two points of view.** Waring, M.; Schofield, Beta; West, Richard. Hatfield, UK, ASE, 1981. p. 215-236. (School science review; 223) (eng). // Association for Science Education (UK)

Although in a British context, the article explores many fundamental issues in education of concern everywhere. Both parts of the article stress that the idea of a common core and equality in education have profound implications and will not be easily achieved. Waring and Schofield explore a number of models (apples, mushy bananas and pips in pomegranate) and conclude that core science might be possible in some form. West, from much more subjective position, regards the notion as dangerous and pernicious nonsense. Since the core is likely to be derived from existing syllabuses, it will simply contribute to hardening of the arteries; a far more radical reconstruction of the school curriculum is required if human and social needs are to be met.

Keywords: core curriculum; general education; educational policy; curriculum development; UK – educational innovations; educational relevance; specialization.

00142 - **CXC integrated science: an appraisal.** Reay, Judith. Port of Spain, Association of Principals of Public Secondary Schools of Trinidad and Tobago, 1981. p. 13-18. (Education forum; I, 4) (eng). // Association of Principals of Public Secondary Schools of Trinidad and Tobago

The concept of an integrated approach to science teaching is explained and Caribbean Examinations Council Integrated Science (Double Award) examined in this Context. The strenghts and weaknesses of CXC integrated science are assessed and alternatives examined.

Keywords: evaluation of education; curriculum evaluation; Caribbean.

Identifiers: Caribbean Examinations Council Integrated Science (Double Award) //

00143 - **Definition, design, utilization: some problems associated with integrated science curricula with special reference to the Project for Science Integration in Ghana.** Lutterodt, Sarah A. Hamburg, Germany FR, Unesco Institute for Education, 1981. p. 301-314. (International review of education; 27, 3) (eng). // Unesco Institute for Education (Germany FR)

Teachers face difficulties in utilizing integrated science curricula worldwide. The author believes that problems result from a lack of provision in definition, and identifies three kinds of dilemma: (a) how far experience can be incorporated before beginning to sacrifice conceptual unity (b) how pupils' understanding of the theoretical implications of practical activities can be achieved (c) how the varying results of individual pupils' experience can be adapted to the successful teaching of prescribed objectives. She stresses the need for a realistic assessment of integrated science teaching over the last decade.

Keywords: secondary school curriculum; evaluation of education; curriculum development; curriculum evaluation; Ghana – conceptualization; practicums.

Identifiers: Project for Science Integration (Ghana) //

00144 - **The Development of an integrated science information scheme.** Blum, Abraham. London, Taylor and Francis, 1981. p. 1-15. (European journal of science education; III, 1) (eng; abstr. in fre, ger).

Towards an information network on integrated science development programmes worldwide, especially in developing countries, a group of science educators developed the INCISE scheme including the testing and development of an instrument. Compared with International Clearinghouse Reports, the scheme aims to be (1) more objective (2) more detailed (3) more even in geographical coverage. Testing of this instrument aimed at inter-scorer consistency. A revised form is appended to the article with a recommendation for large-scale testing and comparative analysis of the results towards futher improvement.

Keywords: international information systems; educational information systems; questionnaires; curriculum development; curriculum research – educational cooperation.

Identifiers: International Network of Centres for Integrated Science Education //

00145 - **The Dilemma of the environmental educator: are we really needed? Some answers and examples in the affirmative.** Newman, Peter W.G. London, Taylor and Francis, 1981. p. 109-122. (Environmental education and information; I, 2) (eng).

Examines the structure of environmental education and defines the discipline as an integration of three streams: environmental sciences (physical and natural sciences), and environmental engineering (engineering sciences). Describes four integrating problem-oriented courses offered at Murdoch University in Western Australia.

Keywords: university curriculum; higher education; environmental education; Australia – engineering education; interdisciplinary approach; physical sciences; social sciences.

Identifiers: Murdoch University (Australia) //

00146 - **Do teachers rate science attitude objectives as highly as cognitive objectives?** Schibeci, R.A. New York, John Wiley, 1981. p. 69-72. (Journal of research in science teaching; XVIII, 1) (eng). // National Association for Research in Science Teaching (USA)

A study showed that Western Australian high school teachers gave strongly positive answers to the question.

Keywords: educational aims; student attitudes; motivation; academic achievement; secondary school teachers; Australia.

00147 - **Earth science in New Zealand secondary schools.** Vallender, G.D. Wellington, New Zealand Science Teachers Association, 1981. p. 5-11. (N Z science teacher; 29) (eng). // New Zealand Science Teachers Association

The writer's view is that earth science does not receive the attention in schools that this expanding science deserves. The article includes a suggested scheme. The emphasis is on upper school.

Keywords: earth sciences; upper secondary education; geology education; curriculum development.

00148 - **The Earth sciences and the core curriculum: a case for consideration.** Perrin, M.; Thompson, D. Hatfield, UK, ASE, 1981. p. 29-31. (Education in science; 95) (eng). // Association for Science Education (UK)

There has been increasing awareness that the earth sciences should be included in general education to 16+. Quoting extensively from a Royal Society publication, this article answers the questions "What is earth science?" and "What use is it?"

Keywords: earth sciences; general education; geology education; secondary school curriculum; UK.

Identifiers: Royal Society (UK) //

00149 - **Education through science: the policy statement of the Association for Science Education, 1981.** Hatfield, UK, ASE, 1981. p. 5-52. (School science review; 222) (eng). // Association for Science Education (UK)

This policy has been gestating for several years. Its components are (1) the place of science in the school curriculum (2) the development of the school science curriculum, including pedagogic implications of science for all, assessment and resources (3) implementation. The summary on pp 45-47 is usefully cross-referenced to the rest of the statement. Although the statement refers only to the UK, it will be of value to planners and anyone reflecting on his own contribution to science education, perhaps in teacher education programmes. The summary is also published in Education in Science, 93 (June 1981).

Keywords: educational policy; curriculum development; general education; teacher role; UK – student evaluation; educational resources; educational planning.

00150 - **The Effects of single sex and coeducation on science subject preferences and choices at 14+.** Ormerod, M.B. Hatfield, UK, ASE, 1981. p. 553-555. (School science review; 220) (eng). // Association for Science Education (UK)

Another survey which seems to show that each subject is assigned a gender, chemistry and physics being extremely "male", and biology mildly "female". With girls, there is some correlation with perceived "easiness". Since children are generally asked to make subject choices at puberty, the choice may be no more rational than an assertion of sex. The solution appears to be a balanced curriculum up to 16+.

Keywords: sex stereotypes; elective courses; student attitudes; secondary school curriculum – physics education; chemistry education; biology education; core curriculum; general education; coeducational schools; sex role; UK.

00151 - **ESTEAM: a curriculum development for exceptionally able children in science.** Screen, Peter. Hatfield, UK, ASE, 1981. p. 350-355. (School science review; 223) (eng). // Association for Science Education (UK)

A summary report of summer schools for 12-13 years olds thought to be in the top 2% of their age group. It is preceded by a discussion of the characteristics of the gifted child in science, and strategies for meeting his needs.

Keywords: gifted students; ability; lower secondary education; teaching strategies; UK.

00152 - **Evaluating school laboratory skills.** Lunetta, V.N.; Hofstein, Avi; Giddings, Geoff. Washington, NSTA, 1981. p. 22-25. (Science teacher; XLVIII, 4801) (eng). // National Science Teachers Association (USA)

The assessment of cognitive achievement is routinely done by most teachers. Practical-based questions are in the minority, however, and

this article may help teachers to include a different type of evaluation procedure in their work.

Keywords: activity learning; school laboratories; practicums; evaluation methods; student evaluation.

00153 - **An Evaluation of the Nigerian Integrated Science Project.** Jegede, Olugbemiro Johnson. Malvern, UK, ICSU-CTS, 1981. p. 26-27. (ICSU-CTS Newsletter; 8) (eng). // International Council of Scientific Unions. Committee on the Teaching of Science

A synopsis of a PhD study. It could be of interest to those concerned about the success of integrated science in general and in Nigeria in particular.

Keywords: curriculum evaluation; lower secondary education; Nigeria.

Identifiers: Science Teachers Association of Nigeria // Nigerian Integrated Science Project //

00154 - **An Evaluation of the Nigerian Integrated Science Project (NISP).** Jegede, Olugbemiro Johnson. Wales, UK, University of Wales, 1981. 321 p. (eng). (Thesis submitted in candidature for the degree of Ph.D of the University of Wales). // University of Wales (UK)

The study focuses on the achievement of the Project's objectives as expressed by the teachers involved; and determines the performance in, and attitude towards, integrated science by the students. Results suggested that integrated science teachers were not favourably disposed towards the Project (due to the lack of appropriate training) and the achievement of cognitive objectives was below expectations. On the other hand, the majority of students had developed positive attitudes towards science through NISP. However, a significantly negative association between attitude towards science and achievement in science was found. Location of school (rural/urban), sex and socio-economic background were found to be correlates of achievement in, and attitudes towards, integrated science. The majority of students found NISP books very difficult to understand, and readability indices indicated that the books were far too advanced for the students for whom they were meant.

Keywords: evaluation of education; educational projects; project evaluation; Nigeria – lower secondary education; teacher attitudes; student attitudes; teacher education; readability; textbooks; academic achievement.

Identifiers: Nigerian Integrated Science Project //

00155 - **Guidelines for early primary science education (5-10 years): concepts and lesson contents.** Ward, Alan. Hatfield, UK, ASE, 1981. p. 540-545. (School science review; 220) (eng). // Association for Science Education (UK)

"Science 5-13" is rather too voluminous for teachers to find their way around quickly. This author identifies concepts to be taught, and suggests ideas for developing them.

Keywords: primary school curriculum; concepts; teaching strategies; lesson plans; UK.

Identifiers: Schools Council Science 5-13 Project (UK) //

00156 - **History and philosophy in school science.** Sherratt, W. J. Hatfield, UK, ASE, 1981. p. 3-71. (School science review; 223) (eng). // Association for Science Education (UK)

This letter observes that the history and philosophy of science as a means of humanizing and liberalizing school science courses has been urged since the beginning of this century. He suggests that more positive action is now needed.

Keywords: science philosophy; history of science; humanism; curriculum development; educational innovations.

00157 - **The Implications of the "Science in Society" project.** Buttle, J.W. Hatfield, UK, ASE, 1981. p. 187-188. (School science review; 222) (eng). // Association for Science Education (UK)

The writer of this letter is critical of what he identifies as a failure to recognise differences in human values in a study of society. He also feels that other subject teachers should have been involved. In short, he appears to believe that the values throughout the course are those of the scientific "establishment".

Keywords: upper secondary education; social values; humanism; interdisciplinary approach; UK.

Identifiers: "Science in Society" (UK) //

00158 - **Instruction and science learning: a quantitative synthesis.** Boulanger, F.D. New York, John Wiley, 1981. p. 113-121. (Journal of research in science teaching; XVIII, 2) (eng). // National Association for Research in Science Teaching (USA)

Many studies have been done on the quality and quantity of science instruction. This article quantitatively synthesises much of this work over the 1963-1978 period. There is an extensive bibliography.

Keywords: educational quality; teaching methods; learning processes; educational trends; USA; bibliographies.

00159 - **An Integrated approach to energy education.** Klaus, M. Washington, National Science Teachers Association, 1981. p. 8-9. (Science and children; XVIII, 8) (eng).

A description of a third grade energy programme which involves mathematics, social studies, economics, household management. It could easily contain lots more.

Keywords: energy education; primary school curriculum; USA.

00160 - **An Integrated lesson on lead.** Lambert, E. Norman. St. Augustine, Trinidad and Tobago, ASETT, 1981. p. 9-10. (Journal of education in science for Trinidad and Tobago; VIII, 2) (eng). // Association for Science Education of Trinidad and Tobago

A short transcript of a lesson conducted by students with minimal teacher input, and illustrating the kinds of interaction possible, and issues raised in an integrated approach to science.

Keywords: upper secondary education; teaching strategies; peer teaching; activity learning; discussion (teaching method); Trinidad and Tobago.

00161 - **Integrated science unit, pt. 2.** Vella-Zarb, T.A. Waterloo, Ont., University of Waterloo, 1981. p. 4-6. (Chem 13 news; 119) (eng). // University of Waterloo (Canada)

The final part of a study on urine, which integrates skills acquired in physics, concepts learned in chemistry, principles of health and topics learned in biology. Much of it can be carried out at home. Full details are given for the teacher, and there should be few logistic problems.

Keywords: secondary school curriculum; teaching strategies; teaching materials; Canada – student projects; practicums.

00162 - **Interrelating science with other subjects.** Main, E.D. Washington, NSTA, 1981. p. 26-27. (Science and children; XVIII, 5) (eng). // National Science Teachers Association (USA)

A brief but interesting description oh how a third grade class involved a wide variety of subjects in a unit on 'the solar system'. With a little imagination on the part of a teacher, such things are surprisingly easy to organize, and allow for enrichment of many subjects.

Keywords: primary school curriculum; interdisciplinary approach; teaching strategies; general education; USA.

00163 - **The Nuclear debate: examination of the issues.** Ellington, H.I.; Addinall, E. London, IoP, 1981. p. 274-281. (Physics education; XVI, 5) (eng). // Institute of Physics (UK)

The article begins with projections about Britain's energy consumption and fuels available, indicating that there is no alternative to the eventual dependence on fast reactors. For other countries, the data would not apply, although the ideas would. The article then goes on to present, without comment, the views of opponents and protagonists of nuclear energy generation. The article would be suitable for 6th form science and non-science students, and could form the basis of a debate. The authors have developed a teaching package for just this purpose.

Keywords: energy education; energy sources; nuclear energy; sixth forms; discussion (teaching method) – social needs; upper secondary education; teaching strategies; learning modules; teaching materials; UK.

00164 - **Nuffield Combined Science: teams for the seventies, themes for the eighties.** Holford, Derek. Driffield, UK, Studies in Education, 1981. p. 38-42. (Education 3-13; IX, 4) (eng).

Appraises new Nuffield Combined Science materials (themes) for teachers of children aged 9-11. Reflects on teaching tactics for the 80s. Suggests reasons for the popularity of the Combined Science course and also for the introduction of the Themes. He suggests a less radical shift in teaching style than discovery learning and guided discovery, and favours a curriculum focused more on the enrichment and mastery of concepts.

Keywords: primary school curriculum; curriculum guides; educational aims; teaching strategies; classroom techniques; UK – heuristic method (teaching); direct method (teaching); concepts; teacher attitudes; activity learning.

Identifiers: Nuffield Combined Science Themes for the Middle Years (UK) //

00165 - **Origins and significance of the science, technology and society movement.** Roby, Keith R. Clayton, Australia, Monash University, 1981. p. 37-43. (Australian science teachers journal; 27, 2) (eng). // Monash University (Australia)

The significance of the inclusion of subject matter pertaining to science, technology and society (STS) in the science curriculum is examined and discussed.

Keywords: biology education; educational aims; secondary school curriculum; technology – curriculum development; educational relevance; Australia.

00166 - **Performance of some Nigerian pupils on some selective concepts in integrated science.** Oyeneyin, A.M.; Balogun, T.A. Ibadan, Nigeria, STAN, 1981. p. 104-111. (Journal of the Science Teachers' Association of Nigeria; XX, 1) (eng). // Science Teachers' Association of Nigeria
A small study of Class 2 pupils which found that achievement at lower cognitive levels was significantly better than at higher levels. No significant differences were found among ease of mastering the various concepts.
Keywords: lower secondary education; academic achievement; concepts; learning processes; Nigeria.

00167 - **Physics for none to 16?** Archenhold, W.F. London, IoP, 1981. 193 p. (Physics education; XVI, 4) (eng).
Expressing his concerns for children and for child-centred teaching, the author appears to support specialist sciences rather than integration.
Keywords: physics education; educational aims; UK.

00168 - **Primary science curriculum development in Africa: strategies, problems and prospects with particular reference to the 'African Primary Science Programme'.** Bajah, Sam Tunde. London, Taylor and Francis, 1981. p. 259-269. (International journal of science education; III, 3) (eng; abstr. in fre, ger).
Discusses problems of introducing the African Primary Science Programme (APSP) in Anglophone African states and its implication for science education in Africa. The background and characteristics of APSP are given and the account of its development is interesting.
Keywords: primary school curriculum; curriculum development; educational innovations; English speaking Africa.
Identifiers: African Primary Science Programme //

00169 - **A Reflection on some meanings of 'interdisciplinary' and 'integration among the sciences'.** Arca, M.; Vicentini-Missoni, M. London, Taylor and Francis, 1981. p. 117-126. (European journal of science education; III, 2) (eng; abstr. in fre, ger).
After the Nijmegen International Conference in 1978, these researchers found it necessary to struggle with the concepts embodied in these and similar terms and thus to clarify needs of science education, starting with primary children.
Keywords: interdisciplinary approach; concepts; educational philosophy; science philosophy – educational needs; primary school curriculum.

00170 - **A Sandwich course for primary science.** Brown, C. A. Hatfield, UK, ASE, 1981. p. 342-343. (School science review; 223) (eng). // Association for Science Education (UK)
This article describes a strategy in one area of England. It arose from the expressed needs of teachers for help in clarifying what is expected of them and in disseminating appropriate science teaching in their own schools. The support of administrators is required, not least for the release of teachers for the college parts of the course. There has so far been no evaluation.
Keywords: primary school curriculum; primary teacher education; inservice teacher education; UK.

00171 - **The School curriculum.** Black, Paul J. London, IOP, 1981. p. 201. (Physics bulletin; XXXII, 7) (eng). // Institute of Physics (UK)
The author, a scientist and a science educator, discusses the quandary of science for all up to 16 while at the same time selecting and training the most talented. He proposes a new type of curriculum – a core about science and scientists, and a spectrum of options.
Keywords: core curriculum; secondary school curriculum; educational aims; elective courses; student selection; gifted students; UK.

00172 - **The School curriculum: a response.** Chapman, B.R. London, IoP, 1981. p. 348. (Physics bulletin; XXXII, 11) (eng). // Institute of Physics (UK)
The writer believes that recent British proposals for restructuring the curriculum are a rear view which take no account of developments in society. He suggests a 13-16 structure in which there are more courses studied for shorter periods, e.g. one-term courses on science and sport, science and music, physics/technology. Then there would be no need to make science compulsory for everyone. In "Phys. Bull., 33,1 (January 1982), 7, R.G. Cawthorne comments critically. He is attracted by much in Chapman's proposals, but points out that they will have to be more carefully marshalled. And in "Phys. Bull., 33, 2 (Febuary 1982), 44, C.A. Crofts argues that employers and all levels of higher education would not be satisfied by such a course.
Keywords: curriculum development; upper secondary education; core curriculum; interdisciplinary approach; UK – education and employment.

00173 - **Science and mathematics in school: towards an interdisciplinary approach.** Ingle, Richard B.; Turner, Anthony D. Hatfield, UK, ASE, 1981. p. 31-33. (Education in science; 93) (eng). // Association for Science Education (UK)
Teachers are well aware that pupils have difficulty transferring their learning in mathematics to their science studies. Yet few schools have done anything about integrating policy and teaching for science and mathematics. Some resources are mentioned, and the article ends with a plea for integration at the teacher education level.
Keywords: mathematics education; interdisciplinary approach; curriculum development; teacher education – educational coordination; educational resources; teacher education curriculum.

00174 - **Science and society in the Australian senior secondary school.** Fensham, Peter J. Malvern, UK, ICSU-CTS, 1981. p. 23-25. (ICSU-CTS newsletter; 8) (eng). // International Council of Scientific Unions. Committee on the Teaching of Science
A brief account of the emphasis in the Australian physical science curriculum, "Man and the Physical World". Uptake and modification in some Australian states is mentioned.
Keywords: physical sciences; upper secondary education; Australia – curriculum development.
Identifiers: "Man and the Physical World" (Australia) //

00175 - **Science curricula: what for?** Shepard, R. Penang, Malaysia, SEAMEO-RECSAM, 1981. 3 p. (Regional centre for education in science and mathematics news; 42) (eng). // SEAMEO. Regional Centre for Education in Science and Mathematics
A specialist in curriculum design suggests that the main learnings in South East Asia school science are the "hidden" curriculum: the ability to tolerate boredom, to accept unquestioningly the statements of authority figures, that schooling is irrelevant to everyday life, etc. In this region as in Western countries, there are few attempts to state the objectives of science education in terms of national goals. Giving some examples of approaches that could be related to national goals, he suggests that South East Asia could develop indigenous curricula which produces autonomous, informed citizens and which could provide a lead for Western countries.
Keywords: science and development; curriculum development; education and development; South East Asia – teaching methods; teacher effectiveness; educational relevance; civic education.

00176 - **Science in a changing society.** Ventura, A.K. Kingston, Jamaica, ASTJ, 1981. p. 25-30. (Science journal; II) (eng). // Association of Science Teachers of Jamaica
The Executive Director of Jamaica's Scientific Research Council describes science as he sees it, and its relationship to society in poor tropical countries like Jamaica. He identifies the emphases needed. Original and creative specialists are needed, as well as a logical and a broad minded population. School courses in science need to include its history, its philosophy, its evolution, its contemporary failings and its future, and must be taught as a method of inquiry.
Keywords: educational goals; science and development; curriculum; social needs; developing countries – science and development; education and development; biotechnology; history of science; science philosophy; Jamaica.

00177 - **Science in men's society.** Harding, Jan. Hatfield, UK, ASE, 1981. p. 368-371. (School science review; 223) (eng). // Association for Science Education (UK)
The "Science in Society materials" are criticised as displaying a massively insensitive and arrogant male interpretation.
Keywords: teaching materials; curriculum guides; sex stereotypes.
Identifiers: "Science in Society" (UK) //

00178 - **The Science in Society course.** Holman, John. York, UK, IUPAC Committee on the Teaching of Chemistry, 1981. p. 14-17. (International newsletter on chemical education; 15) (eng). // International Union of Pure and Applied Chemistry. Committee on the Teaching of Chemistry
This course for sixth form General Studies has been well publicised in various media. Here the article outlines the materials and strategies involved.
Keywords: general education; educational relevance; upper secondary education; teaching materials; UK.
Identifiers: "Science in Society" (UK) //

00179 - **Science in the primary schools: what went wrong?** Plimmer, D. Hatfield, Uk, ASE, 1981. p. 641-647. (School science review; 221) (eng). // Association for Science Education (UK)
This is an exploration of why primary teachers are so reluctant to teach science. Possible factors identified are ability, style of learning, attitudes to science, and difficulty in understanding scientific literature. Primary science is seen as just one link in a vicious circle of events.
Keywords: primary school teachers; teacher attitudes.

00180 - **The Secondary science curriculum: can we learn anything from primary schools?** Baxter, M. Hatfield, UK, ASE, 1981. 37 p. (Education in science; 92) (eng). // Association for Science Education (UK)

It appears that hardly anyone understands the nature of science, and there is often a mis-match between children and the science they are taught. The very best primary school science may have got it right.

Keywords: secondary school curriculum; primary school curriculum; academic achievement; evaluation of education.

00181 - **Sex-role stereotyping by high school females in science.** Vockell, E.L.; Lobonc, S. New York, John Wiley, 1981. p. 209-219. (Journal of research in science teaching; XVIII, 3) (eng). // National Association for Research in Science Teaching (USA)

An interesting study which shows that while science in general is not viewed by girls as a masculine area, physical sciences are. Interestingly, such sex-role stereotyping is far more likely to occur in co-education schools than in all-girls schools. Some possible reasons for this are discussed.

Keywords: sex stereotypes; student attitudes; secondary school students; physical sciences; girls education – coeducational schools; girls schools.

00182 - **Sex-role stereotyping in science textbooks.** Norman, H.; Hiha, A. New Zealand, New New Zealand Science Teachers Association, 1981. p. 20-21. (N Z Science Teacher; 29) (eng). // New Zealand Science Teachers Association

These women examined 80 books, and found a male bias, stronger in secondary than in primary schools. The writers of the article have not been careful enough to exclude the possibility that they may have been biased themselves. Mary Garlick in a brief note at the end of the article gives advice on ways to counter the sex imbalance in science textbooks.

Keywords: textbooks; sex stereotypes; sex role; New Zealand – educational resources; teaching materials; teaching strategies.

00183 - **The Social implications of science and science choices at 14+.** Ormerod, M.B. Hatfield, UK, ASE, 1981. p. 164-167. (School science review; 222) (eng). // Association for Science Education (UK)

Describes an investigation into attitudes to the social implications of science, subject preference and liking for the teachers. After reporting the findings, the author concludes that the work on the social implications of science should be taken before 14+.

Keywords: social values; cultural values; student attitudes; secondary school curriculum; UK.

00184 - **Some science curriculum notes.** Ferguson, D.; Perris, Lyall. Wellington, New Zealand Science Teachers Association, 1981. p. 34-37. (N Z Science Teacher; 29) (eng). // New Zealand Science Teachers Association

An account of developments in agriculture education and moderation of school-based assessment in modular science.

Keywords: agricultural education; examinations; activity learning; student evaluation; modular instruction; New Zealand.

Identifiers: New Zealand Modular Science //

00185 - **Students tell teachers what they want from school.** Javs, H.H. Washington, NSTA, 1981. 30 p. (Science and children; XVIII, 6) (eng). // National Science Teachers Association (USA)

Reports a study involving 224 teachers and their K-6 students. The teachers felt that they knew what their students wanted from school – they were wrong! Only two of the teachers felt that their students would want to learn or do science or learn about a science related career. None of the K-2 students did, but 27-30% of the 3-6 children did. Girls expressed as much interest in science as did the boys. One wonders how many of the teachers were actually teaching science and, if they were, what sort of science they taught if they felt that their students wouldn't want to learn it.

Keywords: primary school students; student attitudes; teacher attitudes; teacher effectiveness; USA – primary school curriculum; sex stereotypes.

00186 - **A Survey of environmental issues treated in science education curricula, before and after 1974.** Blum, Abraham. New York, John Wiley, 1981. p. 221-228. (Journal of research in science teaching; XVIII, 3) (eng). // National Association for Research in Science Teaching (USA)

Environmental science has become very popular in the last decade or so. Unfortunately, less attention has been paid to training teachers in environmental science education. This survey examines how the USA has met this challenge. It draws on ERIC documentation and the 9th International Clearinghouse Report.

Keywords: environmental education; teacher education; bibliographies; USA.

Identifiers: Eric (USA) //

00187 - **Teaching monitoring of practical work.** Brathwaite, WorkeleyE. Kingston, University of the West Indies, 1981. p. 9-13. (Science Education Centre newsletter; XII, 1) (eng). // University of the West Indies (Jamaica). Science Education Centre

The author is disturbed that, although science programmes place considerable emphasis on practical work, assessment of students does not involve much assessment of practical ability, or assesses invalidly and unhelpfully. Sympathising with teachers of large classes, he suggests strategies by means which teachers can keep informative records.

Keywords: activity learning; practicums; student evaluation; class size; evaluation methods – Caribbean.

00188 - **What is science?** Tunnicliffe, S.D. Hatfield, UK, ASE, 1981. p. 548-550. (School science review; 220) (eng). // Association for Science Education (UK)

A primary teacher gives her view of science in the primary school ("tremendous fun"). She has attempted to deal with too many issues in only two pages, but the article could be useful with student teachers, as a starting point for discussion.

Keywords: primary school curriculum; teacher attitudes; primary school teachers; teacher education.

00189 - **What science would year 7 students like to study: some questions, answers and differences.** Dawson, C.J.; Bennett, N. Parkside, South Australian Science Teachers Association, 1981. p. 13-17. (South Australian Science Teachers Association journal; 813) (eng). // South Australian Science Teachers Association

South Australian students were surveyed to determine what science topics they would prefer to study and how they would like to study them. Results for all students (N=753), boys (N=400), and girls (N=353) are reported for the 15 most popular topics and preferred study method. Includes implications for science instruction.

Keywords: interest (learning); sex stereotypes; student attitudes; Australia – upper secondary education; teaching strategies; study methods.

00190 - **Who cares what school biology is for?** Fawns, Rod. Clayton, Australia, Monash University, 1981. p. 23-29. (Australian science teachers journal; 27, 2) (eng). // Monash University (Australia)

Discussed is the question: "If science curricula reflect actions of pressure groups to include or delete certain content, is science a part of a basic, liberal education?"

Keywords: biology education; curriculum; academic freedom; public opinion – curriculum evaluation; educational aims; general education; secondary education; secondary school curriculum; Australia.

00191 - **Caribbean science education: a decade in review.** King, Winston K. Hong Kong, HKASME, 1982. p. 166-177. (Journal of the Hong Kong Association for Science and Mathematics Education; X, 2) (eng). // Hong Kong Association for Science and Mathematics Education

The account, largely about developments in integrated science, dwells on Caribbean Examinations Council Integrated Science (double Award), on teachers' college assessment in the Eastern Caribbean and on the development of science teachers' associations; and touches on science at 11+ and 14+. Predictions for the 80s are made.

Keywords: curriculum development; educational testing; teacher evaluation; Caribbean – examination boards; teacher associations; teacher education; educational trends.

Identifiers: Caribbean Examinations Council Integrated Science (Double Award) //

00192 - **CXC integrated science: to integrate or not to integrate?** Hill, E. Reading, UK, University of Reading, 1982. p. (eng). (Unpublished M.Ed. dissertation). // University of Reading (UK)

CISC is a set of teaching materials put together by Caribbean educators with the aim of helping teachers and candidates for the first CXC science. The author considers whether CISC and integration would be acceptable to teachers and students in Antigua and Barbuda. He concludes that non-integration at this level is preferable, but at lower secondary level the science should be integrated.

Keywords: specialization; teaching materials; upper secondary education; lower secondary education; Antigua and Barbuda; teaching guides – teacher attitudes; student attitudes; curriculum guides; teaching materials.

Identifiers: Caribbean Examinations Council // Caribbean Integrated Science Curriculum // CXC Integrated Science (Double Award) //

00193 - **Did the exam work? (Part 2).** Phillips, R.F. Hatfield, UK, ASE, 1982. p. 15-19. (Education in science; 99) (eng). // Association for Science Education (UK)

Describes how British 16+ papers in biology and integrated science (1981) were analysed in an attempt to determine whether they matched the general objectives and weightings given in the syllabuses. This analysis raises fundamental issues of examining, including the effects of choice in a paper. It also gives guidelines for conducting a similar exercise locally. (Part 1 in EiS 98, p. 13-17, reported similar analyses for chemistry and physics papers.).

Keywords: upper secondary education; examinations; educational aims; biology education; UK.

00194 - **11-13science in middle schools: common practice or common core?** Allsop, R.Terry; Collins, R.C. Hatfield, UK, ASE, 1982. p. 554-555. (School science review; 224) (eng). // Association for Science Education (UK)

In a small survey these writers found that practice was very similar in the various schools, and showed the same deficiencies (familar to those with experience elsewhere). Rethinking of work at this level is imperative.

Keywords: secondary school curriculum; lower secondary education; teaching methods; core curriculum.

00195 - **An Evaluation of the Nigerian Integrated Science Project (NISP) after a decade of use in the classroom.** Jegede, Olugbemiro Johnson. Hamburg, Germany FR, Unesco Institute for Education, 1982. p. 321-336. (International review of education; 18, 3) (eng; abstr. in fre, ger). // Unesco Institute for Education (Germany FR)

Evaluation instruments included a questionaire, assessment, attitude and readability tests, the subject being 482 teachers and 1894 pupils. Problems revealed lack of appropriate teacher training and low achievement of cognitive objectives, but the majority of children had developed positive attitudes towards science. Areas of concern are identified. The project expects too much from the teachers. Doubt is cast on the validity of readability formulae where English is a foreign language (though the official one). Suggests an explanation for the negative association between achievement and attitude.

Keywords: lower secondary education; project evaluation; educational projects; evaluation of education; Nigeria – teacher attitudes; student attitudes; readability; language of instruction; academic achievement.

Identifiers: Nigerian Integrated Science Project //

00196 - **Health development through primary health: from theory into practice.** Monekosso, G.L. Kingston, Jamaica, CFNI, 1982. p. 35-40. (Cajanus; XV, 1) (eng). // Caribbean Food and Nutrition Institute

While much time is devoted to "health and hygiene" in the primary schools of the Caribbean, little attention is paid to these at the secondary level. This article outlines the primary health care model and could provide secondary school teachers with some ideas they could discuss with their students.

Keywords: health education; secondary school curriculum; teaching strategies; teaching materials; Caribbean.

Identifiers: Primary health care model (Caribbean) //

00197 - **Integrated science: should any pupils fail?** Heyworth, Rex. Hong Kong, HKASME, 1982. p. 15-18. (Journal of the Hong Kong Association for Science and Mathematics Education; X, 1) (eng). // Hong Kong Association for Science and Mathematics Education

This article is of interest in the context of purposes and strategies of assessment. The core of the argument is that each pupil should be assessed on the basis of a personal set of objectives. The writer also distinguishes between end-of-term and end-of-unit tests.

Keywords: student evaluation; ability grouping – educational testing; educational aims.

00198 - **Integrated science: what do teachers think?** Allsop, R. Terry; Hassanali, Amena. St Augustine, Trinidad and Tobago, Association for Science Education, 1982. p. 1-6. (Journal of education in science for Trinidad and Tobago ; X, 1) (eng). // Association for Science Education of Trinidad and Tobago

Summarises the findings of a study into the attitudes of teachers towards integrated science for the Caribbean Examinations Council. Chemists held the most favorable attitudes, followed by biologists and then physicists. Interpretations are suggested and recommendations are made for improving the status of integrated science.

Keywords: upper secondary education; teacher attitudes; Trinidad and Tobago.

Identifiers: Caribbean Examinations Council //

00199 - **Integrating with science: one way to bring science back into the elementary school day.** Cohen, Herbert; Staley, Frederick. Bowling Green, Ohio, School Science and Mathematics Association, 1982. p. 565-572. (School science and mathematics; LXXXII, 7) (eng). // School Science and Mathematics Association (USA)

The difficulties of elementary school teachers with science are well-known. The writers argue that integrating science with other disciplines should improve the quality and quantity of science instruction by using science topics, units, themes or curricular materials as vehicles for bringing meaning to the study of other academic disciplines. A classified outline of elementary programmes is provided.

Keywords: interdisciplinary approach; primary school curriculum; teaching strategies; teacher effectiveness; educational quality; USA.

00200 - **Junior secondary science revision: how does it fit with what the experts say?** Dale, Terry. Victoria, B.C., British Columbia Science Teachers' Association of the British Columbia Teachers' Federation, 1982. p. 5-6. (The B C science teacher; XXIV, 822404) (eng). // British Columbia Science Teachers' Association (Canada)

The curriculum, initially with its content organised in an integrated fashion, has been modified so that teachers have a choice of an integrated or discipline-oriented approach. The article outlines the flavour of the revised curriculum.

Keywords: lower secondary education; curriculum development; specialization; Canada.

00201 - **Measuring student attitudes: semantic differential or Likert instruments?** Schibeci, R.A. New York, John Wiley, 1982. p. 565-570. (Science education; 66, 4) (eng).

Following descriptions of a semantic differential (SD) and test of science-related attitudes (TOSRA) – a Likert-type scale – reports results of using the instruments with secondary school students in various Australian schools (N=1 049 for TOSRA and 1 116 for SD). Suggests SD for general attitude and Likert-type scales of specific attitude measurement.

Keywords: student attitudes; educational measurement; comparative analysis; secondary school students – Australia.

Identifiers: Test of Science-related Attitudes (Australia) //

00202 - **Putting science and society in your classroom.** Beisenherz, P.C. Reston, VA, National Association of Biology Teachers, 1982. p. 180-182. (American biology teacher; XLIV, 3) (eng). // National Association of Biology Teachers (USA)

The need for biology teachers to consider society-oriented topics, those which relate to their students' lives, is emphasized. There is evidence that teachers either believe strongly in content-oriented goals or are unable to implement social goals (i.e those not found in the text). Solutions to the latter part are suggested, general rather than specific. The writer emphasises that if the teacher is to follow these up he must already have a strong commitment. If teachers are unwilling to devote the time and effort to go beyond the text, curriculum innovation is unlikely.

Keywords: social needs; educational relevance; educational goals; teacher effectiveness; teacher attitudes – biology education; curriculum development.

00203 - **Resources for science teaching: report of a survey in the Commonwealth Caribbean.** Reay, Judith. London, Commonwealth Secretariat, 1982. 76 p. (eng). // Commonwealth Secretariat

The survey attends particularly to the teaching of integrated science and physics; as such it would embrace resources for most science teaching. There are sections on science and production, improvisions and improvement, science rooms, audiovisual and printed resources, centres and information sources, servicing of equipment and science teachers associations. Appendices include tables of materials in schools for teaching physics and integrated science.

Keywords: educational resources; educational laboratory equipment; audiovisual aids; school laboratories; Caribbean – teacher centres; physics education; primary education; secondary education; teacher associations; Jamaica; Guyana; Trinidad and Tobago; Barbados.

Identifiers: University of the West Indies // Caribbean Examinations Council // Jamaica Science Education Centre // University of the West Indies //

ISBN: 0-85092-212-7.

00204 - **Science education: a select classified bibliography of Nigerian sources, 1960-1982.** Muogilim, Emma S. Ibadan, STAN, 1982. p. 164-178. (Journal of the Science Teachers' Association of Nigeria; XX, 2) (eng). // Science Teachers' Association of Nigeria

The 350-odd items include 55 higher degree disertations, periodical articles and conference papers. The sections on general issues and integrated science are relatively extensive.

Keywords: bibliographies; theses; Nigeria.

00205 - **Science education for citizens: perspectives and issues.** Gaskell, P. James. Leeds, UK, Leeds University Centre for Studies in Science Education, 1982. p. 33-46. (Studies in science education; 9) (eng). // Leeds University (UK). Centre for Studies in Science

Education

The article deals with the interests of various social groups in supporting a thorough revision of the junior secondary science programme in Canada. Attention is drawn to some of the issues in science, technology and society curricula that need to be addressed by science teachers, and to some organisational decisions that need to be made in developing curriculum materials of this type. Deep rooted ethnical and political factors will make it difficult to reach consensus, but teachers must attempt to find answers to the large questions about the social context of science, the political nature of curriculum and what it means to educate a person about a social issue.

Keywords: civic education; educational relevance; pressure groups; lower secondary education; curriculum development; teacher responsibility; Canada.

Identifiers: Junior secondary science (Canada) //

00206 - **Science in society.** Pickup, R.; Lewis, John L.; Payne, V. Hatfield, UK, ASE, 1982. p. 776-779. (School science review; 225) (eng). // Association for Science Education (UK)

These are three letters relating to the ASE's Science in Society materials. One is highly critical, the others are from developers of the materials.

Keywords: upper secondary education; curriculum guides; teaching materials; UK.

Identifiers: "Science in Society" (UK) //

00207 - **Science literacy for all students.** Brown, Peggy. Washington, Association of American Colleges, 1982. 19 p. (Forum for liberal education; 5, 1) (eng). // Association of American Colleges

Describes selected college programmes to increase students' science literacy to prepare them for a world of science and technology.

Keywords: higher education; core curriculum; scientific literacy; general education; USA – educational relevance; social needs.

00208 - **16 + practical assessment.** Biggs, P. Hatfield, UK, ASE, 1982. 43 p. (Education in science; 97) (eng). // Association for Science Education (UK)

This is a brief report of a survey of English science teachers into their views on school based assessment.

Keywords: upper secondary education; examinations; activity learning; student evaluation; UK.

00209 - **Student teachers' attitudes toward science and science teaching.** Lucas, Keith B.; Dooley, John H. New York, John Wiley, 1982. p. 805-809. (Journal of research in science teaching; XIX, 9) (eng). // National Association for Research in Science Teaching (USA)

Investigated attitudes of Australian elementary school student teachers (N=67) towards science and science teaching. No change in attitude was reported (using Moore and Sutman's Attitude Toward Science Teaching Scales) as a result of taking a content-based science unit, suggesting more effort in fostering desirable attitudes among these teachers.

Keywords: student teachers; student attitudes; teacher attitudes; teaching methods; primary school teachers; preservice teacher education; Australia.

00210 - **Teachers' attitudes to the introduction of integrated science in the fourth year of secondary school in Trinidad and Tobago.** Hassanali, Amena. Oxford, UK, Dept of Educational Studies, St Catherine's College, 1982. 110 p. (eng). (Unpublished thesis for Master of Science in Educational Studies). // St. Catherine's College (UK). Dept of Educational Studies

A study undertaken when the Caribbean Examinations Council Integrated Science (Double Award) was relatively new. Results indicated that attitudes were more favourable among (a) trained than untrained teachers (b) chemistry teachers than biology teachers (c) biology teachers than physics teachers (d) teachers of less able pupils than those of more able pupils.

Keywords: teacher attitudes; secondary school curriculum; educational innovations; curriculum development; Trinidad and Tobago.

Identifiers: Caribbean Examinations Council Integrated Science (Double Award) //

00211 - **Teaching about science, technology and society at the secondary school level in the United States: an educational dilemma for the 1980s.** McConnell, Mary C. Leeds, UK, Leeds University Centre for Studies in Science Education, 1982. p. 1-32. (Studies in science education; IX) (eng). // Leeds University (UK). Centre for Studies in Science Education

Summarises some US studies, which show that over the past decade the system of science education in the US has come to be out of harmony with science, the national interest and the needs of the individual. The aims of science education are not understood, and precollege students may receive little or no science courses. Explores attempts to clarify approaches to education about science, technology and society, and exemplifies with some US modules. Closes by identifying some important areas of concern.

Keywords: secondary school curriculum; educational relevance; educational aims; USA – educational trends; individual development; educational needs; learning modules; education and development; secondary school students.

00212 - **Trends in science education and the future of science curriculum in Nigeria.** Oyedum, N.A.; Shuaibu, M.J. Ibadan, Nigeria, STAN, 1982. p. 75-96. (Journal of the Science Teachers' Association of Nigeria; XXI, 1) (eng). // Science Teachers' Association of Nigeria

The article takes an overview of trends worldwide from 1956-57 to 1974-75 in terms of (a) initiation of new projects (b) African projects (c) research and dissertation topics (d) journal articles (USA and UK) by subject (e) themes of new projects in USA and UK. The authors regret that Nigerian science education is influenced, if not dictated, by activity elsewhere. They identify opportunities to face science education problems that are really Nigerian.

Keywords: educational trends; education and culture; curriculum evaluation; Nigeria – educational innovations; educational research; Africa; USA; UK; research priorities.

00213 - **Updating and retraining of science teachers.** Hong Kong, Hong Kong Association for Science and Mathematics Education, 1982. 159 p. (eng). // Hong Kong Association for Science and Mathematics Education // International Council of Associations for Science Education. Asian Symposium, 4th, Hong Kong, 1982

Attention is paid to primary and secondary teachers, to strategies adopted in various countries of Asia, and to teachers of mathematics, science disciplines and integrated science.

Keywords: teacher education; inservice teacher education; Asia – primary teacher education; secondary teacher education; refresher courses; mathematics education.

00214 - **Why do practical work in 11-13 science?** Beatty, J.W.; Woolnough, Brian E. Hatfield, UK, ASE, 1982. p. 768-770. (School science review; 225) (eng). // Association for Science Education (UK)

This article reports the findings from a questionnaire sent to British teachers, and follows up investigations carried out by Kerr and others since 1962. A surprising amount of time was said to be spent on practical work (40-60% was the median, more in comprehensive schools). The most common types of practical work, and the most favored aims, are explored and compared with those of 1962.

Keywords: lower secondary education; activity learning; practicums; educational aims; educational trends; UK – comprehensive schools.

00215 - **Ameliorating current problems in science education.** Gardner, Marjorie H.; Yager, Robert E. New York, John Wiley, 1983. p. 587-594. (Science education; 67, 5) (eng).

Discusses the dangers of quick-fix solutions to the current crisis in science education and the need for a philosophical base and theoretical teaching strategies. Proposes science and mathematics study as requirements for grades K-14 and implementation of a vertically articulated curriculum. Concludes by calling for pluralistic response to the challenge.

Keywords: articulation; curriculum development; educational reform; educational trends; USA – primary school curriculum; secondary school curriculum; higher education; mathematics education.

00216 - **Constraints on the successful implementation of the integrated science programme at the senior secondary level in Nigeria.** Gbamanja, S.P.T. Ibadan, Nigeria, STAN, 1983. p. 72-78. (Journal of the Science Teachers' Association of Nigeria; XXII, 1) (eng). // Science Teachers' Association of Nigeria

Although science teaching in primary and junior secondary schools and teacher education is geared towards integrated science, the senior secondary school segment has been left out. The article examines the feasibility of extending the integrated science programme to this level.

Keywords: upper secondary education; Nigeria.

00217 - **The Development of modular science in Essex and surrounding counties.** Titcombe, A. R. Hatfield, UK, ASE, 1983. p. 619-625. (School science review; 229) (eng). // Association for Science Education (UK)

Gives a brief history of modular science and its development for an examining board. Advantages of the scheme are identified. An outline of the syllabus is given.

Keywords: upper secondary education; learning modules; UK – modular instruction; curriculum development; teaching method innovations; ability grouping.

Identifiers: "Modular Science" (UK) //

00218 - **Educating Americans for the 21st century: a plan of action for improving mathematics, science and technology for all American elementary and secondary students so that their achievement is the best in the world by 1995.** Washington, National Science Board Commission on Precollege Education in Mathematics, Science and Technology, 1983. 124 p. (eng). // USA. National Science Board. Commission on Precollege Education in Mathematics, Science and Technology

The report insists that top priority should be given to retraining and retaining teachers of high quality in mathematics, science and technology and enhancing instruction in these fields in grades K-6. Much more time should be given for these subjects throughout elementary and secondary grades. Implications are explored. Useful appendices include good practices reviewed by the Commission.

Keywords: primary teacher education; secondary teacher education; inservice teacher education; teacher effectiveness; USA – science and technology; mathematics education; curriculum development; teacher recruitment; primary school curriculum; secondary school curriculum; retraining; refresher courses; educational reform.

00219 - **Effects of English language and intellectual ability on performance in integrated science.** Heyworth, Rex. Hong Kong, HKASME, 1983. p. 91-98. (Journal of the Hong Kong Association for Science and Mathematics Education; XI, 1) (eng). // Hong Kong Association for Science and Mathematics Education

Chinese is generally used in class discussion especially with low-ability pupils. New science curricula make new demands. A study on form 2 pupils found that (a) few of the children, especially girls, could think abstractly (b) abstract thinkers (especially girls) do better than concrete thinkers in integrated sciences (c) the most important factor in predicting achievement is English language ability; conventional tests of intelligence show almost no predictive power.

Keywords: language of instruction; language barriers; academic achievement – abstract reasoning; girls education; Hong Kong.

00220 - **Exchange your teaching post and go abroad!** Berry, M.D.S. Hatfield, UK, ASE, 1983. p. 25-26. (Education in science; 104) (eng). // Association for Science Education (UK)

This account is of general interest for its description of the secondary curriculum (and particularly the science aspects) in Western Australia. Inter alia, science is compulsory up to the end of Year 12! Also of interest is the strategy for meeting the needs of children of different abilities.

Keywords: secondary school curriculum; general education; ability grouping; educational policy; Australia – teaching abroad.

00221 - **Integrated science teaching in schools and the new Nigerian policy on education.** Akpan, O.E. Ibadan, Nigeria, STAN, 1983. p. 66-73. (Journal of the Science Teachers' Association of Nigeria; XXI, 2) (eng). // Science Teachers' Association of Nigeria

The article assesses the part to be played by integrated science teaching in the new 3-3-4 education policy which began in 1982. It cites studies undertaken since the inception of the Nigerian Integrated Project about 1970. Generally there have been some successes; however, progress has been painful and the proposals centre on broad efforts to enhance teacher education.

Keywords: secondary school curriculum; core curriculum; educational policy; teacher education; curriculum evaluation; teacher effectiveness; Nigeria.

Identifiers: Nigerian Integrated Science Project //

00222 - **The Issue of sensitive interdisciplinary science-oriented curricula in the social service.** Zoller, Yuri; Weiss, Shoshana. London, Taylor and Francis, 1983. p. 147-155. (International journal of science education; V, 2) (eng; abstr. in fre, ger).

Such curricula are responsive to a social demand for 'relevant' curricula. The illustration given in this paper is "Hashish and Marijuana". Value judgments and decision-making are features, and integration of the cognitive and affective domains is deliberated. Characteristics of and rationale for such programs are listed. The paper also describes how the specimen unit is implemented through "class meetings". Possible problems of acceptability are identified.

Keywords: educational relevance; interdisciplinary approach; social responsibility – learning modules; student attitudes; classroom techniques; discussion (teaching method); Israel.

00223 - **The Nature and problems of curriculum development.** Hamilton, J. Hatfield, UK, ASE, 1983. p. 10-14. (Education in science; 103) (eng). // Association for Science Education (UK)

The Education Permanent Secretary in Britain discusses the need for a central policy and the issues which should be reflected in that policy. Reference is made to a number of recent documents on science education. Although the context is British, the article could be of some interest to educators reflecting on trends in science education.

Keywords: educational policy; curriculum development; educational trends; UK – general education; core curriculum.

00224 - **New trends in primary school education, v.1.** Harlen, Wynne. Paris, Unesco, 1983. 216 p. (The Teaching of basic sciences) (eng; also in ara, fre, spa). // Unesco // Meeting of Experts on the Incorporation of Science and Technology in the Primary School Curriculum, Paris, 1980

The 20 chapters are grouped into 4 sections: aims and constraints; curriculum materials and their development; theory into practice and teacher preparation. There is also a substantial final report which surveys the issues of current significance. Specific accounts of a number of countries are included.

Keywords: primary school curriculum; teaching strategies; primary teacher education; educational trends – educational aims; teaching materials; curriculum development; child development; teaching skills; Brazil; France; Sri Lanka; Indonesia; Bulgaria; Africa.

ISBN: 92-3-102034-x.

00225 - **New trends in school science equipment.** Lowe, Norman K. Paris, Unesco, 1983. 161 p. (eng; also in ara, fre, spa). // Unesco // International Meeting on School Science Equipment, Paris, 1980

This book attempts to provide an overall picture of trends in respect of science equipment, as well as associated problems and factors around the world. Through out the book descriptions of equipment and other resource materials are usually set in the context of curriculum development. The target readership includes teachers, student teachers, teacher educators, research workers, curriculum developers and Ministry of Education officials.

Keywords: educational equipment; school laboratories; educational laboratory equipment; activity learning – curriculum development; educational projects; primary school curriculum; secondary school curriculum; teaching guides; educational expenditure; teacher education; teacher centres.

ISBN: 92-3-102052-8.

00226 - **Organization and integration of learning experiences in a curriculum: a case study.** Everwijn, S.E.M. London, Taylor and Francis, 1983. p. 183-197. (Journal of curriculum studies; XV, 2) (eng).

Describes experience of using the principle of "organizers" from the work of Ausubel, Earl and Tyler in constructing a curriculum which requires students to relate what has been learned in one subject to what is being learned in another. Although the illustrations are from courses for student nurses and in a hotel school, the article could be useful in school science curricula.

Keywords: curriculum development; learning processes; educational psychology; teaching strategies; higher education.

00227 - **Preservice and inservice educaton for science teachers.** Tamir, Pinchas; Hofstein, Avi; Ben-Peretz, M. Rehovot, Israel, Balaban International Science Services, 1983. 634 p. (eng). // International Seminar on Preservice and Inservice Education of Science Teachers, Rehovot, Ein Gedi and Jerusalem, Israel, 1983

The book is organized so that conference papers are pulled together into eight coherent chapters with the following themes: problems and issues; culture, society and teacher eduation; learning and cognition; preservice education; inservice education; teacher education for implementing curriculum materials; practical and vicarious experiences; research.

Keywords: teacher education; inservice teacher education; preservice teacher education; educational quality – educational relevance; educational psychology; curriculum guides; teaching materials; teaching strategies; curriculum research; teacher education curriculum; Israel.

ISBN: 0-86689-022-x.

00228 - **Relative effects of a history/philosophy of science course on student teachers' performance on two models of science.** Ogunniyi, M.B. Carfax Publishing, Oxford, UK, 1983. p. 193-199. (Research in science and technology education; I, 2) (eng).

This study found that a course on the history and philosophy of science enhanced student teachers' understanding of science. It should follow that the views of science held by their own students should also be enhanced.

Keywords: teacher education curriculum; science philosophy; history of science; student teachers; Nigeria – teacher effectiveness; motivation; Africa.

00229 - **Results of a 50-state survey of initiatives in science, mathematics and computer education.** Armstrong, Jane M. Washington, National Science Board Commission on Precollege Education in Mathematics, Science and Technology, 1983. p. 141-203. (Educating Americans for the 21st century) (eng). // USA National Science Board. Commission on Precollege Education in Mathematics, Science and Technology

Provides outlines of innovations (responses to educational challenges) across the nation. There are ideas here for other policy

makers.

Keywords: curriculum; educational innovations; educational policy; USA – mathematics education; computer science education.

00230 - **A Revised and intensified science and technology curriculum grades K-12 urgently needed for our future.** Lomon, Earle L. Washington, National Science Board Commission on Precollege Education in Mathematics, Science and Technology, 1983. p. 25-58. (Educating Americans for the 21st century) (eng). // USA National Science Board. Commission on Precollege Education in Mathematics, Science and Technology // Conference on Goals for Science and Technology Education Grades K-12, Washington, 1983

The conference identified lacks in science and technology in the United States and, as leading causes, deficiencies in precollege science and technology education. Recommendations are made.

Keywords: primary school curriculum; secondary school curriculum; mathematics education; USA – educational reform; curriculum development.

00231 - **Science and technology education and national development.** Morris, Robert W. Paris, Unesco, 1983. 197 p. (eng; also in ara, spa). // Unesco

A number of chapters in this book discuss in broad terms developments and trends in science education, including programmes in integrated science education and non-formal education. Wider issues include professional associations, various levels of education and international cooperation.

Keywords: education and development; educational trends; educational cooperation – nonformal education; professional associations; teacher associations.

Identifiers: Vienna Programme of Action on Science and Technology for Development //

ISBN: 92-3-102144-3.

00232 - **Science education 11-18.** James, E.O. Hatfield, UK, ASE, 1983. p. 18-19. (Education in science; 102) (eng). // Association for Science Education (UK)

This article picks out highlights from a report published by the Royal Society. It is of interest to policy makers who will not be reading the full report.

Keywords: secondary education; educational policy; core curriculum; UK.

Identifiers: Royal Society (UK) // "Science Education 11-18" (UK) //

00233 - **Science education through personal language use: an integrated approach in a primary school.** Carre, Clive G.; Howitt, Bill. Oxford, UK, Carfax Publishing, 1983. p. 243-254. (Educational review; XXXV, 3) (eng).

Suggests a programme which integrates the learning pupils are invited to do and the language they are using to do it. Some experiences are provided.

Keywords: primary school students; interdisciplinary approach; classroom techniques; learning processes.

00234 - **Science in a social context.** Solomon, Joan. Hatfield, UK, ASE, 1983. p. 33-34. (Education in science; 101) (eng). // Association for Science Education (UK)

This is an outline and rationale of the new SISCON course recently developed for new sixth forms.

Keywords: upper secondary education; sixth forms; teaching materials; UK.

Identifiers: "Science in a Social Context" (UK) //

00235 - **Science in primary schools: an HMI discussion paper.** Smith, C. Hatfield, UK, ASE, 1983. p. 23-25. (Education in science; 102) (eng). // Association for Science Education (UK)

A digest of a publication (by Her Majesty's Inspectors) said to be perhaps idealistic but containing much food for thought.

Keywords: primary school curriculum; UK.

00236 - **Science in schools.** London, ASE, 1983. p. 139-140. (Physics bulletin; XXXIV, 4) (eng). // Institute of Physics (UK)

This is a brief account of a report published by the Royal Society. Referring to British education, the recommendations include science for all to 16+, covering the three main branches. Some 20% of the curriculum time should be spent on science, at least in the fourth and fifth secondary years. Many children do not enjoy their science lessons, and a central aim in future enquiries should be to find out why this is so.

Keywords: core curriculum; general education; student attitudes; UK – interest (learning); curriculum research; research priorities; motivation.

Identifiers: Royal Society (UK) //

00237 - **Science teaching and the syllabus.** Perris, Lyall. New Zealand, New Zealand Science Teachers' Association, 1983. p. 19-21. (N Z science teacher; 38) (eng). // New Zealand Science Teachers' Association

Briefly explores the nature of science, which is often not understood by teachers. Goes on to refer to studies on children's science vs scientists' science. Finally attempts to dispel ideas that a national syllabus inhibits teachers from reflecting science in their classrooms. An alternative view is presented by Rob Julian in the next article "An alternative view of science teaching and the curriculum", p. 22-23.

Keywords: secondary school curriculum; science philosophy; teacher responsibility; educational policy; New Zealand.

Identifiers: Learning in Science (New Zealand) //

00238 - **Secondary Science Curriculum Review: an alternative view.** Long, R.R. Hatfield, UK, ASE, 1983. p. 22-24. (Education in science; 103) (eng). // Association for Science Education (UK)

This teacher feels that recent proposals in Britain are unrealistic. He appears to hold the view that priority at this time should be given to the lower ranks of the ability range, and that integrating the sciences is impractical.

Keywords: ability grouping; low achievers; secondary school curriculum; UK – educational goals.

Identifiers: Secondary Science Curriculum Review (UK) //

00239 - **A Single system of examining at 16+.** Hatfield, UK, ASE, 1983. p. 11-12. (Education in science; 104) (eng). // Association for Science Education (UK)

Subtitled "A statement of the position of the ASE", this is a concise response to drafts which have been prepared in Britain.

Keywords: general education; examinations; upper secondary education; UK.

Identifiers: General Certificate of Secondary Education (UK) //

00240 - **Teaching science to the slow learner.** Smith, Veronica. Hatfield, UK, ASE, 1983. p. 138-140. (School science review; 230) (eng). // Association for Science Education (UK)

This teacher describes her experiences first of teaching an integrated science curriculum to a difficult class and then of "throwing away the book". Many successes are mentioned.

Keywords: ability grouping; slow learners; lower secondary education – motivation; teaching strategies; activity learning; UK.

00241 - **What would John Dewey say about science teaching today?** Vandervoort, F.S. Reston, Va., National Association of Biology Teachers, 1983. p. 38-41. (American biology teacher; XLV, 1) (eng). // National Association of Biology Teachers (USA)

Dewey left us with many ideas which should be applicable to science teaching today: (a) inquiry (b) knowledge by means of experience (c) education for citizenship. The writer claims that science curricula are still far from these ideals.

Keywords: educational aims; teaching methods – civic education; activity learning.

Identifiers: Dewey, John //

00242 - **The Differential uptake of science in schools in England, Wales and Northern Ireland.** Driver, Rosalind; Head, Jennifer; Johnson, Sandra. London, Taylor and Francis, 1984. p. 19-29. (International journal of science education; VI, 1) (eng; abstr. in fre, ger).

The study had four purposes: (a) to present findings (b) to comment on the differences among the three areas (c) to note the changes since a survey by Her Majesty's Inspectors in the 70s and (d) to discuss the implications in the light of proposals that all pupils up to the age of 16 should follow a balanced science curriculum. It was found that a sizeable minority of schools, especially in Northern Ireland, do not offer all three sciences. Gender and ability biases were noted. General science was the usual course for pupils of low attainment. The paper contrasts the recommendations of various bodies on (for fourth and fifth forms) integrated science or combined courses versus separate but coordinated teaching of the three main sciences. The study also found only a small proportion of technology based courses.

Keywords: upper secondary education; core curriculum; teacher attitudes; comparative education; UK – sex discrimination; ability; slow learners.

Identifiers: Assessment of Performance Unit (UK) // UK. Dept. of Education and Science // Royal Society (UK) // Secondary Science Curriculum Review (UK) //

00243 - **An Experimental evaluation of the revised edition of the Nigerian Integrated Science Project.** Olarewaju, AdedayoO. Ibadan, Nigeria, STAN, 1984. p. 89-95. (Journal of the Science Teachers' Association of Nigeria; XXII, 2) (eng). // Science Teachers'

Association of Nigeria
The study aimed to find out whether the presentation of instructional objectives before the lesson (as in the revised edition of the Project) would enhance achievement. The finding was that students performed significantly better on the Integrated Science Achievement Test if they were given the objectives in advance.
Keywords: lower secondary education; curriculum evaluation; classroom techniques; teaching strategies; academic achievement; Nigeria.
Identifiers: Nigerian Integrated Science Project //

00244 - **Association of Science Teachers of Nigeria. Annual Conference, 25th, Ibadan, 1984.** Integrated science: annual report. Ibadan, STAN, 1984. p. 189. (eng). // Science Teachers' Association of Nigeria
Reports on a national workshop, its aims, resolutions and propositions.
Keywords: lower secondary education; educational workshops; teacher associations; Nigeria.

00245 - **Integrated science at the senior secondary school: what prospects?** Jegede, Olugbemiro Johnson. Zaria, Ahmadu Bello University, 1984. 26 p. (eng). // Ahmadu Bello University // West African Examinations Council. Monthly Seminar, 1984
The paper reviews the background to integrated science in general and in Nigeria. It presents a variety of arguments for integrated science at the higher level, but also recognises countervailing forces. Implications include teacher education, physical facilities, testing and evaluation. Finally, a project is proposed.
Keywords: upper secondary education; Nigeria – teacher education; educational facilities; educational testing; student evaluation.

00246 - **Integrated science teaching and the need for radical change in schools even with limited resources at our disposal.** Odobunmi, Olagunju. Ibadan, STAN, 1984. p. 147-149. (eng). // Science Teachers' Association of Nigeria // Science Teachers' Association of Nigeria. Annual Conference, 25th, Lagos, 1984
Examines the meaning of integrated science. A brief background to science curriculum development leads into the Nigerian Integrated Science Project of 1970 and the strategies visualized by the Science Teachers' Association of Nigeria. Classroom observation studies indicate that these strategies were not realized in practice. The author advocates retraining and proposes themes for workshops for integrated science teachers and inspectors.
Keywords: secondary school curriculum; curriculum development; inservice teacher education; educational strategies; Nigeria – refresher courses; educational workshops; educational projects; project evaluation; evaluation of education.
Identifiers: Nigerian Integrated Science Project //

00247 - **A Piaget-based integrated math and science program.** Kolodiy, George Oleh. Washington, NSTA, 1984. p. 297-299. (Journal of college science teaching; 13, 4) (eng). // National Science Teachers Association (USA)
Describes a lecture/laboratory course that stresses physical experience and peer interaction in an inquiry-discovery format. The course is required of all incoming freshmen who are non-science majors. Highlights of such course strategies as performing experiments that demonstrate physical properties before introducing mathematical concepts or physical laws are discussed.
Keywords: mathematics education; higher education; general education; USA – activity learning; experiments (lessons).

00248 - **Primary and secondary school science.** New York, UNIPUB, 1984. p. 1-82. (Educational documentation and information; 231) (eng).
This 344-item annotated bibliography presents overview of science teaching in the following categories: science education; primary school science; integrated science teaching; teaching of biology, chemistry, physics, earth/space science; laboratory work; computer technology; out-of-school science; science and society; science education at international, regional, national levels; references and research. The index lists authors and editors.
Keywords: primary education; secondary education; bibliographies – educational equipment; lower secondary education; curriculum development; school laboratories; teaching methods; out of school education; experiments (lessons); computer applications.

00249 - **Reasoning ability of preservice primary teachers: implications for science teaching.** Tobin, Kenneth; Garnett, Patrick J. Melbourne, Australia, ACER, 1984. p. 89-98. (Australian journal of education; XXVIII, 1) (eng). // Australian Council for Educational Research
Results suggest that students with high formal reasoning ability are best equipped to teach primary science. They can utilize formal modes of thinking during science lessons and are more likely to have studied

physical science subjects in Year 12 at school and to have engaged in the science elective studies in the preservice teacher education programme.
Keywords: primary teacher education; student teachers; educational psychology; teacher effectiveness; preservice teacher education; Australia – classroom techniques; elective courses; ability; reasoning.

00250 - **Conference and Workshop on Resources for Science Teaching, Valsayn, Trinidad and Tobago, 1984.** (Report). St. Augustine, Trinidad and Tobago, ASETT, 1984. p. 1-6. (Journal of education in science for Trinidad and Tobago; XII, 1) (eng). // Association for Science Education of Trinidad and Tobago // Conference and Workshop on Resources for Science Teaching, Valsayn, Trinidad and Tobago, 1984
The occasion of ASETT's tenth anniversary was associated with the Committee on Science and Technology in Developing Countries and the International Council of Associations for Science Education. Short reports of the various discussion groups are provided.
Keywords: teacher associations; teaching materials; Trinidad and Tobago – examinations.

00251 - **Science and technology education.** Legg, Keith. Hong Kong, HKASME, 1984. p. 1-6. (Journal of the Hong Kong Association for Science and Mathematics Education; XII, 2) (eng). // Hong Kong Association for Science and Mathematics Education
An address presented in the form of "eleven lessons" for tertiary education. The speaker is Director of the Hong Kong Polytechnic.
Keywords: higher education; university curriculum; teaching methods; educational aims.

00252 - **Science education in Asia and the Pacific.** Bangkok, ROEAP, 1984. p. 1-498. (Bulletin for the Unesco Regional Office for Education in Asia and the Pacific; 25) (eng). // Unesco Regional Office for Education in Asia and the Pacific (Thailand)
Section 1 is an introduction to science and technology education and summarizes practice within the region. At primary level science is a core subject in all countries though approaches vary and severe constraints are faced. At lower secondary level, science is commonly, though not always integrated. At upper secondary level science is more often taught as separate subjects and is optional in most, though not all countries. Generally, secondary science education is academic, elitist and subject oriented. There are notes on equipment and educational technology, science teacher training and non-formal programmes. Section 2 is a country by country account of the state of science education and its development and provides voluminous information on practice in each of the 24 countries. Section 3 consists of some papers describing the development of programmes of science for all. Sections 4 is a 51 page annotated bibliography.
Keywords: science education; primary school curriculum; secondary school curriculum; out of school education; Asia and the Pacific – core curriculum; elective courses; educational technology; science popularization; educational trends; nonformal education; curriculum development; bibliographies; Afghanistan; Australia; Bangladesh; China; India; Indonesia; Iran (Islamic Republic); Japan; Lao PDR; Malaysia; Mongolia; Nepal; New Zealand; Pakistan; Papua New Guinea; Philippines; Korea R; Viet Nam SR; Sri Lanka; Thailand; Turkey; USSR.

00253 - **Science education in Canadian schools; summary of Background Study 52.** Orpwood, Graham; Souque, Jean Pascal. Ottawa, Science Council of Canada, 1984. 26 p. (eng; also in fre). // Science Council of Canada
The summary refers to a study conducted between 1980 and 1983 resulting from criticism about the way science was being taught in elementary and secondary schools. Science education seemed to lack Canadian content and personal, social and national relevance. Specific problems were identified, and four major research projects undertaken. On the basis of these, issues for deliberation are suggested.
Keywords: educational relevance; primary school curriculum; secondary school curriculum; Canada – teaching standards; social needs; educational policy; curriculum development; education and culture; curriculum research.

00254 - **Science for all: implication for higher education.** Blin-Stoyle, Roger J. London, IoP, 1984. p. 168-172. (Physics education; XIX, 4) (eng). // Institute of Physics (UK)
A university professor of theoretical physics and Fellow of the Royal Society has no doubts that secondary science education should move as quickly as possible towards a broad and balanced programme for all up to 16+. The article considers the pressures due to higher education and believes that a core stream could be identified that would flow through 11-16 and into A-level studies. Higher education should then improve its selection system in order to remove the pressure for high A-level performance, thus broadening school education.

Keywords: secondary school curriculum; core curriculum; science and technology; higher education; UK – general education; ability grouping; specialization; student selection.

00255 - **Science for every student: educating Canadians for tomorrow's world.** Ottawa, Science Council of Canada, 1984. 11 p. (eng). // Science Council of Canada

This follows from Background Study 52 on science education in Canadian schools (summary by Orpwood and Souque). The present document analyses the study's findings and presents recommendations for bringing about essential renewal in science education.

Keywords: curriculum evaluation; educational innovations; general education; Canada – educational needs; educational projects; curriculum development.

00256 - **Science subject-choice and students' attitudes to science.** Burns, Janet. Wellington, New Zealand Science Teachers' Association, 1984. p. 7-12. (N Z science teacher; 40) (eng). // New Zealand Science Teachers' Association

Provides analyses of data which show, "inter alia", increasing choice of "science" in secondary school but decreasing choice of individual sciences, especially the physical sciences. There are comparisons by gender, by ethnic origin and by rural/urban areas. The analyses about attitudes include ability and the type of science.

Keywords: elective courses; student attitudes; physical sciences; New Zealand.

00257 - **Submission to the Minister of Education by the New Zealand Institute of Physics (concerning the review of the core curriculum for schools).** Wellington, New Zealand Science Teachers' Association, 1984. p. 19-20. (N Z science teacher; 40) (eng). // New Zealand Science Teachers' Association

For the intermediate level (11-12-year-old) the submission urges the provision of science specialists. This level of schooling is considered the weak link in the chain, and fails to realise children's full potential.

Keywords: lower secondary education; core curriculum; teacher qualifications; specialists; New Zealand – teacher effectiveness; educational opportunities.

Identifiers: New Zealand Core Curriculum Review //

00258 - **Teaching the right stuff: where it's happening today.** Mrachek, Len. Arlington, Va., American Vocational Association, 1984. p. 30-39. (Vocational education journal; LIX, 2) (eng). // American Vocational Association

These five articles discuss the improvement of vocational education programs though the infusion of mathematics and science skills. They include an auto mechanics curriculum; an 11th-grade industrial arts program (orientation, electricity, plumbing); a combination automotive services-small business program; and two programs at one school – engineering processes and materials and electronics technology.

Keywords: vocational school curriculum; industrial arts; technical and vocational education; curriculum development; USA.

00259 - **Towards a social slant in science teaching.** Seecharan, Premlal. St. Augustine, Trinidad and Tobago, ASETT, 1984. p. 1-5. (Journal of education in science for Trinidad and Tobago; XII, 1) (eng). // Association for Science Education of Trinidad and Tobago

The article begins with a distinction between science and technology, but insists that technological development is a powerful reason for teaching science in schools, indeed throughout the school curriculum. The writer goes on to provide sets of intrinsic and extrinsic reasons for science for all. He identifies major problems of science teaching in Trinidad and Tobago, essentially concerned with teachers' attitudes and lack of professional training. Recommendations include integration of science and integration of curricula. In his physics classes this teacher has successfully used exercises and discussions stimulated by newspaper clippings on science in a social context.

Keywords: science and technology; technological change; educational relevance; upper secondary education; core curriculum – education and development; teacher attitudes; teacher education; teaching materials; teaching method innovations; interdisciplinary approach; physics education; Trinidad and Tobago.

00260 - **Towards integrated science teaching consistent with the nature of science and humanistic precepts.** Igwebuike, Thomas B. Ibadan, Nigeria, STAN, 1984. p. 49-58. (Journal of the Science Teachers' Association of Nigeria; XXII, 2) (eng). // Science Teachers' Association of Nigeria

Science teachers and educators appear not to have grasped the philosophical basis for integrating science. Accordingly, this paper attempts to provide a conceptual analysis of the nature of science and a humanistic approach to education. This requires the development of scientific literacy through the use of processes of science while

teaching, and reference to the nature of the child.

Keywords: science philosophy; humanism – scientific literacy; teaching strategies; child development.

00261 - **The Development of primary science education in Trinidad and Tobago.** Fraser-Abder, Pamela. St. Augustine, Trinidad and Tobago, University of the West Indies, 1985. p. 55-67. (Caribbean curriculum; 1) (eng). // University of the West Indies (Trinidad and Tobago)

This describes the effort to ensure the teaching of science in primary schools, a collaborative enterprise of the University and Ministry of Education. The resulting programme is SAPATT (Science: a Process Approach for Trinidad and Tobago), undertaken in 1977 and involving the teachers in its development.

Keywords: primary school curriculum; curriculum development; educational coordination; Trinidad and Tobago.

Identifiers: Science: a Process Approach for Trinidad and Tobago //

00262 - **Engineers for rural well-being.** Arbab, Farzam. Ottawa, IDRC, 1985. p. 132-143. (Science, education and society: perspectives from India and South East Asia) (eng). // International Development Research Centre (Canada) // Seminar on Education, Science Policy, Research and Action, New Delhi, 1984

Outlines FUNDAEC of Colombia, an institution somewhat misleadingly called a rural university. One of the central issues is integration of curricula, though constraints have been recognised.

Keywords: engineering education; rural development; education and development; higher education; Colombia – university curriculum.

Identifiers: Fundación para la Aplicación y Enseñanza de las Ciencias (Colombia) //

00263 - **An Experimental programme in integrated natural science education in Bulgaria.** Golovinski, Evgeny; Lazarov, Dobri. Paris, Unesco, 1985. p. 593-596. (Prospects: quarterly review of education; XV, 4) (eng; also in fre, spa). // Unesco

A problem is how to introduce the latest information from the interface between sciences into the existing curricula of primary and secondary schools. Here is a preliminary report on an integrated subject called "nature study" for 10-12 year olds in 29 schools. Presents rationale and lists "integral foci". An independent learning strategy is used. Students reacted favourably but teachers had some difficulties, being specialists themselves.

Keywords: primary school curriculum; lower secondary education; classroom techniques; Bulgaria – student attitudes; teacher attitudes; teaching methods; learning methods; independent learning.

Identifiers: Nature Study (Bulgaria) //

00264 - **A Framework for curriculum development.** Hatfield, UK, ASE, 1985. p. 12-22. (Planning for science in the curriculum) (eng). // Association for Science Education (UK)

This chapter gives a structure for innovation and could prove useful to teachers.

Keywords: curriculum development; educational aims; teaching method innovations; skill development; teaching skills.

00265 - **The Home as a context for the science curriculum.** Browne, Claudia. St. Augustine, Trinidad and Tobago, ASETT, 1985. p. 14-16. (Journal of education in science for Trinidad and Tobago; XII, 3) (eng). // Association for Science Education of Trinidad and Tobago

A home economics educator suggests that a home context for conventional scientific concepts is one of the needs of children doing no science after lower secondary school, and is also likely to increase motivation. For science teachers she identifies topics and concepts related to nutrition (and economics), food preservation, food preparation, textile and clothing cleaning. The writer draws attention to trends in the direction of social relevance and is concerned that homemakers should have a scientific background for their practices and decision-making in an unpredictable future.

Keywords: home economics education; lower secondary education; educational relevance; general education; motivation; nutrition education; Caribbean.

00266 - **Influences on the practice of science curriculum innovation in the Caribbean, pt. 1: socio-historical.** King, Winston K. St. Augustine, Trinidad and Tobago, ASETT, 1985. p. 1-7. (Journal of education in science for Trinidad and Tobago; XII, 2) (eng). // Association for Science Education of Trinidad and Tobago

An attempt is made to identify the forces contributing to change in the status of science in the school curriculum from the 1960s. These include the relinquishing of colonial ties, the establishment of the university, economic pressures and social movements, advances in science and technology, and curriculum development elsewhere.

Keywords: educational innovations; social change; educational history; educational aims; Caribbean – technological change; education and culture.

00267 - **Influences on the practice of science curriculum innovation in the Caribbean, pt. 2: contextual factors.** King, Winston K. St. Augustine, Trinidad and Tobago, ASETT, 1985. p. 7-13. (Journal of education in science for Trinidad and Tobago; XII, 3) (eng). // Association for Science Education of Trinidad and Tobago

The discussion is set against data from a case study of a primary science innovation in a Caribbean country. Implementation of innovations is influenced by the nature of the subject matter, features of the curriculum, school climate and facilities, and communication of information.

Keywords: teaching method innovations; teacher effectiveness; Caribbean – educational environment; educational facilities.

Identifiers: Science Teacher Observation Schedule (UK) //

00268 - **Influences on the practice of science curriculum innovation in the Caribbean, pt. 3: internal factors.** King, Winston K. St. Augustine, Trinidad and Tobago, ASETT, 1985. p. 1-5. (Journal of education in science for Trinidad and Tobago; XIII, 1) (eng). // Association for Science Education of Trinidad and Tobago

The internal factors refer to those which impinge most directly on the teacher, including training, teacher's perception of aims, teaching style and age and ability of pupils. The author closes by providing a diagram of the influences on the practice of science curriculum innovation. Recommendations are made.

Keywords: teaching method innovations; teacher education; teacher effectiveness – curriculum development; Caribbean.

00269 - **Integrated science as a preparation for 'A' level physics, chemistry and biology.** Chamberlain, Peter J. Oxford, UK, Carfax Publishing, 1985. p. 153-158. (Research in science and technological education; III, 2) (eng).

The author compares performance in A-level science examinations of students in a tertiary college who had taken SCISP with students who had studied the separate sciences to 0-level. Performance was found to be not significantly different between the two groups though SCISP students must have spent considerably less time per science subject in their 11-16 schools. Thus there is no evidence to suggest that SCISP inhibited subsequent progress.

Keywords: academic achievement; sixth forms; specialization; upper secondary education; examinations; UK.

Identifiers: Schools Council Integrated Science Project (UK) //

00270 - **Integrated science teachers' perceived needs for organizational skills relevant to out of school scientific activities.** Onocha, C.O.; Okpala, N.P. Hong Kong, HKASME, 1985. p. 173-181. (Journal of the Hong Kong Association for Science and Mathematics Education; XII, 2) (eng). // Hong Kong Association for Science and Mathematics Education

A study identified the needs of teachers. Regular workshops and inservice courses are recommended since science methods courses do not adequately equip teachers for such activities.

Keywords: out of school education; inservice teacher education; educational workshops; Nigeria.

00271 - **Organising the teaching of science.** Hatfield, UK, ASE, 1985. p. 23-43. (Planning for science in the curriculum) (eng). // Association for Science Education (UK)

The chapter illustrates how some schools have attempted to implement the two major themes of the Association's publication "Education through science": (a) science for all (b) general education through science. Of special interest are different timetable frameworks for integrated science throughout; core science and other science options; core science and other extension courses; core science up to 14 with choice of sciences in years 4-5; physical and biological science for all; coordinated three subjects for all; interdisciplinary courses (science and other subjects).

Keywords: physics education; biology education; curriculum development; core curriculum; UK – interdisciplinary approach; elective courses.

00272 - **'People's science and development theory.** Kumar, Krishna. Ottawa, IDRC, 1985. p. 70-78. (Science, education and society: perspectives from India and South East Asia) (eng). // International Development Research Centre (Canada)

The people's science movement has among its objectives the development of scientific literacy among the masses, the re-assessment of "Western" science and technology and challenging the forces of superstition.

Keywords: science popularization; science and development; scientific literacy; India – education and development; nonformal education.

00273 - **Planning for change.** Hatfield, UK, ASE, 1985. p. 1-11. (Planning for science in the curriculum) (eng). // Association for Science Education (UK)

This chapter advocates, for primary schools, science integrated with the total curriculum. For age 14, the "option system" is deplored, and a broad and balanced science education for all is advocated. The bulk of the chapter is concerned with the practicalities of introducing change.

Keywords: primary school curriculum; secondary school curriculum; educational innovations – curriculum development; elective courses; core curriculum; UK.

00274 - **Planning for science in the curriculum.** Hatfield, UK, ASE, 1985. 65 p. (eng). // Association for Science Education (UK). Working Party on Curriculum Models for Science 5-16

Follows the ASE's "Alternatives for science education" (1979) and "Education through science" (1981), the latter being a policy statement. This report suggests how policy could be turned into practice.

Keywords: primary school curriculum; secondary school curriculum; curriculum development; UK – teaching strategies; educational innovations.
ISBN: 0-86357-034-8.

00275 - **Primary education science and technology: a different PEST in the classroom.** Bellett, D.J. Hatfield, UK, ASE, 1985. p. 39-40. (Education in science; 111) (eng). // Association for Science Education (UK)

An account of an in-school approach involving the cooperation of an engineer and using a dramatic approach (with the children "marooned on a desert island"). Problems solved included making a fire, building a dam, making hunting and fishing equipment, collecting rainwater, collecting salt from sea water, making waterproof shelters, irrigation and, finally, buoyancy for the escape.

Keywords: technology; primary school curriculum; teaching method innovations; classroom techniques; educational games.

00276 - **Progression, continuity and community.** Hatfield, UK, ASE, 1985. p. 44-54. (Planning for science in the curriculum) (eng). // Association for Science Education (UK)

Describes cooperation between primary and secondary schools with local communities and employers.

Keywords: primary schools; secondary schools; school community relationship; industry and education; UK.

00277 - **Pupils' topic preference in integrated science in selected secondary schools in the Ilorin LGA of Kwara State.** Ihebuzor, Noel A.; Adelaiye, Esther O. Ibadan, Nigeria, STAN, 1985. p. 131-137. (Journal of the Science Teachers' Association of Nigeria; XXIII, 1&2) (eng). // Science Teachers' Association of Nigeria

A study on a sample of 300 Form 3 pupils found that pupils tend to prefer topics that are largely biology-related at the expense of either chemistry or physics related topics. Reasons are discussed and recommendations are made.

Keywords: interest (learning); lower secondary education; student attitudes – life sciences; physical sciences; Nigeria.

00278 - **Recent trends and issues in science education in Southeast Asia.** Nielsen, Dean. Ottawa, IDRC, 1985. p. 54-68. (Science, education and society: perspectives from India and South East Asia) (eng). // International Development Research Centre (Canada) // Seminar on Education, Science Policy, Research and Action, New Delhi, 1984

Focuses chiefly on primary and secondary education. Covers curriculum reform, curriculum development, equipment, teacher education, nonformal science education and regional collaboration. Notes numerous examples of integration in Southeast Asia and a variety of approaches to teacher education and teacher support.

Keywords: primary education; secondary education; educational trends; South East Asia – curriculum development; educational equipment; teacher education; nonformal education; regional cooperation.

00279 - **Science, education and society: perspectives from India and South East Asia.** King, Kenneth. Ottawa, IDRC, 1985. 216 p. (eng). // International Development Research Centre (Canada) // Seminar on Education, Science Policy, Research and Action, New Delhi, 1984

Because certain IDRC activities are explicitly interdisciplinary, the Centre has been exploring possible research connections among science, technology, education, employment, manpower and training in three regions of the developing world. The resulting programme is TEED: Technology, Education and Employment for Development. This volume is fundamentally concerned with science above values and science without values. It questions mainstream science, whether in school or in society, and raises alternatives.

Keywords: science and development; education and development; interdisciplinary approach; India; South East Asia – science policy; education and employment; educational relevance.

Identifiers: "Technology, Education and Employment for Development" //

00280 - **Science education in Nigerian secondary schools: a reappraisal.**
Banu, D.P. Ibanan, Nigeria, STAN, 1985. p. 39-44. (Journal of the Science Teachers' Association of Nigeria; XXIII, 1&2) (eng). // Science Teachers' Association of Nigeria

Deplores the absence of social aspects of science, and cites studies which show that the goal dominating the curriculum is the preparation of candidates to pass WASC or GCE. Those studies also showed that the examination questions were very limited. All this is contrary to the goals expressed for Nigerian education. Also absent is attention to personal needs and career awareness in science.

Keywords: upper secondary education; educational goals; educational relevance; examinations; educational needs; education and employment; Nigeria.

00281 - **Science for all: a reflective essay.** Fensham, Peter J. London, Taylor and Francis, 1985. p. 415-435. (Journal of curriculum studies; XVII, 4) (eng).

As "science for all" is a contemporary slogan around the world in the 80s, the author analysises what was done in the 60s and 70s. He believes that there is growing consensus in a number of countries concerning present day science education in schools to the effect that (a) there are much better curricula for the group (approximately 20%) from which future scientists and science related professionals will be drawn (b) we have not achieved an effective science education for the other 80% who will not continue with any formal education in science after they leave school. The adequacy of new curricula in the next decade will depend very considerably on how clearly we can read the realities of the earlier attempts and the realities of the current day.

Keywords: core curriculum; educational trends; ability grouping; evaluation of education – education and employment; scientific literacy; educational relevance; educational goals.

00282 - **Some CXC concepts.** Glasgow, Joyce. St. Augustine, Trinidad and Tobago, ASETT, 1985. p. 7-12. (Journal of education in science for Trinidad and Tobago; XII, 2) (eng). // Association for Science Education of Trinidad and Tobago

This is a tabulation of the concepts reflected in the Caribbean Examinations Council syllabuses for biology, chemistry, integrated science (single award) and physics. The writer aims to identify some of those concepts a Caribbean child, on leaving secondary school, is supposed to have grasped. The list should also prove useful in (a) judging how balanced a particular course of study would be (b) facilitating cooperation among science teachers and (c) acting as a starting point for similar analyses elsewhere.

Keywords: concepts; scientific literacy; upper secondary education; general education; biology education; chemistry education; physics education; Caribbean.

Identifiers: Caribbean Examinations Council //

00283 - **A Study of teaching and learning processes in integrated science classrooms.** Hacker, R.G.; Rowe, M.J. London, Taylor and Francis, 1985. p. 173-180. (International journal of science education; VII, 2) (eng; abstr. in fre, ger).

This report of an empirical study at the lower secondary level focuses on the specialist science teacher with an integrated curriculum and uses the Science Lesson Analysis System for data collection. Informational approaches were found to be more likely when the teacher was outside his specialist discipline, the change being at the expense of problem-solving or inquiry. Subjects had all been trained in teaching an integrated science curriculum and had spent at least six years teaching it. Findings cast doubt on the Nuffield Combined Science recommendation that unification would be best achieved by a single teacher. Science teachers do not share curriculum developers' enthusiasm for teaching outside specialist areas.

Keywords: specialists; teacher attitudes; teacher effectiveness; lower secondary education; teaching methods; UK – teacher education; problem solving; educational research; learning processes.

Identifiers: Nuffield Combined Science (UK) // Science Lesson Analysis System (UK) //

00284 - **Teaching science, mathematics, technical and vocational education in an integrated way.** Bajpai, A.C. London, CASME, 1985. p. 1-13. (Commonwealth Association of Science, Technology and Mathematics Educators journal; V, 2) (eng). // Commonwealth Association of Science, Technology and Mathematics Educators

Shows how a topic "measurement" as a coordinating theme could be prepared and implemented. Physics, chemistry, biology and technical and vocational education are identified. Objectives are

established, each being accompanied by supporting strategies. A student module and teacher's notes are given to illustrate.

Keywords: interdisciplinary approach; technical and vocational education; curriculum development; biology education; chemistry education; learning modules; classroom techniques; teaching strategies.

00285 - **Technology and science: technology and the Secondary Science Curriculum Review.** Ditchfield, Christine. Nottingham, UK, National Centre for School Technology, Trent Polytechnic, 1985. p. 12-14. (School technology; XVIII, 3) (eng). // Trent Polytechnic (UK). National Centre for School Technology

Explains the SSCR of the Association for Science Education, and describes what is being done about technology in the Review.

Keywords: technology; general technical education; secondary school curriculum; educational trends; educational innovations; UK – teacher associations.

Identifiers: Secondary Science Curriculum Review (UK) //

00286 - **Trends in science and technology education.** Holbrook, J.B. Hong Kong, HKASME, 1985. p. 149-162. (Journal of the Hong Kong Association for Science and Mathematics Education; XIII, 2) (eng). // Hong Kong Association for Science and Mathematics Education

Contrasts the aims from the post-Sputnik era with the present goal of science for all, with shifts from science teaching to science learning, from teacher-centered instruction, and towards more process and problem-solving. Characteristics of scientific literacy are cited and associated with technology. Aims are characterised as factual, conceptual and the acquisition of values. A distinction is made among the emphases of different groups. There is a consideration of implications for teacher training and retraining and science teachers' associations.

Keywords: educational aims; scientific literacy; educational trends – teacher education; teacher associations; pressure groups; Canada; USA.

Identifiers: Science Council of Canada // National Science Teachers Association (USA) // Science and technology education and future human needs conference, Bangalore, India, 1985 //

00287 - **The Whole curriculum perspective.** Hatfield, UK, ASE, 1985. p. 55-61. (Planning for science in the curriculum) (eng). // Association for Science Education (UK)

It is stressed that schools need people who are coordinators across the curriculum in order to link scientific concepts, contexts and processes. There are illustrations of ways of achieving this.

Keywords: curriculum development; educational coordination; teacher responsibility; articulation.

00288 - **The Activities of pioneer centres in the USSR.** Grekova, Olga. Paris, Unesco, 1986. p. 155-162. (Innovations in science and technology education; 1) (eng). // Unesco

Out of school institutions are an integral part of the education system and their work is based on the general principles of communist upbringing. The functions are described and illustrated.

Keywords: out of school education; extracurricular activities; youth organizations; USSR.

Identifiers: Pioneer Centres (USSR) //

00289 - **Agriculture in history of science and technology curricula.** De Beaver, Donald. Bethlehem, Pa., STS Program, Lehigh University, 1986. p. 1-4. (Science, technology and society; 57) (eng). // Lehigh University (USA). Science, Technology and Society Program

Points out agriculture's central position in the human economy and advocates its placement in liberal education. Provides a list of topics highlighting agriculture in the history of science and technology curriculum. Discusses the potential for using agriculture material in undergraduate science courses.

Keywords: agricultural engineering; agricultural education; higher education; general education; USA.

00290 - **Application of calculators and computers in science and mathematics education.** Shumway, Richard J. Paris, Unesco, 1986. p. 117-136. (Innovations in science and technology education; 1) (eng). // Unesco

Future-oriented as costs fall, the author assumes that computers and calculators will be available to children. He reviews research done on their use in the classroom. He is clear that responsibility is to help the youth of today learn to use these powerful tools.

Keywords: mathematics education; computer assisted instruction; calculating machines; educational technology – teaching strategies; curriculum development; computer languages; computer programming.

00291 - **The Case for GCSE science: a view from the classroom.** Best, P.H.; Drake, J. Hatfield, UK, ASE, 1986. p. 803-806. (School science review; 241) (eng). // Association for Science Education (UK)

The authors detect confusion in relation to the forthcoming

National Curriculum. They propose a compromise, which is essentially a common core of integrated science in Years 3 and 4 and a choice of four options from ten in Year 5.

Keywords: core curriculum; secondary school curriculum; educational policy; examination boards; UK – specialization; elective courses.

Identifiers: UK National Curriculum //

00292 - **Cognitive acceleration: review and prospects.** Adey, Philip S. St. Augustine, Trinidad and Tobago, University of the West Indies, 1986. p. 84-99. (Science education and research in Latin America and the Caribbean) (eng). // University of the West Indies (Trinidad and Tobago) // Meeting on Science Education Research in Latin America and the Caribbean, Port-of-Spain, 1980

In the face of findings that many curricula make excessive demands on children, an attempt is being made to undertake cognitive acceleration: raising pupils levels of thinking. The paper reviews the literature on cognitive acceleration.

Keywords: mental development; cognition; learning processes; lower secondary education; teaching method innovations; literature reviews; UK – reasoning.

Identifiers: Cognitive Acceleration through Science Education (UK) //

00293 - **Ethics and responsibility in science education.** Frazer, Malcom J.; Kornhauser, Alexandra. Oxford, UK, Pergamon Press, 1986. 264 p. (Science and technology education and future human needs; 2) (eng). // International Council of Scientific Unions // Conference on Science and Technology Education and Future Human Needs, Bangalore, India, 1985

This volume aims to stimulate an awareness of the ethical and social dimensions in science education. Intrinsic and extrinsic problems are presented. Information is given on the efforts being made in education to deal with ethical and social problems. A range of contributors is represented.

Keywords: ethics of science; sociology of science; social responsibility – primary school curriculum; secondary school curriculum; educational relevance.

ISBN: 0-08-033912-3.

00294 - **Health education and science education: changing roles, common goals?** Garrard, Jan. Leeds, UK, Leeds University Centre for Studies in Science Education, 1986. p. 1-26. (Studies in science education; 13) (eng). // Leeds University (UK). Centre for Studies in Science Education

Suggests a sharing of expertise between science education and health education – science education in search of relevance, health education in search of a place in the curriculum. The article aims to provide science educators with some of the broader social science based background of health and health education.

Keywords: health education; educational relevance; educational coordination.

00295 - **Innovators' dilemmas: recontextualizing science and technology education.** Layton, David. Paris, Unesco, 1986. p. 9-28. (Innovations in science and technology education; 1) (eng). // Unesco

Takes an overview of science education and reform movements in the last 30 years and changes in direction in the 1980s. As examples, mention is made of some major policy statements. There appears to be a conflict between curricula for trained scientists and for educated citizenry. Measures to resolve this dilemma are suggested. Only recently has technology education begun to contribute to general education, and another dilemma is its relationship to science education. The cultural context of science and technology education is now a matter for attention. The chapter closes by a realistic discussion of what actually happens in curriculum change.

Keywords: educational innovations; educational trends; education and development; educational reform; curriculum development – education and culture; general technical education; scientific literacy.

Identifiers: "Science for Every Student" (Canada) //

00296 - **An Integrated college freshman natural science curriculum.** Garafalo, Alfred R.; LoPresti, Vincent C. New York, American Chemical Society, 1986. p. 854-858. (Journal of chemical education; 63, 10) (eng). // American Chemical Society

Describes an integrated freshman course sequence which combines biology and chemistry and uses the process of energy flow as a unifying concept. Provides a description of the three-quarters course sequence, along with lists of topics covered in both disciplines. Includes a rationale for developing such interdisciplinary courses.

Keywords: biology education; chemistry education; higher education; interdisciplinary approach; USA – teaching methods; university curriculum.

Identifiers: Massachusetts College of Pharmacy Allied Health Science (USA) //

00297 - **Integrated or co-ordinated science?** Black, PaulJ. Hatfield, UK, ASE, 1986. p. 669-681. (School science review; 241) (eng). // Association for Science Education (UK)

In his Presidential, Address the author discusses the articulation of the three separate sciences at secondary level up to the age of 16. He considers the nature of science, five principles of curriculum design and the needs and entitlement of pupils. He makes practical proposals in the light of recent change in national policy. He advocates a single subject with a single title – Science, or Sciences – and points out the need to attend to public esteem.

Keywords: secondary school curriculum; educational coordination; articulation; examinations; UK – specialization; sociology of science; science philosophy; curriculum development; educational aims; educational needs.

00298 - **Integrating science/mathematics with language arts: gifted child programme suited for all.** Cross, Roger. Hatfield, UK, ASE, 1986. p. 808-812. (School science review; 241) (eng). // Association for Science Education (UK)

As well as trends towards science, technology and society, more attention to the affective domain is needed. The project described here attempts to integrate science, literature and mathematics with gifted lower secondary pupils to provide a more humanistic approach towards mathematics and science.

Keywords: gifted students; mathematics education; humanities; Australia – lower secondary education; educational trends; ability grouping; educational relevance.

00299 - **Making science, technology and mathematics education relevant: overview paper.** Lucas, A.M. London, Commonwealth Secretariat, 1986. p. 4-14. (Making science, technology and mathematics education relevant) (eng). // Commonwealth Secretariat // Commonwealth Association of Science, Technology annd Mathematics Educators. Asia Regional Biennial Workshop, 6th, Singapore, 1986

Brings together the lead papers of the conference, challenges assumptions in them, and raises questions for discussion.

Keywords: general education; technical and vocational education; teacher education; nonformal education; mathematics education; educational relevance.

00300 - **The Nature of science processes and its implications for science education.** Yap Kueh Chin. Penang, Malaysia, SEAMEO-RECSAM, 1986. p. 24-32. (Journal of science and mathematics education in Southeast Asia; IX, 1) (eng). // SEAMEO. Regional Centre for Education in Science and Mathematics

Discusses three issues: (a) Are science processes by nature inductive or deductive? (b) In accordance with the nature of science processes, should an inductive or deductive approach to instruction be emphasized? (c) Should science processes be taught separately or within the context of a science subject? Considers implications for science education and teacher education. There is an extensive list of references.

Keywords: science philosophy; curriculum development; teaching methods; teacher education – deduction; reasoning.

00301 - **Physical science, society and technology: a case study in the sociology of knowledge.** Fensham, Peter J. Melbourne, Australia, ACER, 1988. p. 375-386. (Australian journal of education; XXXI, 3) (eng). // Australian Council for Educational Research

Interest in making science and technology more relevant and more accessible to all school students is evident in many reports. This case study explores the aspects of epistemology and curriculum organisationthat evoke special forces which control content. Some difficulties facing such a direction in science education are identified. There is a description of the effects of pressure groups threatening the spread of courses which incorporate the sociology of education and of science.

Keywords: educational relevance; secondary school curriculum; general education; epistemology – technology; pressure groups; sociology of science; sociology of knowledge.

00302 - **The Place of science and technology in school curricula: a global survey.** Paris, Unesco, 1986. 77 p. (eng). // Unesco

This document arises from responses from 97 Member States to a 1984 questionnaire. It reports practice in those countries classified into five regions. Within each region, findings are given on school systems, science in classes designated 'primary' and 'secondary', practical work in science, mathematics, time allocated for mathematics and science, technology and other subjects. There is also a short subject on issues arising on each of these concerns. Primary science shows wide variation in practice and difficulty in implementation; and it is commonly taught in the context of a broader approach. At the lower secondary level science is commonly taught as an integrated course. At upper levels there may be wide variation in policy.

Keywords: primary education; secondary education; general

technical education; comparative education – Africa; Arab countries; Asia; Oceania; Europe; Latin America; Caribbean; questionnaires.

00303 - **Recent developments in primary and lower secondary school science.** Harlen, Wynne. Paris, Unesco, 1986. p. 29-47. (Innovations in science and technology education) (eng). // Unesco
Considers the science that is appropriate at primary and lower secondary levels and the integration within science and with other subjects. Discusses content selection and organization, continuity from primary to secondary level, teacher training and the provision of resources. Is optimistic about progress in tackling problems of science in primary schools.
Keywords: primary school curriculum; secondary school curriculum; lower secondary education – learning processes; teacher education; teaching materials; teacher attitudes.

00304 - **Relevant education for agriculture and production (REAP).** Eck, D. St. Augustine, Trinidad and Tobago, University of the West Indies, 1986. p. 115-120. (Science education research in Latin America and the Caribbean) (eng). // University of the West Indies (Trinidad and Tobago) // Conference on Science Education and Research in Latin America and the Caribbean, Port-of-Spain, 1986
REAP is a project in Belize which relates the curriculum to the child's environment and uses a practical approach. The integrated curriculum has the following aspects: village/urban study, land and water, ecology, weather, agricultural practices, health and nutrition, and animals and plants. The project is considered highly successful.
Keywords: educational relevance; environmental education; rural environment; agricultural education; health education; nutrition education; Belize.
Identifiers: Rural Education and Agriculture Project (Belize) //

00305 - **Science and technology education towards informed citizenship: the ethics and responsibility related to environment, food and health, industry and information technology and energy.** Tendencia, Cynthia P. Penang, Malaysia, RECSAM, 1986. 145 p. (eng). // SEAMEO. Regional Centre for Education in Science and Mathematics // International Council of Associations for Science Education. Asian Symposium, 5th, Penang, Malaysia, 1986
The objectives for the symposium were as follows: (a) To determine what the average citizen should know on environment, food and health, industry and information technology, land, water and mineral resources and energy as to enable him to make rational decisions. (b) To change and to disseminate teaching/learning materials available from various countries with the intention of promoting the development of science curricula for informed citizenship. (c) To expose science educators to various teaching strategies and approaches for such a curriculum. (d) To foster international exchange of ideas among educators concerned with the need for development of a science curriculum oriented towards informed citizenship. The report includes the texts of papers provided for the meeting and reports of the discussions.
Keywords: science popularization; nonformal education; adult education; Asia – health education; environmental education; nutrition education; teaching strategies; teaching materials; curriculum development; educational cooperation; scientific literacy.

00306 - **Science education for all: an analysis of the issue in the Hong Kong context.** Kee Tao Ping. Hong Kong, Chinese University, 1986. p. 72-78. (Chinese University education journal; 14, 1) (eng). // Chinese University (Hong Kong)
States that the common school curriculum in Hong Kong caters to the academically gifted. Advocates a broad and balanced science curriculum, differentiated to a range of abilities and aptitudes, to be followed by all students throughout the five years of secondary school. Presents four purposes for science education and describes curriculum revisions needed to achieve these purposes.
Keywords: secondary school curriculum; curriculum evaluation; Hong Kong – academic achievement; gifted students; ability grouping; aptitude; curriculum development; educational aims.

00307 - **Science, technology and society courses: problems of implementation in school systems.** Paris, Unesco, 1986. p. 143-154. (Innovations in science and technology education; 1) (eng). // Unesco
In various contents there is a diversity of objectives of such courses and no long-established academic community in higher education and new demands on teachers. There is a review of attempts to incorporate science, technology and society considerations into the curriculum, but few of these for younger children. Needs are identified and strategies suggested.
Keywords: science and technology; social values; curriculum development; teacher role.

00308 - **Science, technology and society: educational implications.** Baez, Albert V. Paris, Unesco, 1986. p. 137-142. (Innovations in science and technology education; 1) (eng). // Unesco
The author takes the environment as an excellent integrating theme which can give relevance and a societal focus to science, technology and society activities. He advocates a strategy to teach science and technology in socially responsible ways in which behavioral changes are considered just as important as scientific information and technological skills. The ultimate aim is to infuse the environmental ethic into all science and technology education, formal and non-formal.
Keywords: environmental education; environmental conservation; educational relevance – environmental perception.
Identifiers: "World Conservation Strategy" //

00309 - **Stimulating innovations at the international level: Unesco's role in science and technology education.** Paris, Unesco, 1986. p. 163-188. (Innovations in science and technology education; 1) (eng). // Unesco
The chapter shows how, since the beginning of the present decade, Unesco's emphasis has been the application of science and technology education to the needs of daily life and development of society. Its role has been to catalyse efforts at various organizational levels and to assist in the initial orientation, facilitating contact and exchanges and providing technical back-up.
Keywords: educational innovations; educational cooperation; educational relevance; general education; educational projects – general technical education; pilot projects; rural education; environmental education; out of school education; extracurricular activities; health education; Africa; Australia; China; India; Philippines; Sri Lanka; Barbados; Brazil; Colombia; Peru; Spain.
Identifiers: Unesco–Aims and activities //

00310 - **'Street science' and the CXC integrated science basic proficiency syllabus.** George, June M. St. Augustine, Trinidad and Tobago, ASETT, 1986. p. 1-4. (Journal of education in science for Trinidad and Tobago; XIII, 2) (eng). // Association for Science Education of Trinidad and Tobago
This article arises from a study into local beliefs for which conventional science has different explanations, of concern to science educators. A Caribbean Examinations Council syllabus has a science-for-the-living focus, and the writer classifies a number of street science items against related CXC syllabus objectives.
Keywords: education and culture; cultural values; teaching strategies; upper secondary education; Caribbean; Trinidad and Tobago.
Identifiers: Caribbean Examinations Council Integrated Science Basic Proficiency //

00311 - **Teaching natural sciences: an integrated approach.** Hecht, Karl. London, IOP, 1986. p. 283-287. (Physics education; XXI, 5) (eng). // Institute of Physics (UK)
The author, a German professor, advocates an integrated course which encompasses central topics. He believes that the aims of science education – especially that of providing useful reference points for later life – will be achieved more effectively by an integrated approach.
Keywords: educational aims; concepts; physical sciences.

00312 - **The Teaching of science and technology in an interdisciplinary context: approaches for the primary school.** McLeod, Sinclair; Mills, George. Paris, Unesco, 1986. 133 p. (Science and technology education document series; 19) (eng). // Unesco
The authors direct the Primary Science Development Project of Scotland. Their thesis is that the teaching of concepts, processes and skills of science may be more effective if linked with other subject areas. In particular, links of science and technology in everyday life may become more "real" to children if presented through interdisciplinary teaching. A number of examples of relevant approaches provide extensive illustrations.
Keywords: primary school curriculum; interdisciplinary approach; teaching methods; UK – teaching strategies; activity learning.
Identifiers: Scottish Primary Science Development Project (UK) //

00313 - **Curriculum development and the concept of "integration" in science: some implications for general education.** Adeniyi, E. Ola. New York, John Wiley, 1987. p. 523-533. (Science education; LXXI, 4) (eng).
Gives the background to the major science education programmes in Nigeria which stress integration. Favours integrated science for primary and lower secondary education, but suggests that there may be problems. Advocates vigorous research and teacher training to improve practice, now that most schools in Nigeria offer the subject.
Keywords: curriculum development; primary school curriculum; lower secondary education – educational research; teacher education; Nigeria.

00314 - **Education and health.** Kelly, Peter J.; Lewis, John L. Oxford, UK, Pergamon Press, 1987. 296 p. (Science and technology and future human needs; 5) (eng). // International Council of Scientific Unions // Conference on Science and Technology Education and Future Human Needs, Bangalore, India, 1985

In the context of education in schools and elsewhere, the book deals with the concept of health, teaching/learning, the quality of life, environment, traditional styles of medicine and modern technologies. There are many short papers from a wide range of contributors.

Keywords: health education; primary education; secondary education; out of school education; teaching methods; learning methods; quality of life; environmental education; traditional medicine; new technologies; ethics of science.

ISBN: 0-08-033947-6.

00315 - **Education, industry and technology.** Waddington, David J. Oxford, UK, Pergamon Press, 1987. 365 p. (Science and technology education and future human needs; 3) (eng). // International Council of Scientific Unions // Conference on Science and Technology Education and Future Human Needs, Bangalore, India, 1985

The sections are as follows: A. Industry, technology and the primary school; B, C, D, E, F. Industry and technological issues in secondary science curricula; G. Education and the world of work; H. The role of tertiary institutions in development; I. Technical training for development; J. Making curricula relevant for industry and the role of teacher training; K. Co-operative education. There are numerous contributions from a variety of sources.

Keywords: science and technology; industry and education – secondary school curriculum; primary school curriculum; higher education; teacher education; education and development; vocational training; technical and vocational education; teaching strategies; teaching materials; educational relevance; examinations; work experience programmes.

ISBN: 0-08-033914-X.

00316 - **Energy resources in science education.** Kirwan, D. F. Oxford, UK, Pergamon Press, 1987. 214 p. (Science and technology and future human needs; 7) (eng). // International Council of Scientific Unions // Conference on Science and Technology Education and Future Human Needs, Bangalore, India, 1985

This book aims to examine the energy perspective in education on all levels and ideas for teaching about the sources and use of energy, the energy problem and conservation and environmental issues. The six sections of the book each contain chapters written by a variety of contributors.

Keywords: energy education; primary education; secondary education – energy conservation; environmental education; higher education.

ISBN: 0-08-033951-4.

00317 - **The Environment and science and technology education.** Baez, Albert V.; Knamiller, Gary W.; Smyth, J.C. Oxford, UK, Pergamon Press, 1987. 430 p. (Science and technology education and future human needs; 8) (eng). // International Council of Scientific Unions // Conference on Science and Technology Education and Future Human Needs, Bangalore, India, 1985

The five parts embrace all levels of formal education as well as public education and the community. Within each part there are contributions from a number of authors; and nearly all parts are rich in case studies.

Keywords: environmental education – primary education; secondary education; higher education; technical and vocational education; nonformal education; school community relationship.

ISBN: 0-08-033953-0.

00318 - **Ethics and scientific activity: implications for science education.** Matete, K. Roma, Lesotho, LSMTA, 1987. p. 6-7. (Lesotho Science and Mathematics Teachers Association newsletter; XX, 1) (eng). // Lesotho Science and Mathematics Teachers Association

Considers the traditional image of ethical neutrality in science and a darker side which has come with scientific advancement. Argues that school teachers must stop teaching science with indifference, because science is a public activity with important social consequences. Suggests steps towards changing the attitudes and updating the skills of teachers. Advocates encouraging teachers to provide open-ended fora in classrooms, leading to reasoned personal decisions by individuals. Liaison with social studies teachers is also recommended.

Keywords: ethics of science; teaching strategies; teacher attitudes – discussion (teaching method); social responsibility; social studies; interdisciplinary approach; Lesotho.

00319 - **Food, agriculture and education.** Rao, A.N. Oxford, UK, Pergamon Press, 1987. 247 p. (Science and technology education and future human needs; 6) (eng). // International Council

of Scientific Unions // Conference on Science and Technology Education and Future Human Needs, Bangalore, India, 1985

This volume identifies and discusses five areas related to food and agriculture: food production, food consumption, preservation and storage, biotechnology and technology tranfer. Section A is a general section with a number of authors writing about agriculture, food and nutrition in education. Section B consists of illustrative case studies. Section C is an account of the discussions that took place at the conference. There is a final section consisting of four papers related to the subject.

Keywords: agricultural education; nutrition education; primary education; secondary education; biotechnology; technology transfer; curriculum development.

ISBN: 0-08-033949-2.

00320 - **Integrated science: a viable alternative.** Skinner, R.R. Hatfield, UK, ASE, 1987. p. 561-565. (School science review; 224) (eng). // Association for Science Education (UK)

A study investigating whether students who had studied SCISP to 0-level were disadvantaged in A-level science. The conclusion is that A-level physics and/or biology candidates were not penalised; only the chemistry candidates who had followed SCISP did less well than those who had done an 0-level chemistry/biology combination.

Keywords: specialization; upper secondary education; examinations; academic achievement; UK – chemistry education; biology education; physics education.

Identifiers: Schools Council Integrated Science Project (UK) // General Certificate of Education (UK) //

00321 - **Land, water and mineral resources in science education.** Graves, Norman J. Oxford, UK, Pergamon Press, 1987. 312 p. (Science and technology and future human needs; 4) (eng). // International Council of Scientific Unions // Conference on Science and Technology Education and Future Human Needs, Bangalore, India, 1985

This book deals with the value of teaching about the earth's resources, the content areas which might be included, and the teaching strategies which might be appropriate. The three main parts represent land use, water resources and mineral resources. There is a wide variety of contributions.

Keywords: natural resources; earth sciences; teaching strategies; curriculum development – water resources; mineral resources; land resources.

ISBN: 0-08-033945-x.

00322 - **Learning and applying integrated science through extra-curricular activities in the junior secondary level.** Perera, L.P.M. London, Junior Club Publications, 1987. p. 34-39. (Commonwealth Association of Science, Technology and Mathematics Educators journal; VII, 3) (eng). // Commonwealth Association of Science, Technology and Mathematics Educators

This enterprise, winner of joint second prize in the 1986 CASTME Awards, is an out-of-school venture in Sri Lanka for 11-16 year olds. The central aim was to teach some concepts in integrated science, and this was approached through stimulating curiosity, creativity skills and attitudes, and the use of scientific method in problem solving. The article includes a detailed illustration of one of the five projects "What's happening outside?". The investigations appear to have been undertaken individually.

Keywords: out of school education; extracurricular activities; interest (learning); secondary education; skill development; student attitudes; Sri Lanka – activity learning; problem solving.

Identifiers: Commonwealth Association of Science, Technology and Mathematics Educators awards //

00323 - **Physics and technology: a modular solution.** Brown, Colin. Bristol, UK, IoP, 1987. p. 245-249. (Physics education; XXII, 4) (eng).

The article describes a working relationship between physics and technology. In the author's school science and technology are unified and all 4th and 5th year pupils spend 25% of their time on it. The advantages of such a curriculum are identified and a list of the 68 units of work is given.

Keywords: science and technology; physics education; learning modules; modular instruction; upper secondary education; UK.

00324 - **Preservice teachers' acquisition and retention of integrated science process skills: a comparison of teacher-directed and self-instructional strategies.** Strawitz, Barbara M.; Malone, Mark R. New York, John Wiley, 1987. p. 53-60. (Journal of research in science teaching; XXIV, 1) (eng). // National Association for Research in Science Teaching (USA)

Results of the study indicate that the self-instructional method was significantly more effective than the teacher-directed method, but both treatments lead to retention.

Keywords: preservice teacher education; teacher education; teaching methods; USA – self instruction; learning methods; retention.

00325 - **International Council of Associations for Science Education. Asian Symposium, 5th, Penang, Malaysia, 1986.** Report. Lee Kwan Ping, Carol. Hong Kong, HKASME, 1987. p. 86-89. (Journal of the Hong Kong Association for Science and Mathematics Education; XV, 1) (eng). // Hong Kong Association for Science and Mathematics Education

The conference focused on "science and technology education towards informed citizenship". Such education could help citizens make responsible and informed decisions on science related issues, particularly those involving ethics and responsibility. If students are to be trained in decision-making, the type of knowledge generated should be tailored to the particular issues that face the students. "Science and technology" includes the knowledge of science itself and also the knowledge that is needed to solve problems. A criticism of existing science courses is included.

Keywords: science and technology; educational relevance; civic education; social responsibility; Asia.

00326 - **Rural science as part of the science curriculum?** Heaney, J.C. Hatfield, UK, ASE, 1987. p. 123-125. (School science review; 246) (eng). // Association for Science Education (UK)

Rural or agricultural science is an example of a technology which children can understand and engage in realistically. The writer maintains that it involves technological matters, social and moral issues, and content in biological science, other sciences, and non-science subjects. He welcomes the possibility that, through the Secondary Science Curriculum Review, many or all science teachers will be able to play an important role in this field.

Keywords: agricultural education; science and technology; educational relevance; social responsibility; interdisciplinary approach; UK – educational trends.

00327 - **School science in West Africa: an assessment of the pedagogic impact of Third World investment.** Urevbu, Andrew O. London, Taylor and Francis, 1987. p. 3-12. (International journal of science education; IX, 1) (eng; abstr. in fre, ger).

The article begins by discussing views of science and criticises the view presented by school science courses. There is a consideration of the content of school science courses. For the junior secondary stage there is as illustration a Nigerian approach which spirals from the immediate personal problems of African children to wider social issues of science. At the senior secondary level, current approaches and textbooks are seen as archaic. The article closes by noting that the African environment and culture hold a rich source of materials for learning about science.

Keywords: science philosophy; sociology of science; educational relevance; West Africa – secondary school curriculum; African cultures; lower secondary education; upper secondary education; teaching strategies; textbooks; Nigeria.
Identifiers: Science Education Programme for Africa //

00328 - **Science and technology education and future human needs.** Lewis, John L.; Kelly, Peter J. Oxford, UK, Pergamon Press, 1987. 185 p. (Science and technology education and future human needs; 1) (eng). // International Council of Scientific Unions // Conference on Science and Technology Education and Future Human Needs, Bangalore, India, 1985

This is the introductory volume to a series of nine associated with the Bangalore Conference. The first part is a historical account of the background to the conference. The second part deals with some of the major issues. The third part lists the contents of the nine volumes of the series; while the fourth part looks toward the future. Appendices provide conference details.

Keywords: education and development; social needs; human resources development; educational planning; educational relevance.
ISBN: 0-08-033910-7.

00329 - **Science education and information transfer.** Taylor, Charles. Oxford, UK, Pergamon Press, 1987. 230 p. (Science and education and future human needs; 9) (eng). // International Council of Scientific Unions // Conference on Science and Technology Education and Future Human Needs, Bangalore, India, 1985

This book is concerned with communication. The 10 chapters, by different authors, cover a wide variety of approaches to communicating with learners. In an appendix there are case studies from various regions (many of them dealing with computers).

Keywords: communication process; computer assisted instruction; information transfer; educational technology; teaching strategies – teaching materials; educational games; audiovisual aids; readability; teacher centres; communication networks.
ISBN: 0-08-033955-7.

00330 - **Social issues: the potential contribution of primary science and technology.** Skamp, Keith. Carton, Australian College of Education, 1987. p. 79-82. (Unicorn; 13, 2) (eng). // Australian College of Education

While the secondary curriculum is often considered an appropriate focus for future-directed studies, elementary science and technology education can contribute significantly to the socialization process. Science education can also help shape youngsters' attitudes and capacity to understand and influence scientific and technogical impacts on themselves and their environment.

Keywords: socialization; primary school curriculum; Australia – student attitudes; technology.

00331 - **Teacher-college students' opinions in Israel and on the West Bank of "what science education is supposed to be"** Jungwirth, Ehud; Zakhalka, Makhmoud. London, Taylor and Francis, 1987. p. 247-257. (International journal of science education; IX, 2) (eng; abstr. in fre, ger). // Hebrew University (Israel)

The author aimed to investigate the effects of a 3 year teacher training programme on views of "what science is supposed to be". That is what socially acceptable responses the subjects think will satisfy "the establishment". Interpretation of the results suggests differences and similarities in school science education and in college education in Jews and Arabs in Israel and Arabs on the West Bank (a three-way comparison). Ethno-cultural variables are expected to apply.

Keywords: teacher education; teacher attitudes; comparative education; Israel; Arabs – higher education; student teachers; student attitudes; survey analysis; educational goals; secondary education.

00332 - **Applications-based science education: should we apply?** Butlin, Chris. Bristol, UK, IoP, 1988. p. 17-23. (Physics education; XXIII, 1) (eng). // Institute of Physics (UK)

The author advocates an application basis for a combined science and technology education. He describes his efforts to develop such an approach, illustrating mostly from physics and (Technical, Vocational and Educational Initiative).

Keywords: science and technology; technical and vocational education; physics education; UK – upper secondary education; examinations.
Identifiers: Technical, Vocational and Educational Initiative (UK) //

00333 - **Assessment of students' learning in science and technology in national and international studies.** Rosier, Malcolm J. Paris, Unesco, 1988. p. 275-282. (Innovations in science and technology education; 2) (eng). // Unesco

Outlines the procedures and concepts in the "Second International science study". Causal models of achievement are given for comparisons among students and among education systems.

Keywords: learning processes; student evaluation; academic achievement; educational measurement; comparative education.
Identifiers: International Association for the Evaluation of Educational Achievement // "Second international science study" //

00334 - **Assessment of students' learning in science education.** Giddings, Geoff; Fraser, Barry J. Paris, Unesco, 1988. p. 257-273. (Innovations in science and technology education; 2) (eng). // Unesco

Deals with assessments often neglected. There are frameworks for the assessment of practical work and attention is drawn to continuous assessment approaches. For the assessment of attitudes to science, particular attention is paid to (Test of Science-related Attitude). Work on the assessment of classroom environment is cited and a typical instrument (ICEQ) is appended.

Keywords: learning processes; student evaluation; school laboratories; practicums; activity learning – student attitudes; classroom environment; evaluation methods; formative evaluation.
Identifiers: Test of Science-related Attitudes (Australia) // Individualized Classroom Environment Questionnaire (Australia) //

00335 - **Balanced science: changes in science education.** Boyle, Alan. Reading, UK, Coles, 1988. p. 9-12. (Careers journal; VIII, 3) (eng). // Institute of Careers Officers (UK)

Distinguishes between balanced science and separate science. Would be useful to disseminate to entrants to a balanced science course, but critical educators will find it partisan.

Keywords: educational trends; specialization; concepts; UK.
Identifiers: "Balanced Science" (UK) // "Separate Science" (UK) //

00336 - **Balanced science equals better science.** Chadwick, Roy. Bristol, UK, IoP, 1988. p. 6. (Physics education; XXIII, 1) (eng). // Institute of Physics (UK)

Presents an analysis of the science background (in terms of number of sciences studied) of students who have qualified to enter a Sixth Form College. Observes that 26% have had a balanced science

curriculum (3 sciences) but probably an unbalanced total curriculum. The rest have had an unbalanced or no science curriculum. Presents arguments for Double Award Balanced Science accounting for 20% of curriculum time.

Keywords: upper secondary education; general education; core curriculum; UK.

Identifiers: Double Award Balanced Science, GCSE (UK) // "Balanced Science" (UK) //

00337 - Balanced science equals better science, pt. II. Chadwick, Roy. Bristol, UK, IoP, 1988. p. 67-68. (Physics education ; XXXII, 2) (eng). // Institute of Physics (UK)

The author presents an analysis of the science background (in terms of sciences studied) of fifth year students in representative 11-16 schools. He concludes that Britain may have the best balanced science education for a very few but the worst balanced education for the vast majority. Some trends for the better are mentioned.

Keywords: upper secondary education; general education; core curriculum; UK – educational policy; educational trends; educational improvement.

Identifiers: General Certificate of Secondary Education (UK) //

00338 - A Case for a process approach: the Warwick experience. Screen, Peter. Bristol, UK, IoP, 1988. p. 146-149. (Physics education; XXIII, 3) (eng). // Institute of Physics (UK)

This approach to science education arises from the belief that it is not the facts themselves but how they are arrived at which constitute an education in science. The six independent processes which form the base are explained. The article ends with a justification.

Keywords: problem solving; activity learning; gifted students – ability grouping; UK.

Identifiers: Warwick Process Science Project (UK) //

00339 - An Evaluation of the nature and function of the CXC Integrated Science (Single Award) syllabuses. George, June M. St. Augustine, University of the West Indies, 1988. 94 p. (eng). // University of the West Indies (Trinidad and Tobago)

The objectives of the study were to determine how well the Caribbean Examinations Council (Single Award) syllabuses (a) provide a functional knowledge of science for young Caribbean adults in a technological world (b) may be considered to support other CXC subjects whose content and orientation require a core of scientific knowledge or elements of science (c) serve in preparing candidates for the world of work, particularly in jobs requiring a basic science background. Analysis of the CXC materials revealed strengths and weaknesses. The impact of the subject on science and non-science students is so far slight. The author found that the subject is too new to gather meaningful data about its value in the world of work.

Keywords: curriculum evaluation; educational relevance; education and employment; Caribbean.

Identifiers: Caribbean Examinations Council //

00340 - Girls and women in science and technology education. Granstam, Ingrid. Paris, Unesco, 1988. p. 47-58. (Innovations in science and technology education; 2) (eng). // Unesco

Strategies for getting more girls interested in technology include practical technology for small girls, special themes and role plays, spare-time activities and theme courses, involvement of engineering students in teaching in schools, talks from female technologists and the creation of activity centres.

Keywords: girls education; womens education; teaching strategies – attitude change; science and technology; teacher role; student attitudes; activity learning; industry and education.

00341 - The Influences of sequenced instructional strategy and locus of control on preservice elementary teachers' understanding of the nature of science. Scharmann, Lawrence C. New York, John Wiley, 1988. p. 589-604. (Journal of research in science teaching; XXV, 7) (eng). // National Association for Research in Science Teaching (USA)

Major conclusions were that (1) logical thinking ability was the most influential predictor of understanding the nature of science and (2) separate experiences rather than those integrating content and teaching method were superior in developing an understanding of the nature of science. Implications for preservice elementary teacher preparations are discussed. There should be an attempt to promote a complementary view of science as content and as process.

Keywords: learning methods; thinking; reasoning; primary teacher education; preservice teacher education; USA.

00342 - Innovations in science and technology education, v.2. Layton, David. Paris, Unesco, 1988. 299 p. (Innovations in technology education; II) (eng; also in spa). // Unesco

The general theme is science and technology education at a time of rapid scientific and technological change. Current trends and issues

are reviewed. The main thematic sections are, in the context of science and technology: an appropriate introduction; interdisciplinary approach; education and active life; materials and methods for education. The target readership includes science educators, ministry of education officials and practising teachers.

Keywords: teaching method innovations – girls education; curriculum development; interdisciplinary approach; teacher education; science and technology; education and productive work; teaching materials; computer assisted instruction; evaluation of education.

ISBN: 92-3-102530-9(eng); 92-3-302530-6(spa).

00343 - Instructional objectives: what effects do they have on students' attitudes towards integrated science? Olarewaju, Adedayo O. New York, John Wiley, 1988. p. 283-291. (Journal of research in science teaching; XXV, 4) (eng). // National Association for Research in Science Teaching (USA)

Reports a study using two experimental groups (objectives given and not given) and a control group. It was found that (a) the experimental groups had more favourable attitudes towards integrated science than the control group and (b) the no objectives group had better attitudes than the objectives group. There was no significant effect due to type of school or sex of the students.

Keywords: educational aims; curriculum evaluation; teaching strategies; classroom techniques; student attitudes; Nigeria.

Identifiers: Nigerian Integrated Science Project //

00344 - Integrality and diversity in science and technology education. Layton, David. Paris, Unesco, 1988. p. 11-24. (Innovations in science and technology education; 2) (eng). // Unesco

As well as movements toward integration of science subjects and of science and technology studies, the author identifies an attempt to make such studies more integral with everyday experiences of the learners and on a continuum from the earliest years to adult life. Alongside this is a tendency towards diversity, which is related to the context of the education and a broadening of perspectives. These ideas are illustrated from the chapters in the volume.

Keywords: educational innovations – diversification of education; educational relevance.

00345 - Integrated science project: How do the A-level science grades of integrated science pupils compare with those of pupils who take all three separate sciences? Skinner, R.R.; Fairbrother, R.W. Oxford, UK, Carfax Publishing, 1988. p. 149-154. (British educational research journal; XIV, 2) (eng).

This reports a comparison of A-level results of candidates who had followed an O-level integrated science course (SCISP) against those who had followed the separate sciences. Only in A-level chemistry was there any significant difference, non-SCISP candidates doing slightly better. However, it seemed that other allied A-level subjects in conjuction with chemistry also affected the grades, a combination of A-level biology and A-level chemistry being particularly beneficial. The writers speculate that the combination accounts for the higher chemistry grades rather than any differences in the O-level background.

Keywords: upper secondary education; examinations; academic achievement; UK – chemistry education; biology education; physics education.

Identifiers: Schools Council Integrated Science Project (UK) //

00346 - Integrating the natural sciences and other school subjects. Lazarov, Dobri; Golovinski, Evgeny. Paris, Unesco, 1988. p. 113-119. (Innovations in science and technology education; 2) (eng). // Unesco

The structure and curriculum of the Bulgarian system is explained. An 8-year experiment in integration in 30 schools is an attempt to overcome some of the shortcomings of the independent teaching of science subjects. The essential requirement is that science is learnt from diverse sources and is seen as both a product and a powerful determinant of its cultural context.

Keywords: primary school curriculum; secondary school curriculum; textbooks; Bulgaria – teacher qualifications; education and culture; physical sciences.

Identifiers: Research Group on Education (Bulgaria) //

00347 - Integrating the two cultures at Georgia Tech: a literature and science introductory course. Armstrong, Paul B. New York, Association of Departments of English, 1988. p. 30-34. (Association of Departments of English bulletin; 88) (eng). // Association of Departments of English (USA)

Describes the success of a Georgia Tech course that integrates science and literature by analyzing the divisions between these "two cultures". Summarizes course organization and content, including section topics; reading material from science, philosophy, and literature; and basic issues confronted in the course.

Keywords: university curriculum; curriculum development; USA –

higher education; literature; philosophy; teaching strategies; interdisciplinary approach; reading materials.
Identifiers: Georgia Tech (USA) //

00348 - Interdisciplinarity in the teaching of science during the first nine to ten years of basic education. Swartland, Jakes. Paris, Unesco, 1988. p. 91-99. (Innovations in science and technology education; 2) (eng). // Unesco
This is an account of the growth of indigenous integrated science curricula in a number of African countries.
Keywords: interdisciplinary approach; teaching methods; Africa – primary school curriculum; lower secondary education; curriculum development.

00349 - An Introduction to technology in the early years of schooling. Mills, George. Paris, Unesco, 1988. p. 31-45. (Innovations in science and technology education; 2) (eng). // Unesco
By the end of compulsory learning a person should be technologically literate and there has recently been seen a need to commence technology education at the earliest stages of schooling. This author sees a fundamental difference between science and technology, but believes when pupils are involved in technology they will be using science. A sequence of process skills is involved in technological problem-solving. Examples are given. Some impediments are identified and recommendations are made for a school policy.
Keywords: primary school curriculum; problem solving; general technical education; activity learning – scientific literacy.

00350 - Low-cost materials for science and technology education. Tobon R., Ramiro. Paris, Unesco, 1988. p. 223-239. (Innovations in science and technology education; 2) (eng). // Unesco
Advantages of low-cost equipment go beyond economic considerations and may have pedagogical aspects. National or local production could have several levels, for example the supply of designs, or parts, or kits. Implications of each are discussed and illustrated.
Keywords: teaching materials; cost reduction – appropriate technology; educational equipment; educational experiments.

00351 - Microworld: the role of the computer in science and technology education. Marx, George. Paris, Unesco, 1988. p. 241-256. (Innovations in science and technology education; 2) (eng). // Unesco
Educational uses and misuses of computers are illustrated. Microcomputers in schools are seen as having the potential to educate students to anticipate alternative futures, analyse possible risks, make appropiate decisions and "save our planet".
Keywords: computer assisted instruction; microcomputers – microbiology.

00352 - Modular science and technology at Peers School. Brown, Colin. Hatfield, UK, ASE, 1988. p. 460-468. (School science review; 248) (eng). // Association for Science Education (UK)
This is an account of what is described as a radical approach to an integrated curriculum (embracing science and craft design technology) and to assessment. The target is children of average ability with an industrial environment. The article provides a rationale, a description of how the system is structured, an outline of the course and some of the experience. The account is not entirely objective, but details could be useful to teachers in other situations.
Keywords: learning modules; modular instruction; secondary school curriculum; teaching materials; student evaluation; UK – vocational education; ability grouping.

00353 - New methods for training and retraining science and technology teachers. Power, Colin. Paris, Unesco, 1988. p. 283-295. (Innovations in science and technology education; 2) (eng). // Unesco
New societal demands in science and technology education are outlined, together with new needs in the teaching force, which must be flexible and forward looking. Examples are given of attempts at reform in preservice courses. The continuing education of teachers is also necessary, and the author illustrates from enterprises around the world, including distance teaching.
Keywords: teacher education; teacher effectiveness; teacher recruitment; preservice teacher education – distance education; refresher courses; inservice teacher education.

00354 - New Nuffield course. Bristol, UK, IoP, 1988. 70 p. (Physics education; XXIII, 2) (eng). // Institute of Physics (UK)
This announces and outlines the characteristics of a course in which each subject keeps its identity but with inter- and cross-curricular links.
Keywords: upper secondary education; specialization; core curriculum; UK – teaching materials.
Identifiers: Nuffield Coordinated Sciences Course (UK) //

00355 - Nuffield Coordinated Sciences: aims and history. Dorling, Geoffrey. Bristol, UK, IoP, 1988. p. 207-211. (Physics education; XXIII, 4) (eng). // Institute of Physics (UK)
This course aims to provide a broad and balanced science course that nevertheless preserves the identities of the separate sciences which were its component parts. The coordination distinguishes it from both integrated science and independent courses in the separate sciences. It matches the National Criteria for "The Sciences: Double Award". The development is described.
Keywords: educational policy; core curriculum; upper secondary education; UK – curriculum guides; curriculum development; examinations; specialization.
Identifiers: Nuffield Coordinated Sciences Course (UK) // National Criteria for the Sciences: Double Award (UK) //

00356 - The Place of process in physics education. Wellington, Jerry J. Bristol, UK, IoP, 1988. p. 150-155. (Physics education; XXIII, 3) (eng). // Institute of Physics (UK)
The article focuses more on general science than the title suggests. Citing recent "process-led" science curricula, the author examines critically this increased emphasis. He concludes that the swing from a content-led curriculum has gone too far and suggests a search for equilibrium between "knowledge that", "knowledge how" and "knowledge why".
Keywords: curriculum development; science philosophy; concepts; activity learning.

00357 - Please mention chemistry. Jenkins, Edgar. London, RSC, 1988. p. 100. (Education in chemistry; XXV, 3) (eng). // Royal Society of Chemistry (UK)
The author articulates some worries about balanced science for all, and hopes that professional associations will act according to their constitutional duty to foster their particular subjects. He advocates encouraging schools to continue teaching separate sciences where they judge it appropriate. His concerns include teacher preparation for integrated science and a shortage of qualified scientific personnel for industry and science.
Keywords: core curriculum; specialization; chemistry education; secondary school curriculum; UK – social needs; secondary teacher education; education and employment; industry and education.

00358 - The Potentiality of distance learning. Tresman, Susan; Thomas, Jeff; Pindar, Katharine. Hatfield, UK, ASE, 1988. p. 687-691. (School science review; 249) (eng). // Association for Science Education (UK)
Innovations in education in the UK include balanced science, which may be taught in secondary schools by specialist-trained teachers. In-service retraining by distance education is one approach to solving the problem, and criteria are identified. The Physics for Science Teachers Project of the Open University is outlined.
Keywords: distance education; inservice teacher education; secondary teacher education; secondary education; UK – specialization; physics education; retraining.
Identifiers: Open University (UK) // "Balanced Science" (UK) // Physics for Science Teachers Project (UK) //

00359 - Practical work in the teaching of science and technology. Badran, Adnan M. Paris, Unesco, 1988. p. 211-221. (Innovations in science and technology education; 2) (eng). // Unesco
In addition to promoting understanding of scientific knowledge and methods of working, practical work should now have social relevance and applicability to problem situations in the real world. The examples given cover geysers, generators, turbines and pollution.
Keywords: practicums; activity learning – educational relevance.

00360 - The Pursuit of the impossible. Millar, Robin. Bristol, UK, IoP, 1988. p. 156-159. (Physics education; XXIII, 3) (eng). // Institute of Physics (UK)
The author suggests that the process view of science curriculum developers is seriously flawed in both primary and secondary education. He concludes that the challenge is to motivate children to use the cognitive skills they already possess to grasp the scientific concepts in order to make sense of their world.
Keywords: science philosophy; educational psychology; primary school curriculum; secondary school curriculum – concepts; motivation; cognition.

00361 - Unesco International Consultation on Recent Developments in Integrated Science Teaching, Canberra, 1988. (Report). Canberra, ICASE, Unesco, 1988. 248 p. (eng). // International Council of Associations for Science Education // Unesco
The consultation aimed to take stock of the current situation and attempted to identify trends and significant changes in integrated science education that had taken place in the ten years since the Nijmegen Conference of 1978. Chapter 2 is a general account of

developments in integrated science courses worldwide since 1967. Chapter 3 consists of reviews of situations in countries in seven regions of the world. Chapter 4 summarizes aspects of the Second International Science Study (SISS). Chapter 5 very briefly summarizes discussions of significant issues (content, curriculum and instructional materials, teaching and assessment, facilities and teacher education). Chapter 6 pinpoints significant issues. The appendices cover a variety of specific topics.

Keywords: educational trends; evaluation of education; comparative education – student evaluation; school laboratories; teacher education; teaching materials; Arab countries; Asia and the Pacific; Latin America; Caribbean; Africa; North America; Europe.

Identifiers: International Conference on Integrated Science Education Worldwide, Nijmegen, Netherlands, 1978 // "Second International Science Study" //

00362 - **Restructuring the curriculum: some implications of studies on learning for curriculum development.** Driver, Rosalind. Paris, Unesco, 1988. p. 59-84. (Innovations in science and technology education; 2) (eng). // Unesco

The author shows how children's ideas influence the sense they make of learning activities, and identifies the general features of these ideas. Strategies for curriculum planning and teaching are discussed.

Keywords: curriculum development; learning processes; educational psychology – primary school curriculum; secondary school curriculum; student attitudes; teaching methods; reasoning; conceptualization.

00363 - **Science and technology abstracts and information resources (STAIR).** Browning, David. Bristol, UK, J.W. Arrowsmith, 1988. 64 p. (STAIR; 01) (eng).

This is an annotated bibliography of journals addressed to teachers and pupils, with advice on obtaining the articles. Over 150 journals (including specialist ones such as "Tin and its Uses", national newspapers and major American journals) are represented. While most of the items are resources for direct classroom use, there are items of interest to the teacher as a professional as well as abstracts of projects. Various indexes are provided.

Keywords: bibliographies; educational resources; teaching materials; technology; reading materials – upper secondary education; student projects.

ISSN: 0952-9535.

00364 - **Science and technology education and agriculture.** Blum, Abraham. Paris, Unesco, 1988. p. 155-165. (Innovations in science and technology education; 2) (eng). // Unesco

The relationship of agriculture to science and to technology are explored in the context of education. The author is particularly concerned about needs in low-income countries. Examples of attempts at integration of agriculture into science curricula come from Zambia, Australia, Israel, Venezuela and Fiji. There are recommendations for stimulating teachers to take a more active part in science and technology education for rural development.

Keywords: agricultural education; secondary school curriculum – science and technology; educational strategies; rural development; educational projects; developing countries; Zambia; Australia; Israel; Venezuela; Fiji.

Identifiers: Agriculture as Environmental Science (Israel) //

00365 - **Science applied in the Caribbean.** Reay, Judith; Steward, John. London, Macmillan Caribbean, 1988. 362 p. (eng).

The chapters in this book have been written by Caribbean scientists demonstrating their commitment to social issues. For each chapter there are suggested exercises for use in school, and cross references to the Caribbean Examinations Council syllabuses in biology, chemistry, physics, integrated science and social studies.

Keywords: science and development; social needs; educational relevance; Caribbean – teaching methods; biology education; chemistry education; physics education; social studies.

Identifiers: Caribbean Examinations Council //

ISBN: 0-333-46333-1.

00366 - **Science for ages 5 to 16.** London, HMSO, 1988. 142 p. (eng). // UK. Dept of Education and Science and the Welsh Office

The bulk of the publication consists of the report from a working group set up to make recommendations on attainment targets and programmes of study for science in the National Curriculum. The rest is the contents of the Secretaries of State. The working group has also made recommendations on assessment and other implications on the National Curriculum. The elements for the proposals are attainment targets, programmes of study, time for science and aplication of orders. The attainment targets are grouped together into knowledge and understanding, exploration and investigation, communication and science in action.

Keywords: educational policy; educational plans; educational

reform; educational programmes; educational aims; UK – primary school curriculum; secondary school curriculum; student evaluation.

Identifiers: UK National Curriculum //

00367 - **The Sciences: double award.** Pople, Stephen. Bristol, UK, Institute of Physics Publishing, 1988. 71 p. (Physics education; XXIII, 2) (eng). // Institute of Physics (UK)

GCSE double award science syllabuses vary widely, but not all offer a balanced curriculum and some can cause problems for A-level studies. The Sciences: Double Award is an attempt to identify criteria from biology, chemistry and physics which would make the double award acceptable as an alternative to awards in these subjects.

Keywords: upper secondary education; educational coordination; examinations; UK – biology education; chemistry education; physics education; educational aims.

Identifiers: The Sciences: Double Award (Joint Council for GCSE, UK) //

00368 - **Sourcebook of science education research in the Caribbean.** Fraser-Abder, Pamela. Paris, Unesco, 1988. 198 p. (Science and technology education document series; 26) (eng). // Unesco

The first part of the sourcebook is an annotated listing of papers about science education and related fields in the wide Caribbean area. It includes journal articles, conference papers and theses and covers the period 1970-1987, with a few references to ealier works. The second half of the book provides information of value to research workers interested in on-going activity in the region.

Keywords: educational research; bibliographies; literature reviews; Caribbean – curriculum development.

00369 - **Structuring investigations in the science curriculum.** Foulds, Ken; Gott, Richard. Bristol, UK, IoP, 1988. p. 347-351. (Physics education; XXIII, 6) (eng). // Institute of Physics (UK)

A curriculum based on investigations is seen as relying on a combination of concepts, procedures and processes. The authors classify and illustrate types of investigation and also the factors which cause difficulties with them. There is a brief account of trials of an investigation-based curriculum with lower secondary pupils.

Keywords: activity learning; lower secondary education; curriculum development; curriculum evaluation; UK.

00370 - **The Suffolk experience.** Dobson, Ken; Watts, Graham; Lloyd, Allan. Bristol, UK, IoP, 1988. p. 162-168. (Physics education; 3) (eng). // Institute of Physics (UK)

A project for Forms 3-5 is outlined. It arose from dissatisfaction with current curricula and assessment. The assessment of processes and laboratory skills stimulates teachers towards innovation in approaches. Content is balanced and arranged in three separate sciences. Development has been made by teachers in workshops. Case studies report problems and positive outcomes.

Keywords: upper secondary education; teaching method innovations; curriculum development; educational workshops; UK – activity learning; biology education; chemistry education; physics education; educational coordination; student evaluation.

Identifiers: Coordinated Science: the Suffolk Development (UK) //

00371 - **Technology education in relation to science education.** Carelse, Xavier F. Paris, Unesco, 1988. p. 101-112. (Innovations in science and technology education; 2) (eng). // Unesco

The separation of science and technology education is undesirable, both in terms of the quality of education as a whole and of the opportunities for the development of every child. Arguments for technology education cover the needs for national development, of the school leaver, of women. Desirable characteristics of technology education are summarised. There are recommendations for implementation and assessment.

Keywords: secondary school curriculum; educational needs; curriculum development – general technical education; teacher qualifications; womens education; evaluation of education; education and development.

00372 - **Training teachers for interdisciplinary work: the state-of-the-art, with special reference to the Caribbean.** Glasgow, Joyce. Paris, Unesco, 1988. p. 121-133. (Innovations in science and technology education; 2) (eng). // Unesco

The chapter covers a spectrum of modification of subject boundaries. Teacher training in each of the fields selected is illustrated by a few case studies. The author's review of the work leads to a set of conclusions to be borne in mind in teacher education for the 'opening up' of science education.

Keywords: interdisciplinary approach; teacher education; Caribbean – agricultural education; nutrition education; environmental education.

00373 - **The Warwick Process Science Project.** Screen, Peter. Hatfield,
UK, ASE, 1988. p. 12-16. (School science review; 242) (eng).
// Association for Science Education (UK)

*The project is developing a "process-led" science curriculum in
contrast to a "knowledge-led" one. The article outlines the
development procedures, rationale and flavour of the curriculum.
Initially it is concerned with ages 11-16, though there is a prospect of
continuing the work for primary children. Its effect on children across
the ability range is mentioned. Initially, the modules are integrated,
but there are plans for later modules on the separate sciences.*

Keywords: curriculum development; learning modules; activity
learning; UK – secondary school curriculum; primary school
curriculum; specialization; ability grouping.

Identifiers: Warwick Process Science Project (UK) //

BIBLIOGRAPHY : SUBJECT INDEX

BIBLIOGRAPHY : PERSONAL NAME INDEX

BIBLIOGRAPHY : TITLE AND SERIES INDEX